FEAR AND TREMBLING

REPETITION

KIERKEGAARD'S WRITINGS, VI

FEAR AND TREMBLING

REPETITION

by Søren Kierkegaard

Edited and Translated
with Introduction and Notes by

Howard V. Hong and
Edna H. Hong

PRINCETON UNIVERSITY PRESS
PRINCETON, NEW JERSEY

Copyright © 1983 by Howard V. Hong
Published by Princeton University Press, 41 William Street, Princeton, New Jersey
In the United Kingdom: Princeton University Press, Guildford, Surrey

All Rights Reserved

Library of Congress Cataloging in Publication Data will be
found on the last printed page of this book

Preparation of this volume has been made possible in part by a grant from
the Translations Program of the National Endowment for the Humanities.

Clothbound editions of Princeton University Press books
are printed on acid-free paper, and binding materials are
chosen for strength and durability. Paperbacks, while satifactory
for personal collections, are not usually suitable for library rebinding.

Printed in the United States of America by Princeton
University Press, Princeton, New Jersey

CONTENTS

Contents

HISTORICAL INTRODUCTION

Of all Kierkegaard's pseudonymous writings, *Fear and Trembling* and *Repetition* are perhaps the most closely personal. At the same time, they exemplify Kierkegaard's view of the optimal relation between a writer's experience and his writing, a relation he formulated later in *Two Ages* (1846):

> The law manifest in poetic production is identical, on a smaller scale, with the law for the life of every person in social intercourse and education. Anyone who experiences anything primitively also experiences in ideality the possibilities of the same thing and the possibility of the opposite. These possibilities are his legitimate literary property. His own personal actuality, however, is not. His speaking and his producing are, in fact, born of silence. The ideal perfection of what he says and what he produces will correspond to his silence, and the supreme mark of that silence will be that the ideality contains the qualitatively opposite possibility. As soon as the productive artist must give over his own actuality, its facticity, he is no longer essentially productive; his beginning will be his end, and his first word will already be a trespass against the holy modesty of ideality. Therefore from an esthetic point of view, such a poetic work is certainly also a kind of private talkativeness and is readily recognized by the absence of its opposite in equilibrium. For ideality is the equilibrium of opposites. For example, someone who has been motivated to creativity by unhappiness, if he is genuinely devoted to ideality, will be equally inclined to write about happiness and about unhappiness. But silence, the brackets he puts around his own personality, is precisely the condition for gaining ideality; otherwise, despite all precautionary measures such as setting the scene in Africa etc., his one-sided preference will still show. An author

certainly must have his private personality as everyone else
has, but this must be his ἄδυτον [inner sanctum], and just
as the entrance to a house is barred by stationing two sol-
diers with crossed bayonets, so by means of the dialectical
cross of qualitative opposites the equality of ideality forms
the barrier that prevents all access.[1]

This text and also the text and the draft on loquacity[2] clearly
express Kierkegaard's view that an author's private experience can legitimately be used in his writing only in transmuted form, that is, as the universally human, not as personal disclosure. Therefore, a reader does not need to know
anything at all about the writer and the leaden personal particulars that have been transmuted into the gold of the imaginatively shaped pseudonymous work.

Kierkegaard expressly employed indirect communication
in works such as *Fear and Trembling* and *Repetition* in order
to take himself as author out of the picture and to leave the
reader alone with the ideas. The pseudonymity or polyonymity of the various works, Kierkegaard wrote in "A First
and Last Declaration," "has not had an accidental basis in
my *person* . . . but an *essential* basis in the *production* itself,
which, for the sake of the lines, of the psychologically varied
differences of the individualities, poetically required a disregard for good and evil, contrition and exuberance, despair
and arrogance, suffering and rhapsody, etc., which are limited only ideally by psychological consistency, which no actual factual person dares allow himself or wishes to allow
himself in the moral limitations of actuality."[3]

---

[1] *Two Ages*, pp. 98-99, *KW* XIV (*SV* VIII 91-92).

[2] Ibid., p. 103 (*SV* VIII 96), and Supplement, p. 130 (*Pap.* VII[1] B 110).

[3] *Concluding Unscientific Postscript, KW* XII (*SV* VII [545]). Louis Mackey
is on sound footing when he writes: "A Kierkegaardian pseudonym is a
persona, an imaginary person created by the author for artistic purposes, not
a *nom de plume*, a fictitious name used to protect his personal identity from
the threats and embarrassments of publicity. When Kierkegaard signed his
books with impossible names like Johannes de Silentio (John of Silence) and
Vigilius Haufniensis (Watchman of Copenhagen), no one in the gossipy
little world of Danish letters had any doubt about their origin. Nor did he

A historical and biographical approach to any work may afford some illumination, but such an approach becomes eccentric if it diverts attention from the author's thought to the author's life. Throughout his authorship, Kierkegaard took special care to prevent his readers from being so diverted, from committing the genetic fallacy. No writer has so painstakingly tried to preclude his readers' collapsing writer and works together and thereby transmogrifying the works into autobiography or memoir. Yet few writers have been approached so consistently from the biographical angle. And none of Kierkegaard's other writings has been so consistently treated from that perspective as have *Fear and Trembling* and *Repetition*.

Kierkegaard was well aware, however, that one reader would inevitably use a biographical approach to whatever he wrote, for she was part of that personal history, the incidental occasion for poetic productions that in their universality are addressed to every individual. She was, of course, Regine Olsen—in a special sense, that single individual (*hiin Enkelte*). In a retrospective journal entry from 1849, Kierkegaard reviewed his motivation for writing *Either/Or* (published February 20, 1843):

> when I began as an author I was "religiously resolved," but this must be understood in another way. *Either/Or*, especially "The Seducer's Diary,"[4] was written for her sake, in order to clear her out of the relationship. On the whole, the very mark of my genius is that Governance broadens and radicalizes whatever concerns me personally. I remember what a pseudonymous writer[5] said about Socrates: ". . . his whole life was personal preoccupation with himself, and then Governance comes and adds world-his-

---

mean they should; his purpose was not mystification but distance. By refusing to answer for his writings he detached them from his personality so as to let their form protect the freedom that was their theme." *Kierkegaard: A Kind of Poet* (Philadelphia: University of Pennsylvania Press, 1971), p. 247.

[4] *Either/Or,* I, *KW* III (*SV* I 273-412).

[5] Johannes Climacus, *Postscript, KW* XII (*SV* VII 120-21 fn.).

torical significance to it." To take another example—I am polemical by nature, and I understood the concept of "that single individual" [*hiin Enkelte*] early. However, when I wrote it for the first time (in *Two Upbuilding Discourses*),[6] I was thinking particularly of *my* reader, for this book contained a little hint to her, and until later it was for me very true personally that I sought only one single reader. Gradually this thought was taken over. But here again Governance's part is so infinite.[7]

The prototype for *Either/Or, Fear and Trembling, Repetition*, and the other polyonymous works was the maieutic method of Socrates. "Viewed Socratically, every point of departure in time is *eo ipso* something accidental, vanishing, an occasion,"[8] according to Johannes Climacus, author of *Philosophical Fragments*. For Socrates, there is "a reciprocal relation, in that life and the situations are for him the occasion to become a teacher and he in turn is an occasion for others to learn something."[9]

The point of departure and, viewed from the vantage point of the completed work, the vanishing occasion of *Either/Or* was the breaking of the engagement between Kierkegaard and Regine Olsen on October 11, 1841. According to a journal entry from May 17, 1843, Kierkegaard broke the engagement primarily out of concern for Regine: "If I had not honored her higher than myself as my future wife, if I had not been prouder of her honor than of my own, then I would have remained silent and fulfilled her wish and mine—I would have married her—there are so many marriages that conceal little stories."[10] But then he would have had to initiate her into his father's melancholy, "the eternal night brooding within

---

[6] The first two (published May 16, 1843) of an eventual series of eighteen discourses published in 1843-1844.

[7] *JP* VI 6388 (*Pap.* X¹ A 266).

[8] *Philosophical Fragments, KW* VII (*SV* IV 181).

[9] Ibid. (*SV* IV 192). On accidental circumstances as occasions, and not as the causes or purposes, of writing, see also *Either/Or*, I, *KW* III (*SV* I 207-10).

[10] *JP* V 5664 (*Pap.* IV A 107).

me," and into his life during the period of estrangement from his father—all of which he thought would crush her. The diary of the imaginary and imaginative seducer was intended to be read by Regine with himself in mind and thus to dissemble and to ease her out of the relationship and the pain of its fracture. This was achieved more easily and more quickly than he had expected, for in June 1843 she became engaged to Johan Frederik Schlegel, who had been her teacher before Kierkegaard met her.

After completing the editor's preface to *Either/Or* (November 11, 1842), Kierkegaard worked on *Two Upbuilding Discourses* (published May 16, 1843; preface dated May 5, 1843, Kierkegaard's thirtieth birthday) and the pseudonymous *Johannes Climacus, or De omnibus dubitandum est*. The two discourses are titled "The Expectancy of Faith," expanded with the subtitle "New Year's Day," and "Every Good and Every Perfect Gift Is from Above." The text of the first is on justification by faith, in which "There is neither Jew nor Greek, there is neither bond nor free, there is neither male nor female . . ." (Galatians 3:23-29). The text of the second is Kierkegaard's "first love," "my only love":[11] "Every good and every perfect gift is from above . . . receive with meekness the engrafted word, which is able to save your souls" (James 1:17-22).

The other work, *Johannes Climacus, or De omnibus dubitandum est* (*Pap*. IV B 1), is a preliminary study of doubt cast in the form of the intellectual biography of Johannes Climacus, a university student who is exploring the implications of the Cartesian methodological dictum that philosophy begins with universal doubt. The piece ends with a brief discussion of consciousness (interest), which doubt presupposes. Consciousness is a relation of opposition between ideality and actuality, an opposition discovered through repetition.[12]

---

[11] *JP* VI 6965 (*Pap*. XI³ B 291:4).

[12] See Supplement, pp. 274-75 (*Pap*. IV B 1).

For earlier uses of the term and a concept of repetition, see *Either/Or*, I, *KW* III (*SV* I 38, 75-76, 203: repetition of making the idea visible; repetition of esthetic moments (*Don Giovanni*); repetition of day and night); II, *KW*

Johannes Climacus was set aside as a work in process, although Johannes Climacus returned the following year (1844) as the author of *Fragments* and again in 1846 as the author of *Concluding Unscientific Postscript*. Kierkegaard returned to the theme of repetition, however, and in a few months during 1843 wrote not only *Repetition* but also *Fear and Trembling* and *Three Upbuilding Discourses*. And just as his relationship with Regine Olsen had been the "point of departure in time . . . an occasion" for the imaginative-reflective work *Either/Or*, especially for "The Seducer's Diary," so again it was the very present but vanishing occasion for the three works written during mid-1843. *Either/Or*, as understood by the secret reader, Regine,[13] was supposed to have been a way of clear-

---

IV (*SV* II 98, 115, 125, 128, 217: esthetic cultivation of the interesting and avoidance of repetition; esthetic view of habit and repetition; "eternity in time," "living in eternity and yet hearing the hall clock strike"; "different conception of time and of the significance of repetition"; repetition in time has no significance for the mystic). In the journals and papers before the writing of *Johannes Climacus, or De omnibus dubitandum est*, there are no entries on repetition as such. See, however, *JP* I 95 (*Pap.* III A 804, 1841: Poul Møller's poem on repetition in a dream or through recollection); *JP* II 1201 (*Pap.* III A 215, 1840: "*redintegratio in statum pristinum*"). See Supplement, p. 274 (*Pap.* IV B 10:3, 4, 8, 9), for an entry from a draft of *Johannes Climacus*.

For earlier entries on "fear and trembling," Abraham, and Abraham and Isaac in the works and in the journals and papers, see *Either/Or*, II, *KW* IV (*SV* II 6, 74: "love with the fear and trembling of a religious love"; "my wife is not the slave woman in Abraham's house"); *JP* III 3269, 3369, 2383 (*Pap.* II A 790, 313, 370: "does not want to have the King of Sodom say: I have made Abraham rich"; "Keep us vigilant in fear and trembling"; "Fear and trembling . . . is not the *primus motor* in the Christian life . . . it is the oscillating balance wheel"); *JP* III 3189, 3380 (*Pap.* II C 8, A 538: "why Paul, in accentuating Abraham as an example of faith, did not take the moment in his life when he was about to sacrifice Isaac"; "pray for me as Abraham prayed for Sodom"); *JP* I 298 (*Pap.* II A 569: "He spared Abraham's firstborn and only tested the patriarch's faith; he spared not his only begotten son"). See Supplement, pp. 239-42 (*Pap.* III C 4; IV A 76, 77).

[13] Regine read the works, as Raphael Meyer testifies in a volume he prepared at her request, *Kierkegaardske Papirer. Forlovelsen [The Engagement]* (Copenhagen and Kristiania: 1904), p. vi: "Already as a newly engaged couple we see them sitting together in Schlegel's room and reading Kierkegaard's works aloud for each other, and indeed they did contain, the one after the other, bits of her past, reminders from the time of engagement,

ing her out of the relationship by the deceptive impression that Kierkegaard was a deceiver or a despairing esthete (volume I) or by the more accurate impression that he thought of love and marriage as Judge William did (volume II) but, because of undeclared hindrances, wronged the beloved precisely out of love.[14] That was Regine's either/or, and Kierkegaard hoped she would choose one or the other interpretation.

During the spring of 1843, Regine met Kierkegaard "every morning between nine and ten." "I made no effort to have it happen. She knew the street I usually walk, I knew the way she . . . . ."[15] Here a sheet is missing from the journal entry, but it may be surmised from Kierkegaard's philosophical work on *Johannes Climacus* and the reconciled composure of *Two Upbuilding Discourses* that the unarranged, silent, momentary meetings were vanishing occasions with no particular consequences. Most likely, Kierkegaard thought she had chosen the second alternative presented in *Either/Or*.

On April 16, 1843, however, there was another chance meeting of considerable consequence.

At vespers on Easter Sunday in Frue Kirke (during Mynster's sermon), she nodded to me. I do not know if it was pleadingly or forgivingly, but in any case very affectionately. I had sat down in a place apart, but she discovered it. Would to God she had not done so. Now a year and a half of suffering and all the enormous pains I took are wasted; she does not believe that I was a deceiver, she has faith in me. What ordeals now lie ahead of her. The next will be that I am a hypocrite. The higher we go, the more dreadful it is. That a man of my inwardness, of my religiousness, could act in such a way. And yet I can no longer live solely for her, cannot expose myself to the contempt of men in order to lose my honor—that I have done.

---

studies of him and her, actuality, which by Kierkegaard's poet-spirit had been transformed into *Dichtung und Wahrheit*" (ed. tr.).

[14] See Supplement, pp. 241–42 (*Pap.* IV A 76).

[15] *JP* V 5653 (*Pap.* IV A 97).

Shall I in sheer madness go ahead and become a villain just
to get her to believe it—ah, what help is that. She will still
believe that I was not that before.[16]

Instead of actually becoming a villain out of sheer madness, Kierkegaard, in what Plato calls the divine madness of
the poet, turned to what became his two most poetic writings, *Repetition* and *Fear and Trembling*, and to the religious
discourses that occupied him before and after the publication
of the two poetic works.[17] The date of the preface to the first
two discourses is May 5, 1843. On May 8, Kierkegaard left
for Berlin.

Two weeks after the conclusive breaking of the engagement in October 1841, Kierkegaard had left Copenhagen for
his first visit to Berlin, where he wrote a large part of
Either/Or.[18] Three weeks after the momentary, silent Easter
meeting in 1843, he left again for Berlin. In a letter to his
old friend Emil Boesen,[19] he reported, "I have finished a work
[*Repetition*][20] of some importance to me, am hard at work on
another [*Fear and Trembling*] . . . ." Inasmuch as his library
was indispensable for the second work and as a printer for
both works had to be found, he informed Boesen that they
would see each other again soon. In the meantime, although
he was ill, he was working long days punctuated only by a
brief morning walk and meals, because "during the past
months I had pumped up a veritable shower bath, and now
I have pulled the string and the ideas are cascading down

---

[16] Ibid.

[17] *Three Upbuilding Discourses*, October 16, 1843; *Four Upbuilding Discourses*, December 6, 1843; *Two Upbuilding Discourses*, March 5, 1844; *Three
Upbuilding Discourses*, June 8, 1844; *Four Upbuilding Discourses*, August 31,
1844. All of them appeared again on May 29, 1845, along with the two
published May 16, 1843, under the title *Eighteen Upbuilding Discourses*.

[18] See, for example, *Kierkegaard: Letters and Documents, KW* XXV, Letters
54, 68, December 14, 1841, and February 6, 1842, to Emil Boesen.

[19] Ibid., Letter 82, May 25, 1843. In an earlier letter, no. 80, May 15, he
had written that "the machinery within me is fully at work, the feelings are
sound, harmonious, etc."

[20] The manuscript of *Repetition* is dated: "Berlin in May 1843." See Supplement, p. 276 (*Pap.* IV B 97:3).

upon me: healthy, happy, merry, gay, blessed children born with ease . . . .."[21] In retrospect, he wrote in a journal entry of 1854:

> Imagination is what providence uses to take men captive in actuality [*Virkeligheden*], in existence [*Tilværelsen*], in order to get them far enough out, or within, or down into existence. And when imagination has helped them get as far out as they should be—then actuality genuinely begins.
>
> Johannes V. Müller says that there are two great powers around which all revolves: ideas and women. This is entirely correct and is consistent with what I say here about the significance of imagination. Women or ideas are what beckon men out into existence. Naturally there is the great difference that for the thousands who run after a skirt there is not always one who is moved by ideas.
>
> As far as I am concerned, it was so difficult to get me out and into an interest in ideas that a girl was used as a middle term against me in a very unusual way.[22]

The young man in *Repetition* becomes awakened as a poet, and Johannes de Silentio of *Fear and Trembling* is a poet-dialectician. Behind them is Kierkegaard, the creator of the pseudonymous authors. Later he wrote, "I am a poet. But long before I became a poet I was intended for the life of religious individuality. And the event whereby I became a poet was an ethical break [a theme in *Repetition*] or a teleological suspension of the ethical [a theme in *Fear and Trembling*]. And both of these things make me want to be something more than 'the poet' . . . ."[23] To be something more or other than a poet might well have been possible for him if *Either/Or* had been successful with the secret reader. Another possibility would have been an act—marriage—against all his

---

[21] See note 19. This is the very opposite of Constantin Constantius's report on his Berlin visit (see p. 169).

[22] *JP* II 1832 (*Pap.* XI¹ A 288). The statement by Johannes von Müller, a German historian (1752-1809), has not been located. None of Müller's books is listed in the auction catalog (*ASKB*).

[23] *JP* VI 6718 (*Pap.* X³ A 789).

best judgment regarding her welfare and his own. In both cases, the momentary, silent meeting of eyes on that late Easter afternoon would scarcely have been the vanishing occasion of the two poetic works, and most likely Johannes Climacus would have completed and published his *De omnibus dubitandum est*, as well as his *Fragments*, in 1843.

Repetition and *Fear and Trembling* were to be a new either/or for Regine. *Repetition* presented one interpretation: the beloved was essentially the muse of the incipient young poet, and he could not fulfill the ethical claims of the engagement because of the probable consequences. "My love cannot find expression in a marriage. If I do that, she is crushed. Perhaps the possibility appeared tempting to her. I cannot help it; it was that to me also. The moment it becomes a matter of actuality, all is lost, then it is too late."[24] Although he rejected Constantius's plan for a deception (intended to clear the beloved out of the relationship just as "The Seducer's Diary" was supposed to have done), he finally despaired of repetition in the ethical sphere, as did Constantius in the esthetic sphere. For the young man, repetition would have been recovery of himself as one able to marry or as a justified exception to the ethical claim. Job not only justified himself but received all that had been lost, and more. The young man could do neither—and then in despair shot himself, according to the penultimate manuscript version.[25] Although Constantius had despaired of the repetition of selected experiences, he had intimations of a third kind of repetition, namely, repetition in the religious sphere—a possibility for the young man when repetition in other ways was manifestly impossible.[26]

Regine's choice of interpretations was between the "either" of *Repetition* and the "or" intimated by Constantius and developed in *Fear and Trembling*: the double-movement of resignation and faith. In the paradox of faith, possibility is affirmed where there is manifestly only impossibility, because

[24] P. 201.
[25] See Supplement, p. 276 (*Pap.* IV B 97:5).
[26] See pp. 228-30.

with God all things are possible. But the author, Johannes de Silentio, is not Abraham; he can make the movement of resignation but not that of faith. He is a poet-dialectician who can think through the nature of faith and poetically celebrate it at a distance. While working on *Fear and Trembling* in Berlin, Kierkegaard opened a journal entry dated May 17, 1843, with a line that Johannes de Silentio could have written *mutatis mutandis*: "If I had had faith, I would have stayed with Regine."[27] Constantius expressed a kindred idea: "If the young man had believed in repetition . . . ."[28]

In order to have the use of his library while completing *Fear and Trembling* and to make printing arrangements for it and *Repetition*, Kierkegaard returned to Copenhagen on May 30, 1843. Having completed the new secret either/or provided by *Repetition* and *Fear and Trembling*, he could proceed with the discourses that had been interrupted by the Easter meeting. During June and July, he finished the manuscript of *Three Upbuilding Discourses* in time to have that work published under his own name simultaneously with the other two. The three discourses have more than a chronological relation to the other two works. They move in the sphere intimated by Constantius and poetically celebrated in ideality by Johannes de Silentio. Although obviously cast in universality, the three discourses are more essentially autobiographical than are *Repetition* and *Fear and Trembling*. The substance of these discourses has a particular appropriateness to those special months of mid-1843. Two are titled "Love Will Cover the Multiplicity of Sins," and the third is titled "Strengthening in the Inner Man." These discourses manifest a continuing and a deepening of Kierkegaard's understanding of himself in a relationship to God, which is clearly indicated in the two discourses begun early in 1843 and published on May 5 of that year. In varying ways, the deepening of self-understanding in a God-relationship is the theme of the eleven discourses published in the eight months before

[27] *JP* V 5664 (*Pap*. IV A 107).
[28] P. 146.

the publication of *Philosophical Fragments* and *The Concept of Anxiety* (June 13 and 17, 1844).

Most unexpectedly, however, a second interruption occurred during the preparation of the manuscript for *Three Upbuilding Discourses*, an interruption that made the second either/or unnecessary for Regine's secret reading and at the same time freed their authors' author. But it did require a revision of the first work, *Repetition*, after *Fear and Trembling* was finished. The second interruption was Kierkegaard's discovery sometime in July of Regine's engagement in June to Johan Frederik Schlegel.

In the bound final copy of *Repetition*, there are marginal remains of five sheets that have been removed. A new ending, consisting of a revision of Constantin Constantius's incidental observations, the final letter from the young man, and Constantius's concluding letter to the reader, had to be written to replace the original pages. Inasmuch as the young man in *Repetition* obtains an accidental repetition through the marriage of his fiancé, the suicide catastrophe was replaced by his future as a poet. References to suicide in earlier portions of the final manuscript clearly had to be altered or omitted.[29] Now Constantius and the young man become parodies of each other: Constantius despairs of esthetic repetition because of the contingency of life, and the young man, despairing of personal repetition in relation to the ethical, obtains esthetic repetition by accident.

Among other changes in the final manuscript or variations in the printed text from the final revised manuscript are the omission of "Berlin in May 1843" on the first page and the change of the date of Constantius's letter to the reader from "July 1843" to "August 1843." Also, the author's name was changed from "Victorinus [added: Constantinus] de bona speranza" to "Constantin [deleted: Walter] Constantius," a change that may have been related to changes in the author's new final portions. The most important changes, however, apart from the change of the outcome of *Repetition*, were the

---

[29] See Supplement, pp. 276-77 (*Pap.* IV B 97:4, 5, 6).

changes in the subtitle.[30] "A Fruitless Venture [*Forsøg*]," "A Venture of Discovery," and, again, "A Fruitless Venture" were replaced by "A Venture in Experimental Philosophy [*Experimental-Philosophie*]," which was changed to "A Venture in Experimenting Philosophy [*experimenterende Philosophie*]." Finally, "Psychology" replaced the term "Philosophy." Of these changes, the most important were the addition of "Experimenting" and the change to "Psychology."

In Danish, the word *Experiment* in its various forms is a loan word.[31] In Kierkegaard's time, the common Danish expression was *Forsøg* (test, trial, venture) or *gjøre Erfaring* (literally, "to make experience") rather than *Experiment* or the verb *experimentere*. Neither Peter E. Müller's *Dansk Synonymik*, I–II (Copenhagen: 1829), nor Christian Molbech's *Dansk Ordbog* (Copenhagen: 1833; *ASKB* 1032) includes *Experiment* in any form. In the proceedings of Det kongelige Videnskabernes Selskab, edited by physicist Hans Christian Ørsted, the term rarely appears (and then usually in treatises by non-Danish members) in the seven volumes covering the years 1823-1845. *Forsøg* and *Undersøgelse* [investigation] are used almost exclusively.

Not only was the term *Experiment* uncommon in Danish

[30] See Supplement, p. 276 (*Pap.* IV B 97:1).

[31] This is also the case in German. Grimms' *Deutsches Wörterbuch* (Leipzig: 1854-1962) does not have *Experiment* as a rubric, only *Erfahrung, Forschung, Versuch*, etc. Kierkegaard owned Anton T. Brück's German translation of Bacon's *Novum Organum* (Leipzig: 1830; *ASKB* 420), in the English version of which "experiment" and similar words are used hundreds of times; in the Latin version, various forms of *experientia* and *experimentum* are used. The German translation very rarely employs *Experiment*, using instead *Versuch, Untersuchung, Empiriker* (for "men of experiment"), etc. In Hegel, according to Hermann Glockner, *Hegel-Lexicon*, I–II (Stuttgart: Fromanns Verlag, 1957), I, p. 581, the term *Experiment* is used only once, in *Wissenschaft der Logik*. See *Georg Wilhelm Friedrich Hegel's Werke. Vollständige Ausgabe*, I–XVIII, ed. Ph. Marheineke et al. (Berlin: 1832-40; *ASKB* 549-65), V, p. 299; *Jubiläumsausgabe* [*J.A.*], I–XXVI (Stuttgart: 1927-40), V, p. 299; *Hegel's Science of Logic*, tr. A. V. Miller (London: Allen & Unwin, 1969; New York: Humanities Press, 1969), p. 802. *Experiment* there refers to the presentation to intuition of a particular case of the specific character apprehended by cognition.

at the time, but the form used in the subtitle, the present participle, *experimenterende*, was even more unusual. The deleted adjectival form, *Experimental*, has not been located anywhere else in the works or in the *Papirer*.[32] The active character of the participle is still more pronounced in Frater Taciturnus's later use of "experiment" as a transitive verb when he says he will *"experimentere en Figur."*[33] Although an English-speaking reader of Danish, as well as most Danish readers, would customarily read *Experiment* as "experiment" and *experimentere* as the verb "to experiment," no one would read "experiment a character" without adding—erroneously—"with" or "on." Instead, however, Kierkegaard's uncommon understanding and use of the transitive verb must be used to define it as "imaginatively construct" or "imaginatively cast in an experiential mode."

Fortunately, the journals and papers and also certain of the works make Kierkegaard's meaning clear. In the autumn of 1837, while reading Johann Erdmann's *Vorlesungen über Glauben und Wissen* (Berlin: 1837; *ASKB* 479), Kierkegaard made note of Erdmann's stress on the role of hypothesis or theory in relation to experiment: "reason experiments when it terminates in making experiences."[34] The universal, the law, the hypothesis are rational abstractions from experience, and then the hypothesis must find confirmation through the experiment; yet the hypothesis is superior and in a sense independent. Reason uses the particularity of the experiment for the sake of the hypothesis, the universal. Erdmann's epistemology is essentially Aristotelian, with more emphasis on the return to experience than is usually attributed to Aristotle.

---

[32] See *Index Verborum til Kierkegaards Samlede Værker*, comp. Alastair McKinnon (Leiden: E. J. Brill, 1973), and indexes to *Søren Kierkegaards Papirer*, XIV–XVI, ed. N. J. Cappelørn (Copenhagen: Gyldendal, 1975-78).

[33] "The Activity of a Traveling Esthetician," *The Corsair Affair*, p. 39, *KW* XIII (*SV* XIII 423). *Ordbog over det danske Sprog*, I–XXVIII (Copenhagen: 1919-56), quotes the expression and notates it with a symbolic comet, meaning "Extremely rare, unique."

[34] *Pap.* II C 4 in suppl. vol. XIII, p. 151. The Danish *gjøre Erfaringer* is translated literally. See *JP* II 2251 (*Pap.* IV C 46, 1837) and note 721.

A journal entry some months later[35] states that poetry transfigures life by explaining, illuminating, and developing it, an idea reinforced later by Kierkegaard's reading of Aristotle in connection with a contemplated series of lectures on esthetics to be opened with a lecture on the concept of poetry.[36] " 'All poetry is imitation' (Aristotle)—'better or worse than we are.' Hence poetry points beyond itself to *actuality* and to the metaphysical ideality."[37] Kierkegaard took note of Aristotle's distinction between ποιεῖν and πράττειν (to make and to act) and of his definition of art (in *Nicomachean Ethics*) as a making.[38] The poet is, then, as the word states, a maker, a maker in the realm of the possible rather than in the realm of what is or has been.[39] Although there is no extant journal reference to Aristotle's dictum that poetry is truer or more philosophical than history, Kierkegaard could hardly have missed it in his reading about poetry as imitation, an observation that appears explicitly two years later in *Stages on Life's Way* (*SV* VI 407).

In a reading entry from 1842, Kierkegaard quotes a poem of unhappy love by Gotthold Ephraim Lessing.[40] In a later retrospective entry, he writes: "Lessing's whole book 'On the Fable' must be read again. . . . It is found in *Sämtl. Werke*, vol. XVIII. On pages 204, 205, especially, there is something on Aristotle's teaching about actuality and possibility, and Lessing's teaching concerning it. It agrees so perfectly with

[35] *JP* I 136 (*Pap.* II A 352, February 5, 1839).

[36] *JP* V 5608 (*Pap.* IV C 127, 1842-43).

[37] *JP* I 144 (*Pap.* IV C 109, 1842-43). See *Stages on Life's Way, KW* XI (*SV* VI 407).

[38] *JP* V 5592 (*Pap.* IV C 24, 1842-43).

[39] Preparation for receptivity to this view of poetry and its substance was most likely provided by Kierkegaard's earlier reading of Plato, particularly the *Phaedo*, in which Socrates says (61 b) that "a poet, if he is to be worthy of the name, ought to work on imaginative themes, not on descriptive ones . . . ." The substance of the dialogue (60 b, 97-99) is drawn upon twice in *Either/Or* (finished in November 1842 and published February 20, 1843), *KW* III (*SV* I 208, 209).

[40] *JP* III 2369 (*Pap.* III A 200). *Gotthold Ephraim Lessing's sämmtliche Schriften,* I–XXXII (Berlin: 1825-28; *ASKB* 1747-62), XVII, p. 281.

what I have developed through several pseudonyms; therefore I have preferred 'the imaginary construction' [*Experi-
mentet*] to the historical-actual."[41] Although the term *Experiment* has not been found in Lessing's volume XVIII or
elsewhere, Johannes Climacus in a draft (1845)[42] and also in
the published text of *Postscript* refers to Lessing and the inverted relationship of one who, "imaginatively constructing
[*experimenterende*, present participle, active], raises doubts
without explaining why he does it, and of one [Climacus]
who, imaginatively constructing, seeks to show forth the religious in its preternatural magnitude without explaining why
he does it."[43]

Numerous entries in the journals and papers[44] may be
summarized to indicate what Kierkegaard and the pseudonymous writers meant by "imaginary construction" [*Experiment*] and "imaginatively constructing" [*experimenterende*] and
how these terms crystallize an epistemology and a philosophy of art involving Aristotle, Plato, and Lessing—and Kierkegaard, who at the last minute added the word to the subtitle of *Repetition*. The task of the poet includes the philosophic
task of casting private and shared experience into reflection,
of penetrating it and grasping its internal coherence and
meaning, the universally human. History and actuality are
thereby transcended, and thus poetry, as well as all art, science, and philosophy, deals only with possibility, "not in the
sense of an idle hypothesis but possibility in the sense of ideal
actuality."[45] Therefore the poet is "one who makes," who
construes, constructs, and composes hypotheses as do philosophers and scientists. What distinguishes the poet is a kind
of imagination that shapes the possibles in palpable form, in
the form of "ideal actuality." The poet's mode is not the

[41] *JP* III 2373 (*Pap.* X¹ A 363, 1849). Lessing's view is epitomized on p.
249 (ed. tr.): "In a fable, the fable maker only wants to bring an idea into
perceptible form [intuition]."
[42] *Pap.* VI B 98:21.
[43] *KW* XII (*SV* VII 48).
[44] See pp. 357-62, note to subtitle.
[45] *JP* I 1059 (*Pap.* X² A 439).

discursive, demonstrative, didactic [*docerende*] mode of the scientist and philosopher or the strict narrative mode of the historian. His mode is that of imaginative construction in the artistic illusion of actuality, or, to borrow a phrase from Climacus in *Fragments*, it is to construct imaginatively or to hypothesize *in concreto*[46] rather than to use the scientific and philosophic mode of abstraction in his presentation.

The poet in this view is an imaginative constructor [*Experimentator*] who presents the possible in experiential (the two words have a common root) verisimilitude. For the existential philosopher, "the portrayal of the existential is chiefly either realization in life or poetic presentation, *loquere ut videam* [speak that I may see]."[47] Kierkegaard is therefore the poetic *Experimentator* who makes or fashions the various pseudonymous, poetic, imaginative constructors, who in turn imaginatively shape characters, scenes, situations, and relations expressive in various ways of the hypothesis(es) informing the work. *Experimentere* is therefore a transitive verb: imaginatively and reflectively to construct a hypothesis and imaginatively to cast it and its implications in the constructed poetic illusion of experiential actuality. Therefore, the task of Frater Taciturnus is to "experiment a character," not to experiment *with* or *on* a character. Likewise, Johannes de Silentio is "a poetic [experimented, imaginatively "made"] person who exists only among poets"[48] and who in turn is the dialectical poet who poetizes or "experiments" ethical-religious issues in the form of ideal actuality in the imagina-

---

[46] *KW* VII (*SV* IV 242).

[47] *JP* I 1058 (*Pap.* X² A 414). See the first page of Frater Taciturnus's "Letter to the Reader," *Stages, KW* XI (*SV* VI 371); *Letters, KW* XXV, Letters 8, 72. John Ruskin had a similar view of the poet and his work: "A poet, or creator, is therefore a person who puts things together, not as a watchmaker steel, or a shoemaker leather, but who puts life into them. His work is essentially this: it is the gathering of and arranging of material by the imagination, so as to have in it at least the harmony or helpfulness of life, and the passion or emotion of life." *Modern Painters*, V, *The Works of John Ruskin*, I–XXIX (London, New York: George Allen, 1905), VII, p. 215.

[48] See Supplement, p. 243 (*Pap.* IV B 79, 1843).

tively constructed work titled *Fear and Trembling*. Accordingly, Aage Henriksen quite justifiably calls that work a novel,[49] a category in which he includes "The Seducer's Diary" in *Either/Or*, *Repetition*, and " 'Guilty?'/'Not Guilty?' " in *Stages*.[50]

For Kierkegaard himself, the use of the terms *Experiment* and *experimentere* had some fateful personal consequences that arose from two misunderstandings. Before Kierkegaard made his "First and Last Declaration" (unnumbered pages at the end of *Postscript*), in which he acknowledged being the poetic fashioner of the pseudonymous authors, who themselves fashioned the imaginary constructions—the works and characters—the pseudonymous works were attributed to him by rumor and even in print.[51] It was also thought by a growing number that these pseudonymous works—especially "The Seducer's Diary" in *Either/Or* and " 'Guilty?'/'Not Guilty?' " in *Stages*, as well as *Fear and Trembling* and *Repetition*—were nothing other than thinly disguised personal history and not categories poetically-dialectically set in motion in the form of imaginary ideal actuality. That Regine would interpret the works as addressed by him to her—and that she would think of him as a scoundrel and deceiver—was part of his plan. But that the poetic-dialectical productions were taken as autobiographical reports was the result of a misconception of the facts and of the works.

The second misunderstanding arose from the ordinary

---

[49] Aage Henriksen, *Kierkegaards Romaner* (Copenhagen: Gyldendal, 1969).

[50] *JP* V 5865 (*Pap.* VII[1] A 83) states that " 'Guilty?'/'Not Guilty?' " in *Stages* is the imaginary construction par excellence, not only because it is in the form of double-reflection, as all the pseudonymous works are, but also because the Quidam of the imaginary construction makes an imaginary construction in order "to poetize himself out of a girl." On the other hand, the second imaginary construction in the Quidam sense is "lacking in *Either/Or*" (*JP* V 5866; *Pap.* VII[1] A 84, 1846), an omission that is explained in *JP* V 5628 (*Pap.* IV A 215, 1843): "The only thing this work lacks is a narrative, which I did begin but omitted, just as Aladdin left a window incomplete. It was to be called 'Unhappy Love.' It was to form a contrast to the Seducer."

[51] See *The Corsair Affair*, p. 24, and note 55, *KW* XIII.

conception of "experiment" and from the surmise that "the Seducer" and Quidam (*Stages*), especially, in Baconian fashion[52] vexed or tortured their subjects experimentally in the practice of a kind of vivisection. Peder Ludvig Møller wrote in *Gæa* (dated 1846 but actually published in December 1845):

> the transparency in our author seems to be a result of poisoning. And, of course, the feminine nature placed on the experimental rack turns into dialectic in the book and vanishes, but in actual life she inevitably must go mad or into Peblinge Lake. . . .
>
> If ordinary common sense may be permitted to intervene here, it perhaps would say in elemental immediacy: If you regard life as a dissecting laboratory and yourself as a cadaver, then go ahead, lacerate yourself as much as you want to; as long as you do not harm anyone else, the police will not disturb your activity. But to spin another creature into your spider web, dissect it alive or torture the soul out of it drop by drop by means of experimentation, that is not allowed, except with insects, and is there not something horrible and revolting to the healthy human mind even in this idea?[53]

The consequences of the twin misunderstandings of the works as factually autobiographical and of "experiment" as the artful vexation of nature in the natural sciences are summarized by Georg Brandes: "Certain features of unreasonableness or hardness towards his betrothed (which, insofar as they were the case, were all due to his efforts to make the young girl weary of him, to put himself in a bad light before her and thereby ease the break for her) were rumored about the city, and the multitude, who had no clue to these singularities in conduct, attributed them to the worst characteristics: coldness of heart, a tendency to play with a human heart in order, as it was called, to make experiments with it,

[52] Francis Bacon, *Novum Organum*, I, xcviii. See note 31 above.
[53] *Gæa*, pp. 176-78. See *The Corsair Affair*, Supplement, pp. 100-04, *KW* XIII. See also pp. 105-08 and 124 in *The Corsair Affair*.

something the bourgeois philistines found all the more terrible the less clear a conception they had of what they actually meant by it."[54]

Regine herself knew that the popular notion of Kierkegaard as an "experimenter" on the human heart—namely, hers—was false. Hanne Mourier, a friend of Regine Schlegel, put portions of some of their conversations into writing, which was then read and approved by Regine. On this point, Hanne Mourier writes:

> After your husband's death, interest in the story of your youth, your engagement to S. Kierkegaard, has again come to the fore, and many direct approaches have been made to you about this. At first you felt overwhelmed by this interest and spoke about the matter reluctantly, because for many years you lived a completely private and happy life with your husband, and almost no one has dared to approach you with indiscreet questions. Now it is your duty to communicate what you and no one else can: what view you and your husband have had of S. Kierkegaard. You desire that later generations shall be informed about S. Kierkegaard and your noble husband in relation to you and see them in the true and good light in which you have known both of them. It must be said and positively maintained that S. Kierkegaard has never misused your love in order to torment you or to conduct mental experiments with you, as has been commonly but erroneously assumed. When he became engaged, it was his earnest intention to marry you. In these later years you speak of this relationship with many people with whom you associate, because you desire that it be understood that S. Kierkegaard's life was not in any way at variance with his work as a religious author.[55]

---

[54] Georg Brandes, *Søren Kierkegaard, Samlede Skrifter*, I–XVIII (Copenhagen: 1899-1910), II, p. 292 (ed. tr.).

[55] The text of the manuscript, dated March 1, 1902, is printed in Hjalmar Helweg, *Søren Kierkegaard* (Copenhagen: 1933), pp. 385-92. The quoted portion is from p. 386 (ed. tr.).

If the term *Experiment* was erroneously and even maliciously misunderstood by the majority of Kierkegaard's contemporaries and eventually by others as well, the terms "psychology" and "psychological" were less misleading at that time but more so later, particularly in the English-speaking world. Psychology in the nineteenth century was part of philosophy, as it had been in classical philosophy since Thales, Socrates, Plato, and Aristotle: a characterization of man's defining nature or distinguishing capacities, that is, philosophical anthropology.

Psychologie (German spelling, changed to Danish spelling in the printed version) finally replaced *Philosophie* on the title page of the final manuscript copy of *Repetition*, a change that may have been influenced by Johann E. Erdmann, whose use of *Experiment* Kierkegaard had noted earlier. Erdmann states in his *Grundriss der Psychologie* (Leipzig: 1840), which Kierkegaard owned (*ASKB* 481), that the first of the three parts of psychology is "philosophical anthropology,"[56] which has as its object "the subjective spirit."[57] "Psychology," however, seems to have meant something more to Kierkegaard than philosophical anthropology, a view of man and its implications for a life-view, particularly when the word was used together with *Experiment* and *experimenterende*. "Psychology" and "psychological" qualify the imaginative constructing by adding an emphasis upon the embodiment of a view or views of man in characters, events, and relations, just as a poet makes the imaginative construction in palpable form, the idea made visible, a philosophy of man *in concreto*.[58]

What is developed under (c) [*Pap*. IV B 117, pp. 281-82] was what I wanted to set forth in *Repetition*, but not in a scientific-scholarly way, still less in a scientific-schol-

---

[56] P. 10. The same terminology is found in Karl Rosenkranz, *Psychologie oder die Wissenschaft vom subjectiven Geist* (Königsberg: 1837; *ASKB* 744), a work cited three times in *The Concept of Anxiety*.

[57] Pp. 1, 11.

[58] See *Fragments, KW* VII (*SV* IV 242), for use of the phrase.

arly way in the sense that every teller in our philosophical bank could count 1, 2, 3. I wanted to depict and make visible psychologically and esthetically; in the Greek sense I wanted to let the concept come into being in the individuality and the situation, working itself forward through all sorts of misunderstanding.[59]

But as soon as the individual is viewed in his freedom, the question becomes a different one: can repetition be realized. It is repetition in this pregnant sense as task for freedom and as freedom that gives the title to my little book and that in my little book has come into being depicted and made visible in the individuality and in the situation, which is the main point to the psychologist, and one is justified in looking for it and demanding that it be esthetically depicted by one who, unlike the scientific psychologist, has very scrupulously designated himself as imaginatively constructing [*experimenterende*].[60]

In brief, "imaginary construction" (*Experiment*), both as an imaginary construction in thought (*Tankeexperiment*) and as an "imaginary psychological construction" (*psychologisk Experiment*), is for Kierkegaard related to "indirect method" or "indirect communication." "Later I again found illumination of the meaning of imaginary construction [*Experiment*] as the form of communication."[61] When the term *Experiment* is used without reference to a category (the pseudonymous works), it means hypothesis,[62] illusion,[63] imaginary construction.[64] With the exception of later retrospective entries in the journals and papers referring to the pseudonymous series that ends with Climacus's *Postscript* (1846) and of the term's par-

[59] See Supplement, p. 302 (*Pap.* IV B 117, p. 282).
[60] See Supplement, pp. 312-13 (*Pap.* IV B 117, p. 293). For use of the term "psychology" in other works and in the journals and papers, see pp. 361-62.
[61] *JP* I 633 (*Pap.* VI B 40:45). See pp. 357-62.
[62] *The Concept of Irony, KW* II (*SV* XIII 171).
[63] *JP* I 188 (*Pap.* X² A 396). See *Two Ages*, pp. 66-67, and note 15, *KW* XIV (*SV* VIII 63).
[64] *The Sickness unto Death*, p. 68, *KW* XIX (*SV* XI 180).

ticularized use in *The Sickness unto Death*, phrases involving *Experiment* are extremely rare in the works and the *Papirer* after 1846.

Although *Fear and Trembling* and *Repetition* constitute a distinguishable island surrounded by the Climacus works and by the eighteen upbuilding discourses, they are not essentially distinct from other works in the authorship. They have a substantive place in the comprehensive plan (*Total-Anlæg*). References to *Fear and Trembling* as a work and to the central concepts in it ("knight of faith," "paradox," "double-movement," "by virtue of the absurd," "teleological suspension," "leap," "offense") appear in the pseudonymous works, particularly in *The Concept of Anxiety, Fragments*, and *Postscript*. Thereafter, however, the concepts, as formulated in *Fear and Trembling*, rarely appear, except for the term used least often, "offense," which becomes increasingly important in *Upbuilding Discourses in Various Spirits, Works of Love, Christian Discourses, The Sickness unto Death, Practice in Christianity*, and *The Moment*.

Apart from a reference in *The Point of View* that categorizes *Fear and Trembling* as an esthetic work,[65] direct references to it in the works are confined to *The Concept of Anxiety* and *Postscript*. In the former, it is pointed out that Johannes de Silentio centers on the collision between ethics and religious ideality and on the possibility of repetition by virtue of the absurd.[66] In *Postscript*, Johannes Climacus briefly discusses *Fear and Trembling* with reference to the paradox and the leap: "Christianity is rooted in the paradoxical . . . the leap."[67] Johannes Climacus's discussion of "spiritual trial [*Anfægtelse*]"[68] clarifies that crucial category in *Fear and Trembling*. Particular attention is given to the "knight of faith," who, Climacus says, was presented "in a state of complete-

---

[65] *The Point of View, KW* XXII (*SV* XIII 521).
[66] *The Concept of Anxiety*, p. 17, *KW* VIII (*SV* IV 289).
[67] *Postscript, KW* XII (*SV* VII 85).
[68] Ibid. (*SV* VII 222, 226-27, 399-400).

ness, and hence in a false medium, instead of in the medium of existence."[69]

The themes of *Fear and Trembling* that reappear in the journals and papers with specific reference to the work are: Abraham,[70] "the leap, becoming open and making manifest, the hero of faith,"[71] the absurd,[72] the single individual,[73] and the poet and hero.[74] An entry on Abraham from 1843 has been turned around by some interpreters of *Fear and Trembling* and used as a justification for a primarily biographical approach to the work: "He who has explained this riddle has explained my life."[75] On the other hand, most readers would agree with the opening lines of an entry from 1849: "Once I am dead, *Fear and Trembling* alone will be enough for an imperishable name as an author. Then it will be read, translated into foreign languages as well."[76]

In *The Point of View*,[77] *Repetition*, as well as *Fear and Trembling*, is placed in the esthetic category. There is some discussion of *Repetition* in *The Concept of Anxiety, Stages*, and *Postscript*. In the first work, Vigilius Haufniensis picks out three portions for special attention: " 'Repetition is the *interest [Interesse]* of metaphysics and also the interest upon which metaphysics comes to grief; repetition is the watchword [*Løsnet*] in every ethical view; repetition is *conditio sine qua non* [the indispensable condition] for every issue of dogmatics' "; "eternity is the true repetition"; " 'Repetition is the earnestness of existence.' "[78] In *Stages*, Frater Taciturnus says that Constantin Constantius failed in his use of the erotic

---

[69] Ibid. (*SV* VII 435).

[70] See Supplement, pp. 266-70 (*Pap.* X³ A 114; X⁴ A 338, 357, 458; X⁵ A 132).

[71] *JP* VI 6405 (*Pap.* X⁶ B 85).

[72] *JP* I 11, 12 (*Pap.* X⁶ B 80, 81).

[73] *JP* VI 6357 (*Pap.* X¹ A 139).

[74] *JP* II 1812 (*Pap.* XI¹ A 476).

[75] See Supplement, pp. 241-42 (*Pap.* IV A 76).

[76] See Supplement, pp. 257-58 (*Pap.* X² A 15).

[77] *The Point of View, KW* XXII (*SV* XIII 521).

[78] *The Concept of Anxiety*, pp. 17-19, 149, 151, *KW* VIII (*SV* IV 290-91, 415, 417). For the cited portions in *Repetition*, see pp. 149, 133, 221.

because "he remained within the esthetic"; on that level, "the collision is resolved without any difficulty."[79] Of the author of *Repetition*, he says: "The reader who has read Constantin Constantius's little book will see that I have a certain resemblance to that author, but am still very different, and the person who imaginatively constructs [*experimenterer*] always does well to conform to the imaginary construction."[80] Climacus in *Postscript* writes that "*Repetition* was called 'an imaginary psychological construction' . . .. That this was a doubly reflected communication form was immediately clear to me."[81] Climacus declines to say whether, apart from the form of communication, *Repetition* and *Fear and Trembling* have any value,[82] but he nevertheless discusses the theme of *Repetition* in relation to *Fear and Trembling*[83] and in relation to *Stages*.[84]

Both *Repetition* and the concept of repetition are sparsely represented in the journals and papers.[85] The paucity of entries, despite the importance of the work and the concept, may be accounted for by assuming, as do the Danish editors of the *Papirer*,[86] that the extant collection of journal entries and papers is incomplete and by taking into account Kierkegaard's use of "spontaneity after reflection" and "faith" as synonyms for essential repetition. Scattered here and there, however, and as late as April 1855, a few entries give an estimate of the concept and of the work. "Repetition comes again everywhere" (1843).[87] " 'Repetition' is and remains a religious category. Constantin Constantius therefore cannot proceed further. He is clever, an ironist, battles the interest-

---

[79] *Stages, KW* XI (*SV* VI 376).

[80] Ibid. (*SV* VI 407).

[81] *Postscript, KW* XII (*SV* VII 223). With reference to "imaginary psychological construction," see pp. 357-62.

[82] Ibid. (*SV* VII 224).

[83] Ibid. (*SV* VII 222-26).

[84] Ibid. (*SV* VII 248).

[85] See Supplement, pp. 274-75, 325-27.

[86] *Pap.* I, p. ix.

[87] *JP* III 3793 (*Pap.* IV A 156). See Supplement, p. 326.

ing—but is not aware that he himself is caught in it" (1844).[88]
"*Eternity is indeed the true repetition*" (1844).[89] "[A]ll pointed
to a repetition, as it therefore stands in the little book *Repetition*: Repetition is the category about which it will revolve"
(1853).[90] "One of my pseudonyms has written a little book
called *Repetition*, in which he denies that there is repetition.
Without being quite in disagreement with him in the deeper
sense, I may very well be of the opinion that there nevertheless is a repetition, yes, it is very fortunate that there is a
repetition. . .." (1855).[91]

The author of *Fear and Trembling*, Johannes de Silentio,
appears in the journals and papers[92] as the possible author of
a collection of aphorisms, some of which later appeared in
The Moment but without Johannes de Silentio's name attached. Constantin Constantius, the author of *Repetition*, does
not appear again either as author or as the possible author of
a proposed work, but he does appear in *Stages* as the arranger
of the banquet and as one of the speakers on the theme of
love, as in Plato's *Symposium*. Worldly wise Constantius's
approach is that woman is properly construed only under the
category of jest.[93] The young man in *Repetition* is also present
and speaks on unhappy love.[94]

Notwithstanding Kierkegaard's belief that *Fear and Trembling* alone was "enough for an imperishable name as an author," the contemporary reception of that work and of *Repetition* was scarcely a prediction of future fame. In the four
years after their simultaneous publication on October 16, 1843,
in editions of 525 copies, only 321 copies of *Fear and Trembling* and 272 copies of *Repetition* had been sold. Of Kierkegaard's first thirteen books, which he himself published, only
one, *Either/Or*, was sold out by July 1847. At that time, *Fear*

---

[88] *JP* III 3794 (*Pap.* IV A 169). See Supplement, p. 326.
[89] *Pap.* V B 60, p. 137. See Supplement, p. 327.
[90] *Pap.* X⁶ B 236. See Supplement, p. 329.
[91] *Pap.* XI³ B 122. See Supplement, p. 330.
[92] *JP* VI 6787 (*Pap.* X⁶ B 253).
[93] *Stages, KW* XI (*SV* VI 49).
[94] Ibid. (*SV* VI 34-35).

and Trembling and *Repetition* were remaindered (204 and 253 copies, respectively), along with seven other titles, to book-seller C. A. Reitzel.[95]

Within a year after the two works had been published, four reviews or notices of *Fear and Trembling*[96] and three re-views or notices of *Repetition*[97] appeared. A point of agree-ment in the first two (anonymous) pieces[98] and in the latest (pseudonymous) review[99] is that *Fear and Trembling* and *Either/Or* are works of the same author. The second anony-mous piece and the pseudonymous review include *Repetition* in the same authorship. The pseudonymous review also links the three works with *Philosophical Fragments* (June 13, 1844), by Johannes Climacus, and *The Concept of Anxiety* (June 17, 1844), by Vigilius Haufniensis, and states that "the public has already linked these two books with the ones discussed here."[100] *Prefaces* (June 17, 1844), by Nicolaus Notabene, is not mentioned.

The first anonymous review was by Johan F. Hagen, who was introduced to Hegelian philosophy by H. L. Martensen and was eventually appointed Professor of Church History at the University of Copenhagen. Hagen states that *Fear and Trembling* and *Either/Or* manifest the same indefatigable dia-lectical talent and the same penchant for paradox. After a lengthy résumé of *Fear and Trembling*, he criticizes the em-phasis on transcendence and on "by virtue of the absurd" and concludes by applying the principle of mediation, whereby

[95] See Frithiof Brandt and Else Rammel, *Søren Kierkegaard og Pengene* (Co-penhagen: 1935), p. 18.

[96] [J. F. Hagen], *Theologisk Tidsskrift*, Ny Række, VIII, 2, February 1844, pp. 191-99; Anon., *Den Frisindede*, 129, Feb. 11, 1843, p. 515; "Kts" [J. P. Mynster], "*Kirkelig Polemik*," *Intelligensblade*, IV, 41-42, 1844, pp. 105-06 (see *The Point of View*, KW XXII [SV XIII 528]); "-v," *For Litteratur og Kritik*, II, 1844, pp. 373-91.

[97] Anon., *Den Frisindede*, 129, Feb. 11, 1843, p. 515; J. L. Heiberg, *Urania Aarbog for 1844* (Copenhagen: 1843; ASKB U 57), pp. 97-102; "-v," *For Litteratur og Kritik*, II, 1844, pp. 373-91.

[98] [Hagen], *Theologisk Tidsskrift*; Anon., *Den Frisindede*. See note 96 above.

[99] "-v," *For Litteratur og Kritik*. See note 96 above.

[100] Ibid., p. 390.

faith is encompassed in the universally rational as a higher wisdom. Kierkegaard wrote a brief, wry reply[101] in Johannes de Silentio's name but did not submit it for publication.

The second anonymous piece is not much more than a notice of *Fear and Trembling* and *Repetition*, with a long quotation from each. The brief estimate, although positive, is mixed. These works, according to the reviewer, are "a heaping up of ideas, thoughts about ideas, paradoxes, philosophical propositions that still do not want to be that, tales, episodes, bold metaphors and similes, etc. that are adroitly gathered together in a unity and presented with a matchless virtuosity of language that only too easily captivates. —We wish that these works, which without a doubt are by the anonymous author of *Either/Or*, may receive critical judgment as unbiased as it is competent, of which there is not much prospect in our day. . . . Incidentally, the works cited are not for hasty readers and are not likely acquisitions for circulating libraries."[102]

The third public reference to *Fear and Trembling* came as an incidental observation in an article by Bishop Jakob P. Mynster,[103] who called it a "remarkable book." "But why is that work called *Fear and Trembling?* Because its author has vividly comprehended, has deeply felt, has expressed with the full power of language the horror that must grip a person's soul when he is confronted by a task whose demands he dare not evade, and when his understanding is yet unable to disperse the appearance with its demand that seems to call him out from the eternal order to which every being shall submit." In an entry from June 29, 1855,[104] Kierkegaard recalls this observation without comment, but in the posthumously published *The Point of View for My Work as an Author*, where he states that *Fear and Trembling* is "a very singular esthetic kind of production," he adds: "And here the most

[101] *JP* V 5709 (*Pap.* IV A 193).
[102] *Den Frisindede*, p. 515. See note 96 above.
[103] See note 96 above.
[104] *Pap.* XI² A 419.

worthy author with the pen name Kts. placed the proper emphasis, which pleased me very much."[105]

The review of *Fear and Trembling* and *Repetition* by "-v" in the journal *For Litteratur og Kritik* is long and perceptive.[106] After some comments on the satisfactions and difficulties in reading an author who knows how to hold fast to his thought and has the courage to think it to the end, the reviewer castigates readers who think a thought halfway and Hegelians who absorb difficulties in thought by employing the handy term "mediation." The remainder of the review consists of an analysis of the two works (plus a comparison with *Either/Or* and an allusion to *Philosophical Fragments* and *The Concept of Anxiety*), regarding each as part of a comprehensive view [*Totalanskuelse*][107] and contrasting all of the works mentioned with Hegelian systematic continuity. The insightful and comprehensive character of this review and the terminology used in it may lead a later reader to compare it with "A Glance at a Contemporary Effort in Danish Literature," a section interpolated in *Concluding Unscientific Postscript*.

In 1850, Theophilus Nicolaus published his *Er Troen et Paradox og "i Kraft af det Absurde"* (*Is Faith a Paradox and "by Virtue of the Absurd"*),[108] in which both *Fear and Trembling* and *Postscript* are considered. Kierkegaard wrote a number of replies, none of which was published, and additional draft paragraphs.[109] His initial response was a lament over poor reading: "This is what comes about when bungling stupidity takes sides directly opposite to an artistic design." "What daily toil, enormous effort, almost sleepless dialectical perseverance it costs me to keep the threads straight in this subtle construction—such is not for others at all. I am identified automatically with my pseudonyms, and some nonsense is concocted which—of course—many more understand—yes,

[105] *The Point of View, KW* XXII (*SV* XIII 528).

[106] See note 96 above.

[107] *For Litteratur og Kritik*, p. 375.

[108] See Supplement, p. 265 (*Pap.* X⁶ B 69).

[109] See Supplement, pp. 259-66 (*Pap.* X⁶ B 68, 69, 77, 82), and *JP* I 9-12 (*Pap.* X⁶ B 78-81).

of course!"[110] The pieces for possible publication are of importance not in relation to the vanishing occasion for the writing but because of Kierkegaard's discussion of "the absurd."

Just as Theophilus Nicolaus's critique of *Fear and Trembling* was the occasion for some discussions of "the absurd," so also J. L. Heiberg's discussion of *Repetition* in his *Urania Aarbog for 1844*[111] provided an occasion for some replies for possible publication on the theme of repetition.[112] Heiberg had not misunderstood, but, having understood the obvious aspects, he had missed the prime concept of repetition. This is apparent in his quotations from *Repetition*,[113] which stop short of the key sentence that epitomizes the range and crucial aspect of repetition,[114] and in his discussions centering largely on cyclical repetitions in nature.

The unpublished responses to the few reviews of both books did not occupy much of Kierkegaard's time and attention. He was already immersed in the writing of thirteen upbuilding discourses,[115] which were published within eight months following the simultaneous publication of *Three Upbuilding Discourses*, *Fear and Trembling*, and *Repetition*. During this period, *Philosophical Fragments* (June 13, 1844) and *The Concept of Anxiety* (June 17, 1844) were also published. Although *Fear and Trembling* and *Repetition* were transcended in substance by the discourses and set aside in form by *Fragments* and *The Concept of Anxiety*,[116] they were not forgotten. A

---

[110] *JP* VI 6597 (*Pap.* X² A 601).

[111] See note 97 above. For the text, see pp. 379-83, note 14.

[112] See Supplement, pp. 281-325 (*Pap.* IV B 101-05, 108-12, 116-18, 120, 124).

[113] *Urania . . . 1844*, pp. 98-100. See pp. 379-83, note 14.

[114] See p. 149.

[115] See note 17 above.

[116] Both works are imaginary constructions in that the authors (Johannes Climacus and Vigilius Haufniensis) have been imaginatively constructed or are poetic creations. *Fragments* is an imaginary construction (*Postscript*, *KW* XII, *SV* VII 61), the work of a poet (*Fragments*, *KW* VII, *SV* IV 202-04), a thought-project (*Fragments*, *SV* IV 119). *The Concept of Anxiety* is a "deliberation" (title page), and its form is different from that of *Fear and Trembling*

sequel to the two works appeared in the form of *Stages on Life's Way* (April 30, 1845). The section in that work titled " 'Guilty?'/'Not Guilty?' "[117] is another approach to the theme of the broken engagement in *Repetition*, and Frater Taciturnus's closing observations[118] are another approach to the theme of the ethical-religious in *Fear and Trembling*.

One year later, Johannes Climacus, whose *Fragments* followed *Repetition* and *Fear and Trembling*, came to the fore again after the appearance of their sequel, *Stages*. *Concluding Unscientific Postscript* (February 27, 1846), as the title indicates, was intended to be not only the last of the series of varied pseudonymous works but also the termination of Kierkegaard's writing career.

---

in that it is "direct and even a little didactic" (*Postscript, SV* VII 229). Both *Anxiety* (pp. 113, 128, 137, *KW* VIII, *SV* IV 382, 395, 403) and *Fragments* (*SV* IV 114) are "algebraic" rather than narrative, impassioned, lyrical.

[117] *Stages, KW* XI (*SV* VI 175-459).

[118] Ibid. (*SV* VI 370-459).

FEAR AND TREMBLING

DIALECTICAL LYRIC

by Johannes de Silentio

Was Tarquinius Superbus in seinem Garten mit den Mohnköpfen sprach, verstand der Sohn, aber nicht der Bote [What Tarquinius Superbus said in the garden by means of the poppies, the son understood but the messenger did not].

HAMANN

Not only in the business world but also in the world of ideas, our age stages *ein wirklicher Ausverkauf* [a real sale]. Everything can be had at such a bargain price that it becomes a question whether there is finally anyone who will make a bid. Every speculative monitor who conscientiously signals the important trends in modern philosophy, every assistant professor, tutor, and student, every rural outsider and tenant incumbent in philosophy is unwilling to stop with doubting everything but goes further.[1] Perhaps it would be premature and untimely to ask them where they really are going, but in all politeness and modesty it can probably be taken for granted that they have doubted everything, since otherwise it certainly would be odd to speak of their having gone further. They have all made this preliminary movement and presumably so easily that they find it unnecessary to say a word about how, for not even the person who in apprehension and concern sought a little enlightenment found any, not one suggestive hint or one little dietetic prescription with respect to how a person is to act in carrying out this enormous task. "But did not Descartes do it?" Descartes,[2] a venerable, humble, honest thinker, whose writings no one can read without being profoundly affected—he did what he said and said what he did. Alas! Alas! Alas! That is a great rarity in our day! As Descartes himself so frequently said, he did not doubt with respect to faith. "Memores tamen, ut jam dictum est, huic lumini naturali tamdiu tantum esse credendum, quamdiu nihil contrarium a Deo ipso revelatur . . . . . Præter cætera autem, memoriæ nostræ pro summa regula est infigendum, ea quæ nobis a Deo revelata sunt, ut omnium certissima esse credenda; et quamvis forte lumen rationis, quam maxime clarum et evidens, aliud quid nobis suggerere videretur, soli tamen auctoritati divinæ potius quam proprio nostro judicio fidem esse adhibendam [but we must keep in mind

what has been said, that we must trust to this natural light
only so long as nothing contrary to it is revealed by God
Himself . . . . . Above all we should impress on our memory
as an infallible rule that what God has revealed to us is incomparably more certain than anything else; and that we ought
to submit to the Divine authority rather than to our own
judgment even though the light of reason may seem to us to
suggest, with the utmost clearness and evidence, something
opposite]." *Principles of Philosophy,* I, para. 28 and para. 76.[3]
He did not shout "Fire! Fire!" and make it obligatory for
everyone to doubt, for Descartes was a quiet and solitary
thinker, not a shouting street watchman; he modestly let it
be known that his method had significance only for him and
was partly the result of his earlier warped knowledge. "Ne
quis igitur putet, me hic traditurum aliquam methodum, quam
unusquisque sequi debeat ad recte regendam rationem; illam
enim tantum, quam ipsemet secutus sum, exponere decrevi.
. . . Sed simul ac illud studiorum curriculum absolvi (sc.
juventutis), quo decurso mos est in eruditorum numerum
cooptari, plane aliud coepi cogitare. Tot enim me dubiis totque
erroribus implicatum esse animadverti, ut omnes discendi
conatus nihil aliud mihi profuisse judicarem, quam quod ig-
norantiam meam magis magisque detexissem [Thus my design is not here to teach the Method which everyone should
follow in order to promote the good conduct of his Reason,
but only to show in what manner I have endeavoured to
conduct my own. . . . But so soon as I had achieved the
entire course of study at the close of which one is usually
received into the ranks of the learned, I entirely changed my
opinion. For I found myself embarrassed with so many doubts
and errors that it seemed to me that the effort to instruct
myself had no effect other than the increasing discovery of
my own ignorance]." *Dissertation on Method,* pp. 2 and 3.[4]

What those ancient Greeks,[5] who after all did know a little
about philosophy, assumed to be a task for a whole lifetime,
because proficiency in doubting is not acquired in days and
weeks, what the old veteran disputant attained, he who had
maintained the equilibrium of doubt throughout all the spe-

cious arguments, who had intrepidly denied the certainty of the senses and the certainty of thought, who, uncompromising, had defied the anxiety of self-love and the insinuations of fellow feeling—with that everyone begins in our age.

In our age, everyone is unwilling to stop with faith but goes further. It perhaps would be rash to ask where they are going, whereas it is a sign of urbanity and culture for me to assume that everyone has faith, since otherwise it certainly would be odd to speak of going further. It was different in those ancient days. Faith was then a task for a whole lifetime, because it was assumed that proficiency in believing is not acquired either in days or in weeks. When the tried and tested oldster approached his end, had fought the good fight and kept the faith,[6] his heart was still young enough not to have forgotten the anxiety and trembling that disciplined the youth, that the adult learned to control, but that no man outgrows—except to the extent that he succeeds in going further as early as possible. The point attained by those venerable personages is in our age the point where everyone begins in order to go further.

[7]The present author is by no means a philosopher.[8] He has not understood the system, whether there is one, whether it is completed; it is already enough for his weak head to ponder what a prodigious head everyone must have these days when everyone has such a prodigious idea. Even if someone were able to transpose the whole content of faith into conceptual form, it does not follow that he has comprehended faith, comprehended how he entered into it or how it entered into him. The present author is by no means a philosopher. He is *poetice et eleganter* [in a poetic and refined way] a supplementary clerk who neither writes the system nor gives *promises* of the system, who neither exhausts himself on the system nor binds himself to the system. He writes because to him it is a luxury that is all the more pleasant and apparent the fewer there are who buy and read what he writes. He easily envisions his fate in an age that has crossed out passion in order to serve science,[9] [10]in an age when an author who desires readers must be careful to write in such a way that

III
59

his book can be conveniently skimmed during the after-dinner nap, must be careful to look and act like that polite gardener's handyman in *Adresseavisen* [The Advertiser] who with hat in hand and good references from his most recent employer recommends himself to the esteemed public.[11] He foresees his fate of being totally ignored; he has a terrible foreboding that the zealous critic will call him on the carpet many times. He dreads the even more terrible fate that some enterprising abstracter, a gobbler of paragraphs (who, in order to save science, is always willing to do to the writing of others what Trop[12] magnanimously did with [his] *The Destruction of the Human Race* in order to "save good taste"), will cut him up into paragraphs and do so with the same inflexibility as the man who, in order to serve the science of punctuation, divided his discourse by counting out the words, fifty words to a period and thirty-five to a semicolon. —I throw myself down in deepest submission before every systematic ransacker: "This is not the system; it has not the least thing to do with the system. I invoke everything good for the system and for the Danish shareholders in this omnibus,[13] for it will hardly become a tower.[14] I wish them all, each and every one, success and good fortune."

Respectfully,
JOHANNES DE SILENTIO

III
60

EXORDIUM[1]

Once upon a time there was a man who as a child had heard that beautiful story of how God tempted [*fristede*][2] Abraham and of how Abraham withstood the temptation [*Fristelsen*], kept the faith, and, contrary to expectation, got a son a second time.[3] When he grew older, he read the same story with even greater admiration, for life had fractured what had been united in the pious simplicity of the child. The older he became, the more often his thoughts turned to that story; his enthusiasm for it became greater and greater, and yet he could understand the story less and less. Finally, he forgot everything else because of it; his soul had but one wish, to see Abraham, but one longing, to have witnessed that event. His craving was not to see the beautiful regions of the East, not the earthly glory of the promised land, not that God-fearing couple whose old age God had blessed, not the venerable figure of the aged patriarch, not the vigorous adolescence God bestowed upon Isaac—the same thing could just as well have occurred on a barren heath. [4]His craving was to go along on the three-day journey when Abraham rode with sorrow before him and Isaac beside him. His wish was to be present in that hour when Abraham raised his eyes and saw Mount Moriah in the distance, the hour when he left the asses behind and went up the mountain alone with Isaac— for what occupied him was not the beautiful tapestry of imagination but the shudder of the idea.

That man was not a thinker.[5] He did not feel any need to go beyond faith; he thought that it must be supremely glorious to be remembered as its father, an enviable destiny to possess it, even if no one knew it.

That man was not an exegetical scholar. He did not know Hebrew; if he had known Hebrew, he perhaps would easily have understood the story and Abraham.

III
63

I.[6]

"And God tempted [fristede][7] Abraham and said to him, take Isaac,
your only son, whom you love, and go to the land of Moriah and
offer him there as a burnt offering on a mountain that I shall show
you."[8]

It was early in the morning when Abraham arose, had the
asses saddled, and left his tent, taking Isaac with him, but
Sarah watched them from the window as they went down
the valley—until she could see them no longer.[9] They rode
in silence for three days. On the morning of the fourth day,
Abraham said not a word but raised his eyes and saw Mount
Moriah in the distance. He left the young servants behind
and, taking Isaac's hand, went up the mountain alone. But
Abraham said to himself, "I will not hide from Isaac where
this walk is taking him." He stood still, he laid his hand on
Isaac's head in blessing, and Isaac kneeled to receive it. And
Abraham's face epitomized fatherliness;[10] his gaze was gentle,
his words admonishing. But Isaac could not understand him,
his soul could not be uplifted; he clasped Abraham's knees,
he pleaded at his feet, he begged for his young life, for his
beautiful hopes; he called to mind the joy in Abraham's house,
he called to mind the sorrow and the solitude. Then Abraham lifted the boy up and walked on, holding his hand, and
his words were full of comfort and admonition. But Isaac

III
64

could not understand him. Abraham climbed Mount Moriah, but Isaac did not understand him. Then Abraham turned
away from him for a moment, but when Isaac saw Abraham's face again, it had changed: his gaze was wild, his whole
being was sheer terror. He seized Isaac by the chest, threw
him to the ground, and said, "Stupid boy, do you think I
am your father?[11] I am an idolater. Do you think it is God's
command? No, it is my desire." Then Isaac trembled and
cried out in his anguish: "God in heaven, have mercy on me,
God of Abraham, have mercy on me; if I have no father on
earth, then you be my father!" But Abraham said softly to

himself, "Lord God in heaven, I thank you; it is better that he believes me a monster than that he should lose faith in you."

When the child is to be weaned, the mother blackens her breast. It would be hard to have the breast look inviting when the child must not have it. So the child believes that the breast has changed, but the mother—she is still the same, her gaze is tender and loving as ever. How fortunate the one who did not need more terrible means to wean the child!

II.

It was early in the morning when Abraham arose: he embraced Sarah, the bride of his old age, and Sarah kissed Isaac, who took away her disgrace, Isaac her pride, her hope for all the generations to come.[12] They rode along the road in silence, and Abraham stared continuously and fixedly at the ground until the fourth day, when he looked up and saw Mount Moriah far away, but once again he turned his eyes toward the ground. Silently he arranged the firewood and bound Isaac; silently he drew the knife—then he saw the ram that God had selected. This he sacrificed and went home. — — —From that day henceforth, Abraham was old; he could not forget that God had ordered him to do this. Isaac flourished as before, but Abraham's eyes were darkened, and he saw joy no more.

[13]When the child has grown big and is to be weaned, the mother virginally conceals her breast, and then the child no longer has a mother. How fortunate the child who has not lost his mother in some other way!

III.

It was early in the morning when Abraham arose: he kissed Sarah, the young mother, and Sarah kissed Isaac, her delight, her joy forever. And Abraham rode thoughtfully down the road; he thought of Hagar and the son, whom he drove out into the desert.[14] He climbed Mount Moriah, he drew the knife.

It was a quiet evening when Abraham rode out alone, and he rode to Mount Moriah; he threw himself down on his face, he prayed God to forgive him his sin, that he had been willing to sacrifice Isaac, that the father had forgotten his duty to his son. He often rode his lonesome road, but he found no peace. He could not comprehend that it was a sin that he had been willing to sacrifice to God the best that he had, the possession for which he himself would have gladly died many times; and if it was a sin, if he had not loved Isaac in this manner, he could not understand that it could be forgiven, for what more terrible sin was there?

[15]When the child is to be weaned, the mother, too, is not without sorrow, because she and the child are more and more to be separated, because the child who first lay under her heart and later rested upon her breast will never again be so close. So they grieve together the brief sorrow. How fortunate the one who kept the child so close and did not need to grieve any more!

IV.

It was early in the morning, and everything in Abraham's house was ready for the journey. He took leave of Sarah, and Eliezer,[16] the faithful servant, accompanied him along the road until he turned back again. They rode along in harmony, Abraham and Isaac, until they came to Mount Moriah. Abraham made everything ready for the sacrifice, calmly and gently, but when he turned away and drew the knife, Isaac saw that Abraham's left hand was clenched in despair, that a shudder went through his whole body—but Abraham drew the knife.

Then they returned home again, and Sarah hurried to meet them, but Isaac had lost the faith. Not a word is ever said of this in the world, and Isaac never talked to anyone about what he had seen, and Abraham did not suspect that anyone had seen it.

[17]When the child is to be weaned, the mother has stronger sustenance at hand so that the child does not perish. How fortunate the one who has this stronger sustenance at hand.

[18]Thus and in many similar ways did the man of whom we speak ponder this event. Every time he returned from a pilgrimage to Mount Moriah, he sank down wearily, folded his hands, and said, "No one was as great as Abraham. Who is able to understand him?"[19]

EULOGY ON ABRAHAM[1]

If a human being did not have an eternal consciousness,[2] if underlying everything there were only a wild, fermenting power that writhing in dark passions produced everything, be it significant or insignificant, if a vast, never appeased emptiness hid beneath everything, what would life be then but despair? If such were the situation, if there were no sacred bond that knit humankind together, if one generation emerged after another like forest foliage,[3] if one generation succeeded another like the singing of birds in the forest, if a generation passed through the world as a ship through the sea, as wind through the desert, an unthinking and unproductive performance, if an eternal oblivion, perpetually hungry, lurked for its prey and there were no power strong enough to wrench that away from it—how empty and devoid of consolation life would be! But precisely for that reason it is not so, and just as God created man and woman, so he created the hero and the poet or orator. The poet or orator can do nothing that the hero does; he can only admire, love, and delight in him. Yet he, too, is happy—no less than that one is, for the hero is, so to speak, his better nature, with which he is enamored—yet happy that the other is not himself, that his love can be admiration. He is recollection's genius. He can do nothing but bring to mind what has been done, can do nothing but admire what has been done; he takes nothing of his own but is zealous for what has been entrusted. He follows his heart's desire, but when he has found the object of his search, he roams about to every man's door with his song and speech so that all may admire the hero as he does, may be proud of the hero as he is. This is his occupation, his humble task; this is his faithful service in the house of the hero. If he remains true to his love in this way, if he contends night and day against the craftiness of oblivion, which wants to trick him out of his hero, then he has fulfilled his task, then he is gathered together with the hero, who has loved him just as faithfully, for the poet is, so to speak, the hero's better nature, powerless, to be sure, just as a memory is, but also transfigured just as a memory is. Therefore, no one who was great will be forgotten, and even though it takes time, even though a cloud[4] of misunderstanding takes away the hero, his lover will nevertheless come, and the longer the passage of time, the more faithfully he adheres to him.

No! No one who was great in the world will be forgotten, but everyone was great in his own way, and everyone in proportion to the greatness of that which *he loved*. He who loved himself became great by virtue of himself, and he who loved other men became great by his devotedness, but he who loved God became the greatest of all. Everyone shall be remembered, but everyone became great in proportion to his *expectancy*. One became great by expecting the possible, another by expecting the eternal; but he who expected the impossible became the greatest of all. Everyone shall be remembered, but everyone was great wholly in proportion to the magnitude of that with which he *struggled*. For he who struggled with the world became great by conquering the world, and he who struggled with himself became great by conquering himself, but he who struggled with God became the greatest of all. Thus did they struggle in the world, man against man, one against thousands, but he who struggled with God was the greatest of all. Thus did they struggle on earth: there was one who conquered everything by his power, and there was one who conquered God by his powerlessness. There was one who relied upon himself and gained everything; there was one who in the security of his own strength sacrificed everything; but the one who believed God was the greatest of all. There was one who was great by virtue of his power, and one who was great by virtue of his wisdom, and one who was great by virtue of his hope, and one who was great by virtue of his love, but Abraham was the greatest of all, great by that power whose strength is powerlessness, great by that wisdom whose secret is foolishness, great by that hope whose form is madness, great by the love that is hatred to oneself.

By faith Abraham emigrated from the land of his fathers and became an alien in the promised land.[5] He left one thing behind, took one thing along: he left behind his worldly understanding, and he took along his faith. Otherwise he certainly would not have emigrated but surely would have considered it unreasonable [*urimeligt*]. By faith he was an alien in the promised land, and there was nothing that reminded him of what he cherished, but everything by its newness tempted his soul to sorrowful longing. And yet he was God's chosen one in whom the Lord was well pleased! As a matter of fact, if he had been an exile, banished from God's grace, he could have better understood it—but now it was as if he and his faith were being mocked. There was also in the world one who lived in exile from the native land he loved.[6] He is not forgotten, nor are his dirges of lamentation when he sorrowfully sought and found what was lost. There is no dirge by Abraham. It is human to lament, human to weep with one who weeps, but it is greater to have faith, more blessed to contemplate the man of faith.

By faith Abraham received the promise that in his seed all the generations of the earth would be blessed.[7] Time passed, the possibility was there, Abraham had faith; time passed, it became unreasonable, Abraham had faith. There was one in the world who also had an expectancy.[8] Time passed, evening drew near; he was not so contemptible as to forget his expectancy, and therefore he will not be forgotten, either. Then he sorrowed, and his sorrow did not disappoint him as life had done, it did everything it could for him; in the sweetness of his sorrow he possessed his disappointed expectancy. It is human to sorrow, human to sorrow with the sorrowing, but it is greater to have faith, more blessed to contemplate the man of faith. We have no dirge of sorrow by Abraham. As time passed, he did not gloomily count the days; he did not look suspiciously at Sarah, wondering if she was not getting old; he did not stop the course of the sun so she would not become old and along with her his expect-

III
70

ancy; he did not soothingly sing his mournful lay for Sarah. Abraham became old, Sarah the object of mockery in the land, and yet he was God's chosen one and heir to the promise that in his seed all the generations of the earth would be blessed. Would it not have been better, after all, if he were not God's chosen? What does it mean to be God's chosen? Is it to be denied in youth one's youthful desire in order to have it fulfilled with great difficulty in one's old age? But Abraham believed and held to the promise. If Abraham had wavered, he would have given it up. He would have said to God, "So maybe it is not your will that this should be; then I will give up my wish. It was my one and only wish, it was my blessedness. My soul is open and sincere; I am hiding no secret resentment because you denied me this." He would not have been forgotten, he would have saved many by his example, but he still would not have become the father of faith, for it is great to give up one's desire, but it is greater to hold fast to it after having given it up; it is great to lay hold of the eternal, but it is greater to hold fast to the temporal after having given it up.

III
71   Then came the fullness of time. If Abraham had not had faith, then Sarah would surely have died of sorrow, and Abraham, dulled by grief, would not have understood the fulfillment but would have smiled at it as at a youthful dream. But Abraham had faith, and therefore he was young, for he who always hopes for the best grows old and is deceived by life, and he who is always prepared for the worst grows old prematurely, but he who has faith—he preserves an eternal youth. So let us praise and honor that story! For Sarah, although well advanced in years, was young enough to desire the pleasure of motherhood, and Abraham with his gray hairs was young enough to wish to be a father. Outwardly, the wonder of it is that it happened according to their expectancy; in the more profound sense, the wonder of faith is that Abraham and Sarah were young enough to desire and that faith had preserved their desire and thereby their youth. He accepted the fulfillment of the promise, he accepted it in faith, and it happened according to the promise and according to

his faith. Moses struck the rock with his staff, but he did not have faith.[9]

So there was joy in Abraham's house when Sarah stood as bride on their golden wedding day.

But it was not to remain that way; once again Abraham was to be tried [*forsøges*].[10] He had fought with that crafty power that devises all things, with that vigilant enemy who never dozes, with that old man who outlives everything—he had fought with time and kept his faith. Now all the frightfulness of the struggle was concentrated in one moment. "And God tempted [*fristede*][11] Abraham and said to him, take Isaac, your only son, whom you love, and go to the land of Moriah and offer him as a burnt offering on a mountain that I shall show you."

So everything was lost, even more appallingly than if it had never happened! So the Lord was only mocking Abraham! He wondrously made the preposterous come true; now he wanted to see it annihilated. This was indeed a piece of folly, but Abraham did not laugh at it as Sarah did when the promise was announced.[12] All was lost! Seventy years[13] of trusting expectancy, the brief joy over the fulfillment of faith. Who is this who seizes the staff from the old man, who is this who demands that he himself shall break it! Who is this who makes a man's gray hairs disconsolate, who is this who demands that he himself shall do it! Is there no sympathy for this venerable old man, none for the innocent child? And yet Abraham was God's chosen one, and it was the Lord who imposed the ordeal [*Prøvelse*].[14] Now everything would be lost! All the glorious remembrance of his posterity, the promise in Abraham's seed—it was nothing but a whim, a fleeting thought that the Lord had had and that Abraham was now supposed to obliterate. That glorious treasure,[15] which was just as old as the faith in Abraham's heart and many, many years older than Isaac, the fruit of Abraham's life, sanctified by prayer, matured in battle, the blessing on Abraham's lips— this fruit was now to be torn off prematurely and rendered meaningless, for what meaning would it have if Isaac should be sacrificed! That sad but nevertheless blessed hour when

III
72

Abraham was to take leave of everything he held dear, when he once more would raise his venerable head, when his face would shine as the Lord's, when he would concentrate all his soul upon a blessing that would be so powerful it would bless Isaac all his days—this hour was not to come! For Abraham would indeed take leave of Isaac, but in such a way that he himself would remain behind; death would separate them, but in such a way that Isaac would become its booty. The old man would not, rejoicing in death, lay his hand in blessing on Isaac, but, weary of life, he would lay a violent hand upon Isaac. And it was God who tested him! Woe to the messenger who brought such news to Abraham! Who would have dared to be the emissary of this sorrow? But it was God who tested [*prøvede*][16] Abraham.

Yet Abraham had faith, and had faith for this life. In fact, if his faith had been only for a life to come, he certainly would have more readily discarded everything in order to rush out of a world to which he did not belong. But Abraham's faith was not of this sort, if there is such a faith at all, for actually it is not faith but the most remote possibility of faith that faintly sees its object on the most distant horizon but is separated from it by a chasmal abyss in which doubt plays its tricks. But Abraham had faith specifically for this life—faith that he would grow old in this country, be honored among the people, blessed by posterity, and unforgettable in Isaac, the most precious thing in his life, whom he embraced with a love that is inadequately described by saying he faithfully fulfilled the father's duty to love the son, which is indeed stated in the command:[17] the son, whom you love. Jacob had twelve sons, one of whom he loved;[18] Abraham had but one, whom he loved.

But Abraham had faith and did not doubt; he believed the preposterous. If Abraham had doubted, then he would have done something else, something great and glorious, for how could Abraham do anything else but what is great and glorious! He would have gone to Mount Moriah, he would have split the firewood, lit the fire, drawn the knife. He would have cried out to God, "Reject not this sacrifice; it is not the best that I have, that I know very well, for what is an old man compared with the child of promise, but it is the best I can give you. Let Isaac never find this out so that he may take comfort in his youth." He would have thrust the knife into his own breast.[19] He would have been admired in the world, and his name would never be forgotten; but it is one thing to be admired and another to become a guiding star that saves the anguished.

But Abraham had faith. He did not pray for himself, trying to influence the Lord; it was only when righteous punishment fell upon Sodom and Gomorrah that Abraham came forward with his prayers.[20]

We read in sacred scripture:[21] "And God tempted [*fristede*] Abraham and said: Abraham, Abraham, where are you? But Abraham answered: Here am I." You to whom these words are addressed, was this the case with you? When in the far distance you saw overwhelming vicissitudes approaching, did you not say to the mountains, "Hide me," and to the hills, "Fall on me"?[22] Or, if you were stronger, did your feet nevertheless not drag along the way, did they not long, so to speak, for the old trails? And when your name was called, did you answer, perhaps answer softly, in a whisper? Not so with Abraham. Cheerfully, freely, confidently, loudly he answered: Here am I. We read on: "And Abraham arose early in the morning." He hurried as if to a celebration, and early in the morning he was at the appointed place on Mount Moriah. He said nothing to Sarah, nothing to Eliezer[23]—who, after all, could understand him, for did not the nature of the temptation [*Fristelsen*] extract from him the pledge of silence? "He split the firewood, he bound Isaac, he lit the fire, he drew the knife."[24] My listener! Many a father has thought himself deprived of every hope for the future when he lost his child, the dearest thing in the world to him; nevertheless, no one was the child of promise in the sense in which Isaac was that to Abraham. Many a father has lost his child, but then it was God, the unchangeable, inscrutable will of the Almighty, it was his hand that took it. Not so with Abraham! A harder test [*Prøve*] was reserved for him, and Isaac's fate was placed, along with the knife, in Abraham's hand. And there he stood, the old man with his solitary hope. But he did not doubt, he did not look in anguish to the left and to the right, he did not challenge heaven with his prayers. He knew it was God the Almighty who was testing [*prøvede*] him; he knew it was the hardest sacrifice that could be demanded of him; but he knew also that no sacrifice is too severe when God demands it—and he drew the knife.

Who strengthened Abraham's arm, who braced up his right arm so that it did not sink down powerless! Anyone who looks upon this scene is paralyzed. Who strengthened Abraham's soul lest everything go black for him and he see neither Isaac nor the ram! Anyone who looks upon this scene is blinded. And yet it perhaps rarely happens that anyone is paralyzed or blinded, and still more rarely does anyone tell what happened as it deserves to be told. We know it all—it was only an ordeal [*Prøvelse*].

If Abraham had doubted as he stood there on Mount Moriah, if irresolute he had looked around, if he had happened to spot the ram before drawing the knife, if God had allowed him to sacrifice it instead of Isaac—then he would have gone home, everything would have been the same, he would have had Sarah, he would have kept Isaac, and yet how changed! For his return would have been a flight, his deliverance an accident, his reward disgrace, his future perhaps perdition. Then he would have witnessed neither to his faith nor to God's grace but would have witnessed to how appalling it is to go to Mount Moriah. Then Abraham would not be forgotten, nor would Mount Moriah. Then it would not be mentioned in the way Ararat,[25] where the ark landed, is mentioned, but it would be called a place of terror, for it was here that Abraham doubted.

Venerable Father Abraham! When you went home from Mount Moriah, you did not need a eulogy to comfort you for what was lost, for you gained everything and kept Isaac—was it not so? The Lord did not take him away from you again, but you sat happily together at the dinner table in your tent, as you do in the next world for all eternity. Venerable Father Abraham! Centuries have passed since those days, but you have no need of a late lover to snatch your memory from the power of oblivion, for every language calls you to mind—and yet you reward your lover more gloriously than anyone else. In the life to come you make him eternally happy in your bosom; here in this life you captivate his eyes and his heart with the wonder of your act. Venerable Father Abraham! Second Father of the race! You who were the first to feel and to bear witness to that prodigious passion that disdains the terrifying battle with the raging elements and the forces of creation in order to contend with God, you who were the first to know that supreme passion, the holy, pure, and humble expression for the divine madness[26] that was admired by the pagans—forgive the one who aspired to speak your praise if he has not done it properly. He spoke humbly, as his heart demanded; he spoke briefly, as is seemly. But he will never forget that you needed 100 years to get the son of your old age against all expectancy, that you had to draw the knife before you kept Isaac; he will never forget that in 130 years[27] you got no further than faith.[28]

PROBLEMATA[1]

From the external and visible world there comes an old adage: "Only one who works gets bread."[3] Oddly enough, the adage does not fit the world in which it is most at home, for imperfection is the fundamental law of the external world, and here it happens again and again that he who does not work does get bread, and he who sleeps gets it even more abundantly than he who works. In the external world, everything belongs to the possessor. It is subject to the law of indifference, and the spirit of the ring[4] obeys the one who has the ring, whether he is an Aladdin or a Noureddin,[5] and he who has the wealth of the world has it regardless of how he got it.

It is different in the world of the spirit. Here an eternal divine order prevails. Here it does not rain on both the just and the unjust; here the sun does not shine on both good and evil.[6] Here it holds true that only the one who works gets bread, that only the one who was in anxiety finds rest, that only the one who descends into the lower world rescues the beloved, that only the one who draws the knife gets Isaac. He who will not work does not get bread but is deceived just as the gods deceived Orpheus[7] with an ethereal phantom instead of the beloved, deceived him because he was soft, not boldly brave, deceived him because he was a zither player and not a man. Here it does not help to have Abraham as father[8] or to have seventeen ancestors. The one who will not work fits what is written about the virgins of Israel:[9] he gives birth to wind—but the one who will work gives birth to his own father.

There is a knowledge that presumptuously wants to introduce into the world of spirit the same law of indifference under which the external world sighs. It believes that it is enough to know what is great—no other work is needed. But for this reason it does not get bread; it perishes of hunger

nd what in fact does it
of Greek contempo-
erations, who knew all
was only one who be-
e countless generations
heart, word for word,

able in that it is always
understood, but here
we are willing to work
g to work, and yet we
fy Abraham, but how?
"The great thing was
he was willing to offer
"the best" is a vague
gize Isaac and the best,
smoke his pipe while
vell stretch out his legs
whom Jesus met along
and given the money
we praise every great
him without working,
aham, even though he
om Abraham's story is
: no ethical obligation,
ghest and holiest. We
Abraham. So we talk
ge the two terms, Isaac
But just suppose that
s from sleeplessness—
und, tragic, and comic
d. He goes home, he
he son, after all, is the
it, he perhaps would
s ecclesiastical dignity
scum of society, what
want to murder your
ticed any heat or per-

spiration when preaching about Abraham, would be surprised at himself, at the wrathful earnestness with which he
thunders at the poor man. He would be pleased with himself, for he had never spoken with such emphasis and emotion. He would say to himself and his wife, "I am an orator—what was lacking was the occasion. When I spoke about
Abraham on Sunday, I did not feel gripped at all." If the
same speaker had a little superfluity of understanding to spare,
I am sure he would have lost it if the sinner had calmly and
with dignity answered: But, after all, that was what you
yourself preached about on Sunday. How could the preacher
ever get such a thing in his head, and yet it was so, and his
only mistake was that he did not know what he was saying.
And to think that there is no poet who could bring himself
to prefer situations such as this to the nonsense and trumpery
with which comedies and novels are stuffed! The comic and
the tragic make contact here in absolute infinitude. By itself,
the preacher's discourse was perhaps ludicrous enough, but
it became infinitely ludicrous through its effect, and yet this
was quite natural. [13]Or suppose that the unprotesting sinner
is convinced by the pastor's severe lecture, suppose that the
zealous pastor goes home happy—happy in the consciousness that he not only was effective in the pulpit but above all
had irresistible power as a spiritual counselor, inasmuch as
on Sunday he inspired the congregation, while on Monday,
like a cherub with a flaming sword, he placed himself in
front of the person whose actions would give the lie to the
old saying that things do not go in the world as the preacher
preaches.*

But if the sinner remains unconvinced, his situation is really
tragic. Then he probably will be executed or sent to the
madhouse. In short, in relation to so-called reality, he be-

---

* In the old days, people said: It is too bad that things do not go in the
world as the preacher preaches. Maybe the time will come, especially with
the aid of philosophy, when they can say: Fortunately things do not go as
the preacher preaches, for there is still some meaning in life, but there is
none in his sermons.

came unhappy; in another sense, I am sure, Abraham made him happy, for he who works does not perish.

How is a contradiction such as that of the speaker to be explained? Is it because Abraham has gained a prescriptive right to be a great man, so that what he does is great and when another man does the same thing it is a sin, an atrocious sin? In that case, I do not wish to participate in such empty praise. If faith cannot make it a holy act to be willing to murder his son, then let the same judgment be passed on Abraham as on everyone else. If a person lacks the courage to think his thought all the way through and say that Abraham was a murderer, then it is certainly better to attain this courage than to waste time on unmerited eulogies. The ethical expression for what Abraham did is that he meant to murder Isaac; the religious expression is that he meant to sacrifice Isaac—but precisely in this contradiction is the anxiety that can make a person sleepless, and yet without this anxiety Abraham is not who he is. Or if Abraham perhaps did not do at all what the story tells, if perhaps because of the local conditions of that day it was something entirely different, then let us forget him, for what is the value of going to the trouble of remembering that past which cannot become a present. Or perhaps the speaker forgot something equivalent to the ethical oversight that Isaac was the son. In other words, if faith is taken away by becoming *Nul* and *Nichts*, all that remains is the brutal fact that Abraham meant to murder Isaac, which is easy enough for anyone to imitate if he does not have faith—that is, the faith that makes it difficult for him.

As for me, I do not lack the courage to think a complete thought. Up to now I have feared none, and if I should encounter such a one, I hope that I at least will have the honesty to say: This thought makes me afraid, it shocks me, and therefore I will not think it. If I am wrong in so doing, my punishment will not fail to come. If I had acknowledged as true the judgment that Abraham was a murderer, I am not sure that I would have been able to silence my reverence for him. But if I did think that, I probably would have said nothing, for one should not initiate others into such thoughts. But Abraham is no illusion, he did not sleep his way to fame, he does not owe it to a whim of fate.

Is it possible to speak unreservedly about Abraham without running the risk that some individual will become unbalanced and do the same thing? If I dare not, I will say nothing at all about Abraham, and the last thing I will do is to scale him down in such a way that he thereby becomes a snare for the weak. As a matter of fact, if one makes faith everything—that is, makes it what it is—then I certainly believe that I dare to speak of it without danger in our day, which is scarcely prodigal in faith. It is only by faith that one achieves any resemblance to Abraham, not by murder. If one makes love into a fleeting mood, a sensual feeling in a person, then one only lays snares for the weak by talking about the achievements of love. Everyone, to be sure, has momentary feelings, but if everyone therefore would do the dreadful thing that love has sanctified as an immortal achievement, then everything is lost, both the achievement and the one led astray.

It is permissible, then, to speak about Abraham, for whatever is great can never do damage when it is understood in its greatness; it is like a two-edged sword that kills and saves. If it fell to my lot to speak about him, I would begin by showing what a devout and God-fearing man Abraham was, worthy of being called God's chosen one. Only a person of that kind is put to such a test [*Prøve*], but who is such a person? Next I would describe how Abraham loved Isaac. For that purpose I would call upon all the good spirits to stand by me so that what I said would have the glow of fatherly love. I hope to describe it in such a way that there would not be many a father in the realms and lands of the king who would dare to maintain that he loved in this way. But if he did not love as Abraham loved, then any thought of sacrificing Isaac would surely be a spiritual trial [*Anfægtelse*].[14] On this point alone, one could talk for several Sundays—after all, one does not need to be in a great hurry. If it were done properly, the result would be that some of

III
83

the fathers would by no means demand to hear more but for the time being would be pleased if they actually succeeded in loving as Abraham loved. But if there was one who, having heard the greatness as well as the dreadfulness in Abraham's deed, ventured to proceed along that path, I would saddle my horse and ride along with him. At every station before coming to Mount Moriah, I would explain to him that he still could turn around, could repent of the misunderstanding that he was called to be tried [*forsøges*] in such a conflict, could confess that he lacked the courage, so that God himself would have to take Isaac if he wanted to have him. It is my conviction that such a man is not repudiated, that he can be blessed along with all the others, but not within time. Even in the periods of the greatest faith, would not such a judgment be passed on a man like that? I knew a man who once could have saved my life if he had been magnanimous. He spoke bluntly, "I see very well what I could do, but I dare not; I fear that eventually I shall lack strength, that I shall regret it." He was not magnanimous, but who would therefore not go on loving him?

III
84

Having spoken thus, having stirred the listeners to an awareness of the dialectical struggles of faith and its gigantic passion, then I would not become guilty of an error on the part of the listeners, [15]so they would think, "He has faith to such a degree that all we have to do is hang onto his coattails." I would add, "By no means do I have faith. By nature I am a shrewd fellow, and shrewd people always have great difficulty in making the movement of faith, but I do not attribute per se any *worth to the difficulty that brought the shrewd person further in the overcoming of it than to the point at which the simplest and most unsophisticated person arrives more easily.*"

Love indeed has its priests in the poets, and occasionally we hear a voice that knows how to honor it, but not a word is heard about faith. Who speaks to the honor of this passion? Philosophy goes further. Theology sits all rouged and powdered in the window and courts its favor, offers its charms to philosophy. It is supposed to be difficult to understand Hegel, but to understand Abraham is a small matter. To go beyond Hegel[16] is a miraculous achievement, but to go beyond Abraham is the easiest of all. I for my part have applied considerable time to understanding Hegelian philosophy and believe that I have understood it fairly well; I am sufficiently brash to think that when I cannot understand particular passages despite all my pains, he himself may not have been entirely clear. All this I do easily, naturally, without any mental strain. Thinking about Abraham is another matter, however; then I am shattered. I am constantly aware of the prodigious paradox that is the content of Abraham's life, I am constantly repelled, and, despite all its passion, my thought cannot penetrate it, cannot get ahead by a hairsbreadth. I stretch every muscle to get a perspective, and at the very same instant I become paralyzed.

I am not unfamiliar with what the world has admired as great and magnanimous. My soul feels its kinship with it and in all humility is certain that the cause for which the hero strives is also my cause, and when I consider it, I cry out to myself: *jam tua res agitur* [now your cause is at stake].[17] I *think* myself *into* the hero; I cannot think myself into Abraham; when I reach that eminence, I sink down, for what is offered me is a paradox. I by no means conclude that faith is something inferior but rather that it is the highest, also that it is dishonest of philosophy to give something else in its place and to disparage faith. Philosophy cannot and must not give faith, but it must understand itself and know what it offers and take nothing away, least of all trick men out of something by pretending that it is nothing. I am not unfamiliar with the hardships and dangers of life. I fear them not and approach them confidently. I am not unfamiliar with the terrifying. My memory is a faithful spouse, and my imagination, unlike myself, is a busy little maid who sits all day at her work and in the evening can coax me so charmingly that I have to look at it, even though it is not always landscapes or flowers or *Schäfer-Historier* [pastoral idylls] that she paints. I have seen the terrifying face to face, and I do not flee from it in horror, but I know very well that even though I advance toward it courageously, my courage is still not the courage

III
85

of faith and is not something to be compared with it. I cannot make the movement of faith, I cannot shut my eyes and plunge confidently into the absurd;[18] it is for me an impossibility, but I do not praise myself for that. I am convinced that God is love; for me this thought has a primal lyrical validity. When it is present to me, I am unspeakably happy; when it is absent, I long for it more vehemently than the lover for the object of his love. But I do not have faith; this courage I lack. To me God's love, in both the direct and the converse sense, is incommensurable with the whole of actuality. Knowing that, I am not so cowardly that I whimper and complain, but neither am I so perfidious as to deny that faith is something far higher. I can bear to live in my own fashion, I am happy and satisfied, but my joy is not the joy of faith, and by comparison with that, it is unhappy. I do not trouble God with my little troubles, details do not concern me; I gaze only at my love and keep its virgin flame pure and clear. Faith is convinced that God is concerned about the smallest things. I am satisfied with a left-handed marriage in this life; faith is humble enough to insist on the right hand, for I do not deny that this is humility and will never deny it.

I wonder if anyone in my generation is able to make the movements of faith? If I am not mistaken, my generation is rather inclined to be proud of doing what it probably does not even believe me capable of—that is, the imperfect. My soul balks at doing what is so often done—talking inhumanly about the great, as if a few centuries were an enormous distance. I prefer to speak humanly about it, as if it happened yesterday, and only let the greatness itself be the distance that either elevates or judges. If I (*in the capacity of tragic hero*, for higher I cannot come) had been ordered to take such an extraordinary royal journey as the one to Mount Moriah, I know very well what I would have done. I would not have been cowardly enough to stay at home, nor would I have dragged and drifted along the road or forgotten the knife in order to cause a delay. I am quite sure that I would have been punctual and all prepared—more than likely, I would have arrived too early in order to get it over sooner. But I also know what else I would have done. The moment I mounted the horse, I would have said to myself: Now all is lost, God demands Isaac, I sacrifice him and along with him all my joy—yet God is love and continues to be that for me, for in the world of time God and I cannot talk with each other, we have no language in common. Perhaps someone in our time would be so foolish, so envious of the great, as to want to delude himself and me into believing that if I had actually done this I would have done something even greater than what Abraham did, for my immense resignation [*Resignation*][19] would be far more ideal and poetic than Abraham's small-mindedness. But this is utterly false, for my immense resignation would be a substitute for faith. I would not be able to do more than make the infinite movement in order to find myself and again rest in myself. Neither would I have loved Isaac as Abraham loved him. That I was determined to make the movement could prove my courage, humanly speaking—that I loved him with my whole soul is the presupposition without which the whole thing becomes a misdeed—nevertheless I would not love as Abraham loved, for then I would have held back at the very last minute, without, however, arriving too late at Mount Moriah. Furthermore, by my behavior I would have spoiled the whole story, for if I had gotten Isaac again, I would have been in an awkward position. What was the easiest for Abraham would have been difficult for me—once again to be happy in Isaac!—for he who with all the infinity of his soul, *proprio motu et propriis auspiciis* [of his own accord and on his own responsibility], has made the infinite movement and cannot do more, he keeps Isaac only with pain.

But what did Abraham do? He arrived neither too early nor too late. He mounted the ass, he rode slowly down the road. During all this time he had faith, he had faith that God would not demand Isaac of him, and yet he was willing to sacrifice him if it was demanded. He had faith by virtue of the absurd, for human calculation was out of the question, and it certainly was absurd that God, who required it of him,

III
87

;

the requirement. He
he moment when the
vould not require Isaac.
tcome, but through a
is first condition, and
lly than the first time.
ly be sacrificed. Abra-
at he would be blessed
ssed here in the world.
l restore to life the one
absurd, for all human
t that sorrow can make
ough; it is also evident
l to the wind so dras-
g, even though a per-
ot intend to disparage
derstanding and along
s the stockbroker, and
again by virtue of the
not make me say it is
rary, it is the one and
d that what faith pro-
arse and boorish piece
natures, but it is far
n is the finest and the
vation of which I can
more than that. I can
ereby I cross over into
ancer's, twisted in my
ne. One, two, three—
but I cannot make the
cannot do—I can only
he moment he swung
himself: Now Isaac is
here at home as ride
not need Abraham,
his name and seventy
, as I can prove by his

really fervent joy on receiving Isaac and by his needing no preparation and no time to rally to finitude and its joy. If it had been otherwise with Abraham, he perhaps would have loved God but would not have had faith, for he who loves God without faith reflects upon himself; he who loves God in faith reflects upon God.

This is the peak on which Abraham stands. The last stage to pass from his view is the stage of infinite resignation. He actually goes further and comes to faith. All those travesties of faith—the wretched, lukewarm lethargy that thinks: There's no urgency, there's no use in grieving beforehand; the despicable hope that says: One just can't know what will happen, it could just possibly be—those travesties are native to the paltriness of life, and infinite resignation has already infinitely disdained them.

Abraham I cannot understand; in a certain sense I can learn nothing from him except to be amazed. If someone deludes himself into thinking he may be moved to have faith by pondering the outcome of that story, he cheats himself and cheats God out of the first movement of faith—he wants to suck worldly wisdom out of the paradox. Someone might succeed, for our generation does not stop with faith, does not stop with the miracle of faith, turning water into wine[22]—it goes further and turns wine into water.

Would it not be best to stop with faith, and is it not shocking that everyone wants to go further? Where will it all end when in our age, as declared in so many ways, one does not want to stop with love? In worldly shrewdness, in petty calculation, in paltriness and meanness, in everything that can make man's divine origin doubtful. Would it not be best to remain standing at faith and for him who stands to see to it that he does not fall,[23] for the movement of faith must continually be made by virtue of the absurd, but yet in such a way, please note, that one does not lose the finite but gains it whole and intact. For my part, I presumably can describe the movements of faith, but I cannot make them. In learning to go through the motions of swimming, one can be suspended from the ceiling in a harness and then presumably

describe the movements, but one is not swimming. In the
same way I can describe the movements of faith. If I am
thrown out into the water, I presumably do swim (for I do
not belong to the waders), but I make different movements,
the movements of infinity, whereas faith makes the opposite
movements: after having made the movements of infinity, it
makes the movements of finitude. Fortunate is the person
who can make these movements! He does the marvelous,
and I shall never weary of admiring him; it makes no difference to me whether it is Abraham or a slave in Abraham's
house, whether it is a professor of philosophy or a poor servant girl—I pay attention only to the movements. But I do
pay attention to them, and I do not let myself be fooled,
either by myself or by anyone else. The knights of the infinite resignation are easily recognizable—their walk is light
and bold. But they who carry the treasure of faith are likely
to disappoint, for externally they have a striking resemblance
to bourgeois philistinism, which infinite resignation, like faith,
deeply disdains.
     I honestly confess that in my experience I have not found
a single authentic instance, although I do not therefore deny
that every second person may be such an instance. Meanwhile, I have been looking for it for many years, but in vain.
Generally, people travel around the world to see rivers and
mountains, new stars, colorful birds, freakish fish, preposterous races of mankind; they indulge in the brutish stupor
that gawks at life and thinks it has seen something. That does
not occupy me. But if I knew where a knight of faith lived,
I would travel on foot to him, for this marvel occupies me
absolutely. I would not leave him for a second, I would watch
him every minute to see how he made the movements; I
would consider myself taken care of for life and would di-
vide my time between watching him and practicing myself,
and thus spend all my time in admiring him. As I said before, I have not found anyone like that; meanwhile, I may
very well imagine him. Here he is. The acquaintance is made,
I am introduced to him. The instant I first lay eyes on him,
I set him apart at once; I jump back, clap my hands, and say

half aloud, "Good Lord, is this the man, is this really the one—he looks just like a tax collector!" But this is indeed the one. I move a little closer to him, watch his slightest movement to see if it reveals a bit of heterogeneous optical telegraphy[24] from the infinite, a glance, a facial expression, a gesture, a sadness, a smile that would betray the infinite in its heterogeneity with the finite. No! I examine his figure from top to toe to see if there may not be a crack through which the infinite would peek. No! He is solid all the way through. His stance? It is vigorous, belongs entirely to finitude; no spruced-up burgher walking out to Fresberg[25] on a Sunday afternoon treads the earth more solidly. He belongs entirely to the world; no bourgeois philistine could belong to it more. Nothing is detectable of that distant and aristocratic nature by which the knight of the infinite is recognized. He finds pleasure in everything, takes part in everything, and every time one sees him participating in something particular, he does it with an assiduousness that marks the worldly man who is attached to such things. He attends to his job. To see him makes one think of him as a pen-pusher who has lost his soul to Italian bookkeeping, so punctilious is he. Sunday is for him a holiday. He goes to church. No heavenly gaze or any sign of the incommensurable betrays him; if one did not know him, it would be impossible to distinguish him from the rest of the crowd, for at most his hearty and powerful singing of the hymns proves that he has good lungs. In the afternoon, he takes a walk to the woods. He enjoys everything he sees, the swarms of people, the new omnibuses,[26] the Sound.[27] Encountering him on Strandveien, one would take him for a mercantile soul enjoying himself. He finds pleasure in this way, for he is not a poet, and I have tried in vain to lure the poetic incommensurability out of him. Toward evening, he goes home, and his gait is as steady as a postman's. On the way, he thinks that his wife surely will have a special hot meal for him when he comes home—for example, roast lamb's head with vegetables. If he meets a kindred soul, he would go on talking all the way to Østerport about this delicacy with a passion befitting a res-

III
90

taurant operator. It so happens that he does not have four shillings[28] to his name, and yet he firmly believes that his wife has this delectable meal waiting for him. If she has, to see him eat would be the envy of the elite and an inspiration to the common man, for his appetite is keener than Esau's.[29] His wife does not have it—curiously enough, he is just the same. On the way he passes a building site and meets another man. They converse for a moment; in an instant he erects a building, and he himself has at his disposition everything required. The stranger leaves him thinking that he surely is a capitalist, while my admired knight thinks: Well, if it came right down to it, I could easily get it. He sits at an open window and surveys the neighborhood where he lives: everything that happens—a rat scurrying under a plank across the gutter, children playing—engages him with an equanimity akin to that of a sixteen-year-old girl. And yet he is no genius, for I have sought in vain to spy out the incommensurability of genius in him. In the evening, he smokes his pipe; seeing him, one would swear it was the butcher across the way vegetating in the gloaming. With the freedom from care of a reckless good-for-nothing, he lets things take care of themselves, and yet every moment of his life he buys the opportune time at the highest price, for he does not do even the slightest thing except by virtue of the absurd. And yet, yet—yes, I could be infuriated over it if for no other reason than envy—and yet this man has made and at every moment is making the movement of infinity. He drains the deep sadness of life in infinite resignation, he knows the blessedness of infinity, he has felt the pain of renouncing everything, the most precious thing in the world, and yet the finite tastes just as good to him as to one who never knew anything higher, because his remaining in finitude would have no trace of a timorous, anxious routine, and yet he has this security that makes him delight in it as if finitude were the surest thing of all. And yet, yet the whole earthly figure he presents is a new creation by virtue of the absurd. He resigned everything infinitely, and then he grasped everything again by virtue of the absurd. He is continually making

III
91

the movement of infinity, but he does it with such precision and assurance that he continually gets finitude out of it, and no one ever suspects anything else. It is supposed to be the most difficult feat for a ballet dancer to leap into a specific posture in such a way that he never once strains for the posture but in the very leap assumes the posture. Perhaps there is no ballet dancer who can do it—but this knight does it. Most people live completely absorbed in worldly joys and sorrows; they are benchwarmers who do not take part in the dance. The knights of infinity are ballet dancers and have elevation. They make the upward movement and come down again, and this, too, is not an unhappy diversion and is not unlovely to see. But every time they come down, they are unable to assume the posture immediately, they waver for a moment, and this wavering shows that they are aliens in the world. It is more or less conspicuous according to their skill, but even the most skillful of these knights cannot hide this wavering. One does not need to see them in the air; one needs only to see them the instant they touch and have touched the earth—and then one recognizes them. But to be able to come down in such a way that instantaneously one seems to stand and to walk, to change the leap into life into walking, absolutely to express the sublime in the pedestrian—only that knight can do it, and this is the one and only marvel.

III
92

Nevertheless, this marvel can so easily deceive that I shall describe the movements in a specific case that can illuminate their relation to actuality, for this is the central issue. A young lad falls in love with a princess, and this love is the entire substance of his life, and yet the relation is such that it cannot possibly be realized, cannot possibly be translated from ideality into reality.* Of course, the slaves of the finite, the frogs in the swamp of life, scream: That kind of love is foolishness;

---

* It goes without saying that any other interest in which an individual has concentrated the whole reality [*Realitet*] of actuality [*Virkelighedens*] can, if it proves to be unrealizable, prompt the movement of resignation. I have chosen a love affair to show the movements, because this interest is far easier to understand and thus frees me from all preliminary considerations that in a deeper sense could be of concern only to very few individuals.

the rich brewer's widow is just as good and solid a match. Let them go on croaking in the swamp. The knight of infinite resignation does not do any such thing; he does not give up the love, not for all the glories of the world. He is no fool. First of all, he assures himself that it actually is the substance of his life, and his soul is too healthy and too proud to waste the least of it in an intoxication. He is not cowardly; he is not afraid to let it steal into his most secret, his most remote thoughts, to let it twist and entwine itself intricately around every ligament of his consciousness—if his love comes to grief, he will never be able to wrench himself out of it. He feels a blissful delight in letting love palpitate in every nerve, and yet his soul is as solemn as the soul of one who has drunk the poisoned cup[30] and feels the juice penetrate every drop of blood—for this is the moment of crisis. Having totally absorbed this love and immersed himself in it, he does not lack the courage to attempt and to risk everything. He examines the conditions of his life, he convenes the swift thoughts that obey his every hint, like well-trained doves, he flourishes his staff, and they scatter in all directions. But now when they all come back, all of them like messengers of grief, and explain that it is an impossibility, he becomes very quiet, he dismisses them, he becomes solitary, and then he undertakes the movement. If what I say here is to have any meaning, the point is that the movement is carried out normatively.* In the first place, the knight will then have the

III
93

---

* This requires passion. Every movement of infinity is carried out through passion, and no reflection can produce a movement. This is the continual leap in existence that explains the movement, whereas mediation is a chimera, which in Hegel[31] is supposed to explain everything and which is also the only thing he never has tried to explain. Just to make the celebrated Socratic distinction between what one understands and what one does not understand[32] requires passion; and even more, of course, [passion is necessary in order] to make the authentic Socratic movement, the movement of ignorance. What our generation lacks is not reflection but passion. In one sense, therefore, our age is actually too tenacious of life to die, for dying is one of the most remarkable leaps, and a little poem has always appealed to me very much because the poet, after beautifully and simply expressing his desire for the good things of life in five or six lines, ends thus:

ein seliger Sprung in die Ewigkeit [a blessed leap into eternity].[33]

power to concentrate the whole substance of his life and the meaning of actuality into one single desire. If a person lacks this concentration, this focus, his soul is dissipated in multiplicity from the beginning, and then he never manages to make the movement; he acts as shrewdly in life as the financiers who put their resources into widely diversified investments in order to gain on one if they lose on another— in short, he is not a knight. In the next place, the knight will have the power to concentrate the conclusion of all his thinking into one act of consciousness. If he lacks this focus, his soul is dissipated in multiplicity from the beginning, and he will never find the time to make the movement; he will continually be running errands in life and will never enter into eternity, for in the very moment he approaches it, he will suddenly discover that he has forgotten something and therefore must go back. In the next moment, he thinks, it will be possible, and this is quite true, but with such observations one will never come to make the movement but with their help will sink deeper and deeper into the mire.

The knight, then, makes the movement, but which one? Will he forget it all, for this, too, constitutes a kind of concentration? No, for the knight does not contradict himself, and it is a contradiction to forget the whole substance of his life and yet remain the same. He feels no inclination to become another person, by no means regards that as something great. Only the lower natures forget themselves and become something new. The butterfly, for example, completely forgets that it was a caterpillar, and may in turn so completely forget that it was a butterfly that it may become a fish. The deeper natures never forget themselves and never become anything other than what they were. The knight, then, will recollect everything, but this recollection is precisely the pain, and yet in infinite resignation he is reconciled with existence. His love for that princess would become for him the expression of an eternal love, would assume a religious character, would be transfigured into a love of the eternal being, which true enough denied the fulfillment but nevertheless did reconcile him once more in the eternal consciousness of its validity in an eternal form that no actuality can take away from

III
94

t everything is possible
gross error. Spiritually
n the finite world there
night, however, makes
ng it spiritually, but he
t. The desire that would
een stranded on impos-
s not therefore lost, nor
ague emotions of desire
netimes he awakens it
villing to let the whole
e been an affair of the
e young, and it grows
. But he needs no finite
oment he has made the
oes not need the erotic
nor does he in the finite
her farewell, because in
nd he knows very well
eing each other for the
e again are justified in
to be the last time, for
He has grasped the deep
erson one ought to be
inifely concerned about
this proves that he has
one has occasion to see
l is authentic or feigned.
that he had made the
he princess did some-
a prince—and his soul
thereby demonstrated
properly, for one who
neself. The knight does
is love just as young as
loses it simply because
What the princess does
wer natures who have

the law for their actions in someone else, the premises for their actions outside themselves. If, however, the princess is similarly disposed, something beautiful will emerge. She will then introduce herself into the order of knighthood into which one is not taken by election but of which everyone is a member who has the courage to enroll oneself, the order of knighthood that proves its immortality by making no distinction between male and female. She, too, will keep her love young and sound; she, too, will have overcome her agony, even though she does not, as the ballad[35] says, lie by her lord's side every night. These two will in all eternity be compatible, with such a rhythmical *harmonia præstabilita*[36] that if the moment ever came—a moment, however, that does not concern them finitely, for then they would grow old— if the moment ever came that allowed them to give love its expression in time, they would be capable of beginning right where they would have begun if they had been united in the beginning. The person who understands this, whether man or woman, can never be deceived, for it is only the baser natures that fancy that they are deceived. No girl who does not have this pride actually understands what it means to love, but if she does have this pride, the craftiness and cunning of the whole world cannot deceive her.

In infinite resignation there is peace and rest; every person who wills it, who has not debased himself by self-disdain— which is still more dreadful than being too proud—can discipline himself to make this movement, which in its pain reconciles one to existence. Infinite resignation is that shirt mentioned in an old legend.[37] The thread is spun with tears, bleached with tears; the shirt is sewn in tears—but then it also gives protection better than iron or steel. The defect in the legend is that a third person can work up this linen. The secret in life is that each person must sew it himself, and the remarkable thing is that a man can sew it fully as well as a woman. In infinite resignation there is peace and rest and comfort in the pain, that is, when the movement is made normatively. I could easily write a whole book if I were to expound the various misunderstandings, the awkward positions, the botched up movements I have encountered in just my own little experience. There is little belief in spirit, and yet the essential thing in making this movement is spirit. It is essential that it not be a unilateral result of a *dira necessitas* [cruel constraint of necessity],[38] and the more this is present, the more doubtful it always is that the movement is normal. Thus, if one believes that cold, barren necessity must necessarily be present, then one is declaring thereby that no one can experience death before one actually dies, which to me seems to be crass materialism. But in our age people are less concerned about making pure movements. If someone who wanted to learn to dance were to say: For centuries, one generation after the other has learned the positions, and it is high time that I take advantage of this and promptly begin with the quadrille—people would presumably laugh a little at him, but in the world of spirit this is very plausible. What, then, is education? I believed it is the course the individual goes through in order to catch up with himself, and the person who will not go through this course is not much helped by being born in the most enlightened age.

Infinite resignation is the last stage before faith, so that anyone who has not made this movement does not have faith, for only in infinite resignation do I become conscious of my eternal validity,[39] and only then can one speak of grasping existence by virtue of faith.

Now let us meet the knight of faith on the occasion previously mentioned. He does exactly the same as the other knight did: he infinitely renounces the love that is the substance of his life, he is reconciled in pain. But then the marvel happens; he makes one more movement even more wonderful than all the others, for he says: Nevertheless I have faith that I will get her—that is, by virtue of the absurd, by virtue of the fact that for God all things are possible.[40] The absurd does not belong to the differences that lie within the proper domain of the understanding. It is not identical with the improbable, the unexpected, the unforeseen. The moment the knight executed the act of resignation, he was convinced of the impossibility, humanly speaking; that was the conclusion

III
97

of the understanding, and he had sufficient energy to think it. But in the infinite sense it was possible, that is, by relinquishing it [*resignere derpaa*], but this having, after all, is also a giving up. Nevertheless, to the understanding this having is no absurdity, for the understanding continues to be right in maintaining that in the finite world where it dominates this having was and continues to be an impossibility. The knight of faith realizes this just as clearly; consequently, he can be saved only by the absurd, and this he grasps by faith. Consequently, he acknowledges the impossibility, and in the very same moment he believes the absurd, for if he wants to imagine that he has faith without passionately acknowledging the impossibility with his whole heart and soul, he is deceiving himself and his testimony is neither here nor there, since he has not even attained infinite resignation.

Precisely because resignation is antecedent, faith is no esthetic emotion but something far higher; it is not the spontaneous inclination of the heart but the paradox of existence. If, for example, in the face of every difficulty, a young girl still remains convinced that her desire will be fulfilled, this assurance is by no means the assurance of faith, even though she has been brought up by Christian parents and perhaps has had confirmation instruction from the pastor for a whole year. She is convinced in all her childlike naiveté and innocence, and this assurance ennobles her nature and gives her a supranatural magnitude so that like a thaumaturge she can invoke the finite powers of existence and bring the very stones to tears, while on the other hand in her perplexity she can just as well run to Herod as to Pilate and move the whole world with her pleas. Her assurance is most captivating, and one can learn much from her, but there is one thing that cannot be learned from her—how to make movements—for her assurance does not dare, in the pain of resignation, to look the impossibility in the eye.

So I can perceive that it takes strength and energy and spiritual freedom to make the infinite movement of resignation; I can also perceive that it can be done. The next [movement] amazes me, my brain reels, for, after having made the movement of resignation, then by virtue of the absurd to get everything, to get one's desire totally and completely—that is over and beyond human powers, that is a marvel. But this I can perceive: that the young girl's assurance is nothing but rashness compared with the unshakability of faith in the full recognition of the impossibility. Every time I want to make this movement, I almost faint; the very same moment I admire absolutely, I am seized with great anxiety. For what is it to tempt [*friste*] God? And yet this is the movement of faith and continues to be that, even though philosophy, so as to confuse the concepts, wants to delude us into thinking it has faith, even though theology is willing to sell it off at a low price.

The act of resignation does not require faith, for what I gain in resignation is my eternal consciousness. This is a purely philosophical movement that I venture to make when it is demanded and can discipline myself to make, because every time some finitude will take power over me, I starve myself into submission until I make the movement, for my eternal consciousness is my love for God, and for me that is the highest of all. The act of resignation does not require faith, but to get the least little bit more than my eternal consciousness requires faith, for this is the paradox. The movements are often confused. It is said that faith is needed in order to renounce everything. Indeed, one hears what is even more curious: a person laments that he has lost his faith, and when a check is made to see where he is on the scale, curiously enough, he has only reached the point where he is to make the infinite movement of resignation. Through resignation I renounce everything. I make this movement all by myself, and if I do not make it, it is because I am too cowardly and soft and devoid of enthusiasm and do not feel the significance of the high dignity assigned to every human being, to be his own censor, which is far more exalted than to be the censor general of the whole Roman republic. This movement I make all by myself, and what I gain thereby is my eternal consciousness in blessed harmony with my love for the eternal being. By faith I do not renounce anything; on the contrary, by faith I receive everything exactly in the sense in which it is said that one who has faith like a mustard seed can move mountains.[41] It takes a purely human courage to renounce the whole temporal realm in order to gain eternity, but this I do gain and in all eternity can never renounce—it is a self-contradiction. But it takes a paradoxical and humble courage to grasp the whole temporal realm now by virtue of the absurd, and this is the courage of faith. By faith Abraham did not renounce Isaac, but by faith Abraham received Isaac. By virtue of resignation, that rich young man[42] should have given away everything, but if he had done so, then the knight of faith would have said to him: By virtue of the absurd, you will get every penny back again—believe it! And the formerly rich young man should by no means treat these words lightly, for if he were to give away his possessions because he is bored with them, then his resignation would not amount to much.

Temporality, finitude—that is what it is all about. I can resign everything by my own strength and find peace and rest in the pain; I can put up with everything—even if that dreadful demon, more horrifying than the skeletal one who terrifies men, even if madness held its fool's costume before my eyes and I understood from its face that it was I who should put it on—I can still save my soul as long as my concern that my love of God conquer within me is greater than my concern that I achieve earthly happiness. In his very last moment, a person can still concentrate his whole soul in one single look to heaven, from whence come all good gifts, and this look will be understood by himself and by him whom it seeks to mean that he has been true to his love. Then he will calmly put on the costume. He whose soul lacks this romanticism has sold his soul, whether he gets a kingdom or a wretched piece of silver for it. By my own strength I cannot get the least little thing that belongs to finitude, for I continually use my strength in resigning everything. By my own strength I can give up the princess, and I will not sulk about it but find joy and peace and rest in my pain, but by my own strength I cannot get her back again, for I use all my strength in resigning. On the other hand, by faith, says that marvelous knight, by faith you will get her by virtue of the absurd.

But this movement I cannot make. As soon as I want to begin, everything reverses itself, and I take refuge in the pain of resignation. I am able to swim in life, but I am too heavy for this mystical hovering. To exist [*existere*] in such a way that my contrast to existence constantly expresses itself as the most beautiful and secure harmony with it—this I cannot do. And yet, I repeatedly say, it must be wonderful to get the princess. The knight of resignation who does not say this is a deceiver; he has not had one single desire, and he has not kept his desire young in his pain. There may be someone who found it quite convenient that the desire was no longer alive and that the arrow of his pain had grown dull, but such a person is no knight. A free-born soul who caught himself doing this would despise himself and begin all over again, and above all would not allow his soul to be self-deceived. And yet it must be wonderful to get the princess, and the knight of faith is the only happy man, the heir to the finite, while the knight of resignation is a stranger and an alien. To get the princess this way, to live happily with her day after day (for it is also conceivable that the knight of resignation could get the princess, but his soul had full insight into the impossibility of their future happiness), to live happily every moment this way by virtue of the absurd, every moment to see the sword hanging over the beloved's head, and yet not to find rest in the pain of resignation but to find joy by virtue of the absurd—this is wonderful. The person who does this is great, the only great one; the thought of it stirs my soul, which never was stingy in admiring the great.

If everyone in my generation who does not wish to stop with faith is actually a person who has grasped the horror of life, has grasped the meaning of Daub's statement that a soldier standing alone with a loaded rifle at his post near a powder magazine on a stormy night thinks strange thoughts;[43] if everyone who does not wish to stop with faith is actually a person who has the spiritual power to comprehend that the wish was an impossibility and then to take time to be alone with the thought; if everyone who does not wish to stop with faith is a person who in pain is reconciled and is reconciled through pain; if everyone who does not wish to stop with faith is a person who subsequently (and if he has not done all the foregoing, then he should not trouble himself when the issue is that of faith) performed the marvel and grasped existence in its totality by virtue of the absurd—then what I am writing is the loftiest eulogy upon the generation by its most inferior member, who could make only the movement of resignation. But why are they not willing to stop with faith? Why do we sometimes hear that people are ashamed to acknowledge that they have faith? I cannot comprehend it. If I ever manage to be able to make this movement, I will in the future drive with four horses.

III
101

Is it actually the case that all the bourgeois philistinism I see in life—which I do not permit myself to condemn with my words but with my deeds—is actually not what it seems, is the marvel? It is indeed conceivable, for that hero of faith did, after all, have a striking resemblance to it, for that hero of faith was not even an ironist and humorist but something much higher. There is a lot of talk these days about irony and humor, especially by people who have never been able to practice them but nevertheless know how to explain everything. I am not completely unfamiliar with these two passions;[44] I know a little more about them than is found in German and German-Danish compendiums. Therefore I know that these two passions are essentially different from the passion of faith. Irony and humor are also self-reflective and thus belong to the sphere of infinite resignation; their elasticity is owing to the individual's incommensurability with actuality.

Be it a duty or whatever, I cannot make the final movement, the paradoxical movement of faith, although there is nothing I wish more. Whether a person has the right to say this must be his own decision; whether he can come to an amicable agreement in this respect is a matter between himself and the eternal being, who is the object of faith. Every person can make the movement of infinite resignation, and for my part I would not hesitate to call a coward anyone who imagines that he cannot do it. Faith is another matter, but no one has the right to lead others to believe that faith is something inferior or that it is an easy matter, since on the contrary it is the greatest and most difficult of all.

The story of Abraham is understood in another way. We praise God's mercy, that he gave him Isaac again and that the whole thing was only an ordeal [*Prøvelse*]. An ordeal, this word can say much and little, and yet the whole thing is over as soon as it is spoken. We mount a winged horse, and in the same instant we are on Mount Moriah, in the same instant we see the ram. We forget that Abraham only rode an ass, which trudges along the road, that he had a journey of three days, that he needed some time to chop the firewood, to bind Isaac, and to sharpen the knife.

III
102
And yet we pay tribute to Abraham. The speaker can just as well sleep until the last quarter hour before he has to speak; the listener can just as well go to sleep during the speech, for everything goes along splendidly without any trouble on either side. If someone were present who suffered from sleeplessness, he would perhaps go home, sit down in a corner, and think: The whole thing is over in a moment; all you have to do is wait for a minute and you will see the ram, and the ordeal will be over. If the speaker were to meet him in this situation, I think he would step up to him in all his dignity and say, "What a wretched man, to let your soul sink into such foolishness; no miracle takes place, and all life is an ordeal." As the speaker grew more effusive, he would become more and more emotional, more and more pleased with himself, and although he noticed no gorged blood vessels when he was talking about Abraham, he now would feel the veins on his forehead swell. Perhaps he would be dumbfounded if the sinner quietly and with dignity answered: After all, that was what you preached about last Sunday.

Let us then either cancel out Abraham or learn to be horrified by the prodigious paradox that is the meaning of his life, so that we may understand that our age, like every other age, can rejoice if it has faith. If Abraham is not a nobody, a phantom, a showpiece used for diversion, then the sinner can never err in wanting to do likewise, but the point is to perceive the greatness of what Abraham did so that the person can judge for himself whether he has the vocation and the courage to be tried [*forsøges*] in something like this. The comic contradiction in the speaker's behavior was that he made a nonentity of Abraham and yet wanted to forbid the other to conduct himself in the same way.

Should we, then, not dare to speak about Abraham? I surely think we can. If I were to speak about him, I would first of all describe the pain of the ordeal. To that end, I would, like a leech, suck all the anxiety and distress and torment out of a father's suffering in order to describe what Abraham suffered, although under it all he had faith. I would point out that the journey lasted three days and a good part of the fourth; indeed, these three and a half days could be infinitely longer than the few thousand years that separate me from Abraham. I would point out—and this is my view—that every person may still turn back before he begins such a thing and at any time may repentantly turn back. If one does this, I am not apprehensive; I do not fear arousing a desire in people to be tried as Abraham was. But to sell a cheap edition of Abraham and yet forbid everyone to do likewise is ludicrous.

In order to perceive the prodigious paradox of faith, a paradox that makes a murder into a holy and God-pleasing act, a paradox that gives Isaac back to Abraham again, which no thought can grasp, because faith begins precisely where thought stops—in order to perceive this, it is now my intention to draw out in the form of problemata the dialectical aspects implicit in the story of Abraham.[45]

III
103

Is there a Teleological Suspension of the Ethical?

The ethical as such is the universal,[1] and as the universal it applies to everyone, which from another angle means that it applies at all times. It rests immanent in itself, has nothing outside itself that is its τέλος [end, purpose] but is itself the τέλος for everything outside itself, and when the ethical has absorbed this into itself, it goes not further. The single individual,[2] sensately and psychically qualified in immediacy, is the individual who has his τέλος in the universal, and it is his ethical task continually to express himself in this, to annul his singularity in order to become the universal. As soon as the single individual asserts himself in his singularity before the universal, he sins, and only by acknowledging this can he be reconciled again with the universal. Every time the single individual, after having entered the universal, feels an impulse to assert himself as the single individual, he is in a spiritual trial [*Anfægtelse*],[3] from which he can work himself only by repentantly surrendering as the single individual in the universal. If this is the highest that can be said of man and his existence, then the ethical is of the same nature as a person's eternal salvation, which is his τέλος forevermore and at all times, since it would be a contradiction for this to be capable of being surrendered (that is, teleologically suspended), because as soon as this is suspended it is relinquished, whereas that which is suspended is not relinquished but is preserved in the higher, which is its τέλος.

If this is the case, then Hegel is right in "The Good and Conscience,"[4] where he qualifies man only as the individual and considers this qualification as a "moral form of evil"[5] (see especially *The Philosophy of Right*), which must be annulled [*ophævet*] in the teleology of the moral in such a way that the single individual who remains in that stage either sins or is immersed in spiritual trial. But Hegel is wrong in speaking about faith; he is wrong in not protesting loudly and clearly against Abraham's enjoying honor and glory as a father of faith when he ought to be sent back to a lower court and shown up as a murderer.

Faith is namely this paradox that the single individual is higher than the universal—yet, please note, in such a way that the movement repeats itself, so that after having been in the universal he as the single individual isolates himself as higher than the universal. If this is not faith, then Abraham is lost, then faith has never existed in the world precisely because it has always existed.[6] For if the ethical—that is, social morality[7]—is the highest and if there is in a person no residual incommensurability in some way such that this incommensurability is not evil (i.e., the single individual, who is to be expressed in the universal), then no categories are needed other than what Greek philosophy had or what can be deduced from them by consistent thought. Hegel should not have concealed this, for, after all, he had studied Greek philosophy.

People who are profoundly lacking in learning and are given to clichés are frequently heard to say that a light shines over the Christian world, whereas a darkness enshrouds paganism. This kind of talk has always struck me as strange, inasmuch as every more thorough thinker, every more earnest artist still regenerates himself in the eternal youth of the Greeks. The explanation for such a statement is that one does not know what one should say but only that one must say something. It is quite right to say that paganism did not have faith, but if something is supposed to have been said thereby, then one must have a clearer understanding of what faith is, for otherwise one falls into such clichés. It is easy to explain all existence, faith along with it, without having a conception of what faith is, and the one who counts on being admired for such an explanation is not such a bad calculator, for it is as Boileau[8] says: *Un sot trouve toujours un plus sot, qui l'admire* [One fool always finds a bigger fool, who admires him].

Faith is precisely the paradox that the single individual as the single individual is higher than the universal, is justified before it, not as inferior to it but as superior—yet in such a way, please note, that it is the single individual who, after being subordinate as the single individual to the universal, now by means of the universal becomes the single individual who as the single individual is superior, that the single individual as the single individual stands in an absolute relation to the absolute. This position cannot be mediated, for all mediation takes place only by virtue of the universal; it is and remains for all eternity a paradox, impervious to thought. And yet faith is this paradox, or else (and I ask the reader to bear these consequences *in mente* [in mind] even though it would be too prolix for me to write them all down) or else faith has never existed simply because it has always existed, or else Abraham is lost.

It is certainly true that the single individual can easily confuse this paradox with spiritual trial [*Anfægtelse*],[9] but it ought not to be concealed for that reason. It is certainly true that many persons may be so constituted that they are repulsed by it, but faith ought not therefore to be made into something else to enable one to have it, but one ought rather to admit to not having it, while those who have faith ought to be prepared to set forth some characteristics whereby the paradox can be distinguished from a spiritual trial.

The story of Abraham contains just such a teleological suspension of the ethical. There is no dearth of keen minds and careful scholars who have found analogies to it. What their wisdom amounts to is the beautiful proposition that basically everything is the same. If one looks more closely, I doubt very much that anyone in the whole wide world will find one single analogy, except for a later one, which proves nothing if it is certain that Abraham represents faith and that it is manifested normatively in him, whose life not only is the most paradoxical that can be thought but is also so paradoxical that it simply cannot be thought. He acts by virtue of the absurd, for it is precisely the absurd that he as the single individual is higher than the universal. This paradox cannot be mediated, for as soon as Abraham begins to do so, he has to confess that he was in a spiritual trial, and if that is the case, he will never sacrifice Isaac, or if he did sacrifice Isaac, then in repentance he must come back to the universal. He gets Isaac back again by virtue of the absurd. Therefore, Abraham is at no time a tragic hero but is something entirely different, either a murderer or a man of faith. Abraham does not have the middle term that saves the tragic hero. This is why I can understand a tragic hero but cannot understand Abraham, even though in a certain demented sense I admire him more than all others.

In ethical terms, Abraham's relation to Isaac is quite simply this: the father shall love the son more than himself. But within its own confines the ethical has various gradations. We shall see whether this story contains any higher expression for the ethical that can ethically explain his behavior, can ethically justify his suspending the ethical obligation to the son, but without moving beyond the teleology of the ethical.

When an enterprise of concern to a whole nation[10] is impeded, when such a project is halted by divine displeasure, when the angry deity sends a dead calm that mocks every effort, when the soothsayer carries out his sad task and announces that the deity demands a young girl as sacrifice— then the father must heroically bring this sacrifice. He must nobly conceal his agony, even though he could wish he were "the lowly man who dares to weep"[11] and not the king who must behave in a kingly manner. Although the lonely agony penetrates his breast and there are only three persons[12] in the whole nation who know his agony, soon the whole nation will be initiated into his agony and also into his deed, that for the welfare of all he will sacrifice her, his daughter, this lovely young girl. O bosom! O fair cheeks, flaxen hair (v. 687).[13] And the daughter's tears will agitate him, and the father will turn away his face, but the hero must raise the knife. And when the news of it reaches the father's house, the beautiful Greek maidens will blush with enthusiasm, and if the daughter was engaged, her betrothed will not be angry but will be proud to share in the father's deed, for the girl belonged more tenderly to him than to the father.

When the valiant judge[14] who in the hour of need saved Israel binds God and himself in one breath by the same promise, he will heroically transform the young maiden's jubilation, the beloved daughter's joy to sorrow, and all Israel will sorrow with her over her virginal youth. But every freeborn man will understand, every resolute woman will admire Jephthah, and every virgin in Israel will wish to behave as his daughter did, because what good would it be for Jephthah to win the victory by means of a promise if he did not keep it—would not the victory be taken away from the people again?

When a son forgets his duty,[15] when the state entrusts the sword of judgment to the father, when the laws demand punishment from the father's hand, then the father must heroically forget that the guilty one is his son, he must nobly hide his agony, but no one in the nation, not even the son, will fail to admire the father, and every time the Roman laws are interpreted, it will be remembered that many interpreted them more learnedly but no one more magnificently than Brutus.

But if Agamemnon, while a favorable wind was taking the fleet under full sail to its destination, had dispatched that messenger who fetched Iphigenia to be sacrificed; if Jephthah, without being bound by any promise that decided the fate of the nation, had said to his daughter: Grieve now for two months over your brief youth, and then I will sacrifice you; if Brutus had had a righteous son and yet had summoned the lictors to put him to death—who would have understood them? If, on being asked why they did this, these three men had answered: It is an ordeal in which we are being tried [*forsøges*]—would they have been better understood?

When in the crucial moment Agamemnon, Jephthah, and Brutus heroically have overcome the agony, heroically have lost the beloved, and have only to complete the task externally, there will never be a noble soul in the world without tears of compassion for their agony, of admiration for their deed. But if in the crucial moment these three men were to append to the heroic courage with which they bore the agony the little phrase: But it will not happen anyway—who then would understand them? If they went on to explain: This we believe by virtue of the absurd—who would understand them any better, for who would not readily understand that it was absurd, but who would understand that one could then believe it?

The difference between the tragic hero and Abraham is very obvious. The tragic hero is still within the ethical. He allows an expression of the ethical to have its τέλος in a higher expression of the ethical; he scales down the ethical relation between father and son or daughter and father to a feeling that has its dialectic in its relation to the idea of moral conduct. Here there can be no question of a teleological suspension of the ethical itself.

Abraham's situation is different. By his act he transgressed the ethical altogether and had a higher τέλος outside it, in relation to which he suspended it. For I certainly would like to know how Abraham's act can be related to the universal, whether any point of contact between what Abraham did and the universal can be found other than that Abraham transgressed it. It is not to save a nation, not to uphold the idea of the state that Abraham does it; it is not to appease the angry gods. If it were a matter of the deity's being angry, then he was, after all, angry only with Abraham, and Abraham's act is totally unrelated to the universal, is a purely private endeavor. Therefore, while the tragic hero is great because of his moral virtue,[16] Abraham is great because of a purely personal virtue. There is no higher expression for the ethical in Abraham's life than that the father shall love the son. The ethical in the sense of the moral is entirely beside the point. Insofar as the universal was present, it was cryptically in Isaac, hidden, so to speak, in Isaac's loins, and must cry out with Isaac's mouth: Do not do this, you are destroying everything.

Why, then, does Abraham do it? For God's sake and—the two are wholly identical—for his own sake.[17] He does it for God's sake because God demands this proof of his faith; he

does it for his own sake so that he can prove it. The unity
of the two is altogether correctly expressed in the word already used to describe this relationship. It is an ordeal, a
temptation.[18] A temptation—but what does that mean? As a
rule, what tempts a person is something that will hold him
back from doing his duty, but here the temptation is the
ethical itself, which would hold him back from doing God's
will. But what is duty? Duty is simply the expression for
God's will.

III
110

Here the necessity of a new category for the understanding
of Abraham becomes apparent. Paganism does not know such
a relationship to the divine. The tragic hero does not enter
into any private relationship to the divine, but the ethical is
the divine, and thus the paradox therein can be mediated in
the universal.

Abraham cannot be mediated; in other words, he cannot
speak.[19] As soon as I speak, I express the universal, and if I
do not do so, no one can understand me. As soon as Abraham wants to express himself in the universal, he must declare that his situation is a spiritual trial [*Anfægtelse*], for he
has no higher expression of the universal that ranks above
the universal he violates.

Therefore, although Abraham arouses my admiration, he
also appalls me. The person who denies himself and sacrifices
himself because of duty gives up the finite in order to grasp
the infinite and is adequately assured; the tragic hero gives
up the certain for the even more certain, and the observer's
eye views him with confidence. But the person who gives
up the universal in order to grasp something even higher that
is not the universal—what does he do? Is it possible that this
can be anything other than a spiritual trial? And if it is possible, but the individual makes a mistake, what salvation is
there for him? He suffers all the agony of the tragic hero, he
shatters his joy in the world, he renounces everything, and
perhaps at the same time he barricades himself from the sublime joy that was so precious to him that he would buy it at
any price. The observer cannot understand him at all; neither

can his eye rest upon him with confidence. Perhaps the believer's intention cannot be carried out at all, because it is
inconceivable. Or if it could be done but the individual has
misunderstood the deity—what salvation would there be for
him? The tragic hero needs and demands tears, and where is
the envious eye so arid that it could not weep with Agamemnon, but where is the soul so gone astray that it has the
audacity to weep for Abraham? The tragic hero finishes his
task at a specific moment in time, but as time passes he does
what is no less significant: he visits the person encompassed
by sorrow, who cannot breathe because of his anguished sighs,
whose thoughts oppress him, heavy with tears. He appears
to him, breaks the witchcraft of sorrow, loosens the bonds,
evokes the tears, and the suffering one forgets his own sufferings in those of the tragic hero. One cannot weep over
Abraham. One approaches him with a *horror religiosus*, as Israel approached Mount Sinai.[20] What if he himself is dis-
traught, what if he had made a mistake, this lonely man who
climbs Mount Moriah, whose peak towers sky-high over the
flatlands of Aulis, what if he is not a sleepwalker safely cross-
ing the abyss while the one standing at the foot of the mountain looks up, shakes with anxiety, and then in his deference
and horror does not even dare to call to him? —Thanks, once
again thanks, to a man who, to a person overwhelmed by
life's sorrows and left behind naked, reaches out the words,
the leafage of language by which he can conceal his misery.
Thanks to you, great Shakespeare,[21] you who can say everything, everything, everything just as it is—and yet, why did
you never articulate this torment? Did you perhaps reserve
it for yourself, like the beloved's name that one cannot bear
to have the world utter, for with his little secret that he cannot divulge the poet buys this power of the word to tell
everybody else's dark secrets. A poet is not an apostle; he
drives out devils only by the power of the devil.[22]

But if the ethical is teleologically suspended in this manner, how does the single individual in whom it is suspended
exist? He exists as the single individual in contrast to the

universal. Does he sin, then, for from the point of view of the idea, this is the form of sin. Thus, even though the child does not sin, because it is not conscious of its existence as such, its existence, from the point of view of the idea, is nevertheless sin, and the ethical makes its claim upon it at all times. If it is denied that this form can be repeated in such a way that it is not sin, then judgment has fallen upon Abraham. How did Abraham exist? He had faith. This is the paradox by which he remains at the apex, the paradox that he cannot explain to anyone else, for the paradox is that he as the single individual places himself in an absolute relation to the absolute. Is he justified? Again, his justification is the paradoxical, for if he is, then he is justified not by virtue of being something universal but by virtue of being the single individual.

III
112
How does the single individual reassure himself that he is legitimate? It is a simple matter to level all existence to the idea of the state or the idea of a society. If this is done, it is also simple to mediate, for one never comes to the paradox that the single individual as the single individual is higher than the universal, something I can also express symbolically in a statement by Pythagoras to the effect that the odd number is more perfect than the even number.[23] If occasionally there is any response at all these days with regard to the paradox, it is likely to be: One judges it by the result. Aware that he is a paradox who cannot be understood, a hero who has become a σκάνδαλον [offense] to his age will shout confidently to his contemporaries: The result will indeed prove that I was justified. This cry is rarely heard in our age, inasmuch as it does not produce heroes—this is its defect—and it likewise has the advantage that it produces few caricatures. When in our age we hear these words: It will be judged by the result—then we know at once with whom we have the honor of speaking. Those who talk this way are a numerous type whom I shall designate under the common name of assistant professors.[24] With security in life, they live in their thoughts: they have a *permanent* position and a *secure* future

in a well-organized state. They have hundreds, yes, even thousands of years between them and the earthquakes of existence; they are not afraid that such things can be repeated, for then what would the police and the newspapers say? Their life task is to judge the great men, judge them according to the result. Such behavior toward greatness betrays a strange mixture of arrogance and wretchedness—arrogance because they feel called to pass judgment, wretchedness because they feel that their lives are in no way allied with the lives of the great. Anyone with even a smattering *erectioris ingenii* [of nobility of nature] never becomes an utterly cold and clammy worm, and when he approaches greatness, he is never devoid of the thought that since the creation of the world it has been customary for the result to come last and that if one is truly going to learn something from greatness one must be particularly aware of the beginning. If the one who is to act wants to judge himself by the result, he will never begin. Although the result may give joy to the entire world, it cannot help the hero, for he would not know the result until the whole thing was over, and he would not become a hero by that but by making a beginning.

III
113

Moreover, in its dialectic the result (insofar as it is finitude's response to the infinite question) is altogether incongruous with the hero's existence. Or should Abraham's receiving Isaac by a *marvel* be able to prove that Abraham was justified in relating himself as the single individual to the universal? If Abraham actually had sacrificed Isaac, would he therefore have been less justified?

But we are curious about the result, just as we are curious about the way a book turns out. We do not want to know anything about the anxiety, the distress, the paradox. We carry on an esthetic flirtation with the result. It arrives just as unexpectedly but also just as effortlessly as a prize in a lottery, and when we have heard the result, we have built ourselves up. And yet no manacled robber of churches is so despicable a criminal as the one who plunders holiness in this way, and not even Judas, who sold his Lord for thirty pieces of silver, is more contemptible than someone who peddles greatness in this way.

It is against my very being to speak inhumanly about greatness, to make it a dim and nebulous far-distant shape or to let it be great but devoid of the emergence of the humanness without which it ceases to be great, for it is not what happens to me that makes me great but what I do, and certainly there is no one who believes that someone became great by winning the big lottery prize. A person might have been born in lowly circumstances, but I would still require him not to be so inhuman toward himself that he could imagine the king's castle only at a distance and ambiguously dream of its greatness, and destroy it at the same time he elevates it because he elevated it so basely. I require him to be man enough to tread confidently and with dignity there as well. He must not be so inhuman that he insolently violates everything by barging right off the street into the king's hall—he loses more thereby than the king. On the contrary, he should find a joy in observing every bidding of propriety with a happy and confident enthusiasm, which is precisely what makes him a free spirit. This is merely a metaphor, for that distinction is only a very imperfect expression of the distance of spirit. I require every person not to think so inhumanly of himself that he does not dare to enter those palaces where the memory of the chosen ones lives or even those where they themselves live. He is not to enter rudely and foist his affinity upon them. He is to be happy for every time he bows before them, but he is to be confident, free of spirit, and always more than a charwoman, for if he wants to be no more than that, he will never get in. And the very thing that is going to help him is the anxiety and distress in which the great were tried, for otherwise, if he has any backbone, they will only arouse his righteous envy. And anything that can be great only at a distance, that someone wants to make great with empty and hollow phrases—is destroyed by that very person.

Who was as great in the world as that favored woman, the

mother of God, the Virgin Mary?[25] And yet how do we speak of her? That she was the favored one among women does not make her great, and if it would not be so very odd for those who listen to be able to think just as inhumanly as those who speak, then every young girl might ask: Why am I not so favored? And if I had nothing else to say, I certainly would not dismiss such a question as stupid, because, viewed abstractly, vis-à-vis a favor, every person is just as entitled to it as the other. We leave out the distress, the anxiety, the paradox. My thoughts are as pure as anybody's, and he who can think this way surely has pure thoughts, and, if not, he can expect something horrible, for anyone who has once experienced these images cannot get rid of them again, and if he sins against them, they take a terrible revenge in a silent rage, which is more terrifying than the stridency of ten ravenous critics. To be sure, Mary bore the child wondrously, but she nevertheless did it "after the manner of women,"[26] and such a time is one of anxiety, distress, and paradox. The angel was indeed a ministering spirit, but he was not a meddlesome spirit who went to the other young maidens in Israel and said: Do not scorn Mary, the extraordinary is happening to her. The angel went only to Mary, and no one could understand her. Has any woman been as infringed upon as was Mary, and is it not true here also that the one whom God blesses he curses in the same breath? This is the spirit's view of Mary, and she is by no means—it is revolting to me to say it but even more so that people have inanely and unctuously made her out to be thus—she is by no means a lady idling in her finery and playing with a divine child. When, despite this, she said: Behold, I am the handmaid of the Lord[27]—then she is great, and I believe it should not be difficult to explain why she became the mother of God. She needs worldly admiration as little as Abraham needs tears, for she was no heroine and he was no hero, but both of them became greater than these, not by being exempted in any way from the distress and the agony and the paradox, but became greater by means of these.

III
115

It is great when the poet in presenting his tragic hero for public admiration dares to say: Weep for him, for he deserves it. It is great to deserve the tears of those who deserve to shed tears. It is great that the poet dares to keep the crowd under restraint, dares to discipline men to examine themselves individually to see if they are worthy to weep for the hero, for the slop water of the snivellers is a debasement of the sacred. —But even greater than all this is the knight of faith's daring to say to the noble one who wants to weep for him: Do not weep for me, but weep for yourself.[28]

We are touched, we look back to those beautiful times. Sweet sentimental longing leads us to the goal of our desire, to see Christ walking about in the promised land. We forget the anxiety, the distress, the paradox. Was it such a simple matter not to make a mistake? Was it not terrifying that this man walking around among the others was God? Was it not terrifying to sit down to eat with him? Was it such an easy matter to become an apostle? But the result, the eighteen centuries—that helps, that contributes to this mean deception whereby we deceive ourselves and others. I do not feel brave enough to wish to be contemporary[29] with events like that, but I do not for that reason severely condemn those who made a mistake, nor do I depreciate those who saw what was right.

But I come back to Abraham. During the time before the result, either Abraham was a murderer every minute or we stand before a paradox that is higher than all mediations.

The story of Abraham contains, then, a teleological suspension of the ethical. As the single individual he became higher than the universal. This is the paradox, which cannot be mediated. How he entered into it is just as inexplicable as how he remains in it. If this is not Abraham's situation, then Abraham is not even a tragic hero but a murderer. It is thoughtless to want to go on calling him the father of faith, to speak of it to men who have an interest only in words. A person can become a tragic hero through his own strength— but not the knight of faith. When a person walks what is in one sense the hard road of the tragic hero, there are many

who can give him advice, but he who walks the narrow road
of faith has no one to advise him—no one understands him.
Faith is a marvel, and yet no human being is excluded from
it; for that which unites all human life is passion,* and faith
is a passion.

* Lessing has somewhere said something similar from a purely esthetic
point of view. He actually wants to show in this passage that grief, too, can
yield a witty remark. With that in mind, he quotes the words spoken on a
particular occasion by the unhappy king of England, Edward II. In contrast
he quotes from Diderot a story about a peasant woman and a remark she
made. He goes on to say: Auch das war Witz, und noch dazu Witz einer
Bäuerin; aber die Umstände machten ihn unvermeidlich. Und folglich auch
muss man die Entschuldigung der witzigen Ausdrücke des Schmerzes und
der Betrübniss nicht darin suchen, dass die Person, welche sie sagt, eine
vornehme, wohlerzogene, verständige, und auch sonst witzige Person sey;
denn die Leidenschaften machen alle Menschen wieder gleich: sondern darin, dass
wahrscheinlicher Weise ein jeder Mensch ohne Unterschied in den näm-
lichen Umständen das nämliche sagen würde. Den Gedanken der Bäuerin
hätte eine Königin haben können und haben müssen: so wie das, was dort
der König sagt, auch ein Bauer hätte sagen können und ohne Zweifel würde
gesagt haben [That also was wit, and the wit of a peasant woman, besides;
but the situation made it inevitable. And consequently one must not seek
the excuse for the witty expressions of pain and sorrow in the fact that the
person who said them was a distinguished, well-educated, intelligent, and
also witty person; *for the passions make all men equal again*: but in this, that in
the same situation probably every person, without exception, would have
said the same thing. A queen could have had and must have had the thought
of a peasant woman, just as a peasant could have said and no doubt would
have said what the king said there]. See *Sämmtliche Werke*, XXX, p. 223.[30]

PROBLEMA II

Is there an Absolute Duty to God?[1]

The ethical is the universal,[2] and as such it is also the divine. Thus it is proper to say that every duty is essentially duty to God, but if no more can be said than this, then it is also said that I actually have no duty to God. The duty becomes duty by being traced back to God, but in the duty itself I do not enter into relation to God. For example, it is a duty to love one's neighbor. It is a duty by its being traced back to God, but in the duty I enter into relation not to God but to the neighbor I love. If in this connection I then say that it is my duty to love God, I am actually pronouncing only a tautology, inasmuch as "God" in a totally abstract sense is here understood as the divine—that is, the universal, that is, the duty. The whole existence of the human race rounds itself off as a perfect, self-contained sphere, and then the ethical is that which limits and fills at one and the same time. God comes to be an invisible vanishing point, an impotent thought; his power is only in the ethical, which fills all of existence. Insofar, then, as someone might wish to love God in any other sense than this, he is a visionary, is in love with a phantom, which, if it only had enough power to speak, would say to him: I do not ask for your love—just stay where you belong. Insofar as someone might wish to love God in another way, this love would be as implausible as the love Rousseau mentions, whereby a person loves the Kaffirs instead of loving his neighbor.[3]

Now if this train of thought is sound, if there is nothing incommensurable in a human life, and if the incommensurable that is present is there only by an accident from which nothing results insofar as existence is viewed from the idea, then Hegel was right. But he was not right in speaking about faith or in permitting Abraham to be regarded as its father, for in the latter case he has pronounced judgment both on

Abraham and on faith. In Hegelian philosophy,[4] *das Äussere* (*die Entäusserung*) [the outer (the externalization)] is higher than *das Innere* [the inner]. This is frequently illustrated by an example. The child is *das Innere*, the adult *das Äussere*, with the result that the child is determined by the external and, conversely, the adult as *das Äussere* by the inner. But faith is the paradox that interiority is higher than exteriority, or, to call to mind something said earlier, the uneven number is higher than the even.[5]

Thus in the ethical view of life, it is the task of the single individual to strip himself of the qualification of interiority and to express this in something external. Every time the individual shrinks from it, every time he withholds himself in or slips down again into the qualifications of feeling, mood, etc. that belong to interiority, he trespasses, he is immersed in spiritual trial [*Anfægtelse*]. The paradox of faith is that there is an interiority that is incommensurable with exteriority, an interiority that is not identical, please note, with the first but is a new interiority.[6] This must not be overlooked. Recent philosophy has allowed itself simply to substitute the immediate for "faith."[7] If that is done, then it is ridiculous to deny that there has always been faith. This puts faith in the rather commonplace company of feelings, moods, idiosyncrasies, *vapeurs* [vagaries], etc. If so, philosophy may be correct in saying that one ought not to stop there. But nothing justifies philosophy in using this language. Faith is preceded by a movement of infinity; only then does faith commence, *nec opinate* [unexpected], by virtue of the absurd. This I can certainly understand without consequently maintaining that I have faith. If faith is nothing more than philosophy makes it out to be, then even Socrates went further, much further, instead of the reverse—that he did not attain it. In an intellectual sense, he did make the movement of infinity. His ignorance is the infinite resignation. This task alone is a suitable one for human capabilities, even though it is disdained these days; but only when this has been done, only when the individual has emptied himself in the infinite, only then has the point been reached where faith can break through.

The paradox of faith, then, is this: that the single individual is higher than the universal, that the single individual—to recall a distinction in dogmatics rather rare these days—determines his relation to the universal by his relation to the absolute, not his relation to the absolute by his relation to the universal. The paradox may also be expressed in this way: that there is an absolute duty to God, for in this relationship of duty the individual relates himself as the single individual absolutely to the absolute. In this connection, to say that it is a duty to love God means something different from the above, for if this duty is absolute, then the ethical is reduced to the relative. From this it does not follow that the ethical should be invalidated; rather, the ethical receives a completely different expression, a paradoxical expression, such as, for example, that love to God may bring the knight of faith to give his love to the neighbor—an expression opposite to that which, ethically speaking, is duty.

If this is not the case, then faith has no place in existence, then faith is a spiritual trial and Abraham is lost, inasmuch as he gave in to it.

This paradox cannot be mediated, for it depends specifically on this: that the single individual is only the single individual. As soon as this single individual wants to express his absolute duty in the universal, becomes conscious of it in the universal, he recognizes that he is involved in a spiritual trial, and then, if he really does resist it, he will not fulfill the so-called absolute duty, and if he does not resist it, then he sins, even though his act *realiter* [as a matter of fact] turns out to be what was his absolute duty. What should Abraham have done, for instance? If he had said to someone: I love Isaac more than anything in the world and that is why it is so hard for me to sacrifice him—the other person very likely would have shaken his head and said: Why sacrifice him, then? Or, if the other had been smart, he probably would have seen through Abraham and perceived that he was manifesting feelings that glaringly contradicted his action.

The story of Abraham contains such a paradox. The ethical expression for his relation to Isaac is that the father must

love the son. This ethical relation is reduced to the relative
in contradistinction to the absolute relation to God. To the
question "Why?" Abraham has no other answer than that it
is an ordeal, a temptation[8] that, as noted above, is a synthesis
of its being for the sake of God and for his own sake. In fact,
these two determinants correspond in ordinary language. For
instance, if we see someone doing something that does not
conform to the universal, we say that he is hardly doing it
for God's sake, meaning thereby that he is doing it for his
own sake. The paradox of faith has lost the intermediary,
that is, the universal. On the one side, it has the expression
for the highest egotism (to do the terrible act, do it for one's
own sake), on the other side, the expression for the most
absolute devotion, to do it for God's sake. Faith itself cannot
be mediated into the universal, for thereby it is canceled.
Faith is this paradox, and the single individual simply cannot
make himself understandable to anyone. People fancy that
the single individual can make himself understandable to another single individual in the same situation. Such a view
would be unthinkable if in our day we were not trying in so
many ways to sneak slyly into greatness. The one knight of
faith cannot help the other at all. Either the single individual
himself becomes the knight of faith by accepting the paradox
or he never becomes one. Partnership in these areas is utterly
unthinkable. Only the single individual can ever give himself
a more explicit explanation of what is to be understood by
Isaac. And even though an ever so precise determination could
be made, generally speaking, of what is to be understood by
Isaac (which, incidentally, would be a ridiculous self-contradiction—to bring the single individual, who in fact stands
outside the universal, under universal categories when he is
supposed to act as the single individual who is outside the
universal), the single individual would never be able to be
convinced of this by others, only by himself as the single
individual. Thus, even if a person were craven and base enough
to want to become a knight of faith on someone else's responsibility, he would never come to be one, for only the
single individual becomes that as the single individual, and

III
120

this is the greatness of it—which I certainly can understand without becoming involved in it, since I lack the courage—but this is also the terribleness of it, which I can understand even better.

As we all know, Luke 14:26 offers a remarkable teaching on the absolute duty to God: "If any one comes to me and does not hate his own father and mother and wife and children and brothers and sisters, yes, and even his own life, he cannot be my disciple." This is a hard saying. Who can bear to listen to it?[9] This is the reason, too, that we seldom hear it. But this silence is only an escape that is of no avail. Meanwhile, the theological student learns that these words appear in the New Testament, and in one or another exegetical resource book[10] he finds the explanation that μισεῖν [to hate] in this passage and in a few other passages *per* μείωσιν [by weakening] means: *minus diligo, posthabeo, non colo, nihili facio* [love less, esteem less, honor not, count as nothing]. The context in which these words appear, however, does not seem to confirm this appealing explanation. In the following verse we are told that someone who wants to erect a tower first of all makes a rough estimate to see if he is able to finish it, lest he be mocked later. The close proximity of this story and the verse quoted seems to indicate that the words are to be taken in their full terror in order that each person may examine himself to see if he can erect the building.

If that pious and accommodating exegete, who by dickering this way hopes to smuggle Christianity into the world, succeeded in convincing one person that grammatically, linguistically, and κατ' ἀναλογίαν [by analogy] this is the meaning of that passage, then it is to be hoped that he at the same time would succeed in convincing the same person that Christianity is one of the most miserable things in the world. The teaching that in one of its most lyrical outpourings, in which the consciousness of its eternal validity overflows most vigorously, has nothing to offer except an overblown word that signifies nothing but only suggests that one should be less kind, less attentive, more indifferent, the teaching that in the moment it gives the appearance of wanting to say

something terrible ends by slavering instead of terrifying—
that teaching certainly is not worth standing up for.[11]

The words are terrible, but I dare say that they can be
understood without the necessary consequence that the one
who has understood them has the courage to do what he has
understood. One ought to be sufficiently honest, however,
to admit what it says, to admit that it is great even though
one himself lacks the courage to do it. Anyone who acts thus
will not exclude himself from participation in this beautiful
story, for in a way it does indeed have a kind of comfort for
the person who does not have the courage to begin construction of the tower. But honest he must be, and he must not
speak of this lack of courage as humility, since, on the contrary, it is pride, whereas the courage of faith is the one and
only humble courage.

It is easy to see that if this passage is to have any meaning
it must be understood literally. God is the one who demands
absolute love. Anyone who in demanding a person's love
believes that this love is demonstrated by his becoming indifferent to what he otherwise cherished is not merely an
egotist but is also stupid, and anyone demanding that kind
of love simultaneously signs his own death sentence insofar
as his life is centered in this desired love. For example, a man
requires his wife to leave her father and mother, but if he
considers it a demonstration of her extraordinary love to him
that she for his sake became an indifferent and lax daughter
etc., then he is far more stupid than the stupid. If he had any
idea of what love is, he would wish to discover that she was
perfect in her love as a daughter and sister, and he would see
therein that she would love him more than anyone in the
kingdom. Thus what would be regarded as a sign of egotism
and stupidity in a person may by the help of an exegete be
regarded as a worthy representation of divinity.

But how to hate them [Luke 14:26]? I shall not review here
the human distinction, either to love or to hate, not because
I have so much against it, for at least it is passionate, but
because it is egotistic and does not fit here. But if I regard
the task as a paradox, then I understand it—that is, I under-

III
122

stand it in the way one can understand a paradox. The absolute duty can lead one to do what ethics would forbid, but it can never lead the knight of faith to stop loving. Abraham demonstrates this. In the moment he is about to sacrifice Isaac, the ethical expression for what he is doing is: he hates Isaac. But if he actually hates Isaac, he can rest assured that God does not demand this of him, for Cain[12] and Abraham are not identical. He must love Isaac with his whole soul. Since God claims Isaac, he must, if possible, love him even more, and only then can he *sacrifice* him, for it is indeed this love for Isaac that makes his act a sacrifice by its paradoxical contrast to his love for God. But the distress and the anxiety in the paradox is that he, humanly speaking, is thoroughly incapable of making himself understandable. Only in the moment when his act is in absolute contradiction to his feelings, only then does he sacrifice Isaac, but the reality of his act is that by which he belongs to the universal, and there he is and remains a murderer.

III
123

Furthermore, the passage in Luke must be understood in such a way that one perceives that the knight of faith can achieve no higher expression whatsoever of the universal (as the ethical) in which he can save himself. Thus if the Church were to insist on this sacrifice from one of its members, we would have only a tragic hero. The idea of the Church is not qualitatively different from the idea of the state. As soon as the single individual can enter into it by a simple mediation, and as soon as the single individual has entered into the paradox, he does not arrive at the idea of the Church; he does not get out of the paradox, but he must find therein either his salvation or his damnation. A Church-related hero such as that expresses the universal in his act, and there will be no one in the Church, not even his father and mother, who does not understand him. But a knight of faith he is not, and in fact he has a response different from Abraham's; he does not say that this is an ordeal [*Prøvelse*] or a temptation [*Fristelse*] in which he is being tried [*forsøges*].[13]

As a rule, passages such as this one in Luke are not quoted. We are afraid to let people loose; we are afraid that the worst will happen as soon as the single individual feels like behaving as the single individual. Furthermore, existing as the single individual is considered to be the easiest thing in the world, and thus people must be coerced into becoming the universal. I can share neither that fear nor that opinion, and for the same reason. Anyone who has learned that to exist as the single individual is the most terrible of all will not be afraid to say that it is the greatest of all, but he must say this in such a way that his words do not become a pitfall for one who is confused but instead help him into the universal, although his words could create a little room for greatness. Anyone who does not dare to mention such passages does not dare to mention Abraham, either. Moreover, to think that existing as the single individual is easy enough contains a very dubious indirect concession with respect to oneself, for anyone who actually has any self-esteem and concern for his soul is convinced that the person who lives under his own surveillance alone in the big wide world lives more stringently and retired than a maiden in her virgin's bower. It may well be that there are those who need coercion, who, if they were given free rein, would abandon themselves like unmanageable animals to selfish appetites. But a person will demonstrate that he does not belong to them precisely by showing that he knows how to speak in fear and trembling, and speak he must out of respect for greatness, so that it is not forgotten out of fear of harm, which certainly will not come if he speaks out of a knowledge of greatness, a knowledge of its terrors, and if one does not know the terrors, one does not know the greatness, either.

III
124

Let us consider in somewhat more detail the distress and anxiety in the paradox of faith. The tragic hero relinquishes himself in order to express the universal; the knight of faith relinquishes the universal in order to become the single individual. As said previously, everything depends on one's position. Anyone who believes that it is fairly easy to be the single individual can always be sure that he is not a knight of faith, for fly-by-nights and itinerant geniuses are not men of faith. On the contrary, this knight knows that it is glo-

rious to belong to the universal. He knows that it is beautiful
and beneficial to be the single individual who translates himself into the universal, the one who, so to speak, personally
produces a trim, clean, and, as far as possible, faultless edition of himself, readable by all. He knows that it is refreshing to become understandable to himself in the universal in
such a way that he understands it, and every individual who
understands him in turn understands the universal in him,
and both rejoice in the security of the universal. He knows
it is beautiful to be born as the single individual who has his
home in the universal, his friendly abode, which immediately receives him with open arms if he wants to remain in
it. But he also knows that up higher there winds a lonesome
trail, steep and narrow; he knows it is dreadful to be born
solitary outside of the universal, to walk without meeting
one single traveler. He knows very well where he is and how
he relates to men. Humanly speaking, he is mad and cannot
make himself understandable to anyone. And yet "to be mad"
is the mildest expression. If he is not viewed in this way,
then he is a hypocrite, and the higher he ascends this path,
the more appalling a hypocrite he is.

The knight of faith knows that it is inspiring to give up
himself for the universal, that it takes courage to do it, but
that there also is a security in it precisely because it is a giving
up for the universal. He knows that it is glorious to be
understood by everyone of noble mind and in such a way
that the observer himself is ennobled thereby. This he knows,
and he feels as if bound; he could wish that this was the task
that had been assigned to him. In the same way, Abraham
now and then could have wished that the task were to love
Isaac as a father would and should, understandable to all,
memorable for all time; he could have wished that the task
were to sacrifice Isaac to the universal, that he could inspire
fathers to laudable deeds—and he is almost shocked at the
thought that for him such wishes constitute a spiritual trial
[*Anfægtelse*] and must be treated as such, for he knows that
he is walking a lonesome path and that he is accomplishing
nothing for the universal but is himself only being tried [*for-*

søges] and tested [*prøves*]. What did Abraham accomplish for the universal? Let me speak humanly about it, purely humanly! It takes him seventy years to have the son of old age.[14] It takes him seventy years to get what others get in a hurry and enjoy for a long time. Why? Because he is being tested and tempted [*fristes*]. Is it not madness! But Abraham had faith, and only Sarah vacillated and got him to take Hagar as concubine, but this is also why he had to drive her away.[15] He receives Isaac—then once again he has to be tested. He knew that it is glorious to express the universal, glorious to live with Isaac. But this is not the task. He knew that it is kingly to sacrifice a son like this to the universal; he himself would have found rest therein, and everybody would have rested approvingly in his deed, as the vowel rests in its quiescent letter.[16] But that is not the task—he is being tested. That Roman commander widely known by his nickname Cunctator[17] stopped the enemy by his delaying tactics—in comparison with him, what a procrastinator Abraham is—but he does not save the state. This is the content of 130 years. Who can endure it? Would not his contemporaries, if such may be assumed, have said, "What an everlasting procrastination this is; Abraham finally received a son, it took long enough, and now he wants to sacrifice him—is he not mad? If he at least could explain why he wants to do it, but it is always an ordeal [*Prøvelse*]." Nor could Abraham explain further, for his life is like a book under divine confiscation and never becomes *publice juris* [public property].

This is the terrifying aspect of it. Anyone who does not perceive this can always be sure that he is no knight of faith, but the one who perceives it will not deny that even the most tried of tragic heroes dances along in comparison with the knight of faith, who only creeps along slowly. Having perceived this and made sure that he does not have the courage to understand it, he may then have an intimation of the wondrous glory the knight attains in becoming God's confidant, the Lord's friend, if I may speak purely humanly, in saying "You"[18] to God in heaven, whereas even the tragic hero addresses him only in the third person.

The tragic hero is soon finished, and his struggles are soon over; he makes the infinite movement and is now secure in the universal. The knight of faith, however, is kept in a state of sleeplessness, for he is constantly being tested [*prøves*], and at every moment there is the possibility of his returning penitently to the universal, and this possibility may be a spiritual trial [*Anfægtelse*] as well as the truth. He cannot get any information on that from any man, for in that case he is outside the paradox.

First and foremost, then, the knight of faith has the passion to concentrate in one single point the whole of the ethical that he violates, in order that he may give himself the assurance that he actually loves Isaac with his whole soul.* If he cannot, he is undergoing spiritual trial. Next, he has the passion to produce this assurance instantaneously and in such a way that it is fully as valid as in the first moment. If he cannot do this, then he never moves from the spot, for then he always has to begin all over again. The tragic hero also concentrates in one point the ethical he has teleologically overstepped, but in that case he has a stronghold in the universal. The knight of faith has simply and solely himself, and therein lies the dreadfulness. Most men live in adherence to an ethical obligation in such a way that they let each day have its cares,[19] but then they never attain this passionate

---

* May I once again throw some light on the distinction between the collisions of the tragic hero and of the knight of faith. The tragic hero assures himself that the ethical obligation is totally present in him by transforming it into a wish. Agamemnon, for example, can say: To me the proof that I am not violating my fatherly duty is that my duty is my one and only wish. Consequently we have wish and duty face to face with each other. Happy is the life in which they coincide, in which my wish is my duty and the reverse, and for most men the task in life is simply to adhere to their duty and to transform it by their enthusiasm into their wish. The tragic hero gives up his wish in order to fulfill this duty. For the knight of faith, wish and duty are also identical, but he is required to give up both. If he wants to relinquish by giving up his wish, he finds no rest, for it is indeed his duty. If he wants to adhere to the duty and to his wish, he does not become the knight of faith, for the absolute duty specifically demanded that he should give it up. The tragic hero found a higher expression of duty but not an absolute duty.

concentration, this intense consciousness. In achieving this, the tragic hero may find the universal helpful in one sense, but the knight of faith is alone in everything. The tragic hero does it and finds rest in the universal; the knight of faith is constantly kept in tension. Agamemnon gives up Iphigenia and thereby finds rest in the universal, and now he proceeds to sacrifice her. If Agamemnon had not made the movement, if at the crucial moment his soul, instead of being passionately concentrated, had wandered off into the usual silly talk about having several daughters and that *vielleicht das Ausserordentliche* [perhaps the extraordinary] still could happen—then, of course, he is no hero but a pauper. Abraham, too, has the concentration of the hero, although it is far more difficult for him, since he has no stronghold at all in the universal, but he makes one movement more, whereby he gathers his soul back to the marvel. If Abraham had not done this, he would have been only an Agamemnon, insofar as it can be otherwise explained how wanting to sacrifice Isaac can be justified when the universal is not thereby benefited.[20]

Whether the single individual actually is undergoing a spiritual trial or is a knight of faith, only the single individual himself can decide. But from the paradox itself several characteristic signs may be inferred that are understandable also to someone not in it. The true knight of faith is always absolute isolation; the spurious knight is sectarian. This is an attempt to jump off the narrow path of the paradox and become a tragic hero at a bargain price. The tragic hero expresses the universal and sacrifices himself for it. In place of that, the sectarian Punchinello has a private theater, a few good friends and comrades who represent the universal just about as well as the court observers in *Gulddaasen*[21] represent justice. But the knight of faith, on the other hand, is the paradox; he is the single individual, simply and solely the single individual without any connections and complications. This is the dreadfulness the sectarian weakling cannot endure. Instead of learning from this that he is incapable of doing the great and then openly admitting it—naturally something I cannot but approve, since it is what I myself do—the poor wretch thinks that by joining up with other poor wretches he will be able to do it. But it does not work; in the world of spirit cheating is not tolerated. A dozen sectarians go arm in arm with one another; they are totally ignorant of the solitary spiritual trials that are in store for the knight of faith and that he dares not flee precisely because it would be still more dreadful if he presumptuously forced his way forward. The sectarians deafen one another with their noise and clamor, keep anxiety away with their screeching. A hooting carnival crowd like that thinks it is assaulting heaven, believes it is going along the same path as the knight of faith, who in the loneliness of the universe never hears another human voice but walks alone with his dreadful responsibility.

The knight of faith is assigned solely to himself; he feels the pain of being unable to make himself understandable to others, but he has no vain desire to instruct others. The pain is his assurance; vain desire he does not know—for that his soul is too earnest. The spurious knight quickly betrays himself by this expertise that he has acquired instantly. He by no means grasps what is at stake: that insofar as another individual is to go the same path he must become the single individual in the very same way and then does not require anyone's advice, least of all the advice of one who wants to intrude. Here again, unable to endure the martyrdom of misunderstanding, a person jumps off this path and conveniently enough chooses the worldly admiration of expertise. The true knight of faith is a witness, never the teacher, and therein lies the profound humanity, which has much more to it than this trifling participation in the woes and welfare of other people that is extolled under the name of sympathy, although, on the contrary, it is nothing more than vanity. He who desires only to be a witness confesses thereby that no man, not even the most unimportant man, needs another's participation or is to be devalued by it in order to raise another's value. But since he himself did not obtain at bargain price what he obtained, he does not sell it at bargain price, either. He is not so base that he accepts the admiration of men and in return gives them his silent contempt; he knows that true greatness is equally accessible to all.

Therefore, either there is an absolute duty to God—and if there is such a thing, it is the paradox just described, that the single individual as the single individual is higher than the universal and as the single individual stands in an absolute relation to the absolute—or else faith has never existed because it has always existed, or else Abraham is lost, or else one must interpret the passage in Luke 14 as did that appealing exegete and explain the similar and corresponding passages[22] in the same way.

III
129

*Was It Ethically Defensible for Abraham to Conceal His Under-
taking from Sarah, from Eliezer, and from Isaac?*

The ethical as such is the universal;[1] as the universal it is in
turn the disclosed. The single individual, qualified as immediate, sensate, and psychical, is the hidden. Thus his ethical
task is to work himself out of his hiddenness and to become
disclosed in the universal. Every time he desires to remain in
the hidden, he trespasses and is immersed in spiritual trial
from which he can emerge only by disclosing himself.

Once again we stand at the same point. If there is no hiddenness rooted in the fact that the single individual as the
single individual is higher than the universal, then Abraham's conduct cannot be defended, for he disregarded the
intermediary ethical agents. But if there is such a hiddenness,
then we face the paradox, which cannot be mediated, since
it is based precisely on this: the single individual as the single
individual is higher than the universal, whereas the universal
is in fact mediation. The Hegelian philosophy assumes no
justified hiddenness, no justified incommensurability. It is,
then, consistent for it to demand disclosure, but it is a little
bemuddled when it wants to regard Abraham as the father
of faith and to speak about faith. Faith is not the first immediacy but a later immediacy.[2] The first immediacy is the
esthetic, and here the Hegelian philosophy certainly may very
well be right. But faith is not the esthetic, or else faith has
never existed because it has always existed.

It would be best at this point to consider the whole question purely esthetically[3] and to that end enter into an esthetic
inquiry, to which I invite the reader to give his entire attention momentarily, while I for my part shall adapt my comments to the subjects. The category I shall consider in more
detail is the *interesting*,[4] a category that especially now—since
the age lives *in discrimine rerum* [at a turning point in his-
tory]—has become very important, for it is actually the cat-

egory of the turning point. Therefore one should not, as sometimes happens after one has been personally enamored of it *pro virili* [with all one's might], disdain that category because it grew away from one, but neither should a person be all too greedy for it, for one thing is sure, to become interesting, to have an interesting life, is not a handicraft task but a momentous privilege, which, like every privilege in the world of spirit, is purchased only in severe pain. Thus Socrates was the most interesting man who ever lived, his life the most interesting life ever led, but this existence was allotted to him by the god [*Guden*], and inasmuch as he himself had to acquire it, he was not a stranger to trouble and pain. To take such an existence in vain is not becoming to anyone who thinks more earnestly about life, and yet in our age we frequently see examples of such an effort. Furthermore, the interesting is a border category, a *confinium* [border territory] between esthetics and ethics. Accordingly, this examination must constantly wander into the territory of ethics, while in order to be of consequence it must seize the problem with esthetic fervor and concupiscence. These days, ethics rarely involves itself with a question like this. The reason must be that the system has no room for it. Therefore, one could do it in monographs, and, moreover, if one did not wish to go into detail, it could be made brief and yet achieve the same result—that is, if one has the predicate in his power, for one or two predicates can betray a whole world. Should there not be room in the system for such little words?

In his immortal *Poetics* (Chapter 11), Aristotle[5] says: δύο μὲν οὖν τοῦ μύθου μέρη, περὶ ταῦτ' ἐστί, περιπέτεια καὶ ἀναγνώρισις [two parts of the plot, then, peripety and discovery (recognition), are on matters of this sort]. It is, of course, only the second element that concerns me here: ἀναγνώρισις, recognition. Whenever and wherever it is possible to speak of recognition, there is *eo ipso* a prior hiddenness. Just as the recognition is the resolving, the relaxing element in dramatic life, so hiddenness is the tension-creating factor. What Aristotle develops earlier in the same chapter with regard to the various merits of tragedy, all in relation to the

way περιπέτεια and ἀναγνώρισις *carambolere* [converge], as
well as what he writes about the single and the double recognition, I cannot deal with here, even if tempted by its interiority and its quiet absorption, especially tempting to one
who for a long time has been weary of the superficial om-
niscience of the survey writers. A broader comment may
have its place here. In Greek tragedy, the hiddenness (and as
a result of it the recognition) is an epic remnant based on a
fate in which the dramatic action vanishes and in which it
has its dark, mysterious source. Because of this, a Greek
tragedy has an effect similar to that of a marble statue, which
lacks the potency of the eye. Greek tragedy is blind. Therefore it takes a certain abstraction if one is to be influenced by
it properly. A son murders his father,[6] but not until later
does he learn that it was his father. A sister is going to sacrifice her brother[7] but realizes it at the crucial moment. Our
reflecting age is not very concerned with this kind of tragedy.
Modern drama[8] has abandoned destiny, has dramatically
emancipated itself, is sighted, gazes inward into itself, ab-
sorbs destiny in its dramatic consciousness. Hiddenness and
disclosure, then, are the hero's free act, for which he is responsible.

Recognition and hiddenness are also an essential element
of modern drama. It would belabor the point to give examples. I am sufficiently courteous to assume that everyone in
our age—which is so esthetically voluptuous, so potent and
inflamed, that it conceives just as easily as the partridge that,
according to Aristotle,[9] needs only to hear the cock's voice
or its flight over her head—I assume that everyone who merely
hears the word "hiddenness" will easily be able to shake a
dozen novels and comedies out of his sleeve. I can therefore
be brief and promptly suggest a rather broad observation.[10]
If anyone in playing the hiding game, and thereby providing
the piece with dramatic yeast, hides some *nonsense*, we get a
comedy; but if he is related to the idea, he may come close
to being a tragic hero. To cite just one example of the comic:
a man puts on makeup and wears a wig. The same man is
eager to make a hit with the fair sex and is sure of success

III
133

with the aid of the makeup and wig, which make him altogether irresistible. He catches a girl and is at the pinnacle of
happiness. Now comes the point of the story. If he is able
to admit to his deception, does he not lose all his charm? If
he reveals himself as a plain, yes, even bald male, does he
not thereby lose the beloved? The hiddenness is his free act,
for which esthetics also makes him responsible. This branch
of knowledge is no friend of bald hypocrites and abandons
him to laughter. This illustration may be sufficient merely to
suggest what I mean; the comic cannot be the subject of interest for this investigation.

The road I must take is dialectically to pursue hiddenness
through esthetics and ethics, for the point is to have esthetic
hiddenness and the paradox appear in their absolute dissimilarity.

A few examples. A girl is secretly in love with someone
without the pair's having definitively confessed their love to
each other as yet. Her parents force her to marry another
(she may also be motivated by daughterly devotion); she obeys
her parents, keeps her love hidden "in order not to make the
other unhappy, and no one will ever find out what she suffers." —A young swain has but to say one word to possess
the object of his longings and restless dreams. But this little
word will compromise, indeed, perhaps (who knows?) destroy a whole family. He nobly decides to remain in hiding:
"The girl must never find out, in order that she perhaps may
find happiness with another." What a pity that here two persons, both of whom are hidden from their respective be-
loveds, are also hidden from each other; otherwise, a remarkable higher unity could be brought about here. —Their
hiddenness is a free act, for which they are responsible also
to esthetics. But esthetics is a courteous and sentimental branch
of knowledge that knows more ways out than any pawnshop
manager. What does it do? It makes everything possible for
the lovers. By a coincidence, the respective partners in the
prospective marriage get a hint of the other party's magnanimous decision. There is an explanation, the lovers get each
other and also a place among authentic heroes, for even though

they never had time to sleep on their heroic resolution, es- thetics regards them as having bravely battled their intention through over a period of many years. As a matter of fact, esthetics is not much concerned about time; be it jest or ear- nestness, time goes just as fast for esthetics.

But ethics knows nothing either of that coincidence or of that sentimentality; neither does it have such a fleeting con- cept of time. This puts a quite different face on the matter. Ethics does not lend itself to debate, for it has pure cate- gories. It does not appeal to experience, which of all ridicu- lous things is about the most ridiculous; far from making a man wise, it makes him mad if he knows nothing higher than that. Ethics has no room for coincidence; consequently, there is no eventual explanation. It does not trifle with dig- nities, it places a heavy responsibility on the hero's frail shoulders, it denounces as arrogant his wanting to play prov- idence with his act, but it also denounces his wanting to do that with his suffering. It enjoins believing in actuality and having courage to do battle with all the sufferings of actual- ity, especially those anemic tribulations that he on his own responsibility has brought upon himself. It warns against having faith in the cunning calculations of the understanding, which are less to be trusted than the ancient oracles. It warns against any misplaced magnanimity—let actuality handle it— then it is time to show courage, but then ethics itself offers all possible aid. Meanwhile, if there was anything more pro- found stirring in this pair, if they were earnest about the task, earnest about getting started, then something will surely come of them, but ethics cannot help them. It is offended because they are keeping a secret from it, a secret that they took upon themselves on their own responsibility.

Esthetics, then, demanded the hiddenness and rewarded it; ethics demanded the disclosure and punished the hiddenness.

Now and then, however, esthetics itself demands disclo- sure. When the hero, prey to esthetic illusion, thinks to save another person by his silence, then it demands silence and rewards it. But when the hero by his action has a disturbing effect on another man's life, it demands disclosure. I have

now come to the tragic hero and for a moment would like
to consider *Iphigenia in Aulis* by Euripides. Agamemnon is
about to sacrifice Iphigenia. Esthetics demands silence of
Agamemnon, inasmuch as it would be unworthy of the hero
to seek comfort from any other person, just as out of solicitude for the women he ought to hide it from them as long
as possible. On the other hand, in order to be a hero, the
hero also has to be tried in the dreadful spiritual trial that the
tears of Clytemnestra and Iphigenia will cause. What does
esthetics do? It has a way out; it has the old servant[11] in
readiness to disclose everything to Clytemnestra. Now
everything is in order.

III
135

But ethics has no coincidence and no old servant at its
disposal. The esthetic idea contradicts itself as soon as it is to
be implemented in actuality. For this reason ethics demands
disclosure. The tragic hero demonstrates his ethical courage
in that he himself, not prey to any esthetic illusion, announces Iphigenia's fate to her. If he does that, then the tragic
hero is ethics' beloved son in whom it is well pleased.[12] If he
remains silent, it may be because he believes he thereby makes
it easier for others, but it may also be because he thereby
makes it easier for himself. But he knows he is free of that.
If he remains silent, he takes a responsibility upon himself as
the single individual, inasmuch as he disregards any argument that may come from outside. As the tragic hero he
cannot do this, because ethics loves him for the very reason
that he always expresses the universal. His heroic deed requires courage, but part of this courage is that he does not
avoid any argument. Now it is certainly true that tears are a
dreadful *argumentum ad hominem* [argumentation based on the
opponent's personal circumstances], and one who is touched
by nothing may well be moved by tears. In the play, Iphigenia is permitted to weep; in real life, she ought to be permitted, as was Jephthah's daughter,[13] to weep for two months,
not in solitude but at her father's feet, and to use all her art,
"which is tears alone," and to entwine herself instead of an
olive branch around his knees (see v. 1224).[14]

Esthetics demanded disclosure but aided itself with a co-

incidence; ethics demanded disclosure and found its fulfillment in the tragic hero.

Despite the rigorousness with which ethics demands disclosure, it cannot be denied that secrecy and silence make a
man great simply because they are qualifications of inwardness. When Amor leaves Psyche, he says to her: You will
bear a child who will be divine if you remain silent but will
be human if you betray the secret.[15] The tragic hero, who is
the favorite of ethics, is the purely human; him I can understand, and all his undertakings are out in the open. If I go
further, I always run up against the paradox, the divine and
the demonic, for silence is both. Silence is the demon's trap,
and the more that is silenced, the more terrible the demon,
but silence is also divinity's mutual understanding with the
single individual.

Before proceeding to the story of Abraham, I shall summon a pair of poetic individualities. With the power of dialectics, I shall hold them at the apex, and by disciplining
them with despair, I may prevent them from standing still,
so that in their anxiety they may possibly be able to bring
something or other to light.*

III
136

---

* These movements and positions[16] presumably may still become subjects
for esthetic treatment, but to what extent faith and the whole life of faith
can be that, I leave undecided here. Inasmuch, however, as it is always a
joy for me to thank anyone to whom I owe something, I shall only thank
Lessing for the several hints about a Christian drama found in his *Hamburgische Dramaturgie*.[17] But he fixed his eyes on the purely divine side of this
life (the consummate victory), and therefore he had doubts; perhaps he would
have formed another judgment if he had been more aware of the purely
human side. (*Theologia viatorum* [theology of wayfarers].)[18] What he says is
undeniably very brief, somewhat evasive, but since I am always very happy
when I can find an opportunity to include Lessing, I promptly do so. Lessing was not only one of the most comprehensive minds Germany has had,
he not only displayed an extremely rare precision in his knowledge, which
enables one to rely on him and his autopsies without fear of being taken in
by loose, undocumented quotations, half-understood phrases picked up in
unreliable compendiums, or of being disoriented by a stupid trumpeting of
something new that the ancients have presented far better—but Lessing also
had a most uncommon gift of explaining what he himself had understood.
With that he stopped; in our day people go further and explain more than
they themselves have understood.

In his *Politics*,[19] Aristotle tells a story about a political disturbance in Delphi that grew out of a marriage affair. *The bridegroom, to whom the augurs prophesied a calamity that would have its origin in his marriage, suddenly changes his plans at the crucial moment when he comes to get his bride*—he refuses to be married. More than this I do not need.* In Delphi this event could hardly come to pass without tears. If a poet were to make use of it, he no doubt could safely count on sympathy.[20] Is it not dreadful that the love that so often was an exile in life is now deprived of heaven's aid as well? Does this not give the lie to the old saying that marriages are made in heaven? Generally, it is all the troubles and difficulties of finitude that, like evil spirits, want to separate the lovers, but love has heaven on its side and therefore this holy alliance triumphs over all enemies. Here it is heaven itself that separates what heaven itself, after all, has brought together. Who would have suspected this? Least of all the young bride. Just a moment ago she was sitting in her room in all her beauty, and the lovely maidens had so carefully adorned her that they could feel justified before the whole world, that they could not merely have joy from it but also envy—yes, joy that it was impossible for them to become more envious because it was impossible for her to be more beautiful. She sat alone in her room and was transformed from beauty to beauty, for every feminine art available was used to adorn worthily the worthy one. Yet one thing was still lacking, which the young maidens had not dreamed of—a veil, a more delicate, lighter, and yet more concealing veil than the one in which the maidens had enveloped her, a bridal dress that no young maiden knew anything about or could help her with. Indeed, even the bride did not understand how to help herself. It was an

---

* According to Aristotle, the historical catastrophe was as follows. In revenge, the family places a temple vessel among his kitchen utensils, and he is condemned as a temple thief. But this is immaterial, for the question is not whether the family is ingenious or stupid in taking revenge. The family gains ideal significance only to the extent that it is drawn into the dialectic of the hero. Moreover, it is fateful enough that he plunges into danger while trying to avoid it by not marrying and also that he comes in contact with the divine in a double manner—first by the augurs' pronouncement and next by being condemned as a temple thief.

invisible, a friendly power, one that finds its pleasure in adorning a bride, that enveloped her in it without her knowing it, for all she saw was the bridegroom walking by on his way to the temple. She saw the door shut after him, and she became even more calm and blissful, for she knew that he now belonged to her more than ever. The door of the temple opened, he came out; she, however dropped her eyes in maidenly modesty and did not see that his countenance was disturbed, but he saw that heaven seemed to be envious of the bride's loveliness and of his happiness. The door of the temple opened, the young maidens saw the bridegroom come out, but they did not see that his countenance was disturbed, for they were busy bringing the bride. Then she advanced in all her maidenly humility, and yet like a mistress surrounded by her staff of young maidens, who curtseyed to her as young girls always curtsey to a bride. Thus did she stand at the head of this beautiful throng and waited—it was only a moment, for the temple was close by—and the bridegroom came—but he walked past her door.

But here I stop; I am not a poet, and I go at things only dialectically.[21] In the first place, note that the hero obtains that information in the crucial moment. Therefore he is unstained and unremorseful; he has not irresponsibly bound himself to the beloved. In the next place, he has the divine pronouncement before him, or, more correctly, against him; thus he is not directed by self-opinionated sagacity as fickle lovers are. That testimony, of course, makes him just as unhappy as the bride, in fact, a little more so, because he is the occasion. To be sure, it is true that the augurs predicted a disaster only for *him*, but the question is whether this disaster is not of such a kind that in affecting him it will also affect their marital happiness. What should he do now? (1) Should he remain silent and get married, thinking: Maybe the disaster will not happen right away, and in any case I have maintained love and have not feared to make myself unhappy; but I must remain silent, for otherwise even this brief moment is lost. This seems plausible but definitely is not, for in that case he has offended against the girl. In a sense,

he has made the girl guilty by his silence, for if she had
known of the prophecy, she certainly would never have given
her assent to such an alliance. Then, in his hour of distress,
he will have to bear not only the disaster but also the responsibility for remaining silent and her righteous anger over
his remaining silent. (2) Should he remain silent and not get
married? In that case, he has to involve himself in a hoax
whereby he will destroy himself in his relation to her. Esthetics perhaps would sanction this. The catastrophe could
then be shaped along the lines of the actual event, except that
it would eventuate in a last-moment explanation, which
nevertheless would come afterwards, inasmuch as the esthetic point of view requires that he die,[22] unless this branch
of knowledge finds itself able to cancel that fated prophecy.
But however noble this conduct is, it is an offense against
the girl and the reality of her love. (3) Should he speak? We
must not forget, of course, that our hero is too poetic for
renunciation of his love to mean no more to him than a frus-
trated business venture. If he speaks, the whole thing becomes an unhappy love affair in the same style as Axel and
Valborg.*[23] They become a couple whom heaven itself sep-

---

* For that matter, it is possible to take another dialectical direction at this
point. Heaven prophesies that his marriage will result in a disaster, so he
could indeed dispense with getting married without therefore giving up the
girl; he could live in a romantic alliance with her, which would be more
than adequate for the lovers. This, however, implies an offense against the
girl, for he is not expressing the universal in his love for her. In any case,
it would be a subject for both a poet and an ethicist who wishes to champion
marriage. Generally, if poetry becomes aware of the religious and of the
inwardness of individuality, it will acquire far more meaningful tasks than
those with which it busies itself now. Again and again we hear this story in
poetry: A man is bound to one girl whom he once loved or perhaps never
loved properly, for he has seen another girl who is the ideal. A man makes
a mistake in life; it was the right street but the wrong house, for directly
across the street on the second floor lives the ideal—this is supposed to be a
subject for poetry. A lover has made a mistake, he has seen the beloved by
artificial light and thought she had dark hair, but look, on close scrutiny she
is a blonde—but her sister is the ideal. This is supposed to be a subject for
poetry. In my opinion, any man like that is an impudent young pup who
can be unbearable enough in life but ought to be hissed off stage as soon as

III
140

arates. But in the situation at hand the separation is to be regarded somewhat differently, because it, too, results from the individuals' free act. The great difficulty in the dialectics of this affair is that the disaster is supposed to strike only him. Unlike Axel and Valborg, they do not achieve a common expression for their suffering, whereas heaven separates Axel and Valborg equally because they are equally close to each other. If this were the case here, then there would have been a way out. Since heaven does not use any visible force to separate them but leaves it up to them, it is conceivable that they would decide together to defy heaven along with its disaster.

But ethics demands that he speak. His heroism, then, essentially consists in abandoning the esthetic magnanimity, which *in casu* [in this case], however, cannot easily be imagined to have any infusion of the vanity that is implicit in being concealed, since it certainly must be clear to him that he is making the girl unhappy. The reality of this heroism is that he had his presupposition and canceled it; for otherwise plenty of heroes could be had, especially in our day, which has developed an exceptional skill in the forgery that does the highest by leaping over what lies between.

But why this sketch, since I still get no further than the tragic hero? Because it was, after all, possible that it could throw some light on the paradox. Everything depends upon the relation in which the bridegroom stands to the augurs' pronouncement, which in one way or another will be decisive for his life. Is this pronouncement *publici juris* [public property] or a *privatissimum* [private matter]? The scene is Greece; an augur's pronouncement is understandable by all. I think that the single individual not only can understand the contents lexically but is also able to understand that an augur is declaring heaven's decision to the single individual. Thus

---

he wants to put on airs in poetry. Only passion against passion provides a poetic collision, not this hurly-burly of minutiae within the same passion. In the Middle Ages, for example, when a girl, after having fallen in love, becomes convinced that earthly love is a sin and prefers a heavenly love, this is a poetic collision, and the girl is poetic, because her life is in the idea.

the augur's pronouncement is intelligible not only to the hero but also to all and does not eventuate in any private relation to the divine. He can do what he wants; whatever has been predicted will happen. He does not enter into a closer relation to the divine either by doing it or by not doing it; he does not become the object of the divine's mercy or wrath. The outcome will be just as understandable to anyone as to the hero, and there is no secret code that only the hero can decipher. If he wants to speak, he can very well do that, for he can make himself understandable; if he wants to be silent, it is because in the capacity of being the single individual he wants to be higher than the universal, wants to delude himself with all sorts of fantastic ideas about how she will quickly forget this sorrow etc. But if the will of heaven had not been declared to him by an augur, if it had come to his knowledge quite privately, if it had entered into a purely private relation to him, then we are in the presence of the paradox, if there is any at all (for my deliberation is dilemmatic)—then he could not speak, however willing he might be to do so. Then he would not enjoy his silence but would suffer the agony, but this indeed would be the assurance that he was justified. Then his silence would not be due to his wanting to place himself as the single individual in an absolute relation to the *universal* but to his having been placed as the single individual in an absolute relation to the *absolute*. Then, as far as I can see, he would also be able to find inner peace therein, whereas his noble silence would always be disturbed by the demands of the ethical. It would be altogether desirable if esthetics would sometime attempt to begin where for so many years it has ended—in the illusion of magnanimity. As soon as it did this, it would be working hand in hand with the religious, for this is the only power that can rescue the esthetic from its battle with the ethical. Queen Elizabeth sacrificed to the state her love for Essex by signing his death decree.[24] This was a heroic act, even though there was a little personal resentment involved because he had not sent her the ring. As is known, he had in fact done so, but a spiteful lady-in-waiting had held it back. It is said, *ni fallor* [if I am not mistaken],

III
141

that Elizabeth learned of this and sat for ten days with one
finger in her mouth, biting it and not saying one word, and
thereupon she died. This would be a subject for a poet who
knew how to pry secrets out of people; otherwise, it can best
be used by a ballet master, with whom the poet frequently
confounds himself these days.

Now I shall develop a sketch along the lines of the demonic, and for that I can use the legend about Agnes and the
merman.[25] The merman is a seducer who rises up from his
hidden chasm and in wild lust seizes and breaks the innocent
flower standing on the seashore in all her loveliness and with
her head thoughtfully inclined to the soughing of the sea.
This has been the poets' interpretation[26] until now. Let us
make a change. The merman was a seducer. He has called to
Agnes and by his wheedling words has elicited what was
hidden in her. In the merman she found what she was seeking, what she was searching for as she stared down to the
bottom of the sea.[27] Agnes is willing to go with him. The
merman takes her in his arms. Agnes throws her arms around
his neck; trusting with all her soul, she gives herself to the
stronger one. He is already standing on the beach, crouching
to dive out into the sea and plunge down with his booty—
then Agnes looks at him once more, not fearfully, not de-
spairingly, not proud of her good luck, not intoxicated with
desire, but in absolute faith and in absolute humility, like the
lowly flower she thought herself to be, and with this look
she entrusts her whole destiny to him in absolute confidence.
And look! The sea no longer roars, its wild voice is stilled;
nature's passion, which is the merman's strength, forsakes
him, and there is a deadly calm—and Agnes is still looking
at him this way. Then the merman breaks down. He cannot
withstand the power of innocence, his natural element is dis-
loyal to him, and he cannot seduce Agnes. He takes her home
again, he explains that he only wanted to show her how
beautiful the sea is when it is calm, and Agnes believes him.
Then he returns alone, and the sea is wild, but not as wild
as the merman's despair. He can seduce Agnes, he can seduce
a hundred Agneses, he can make any girl infatuated—but

Agnes has won, and the merman has lost her. Only as booty can she be his; he cannot give himself faithfully to any girl, because he is indeed only a merman. I have taken the liberty of changing* the merman somewhat, and essentially I have also changed Agnes a little, for in the legend Agnes is not entirely without guilt, since generally it is pure nonsense and game-playing and an insult to the female sex to imagine a seduction in which the girl is utterly, utterly, utterly innocent. To modernize my idioms a bit, the Agnes of the legend is a woman who demands the interesting,[30] and anyone like that can always be sure of having a merman close by, for mermen discover this kind with half an eye and dive after them like the shark after his prey. Thus it is very stupid to say—or perhaps it is a rumor that a merman has helped to circulate—that so-called culture protects a girl from seduction. No, existence is more impartial and equitable; there is only one means, and that is innocence.

III
143

---

* The legend could be treated in another way as well. Even though he has seduced many girls before, the merman is reluctant to seduce Agnes. He is no longer a merman, or, if you please, he is a poor miserable merman who for some time now has sat down there at the bottom of the sea and grieved. But he knows—as the legend[28] in fact tells us—that he can be saved by the love of an innocent girl. But he has a bad conscience about girls and does not dare to approach them. Then he sees Agnes. Hidden in the rushes, he has already seen her many times wandering along the beach.[29] He is captured by her beauty, her quiet self-engagement, but his soul is filled with sadness, not wild desire. And when the merman's sighs blend with the whispering of the rushes, she stands still and listens and loses herself in dreams; she is lovelier than any other woman and even as beautiful as a guardian angel who inspires the merman's confidence. The merman takes courage, approaches Agnes, wins her love, and hopes for his salvation. But Agnes is not a quiet, tranquil girl; she enjoyed the roar of the sea, and the sad sighing of the waves gave her pleasure only because the internal storm raged more violently. She wants to be off and away, to storm wildly out into the infinite with the merman, whom she loves—so she inflames the merman. She disdained his humility and now his pride awakens. And the sea roars and the waves froth, and the merman locks Agnes in his embrace and plunges into the abyss with her. Never had he been so wild, never so full of lust, because in this girl he had hoped for his salvation. Soon he grew tired of Agnes, but no one has ever found her corpse, for she became a mermaid who lured men with her songs.

III
142

III
143

We shall now give the merman a human consciousness and let his being a merman signify a human preexistence,[31] in consequence of which his life was entrapped. There is nothing to hinder his becoming a hero, for the step he now takes is reconciling. He is saved by Agnes; the seducer is crushed, he has submitted to the power of innocence, he can never seduce again. But immediately two forces struggle over him: repentance, Agnes and repentance. If repentance alone gets him, then he is hidden; if Agnes and repentance get him, then he is disclosed.

But now if the merman is seized by repentance and he remains hidden, he certainly will make Agnes unhappy, for Agnes loved him in all her innocence; even when he seemed to her to be changed, however well he concealed it, she still thought it was true that he merely wished to show her the beautiful stillness of the sea. Meanwhile, in his passion the merman himself becomes even more unhappy, for he loved Agnes with a complexity of passions and in addition had a new guilt to bear. Now the demonic in repentance probably will explain that this is indeed his punishment, and the more it torments him the better.

If he surrenders to this demonic element, he perhaps will make another attempt to save Agnes, just as in a sense one can save a person with the aid of evil. He knows that Agnes loves him. If he could tear this love away from Agnes, then in a way she would be saved. But how? The merman is too sensible to reckon that a frank confession will arouse her loathing. Maybe he will endeavor to incite all the dark passions in her, to belittle her, to ridicule her, to make her love ludicrous, and, if possible, to arouse her pride. He [32]will spare himself no anguish, for this is the deep contradiction in the demonic, and in a certain sense there is ever so much more good in a demoniac than in superficial people. The more selfish Agnes is, the more easily she will be deceived (for it is only the very inexperienced who think that it is easy to deceive innocence; existence is very profound, and it is easiest for the clever to fool the clever), but all the more terrible will be the merman's sufferings. The more ingeniously he

III
144

designs his deception, the less Agnes will modestly hide her suffering from him; she will use every resource, and they will not be without effect—that is, not of dislodging him but of tormenting him.

With the assistance of the demonic, therefore, the merman would be the single individual who as the single individual was higher than the universal. The demonic has the same quality as the divine, namely, that the single individual is able to enter into an absolute relation to it. This is the analogy, the counterpart to that paradox of which we speak. It has, therefore, a certain similarity that can be misleading. Thus, all the anguish the merman suffers in silence seems proof that his silence is justified. Meanwhile, there is no doubt that he can speak. So if he speaks, he can become a tragic hero, in my opinion a grandiose tragic hero. There are perhaps few who grasp what constitutes the grandeur.* He will then have the courage to divest himself of every illusion that he can make Agnes happy by his art; he will have the courage, humanly speaking, to crush Agnes. Incidentally, I would like to make just one psychological comment here. The more selfishly Agnes has been developed, the more glaring the self-deception will be. Indeed, it is not inconceivable that in real life the demonic ingenuity of a merman could not only save Agnes, humanly speaking, but could also elicit something extraordinary from her, for a demoniac knows how to extort

III
145

---

* Esthetics sometimes treats a similar situation in its usual game-playing way. The merman is saved by Agnes, and the whole thing ends with a happy marriage! A happy marriage—that is easy enough. But if ethics were to speak at the wedding, I think it would be another matter. Esthetics throws the cloak of love over the merman, and everything is forgotten. It is also superficial to believe that marriage is like an auction, where everything is sold in whatever condition it is when the auctioneer's hammer falls. Esthetics just sees to it that the lovers find each other and does not concern itself about the rest. If only it would see what happens afterwards, but it has no time for that and promptly proceeds to slap a new pair of lovers together. Of all the branches of knowledge, esthetics is the most faithless. Anyone who has really loved it becomes in one sense unhappy, but he who has never loved it is and remains a *pecus* [dumb brute].

III
144

III
145

powers out of even the weakest of people, and in his own way he can be very well meaning with a person.

The merman stands at a dialectical apex. If he is rescued from the demonic in repentance, there are two possibilities. He can hold himself back, remain in hiding, but not depend upon his sagacity. Then he does not as the single individual enter into an absolute relation to the demonic, but he finds peace of mind in the counterparadox that the divine will save Agnes. (This is how the Middle Ages would make the movement, for according to its way of thinking the merman is obviously turned over to the monastery.) Or he can be saved by Agnes. This must not be interpreted to mean that by Agnes's love he would be saved from becoming a seducer in the future (this is an esthetic rescue attempt that always evades the main point, the continuity in the merman's life), for in that respect he is saved—he is saved insofar as he becomes disclosed. Then he marries Agnes. He must, however, take refuge in the paradox. In other words, when the single individual by his guilt has come outside the universal, he can return only by virtue of having come as the single individual into an absolute relation to the absolute. Now here I would like to make a comment that says more than has been said at any point previously.* Sin is not the first immediacy; sin is a later immediacy. In sin, the single individual is already higher (in the direction of the demonic paradox) than the universal, because it is a contradiction on the part of the universal to want to demand itself from a person who lacks the *conditio sine qua non* [indispensable condition]. If, along with other things, philosophy were also to think that it just might enter a man's head to want to act according to its teaching, we would get a strange kind of comedy out of it. An ethics that ignores sin is a completely futile disci-

III
146

---

* Up until now I have assiduously avoided any reference to the question of sin and its reality [*Realitet*]. The whole work is centered on Abraham, and I can still encompass him in immediate categories—that is, insofar as I can understand him. As soon as sin emerges, ethics founders precisely on repentance; for repentance is the highest ethical expression, but precisely as such it is the deepest ethical self-contradiction.

pline, but if it affirms sin, then it has *eo ipso* exceeded itself. Philosophy teaches that the immediate should be annulled. This is true enough, but what is not true is that sin is directly the immediate,[33] any more than faith is directly the immediate.[34]

As long as I move around in these spheres, everything is easy, but nothing of what has been said here explains Abraham, for Abraham did not become the single individual by way of sin—on the contrary, he was a righteous man, God's chosen one. The analogy to Abraham will not become apparent until after the single individual has been brought to a position where he is capable of fulfilling the universal, and now the paradox repeats itself.

Therefore, I can understand the movements of the merman, whereas I cannot understand Abraham, for it is precisely by way of the paradox that the merman reaches the point of wishing to realize the universal. If he remains hidden and is initiated into all the anguish of repentance, he becomes a demoniac and as such is destroyed. If he remains hidden but does not sagaciously think that by his being tormented in the bondage of repentance he can work Agnes free, then he no doubt finds peace but is lost to this world. If he becomes disclosed, if he lets himself be saved by Agnes, then he is the greatest human being I can imagine, for it is only esthetics that thoughtlessly supposes it is praising the power of love by having the prodigal be loved by an innocent girl and thereby saved; it is only esthetics that perceives mistakenly and believes that the girl is the heroic figure instead of the merman. The merman, therefore, cannot belong to Agnes without, after having made the infinite movement of repentance, making one movement more: the movement by virtue of the absurd. He can make the movement of repentance under his own power, but he also uses absolutely all his power for it and therefore cannot possibly come back under his own power and grasp actuality again. If a person does not have sufficient passion to make either of the movements, if he skulks through life repenting a little and thinking everything will come out in the wash, then he has once and for all renounced living in the idea, and in this way he can very easily achieve the highest and help others achieve it as well—that is, beguile himself and others into thinking that things happen in the world of spirit as in a game in which everything happens by chance.[35] Then it is amusing to think how odd it is that doubt about the immortality of the soul[36] can be so prevalent in the very age when everyone can achieve the highest, for the person who has actually made just the movement of infinity scarcely doubts. The conclusions of passion are the only dependable ones—that is, the only convincing ones. Fortunately, existence is here more affectionate and loyal than the wise assert it is, for it excludes no human being, not even the lowest; it fools no one, for in the world of spirit only he is fooled who fools himself. It is everyone's opinion—and if I may be permitted to make a judgment about it, it is also my opinion—that to enter a monastery is not the highest, but by no means do I therefore believe that everyone in our day, when no one enters the monastery, is greater than the deep and earnest souls who found rest in a monastery. How many in our time have sufficient passion to think this and then to judge themselves honestly? The very idea of being conscientious about time this way, of taking the time to scrutinize in sleepless vigilance every single secret thought, so that if a person does not always make the movement by virtue of the noblest and holiest in him, he may in anxiety and horror discover* and lure forth—if in no other way, then through anxiety—the dark emotions hiding in every human life, whereas in association with others one so easily forgets, so easily evades this, is stopped in so many ways, get the opportunity to begin afresh—this thought alone, conceived with due deference, could, I believe, chastise many a man in our day who believes he has already attained the highest. But

III
148

III
148
* Our earnest age does not believe this, and yet, oddly enough, even in the inherently more irresponsible and less reflective paganism the two authentic representatives of the Greek view of life, γνῶθι σαυτόν [know your- III
149 self], each in his own way hinted that, by penetratingly concentrating on oneself, one first and foremost discovers the disposition to evil. I scarcely need to say that I am thinking of Pythagoras and Socrates.[37]

this is of small concern in our generation, which believes it has attained the highest, whereas in fact no generation has been so much at the mercy of the comic as this one. And it is inconceivable that it has not already happened that by a *generatio aequivoca* [self-procreation] our generation has itself given birth to its hero, the demon, who ruthlessly puts on the dreadful theatrical piece that makes the whole generation laugh and forget that it is laughing at itself. Indeed, what other value does existence have than to be laughed at—when one has already attained the highest by the age of twenty. And what higher movement has the age discovered, now that entering the monastery has been abandoned? Is it not a wretched worldly wisdom, sagacity, pusillanimity, that sits in the place of honor, that cravenly deludes men into thinking that they have performed the highest and slyly keeps them from even attempting the lesser? The person who has made the monastic movement has only one movement left, the movement of the absurd. How many in our day understand what the absurd is? How many in our day live in such a way that they have renounced everything or have received everything? How many are merely so honest that they know what they are able to do and what they are unable to do? And is it not true that if there are any such people at all, they are most likely to be found among the less educated and in part among women? The age reveals its defect in a kind of clairvoyance, just as a demoniac discloses himself without understanding himself, for again and again the age demands the comic. If this were actually what our generation needed, then the theater perhaps needs a new play in which someone's dying for love is made ludicrous, or would it not perhaps be more salutary for the age if such a thing occurred among us, if the age were to witness an event such as this, so that for once it could find the courage to believe in the power of the spirit, the courage to stop cravenly suffocating the better side of itself, jealously smothering it in others— through laughter. Should it be necessary for our age to have the ridiculous *Erscheinung* [appearance] of an enthusiast in order to find something to laugh at, or is it not rather more

III
149

necessary that such an inspired character would remind it of what has been forgotten?

If a similar but even more moving plot is wanted, because the passion of repentance was not set in motion, one could use a story from the book of Tobit.[38] The young Tobias wishes to marry Sarah, the daughter of Raguel and Edna. But this girl has a tragic background. She has been given to seven men, all of whom perished in the bridal chamber. For my plot, this is a defect in the story, for the comic effect is almost unavoidable when one thinks of a girl's seven futile attempts to get married, although she was very close to it, about as close as a student who failed his examination seven times. In the book of Tobit, the accent lies elsewhere, and this is why the high number is important and in a certain sense contributes to the tragedy, because the young Tobias's magnanimity is all the greater, partly because he is his parents' only son (6:14), partly because the appalling aspect obtrudes all the more. Consequently, this must be put aside. Sarah, then, is a girl who has never been in love, who still has a young girl's beatific treasure, her prodigious, enormous mortgage on life, her *"Vollmachtbrief zum Glücke"* [full warrant for happiness][39]—[the capacity] to love a man with all her heart. And yet she is unhappier than anyone else, for she knows that the evil demon who loves her will kill her bridegroom on the wedding night. I have read about many griefs, but I doubt that there is to be found a grief as profound as the one in this girl's life. But if the unhappiness comes from without, consolation is still to be found. If existence has not provided a person with that which could have made him happy, it is still consoling to know that he could have received it. But what an unfathomable grief that no amount of time can chase away, no amount of time can cure—to know that it would be of no help if existence did everything! A Greek author hides so infinitely much in his simple naiveté when he says: πάντως γὰρ οὐδείς Ἔρωτα ἔφυγεν ἢ φεύξεται, μέχρι ἂν κάλλος ἦ καὶ ὀφθαλμοὶ βλέπωσιν [For there was never any yet that wholly could escape love, and never shall there be any, never so long as beauty shall be, never so long as eyes can see] (cf. Longus, *Pastoralia*).[40] Many a girl has become unhappy in love, but she nevertheless did *become* that; Sarah *was* that before she became that. It is grievous not to find the person to whom one can give oneself, but it is *unspeakably* grievous not to be able to give oneself. A young girl gives herself, and then it is said: Now she is no longer free. But Sarah was never free, and yet she had never given herself. It is grievous if a girl gives herself and is deceived, but Sarah was deceived before she gave herself. What a world of sorrow will come as a consequence of Tobias's finally marrying her! What wedding preparations, what ceremonials! No girl has been as defrauded as Sarah was, for she was defrauded of the highest bliss, the absolute richness possessed by even the poorest of maidens, defrauded out of the assured, unlimited, unbounded, uninhibited devotedness, for there should indeed first be smoke from the placement of the heart and liver of the fish on the glowing embers.[41] And how must the mother take leave of her daughter, who, just as she herself is defrauded of everything, must in turn defraud the mother of the most beautiful of all. But read the story. Edna prepared the chamber, and she escorted Sarah into it and wept, and she received her daughter's weeping. And she said to her: My child, take heart. The Lord of heaven and earth may exchange your sorrow for joy! Daughter, take heart. And now comes the time of the wedding. We read on—if we can read at all through our tears: But when the door was shut and they were together, Tobias rose from the bed and said: Rise up, sister, and we will pray that the Lord may have mercy upon us (8:4).

If a poet read this story and were to use it, I wager a hundred to one that he would make everything center on the young Tobias. The heroic courage to be willing to risk his life in such obvious danger—as the story reminds us once again, for the morning after the wedding Raguel says to Edna: Send one of the maids to see if he is alive, so that, if not, I can bury him and no one will know it (see 8:13)—this heroic courage would be the subject. I venture to propose another. Tobias behaves gallantly and resolutely and chivalrously, but any man who does not have the courage for that is a milksop who does not know what love is or what it is to be a man or what is worth living for; he has not even grasped the little mystery that it is better to give than to receive and has no intimation of the great mystery that it is far more difficult to receive than to give, that is, if one has had the courage to do without and in the hour of distress did not prove a coward. No, Sarah is the heroic character. She is the one I want to approach as I have never approached any girl or been tempted in thought to approach anyone of whom I have read. For what love for God it takes to be willing to let oneself be healed when from the very beginning one in all innocence has been botched, from the very beginning has been a damaged specimen of a human being! What ethical maturity to take upon oneself the responsibility of permitting the beloved to do something so hazardous! What humility before another person! What faith in God that she would not in the very next moment hate the man to whom she owed everything!

Imagine Sarah to be a man, and the demonic is immediately present. The proud, noble nature can bear everything, but one thing it cannot bear—it cannot bear sympathy. In it there is a humiliation that can be inflicted on a person only by a higher power, for he can never become the object of it by himself. If he has sinned, he can bear the punishment without despairing, but to be without guilt from his mother's womb and yet to be destined as a sacrifice to sympathy, a sweet fragrance in its nostrils—this he cannot endure. Sympathy has a curious dialectic: it demands guilt one moment and refuses it the next, and that is why being predestined to sympathy becomes progessively more dreadful the more the individual's unhappiness is oriented to the spiritual. But Sarah has no guilt; she is thrown as prey to every suffering and then in addition is to be tormented by human sympathy, for even I, who admire her more than Tobias loved her, even I cannot mention her name without saying: The poor girl!

Imagine a man in Sarah's place; let him learn that if he loves a girl an infernal spirit will come and murder the beloved on the wedding night. He might possibly choose the demonic, inclose himself up in himself, and speak the way a demonic nature speaks in secret: "Thanks, I'm no friend of ceremonies and complexities; I do not demand the delight of love at all, for I can in fact be a Bluebeard and have my delight in seeing maidens die on their wedding night." As a rule, we get to know very little about the demonic, even though this is a subject that has a valid claim to be discovered especially in our time, and even though the observer—if he knows anything at all about making contact with the de- monic—can use practically anybody, at least momentarily. In that kind of thing, Shakespeare is and remains a hero. That horrible demoniac, the most demonic figure Shake- speare has depicted but also depicted in a matchless way— Gloucester (later Richard III)—what made him into a de- moniac? Apparently his inability to bear the sympathy heaped upon him from childhood. His monologue in the first act of *Richard III*[42] has more value than all the systems of morality, which have no intimation of the nightmares of existence or of their explanation.

III
152

> . . . Ich, roh geprägt, und aller Reize baar.
> Vor leicht sich dreh'nden Nymphen mich zu brüsten;
> Ich, so verkürzt um schönes Ebenmass,
> Geschändet von der tückischen Natur,
> Entstellt, verwahrlost, vor der Zeit gesandt
> In diese Welt des Athmens, halb kaum fertig
> Gemacht, und zwar so lahm und ungeziemend,
> Dass Hunde bellen, hink' ich wo vorbei.

> [I, that am rudely stamp'd, and want love's majesty
> To strut before a wanton ambling nymph;
> I, that am curtail'd of this fair proportion,
> Cheated of feature by dissembling Nature,
> Deform'd, unfinish'd, sent before my time
> Into this breathing world, scarce half made up,
> And that so lamely and unfashionable
> That dogs bark at me as I halt by them—.]

Natures such as Gloucester's cannot be saved by mediating them into an idea of society. Ethics actually only makes sport of them, just as it would be a taunting of Sarah for ethics to say to her: Why do you not express the universal and get married? Natures such as those are basically in the paradox, and they are by no means more imperfect than other people, except that they are either lost in the demonic paradox or saved in the divine paradox. Time and again people have been pleased that witches, nisses, trolls, etc. are malformed creatures, and no doubt everyone has an inclination, when he sees a malformed person, to attach to him the idea of moral depravity. What a glaring injustice, since the relation ought to be turned around: existence itself has damaged them, just as a stepmother makes the children perverse. The demonic, for which the individual himself has no guilt, has its beginning in his originally being set outside the universal by nature or by a historical situation. Thus Cumberland's Jew[43] is also a demoniac, even though he does good. The demonic can also express itself as contempt for men, a contempt, please note, that does not lead the demoniac himself to act contemptuously; on the contrary, he has his strength in his awareness that he is better than all those who judge him.

With regard to all such things, the poets ought to be almost the first to sound the alarm. God only knows what books the present generation of young versifiers is reading! Their study probably consists of learning rhymes by heart. God knows what importance they have in this world! At this moment, I know of no benefit from them other than that they provide an edifying proof of the immortality of the soul, since of them one may safely say to oneself what Baggesen[44] says about the local poet Kildevalle: If he becomes immortal, then all of us will.

Everything said here about Sarah, chiefly with regard to poetic presentation and therefore with an imaginary presupposition, has its full meaning when with a psychological interest one explores the meaning of the old saying: *Nullum unquam exstitit magnum ingenium sine aliqua dementia* [No great genius has ever existed without some touch of madness].[45]

For such dementia is the suffering of genius in this world, is the expression, if I dare say so, of divine envy, whereas the genius aspect is the expression of preferment. Thus from the beginning the genius is disoriented with respect to the universal and is placed in relation to the paradox—whether he, in despair over his limitations (which in his eyes transform his omnipotence to impotence), seeks a demonic reassurance and for this reason does not wish to admit it either to God or to men, or whether he religiously reassures himself in love for the divine. Here are the psychological subjects to which, it seems to me, one could joyfully give one's whole life, and yet we seldom hear a word about them. What is the relation between mental derangement and genius; can one be construed from the other? In what sense and to what extent is the genius master of his mental derangement? It goes without saying that up to a point he is its master; otherwise he would actually be insane. But such observations require love and a high degree of ingenuity, for observation of the superior person is very difficult. If one paid attention to this in reading a few authors of the greatest genius, it might be possible just once, although with great difficulty, to find out a little.

To take yet another case, let us imagine that an individual, by being hidden and by remaining silent, wants to save the universal. For this I can use the legend of *Faust*. Faust is a doubter,* an apostate of the spirit who goes the way of the

---

* If we do not wish to use a doubter, we could choose a similar figure, for example, an ironist whose sharp eye has radically seen through the ludicrousness of life and whose secret understanding with life forces has made sure of what the patient desires. He knows that he has the power of laughter, and if he wishes to use it, he is sure of his own success—indeed, what is more, of his own happiness. He knows that one solitary voice will speak up to restrain him, but he knows that he is the stronger. He knows that men can still be made to seem earnest momentarily, but he also knows that secretly they yearn to laugh with him; he knows that a woman can still be made to hold the fan momentarily before her eyes when he speaks, but he knows that she is laughing behind the fan. He knows that the fan is not completely opaque; he knows that one can write an invisible message on it; he knows that when a woman flutters her fan at him it is because she has

III
155

flesh. This is the poet's interpretation, and although it is repeated again and again that every age has its Faust, nevertheless one poet after the other undauntedly walks this beaten path. Let us make a little change. Faust is the doubter κατ' ἐξοχήν [par excellence], but he has a sympathetic nature. Even in Goethe's version of Faust, I miss a profound psychological insight into doubt's secret conversations with itself. In our age, when indeed all have experienced doubt, no poet as yet has made any step in this direction. I feel like offering them government bonds on which to write the sum total of their experiences in this respect—they would scarcely write any more than could be accommodated on the top margin.

Only when one turns Faust into himself can doubt take on a poetic aspect; only then does he actually discover within himself all the sufferings of doubt. Then he knows that it is spirit that maintains existence, but he also knows that the security and joy in which men live are not grounded in the power of the spirit but are easily explained as an unreflected bliss. As doubter, as the doubter, he is higher than all this,

---

understood him. He has infallible information about the way laughter sneaks in and lives secretly in a person, and once it has taken up residence, it watches and waits. Let us imagine such an Aristophanes, such a slightly altered Voltaire, for he is also sympathetic: he loves existence, he loves men, and he knows that even if denunciation by laughter may rear up a new, redeemed generation, at the same time a great number of his contemporaries will be destroyed. So he remains silent and as far as possible forgets himself how to laugh. But dare he remain silent? There may be some who simply do not understand the difficulty of which I speak. They presumably think it was an admirable magnanimity to remain silent. I cannot agree at all, for I believe that anyone so constituted, if he has not had the magnanimity to remain silent, is a traitor to existence. Consequently, I demand this magnanimity of him; but if he has it, dare he then remain silent? Ethics is a dangerous branch of knowledge, and it was surely possible that Aristophanes for purely ethical reasons decided to let laughter pass judgment on the perverse age. Esthetic nobility cannot help, because one does not venture such things on that score. If he is to remain silent, he must enter into the paradox.

As yet another plot, I suggest, for example, that someone has an explanation of a hero's life, but one that explains it in a lamentable way, and yet a whole generation has absolute confidence in this hero without suspecting anything like this.

and if someone wants to delude him into fancying that he has passed through doubt, he easily sees through it, for anyone who has made a movement in the world of spirit, consequently an infinite movement, can immediately hear from the response whether it is a tried and tested person who is speaking or a Münchhausen.[46] What a Tamerlane[47] was able to do with his Huns, Faust knows how to do with his doubt—to rouse men up horrified, to make the world totter under their feet, to split men apart, to make the shriek of alarm sound everywhere. And if he does that, then he is no Tamerlane; in a certain sense he is authorized and has the mandate of thought. But Faust has a sympathetic nature, he loves existence, his soul knows no envy, he perceives that he cannot stop the fury he certainly can arouse, he aspires to no Herostratic honor[48]—he remains silent, he hides doubt more carefully in his soul than the girl who hides a sinful fruit of love under her heart, he tries as much as possible to walk in step with other men, but what goes on inside himself he consumes and thus brings himself as a sacrifice for the universal.

Now and then, when some unconventional fellow churns up a whirlwind of doubt, we hear people say: Would that he had remained silent. Faust fulfills this idea. Anyone who has a notion of what it means for a person to live on spirit also knows what the hunger of doubt means and knows that the doubter hungers just as much for the daily bread of life as for the nourishment of spirit. Notwithstanding the possibility that all Faust's agonies may be a very good argument that it is not pride that has possessed him, I shall nevertheless take a precautionary measure, which is easy for me to devise, for just as Gregory of Rimini[49] was called *tortor infantium* [tormentor of infants] because he accepted the damnation of infants, I could be tempted to call myself *tortor heroum* [tormentor of heroes], for I am very inventive when it comes to tormenting heroes. Faust sees Margaret, but not after having chosen lust, for my Faust does not choose lust at all; he sees Margaret not in Mephistopheles's concave mirror[50] but in all her adorable innocence, and since his soul has retained its

III
156

love for people, he can also very easily fall in love with her. But he is a doubter; his doubt has destroyed actuality for him, for my Faust is so ideal that he is not one of those scientific doubters who doubt one hour every semester on the podium but otherwise are able to do everything else, as they do even this, without the help of the spirit or the power of the spirit. He is a doubter, and the doubter hungers just as much for the daily bread of joy as for the nourishment of spirit. But he holds to his resolution and remains silent and does not tell anyone of his doubt, nor does he tell Margaret of his love.

It goes without saying that Faust is too ideal a figure to be satisfied with the nonsense that if he spoke he would prompt a general discussion, or that the whole affair would pass without any consequences, or perhaps this or perhaps that. (Here, as any poet will readily see, is the dormant comic element in the plot, that is, bringing Faust into an ironic relation to those slapstick fools who chase after doubt in our day, present external arguments to prove that they actually have doubted—for example, a doctoral diploma—or swear that they have doubted everything, or prove it by once having met a doubter in their travels, those couriers and sprint-

III
157

ers in the world of spirit who very hastily pick up a little tip about doubt from one person and something about faith from another and then *wirthschafte* [do business] in the best manner, all according to whether the congregation wants to have fine sand or gravel.)[51] Faust is too ideal a figure to go around in bedroom slippers. Anyone who does not have an infinite passion is not ideal, and anyone who has an infinite passion has long since saved his soul from such rubbish. He remains silent in order to sacrifice himself—or he speaks in the awareness that he will throw everything into disorder.

If he remains silent, then ethics condemns him, saying, "You must acknowledge the universal, and you acknowledge it specifically by speaking, and you dare not to have compassion on the universal." This observation should not be forgotten when at times a doubter is judged severely because he speaks. I am not inclined to judge such conduct mildly, but here, as everywhere, the point is that the movements take place normatively. If worst comes to worst, a doubter—even though by speaking he brings every misfortune possible down upon the world—is still to be preferred to these wretched sweet-tooths who taste of everything and want to cure doubt without recognizing it and who then as a rule are themselves the chief reason why doubt breaks out wildly and uncontrollably.[52] If he speaks, he throws everything into disorder, for even if it does not happen, he does not find that out until later, and the outcome cannot help a person either in the moment of action or with respect to responsibility.

If he remains silent on his own responsibility, he can presumably act magnanimously, but he will add a little spiritual trial to his other agonies, for the universal will constantly torment him and say: You should have spoken. How are you going to be sure that your resolution was not prompted by cryptic pride?

But if the doubter can become the single individual who as the single individual stands in an absolute relation to the absolute, then he can get authorization for his silence. In that case, he must make his doubt into guilt. In that case, he is within the paradox, but then his doubt is healed, even if he may have another doubt.

Even the New Testament would acknowledge such a silence. There are even places in the New Testament that praise irony, provided that it is used to conceal the better part.[53] But this movement is just as much one of irony as is everything else that is based on the premise that subjectivity is higher than actuality. Our age does not want to know anything about this; on the whole, it does not want to know more about irony than was said by Hegel,[54] who, curiously enough, did not understand much about it and bore a grudge against it, which our age has good reason not to give up, for it has to guard itself against irony. In the Sermon on the Mount,[55] it says: When you fast, anoint your head and wash your face, that your fasting may not be seen by men. This passage shows clearly that subjectivity is incommensurable with actuality, indeed, that it has the right to deceive. If only the people who traipse about these days talking loosely about the idea of congregation would read the New Testament, maybe they would get some other ideas.[56]

But now to Abraham—how did he act? For I have not forgotten, and the reader will please remember, that I got involved in the previous discussion to make that subject an obstacle, not as if Abraham could thereby become more comprehensible, but in order that the incomprehensibility could become more salient, for, as I said before, I cannot understand Abraham—I can only admire him. It was also pointed out that none of the stages described contains an analogy to Abraham; they were explained, while being demonstrated each within its own sphere, only in order that in their moment of deviation they could, as it were, indicate the boundary of the unknown territory. If there is any question of an analogy, it must be the paradox of sin, but this again is in another sphere and cannot explain Abraham and is itself far easier to explain than Abraham.

So Abraham did not speak, he did not speak to Sarah, or to Eliezer, or to Isaac; he bypassed these three ethical authorities, since for Abraham the ethical had no higher expression than family life.

Esthetics allowed, indeed demanded, silence of the single individual if he knew that by remaining silent he could save another. This alone adequately shows that Abraham is not within the scope of esthetics. His silence is certainly not in order to save Isaac; in fact, his whole task of sacrificing Isaac for his own and for God's sake is an offense to esthetics, because it is able to understand that I sacrifice myself but not that I sacrifice someone else for my own sake. The esthetic hero was silent. Meanwhile, ethics passed judgment on him because he was silent on account of his accidental particularity. It was his human prescience that led him to remain silent. Ethics cannot forgive this. Any human knowing of that sort is only an illusion. Ethics demands an infinite movement, it demands disclosure. The esthetic hero, then, can speak but will not.

The authentic tragic hero sacrifices himself and everything that is his for the universal; his act and every emotion in him belong to the universal; he is open, and in this disclosure he is the beloved son of ethics. This does not fit Abraham; he does nothing for the universal and is hidden.

Now we are face to face with the paradox. Either the single individual as the single individual can stand in an absolute relation to the absolute, and consequently the ethical is not the highest, or Abraham is lost: he is neither a tragic hero nor an esthetic hero.[57]

Here again it may seem that the paradox is the simplest and easiest of all. May I repeat, however, that anyone who remains convinced of this is not a knight of faith, for distress and anxiety are the only justification conceivable, even if it is not conceivable in general, for then the paradox is canceled.

Abraham remains silent—but he *cannot* speak. Therein lies the distress and anxiety. Even though I go on talking night and day without interruption, if I cannot make myself understood when I speak, then I am not speaking. This is the case with Abraham. He can say everything, but one thing he cannot say, and if he cannot say that—that is, say it in such a way that the other understands it—then he is not speaking. The relief provided by speaking is that it translates me into the universal. Now, Abraham can describe his love for Isaac in the most beautiful words to be found in any language. But this is not what is on his mind; it is something deeper, that he is going to sacrifice him because it is an ordeal. No one can understand the latter, and thus everyone can only misunderstand the former. The tragic hero does not know this distress. In the first place, he has the consolation that every counterargument has had its due, that he has given everyone an opportunity to stand up against him: Clytemnestra, Iphigenia, Achilles, the chorus, every living person, every voice from humanity's heart, every cunning, every alarming, every incriminating, every commiserating thought.

He can be sure that everything permitted to be said against
him has been said ruthlessly, mercilessly—and to fight against
the whole world is a consolation, to fight against oneself is
frightful. He does not have to fear having overlooked anything, so that later on he perhaps must cry out as King Edward IV did on hearing of the murder of Clarence:[58]

> Wer bat für ihn? Wer kniet' in meinem Grimm
> Zu Füssen mir und bat mich überlegen?
> Wer sprach von Bruderpflicht? Wer sprach von Liebe?*

> [Who sued to me for him? Who (in my wrath)
> Kneel'd at my feet and bid me be advis'd?
> Who spoke of brotherhood? Who spoke of love?]

The tragic hero does not know the dreadful responsibility
of loneliness. Moreover, he has the consolation that he can
weep and lament with Clytemnestra and Iphigenia[59]—and tears
and cries are relieving, but groanings that cannot be uttered
are torturing. Agamemnon can quickly concentrate his whole
being in the certainty that he is going to act, and then he still
has time to comfort and encourage. This Abraham cannot
do. When his heart is moved, when his words would provide blessed comfort to the whole world, he dares not to
offer comfort, for would not Sarah, would not Eliezer, would
not Isaac say to him, "Why do you want to do it, then? After
all, you can abstain." And if in his distress he wanted to
unburden himself and clasp to himself all that he held dear
before he proceeded to the end, the terrible consequence might
be that Sarah, Eliezer, and Isaac would take offense at him
and believe him to be a hypocrite. Speak he cannot; he speaks
no human language. And even if he understood all the languages of the world, even if those he loved also understood
them, he still could not speak—he speaks in a divine language, he speaks in tongues.[60]

This distress I can understand very well. I can admire
Abraham. I have no fear that anyone reading this story will
be tempted rashly to want to be the single individual. But I

* Cf. II, 1.

also confess that I do not have the courage for it and that I would gladly renounce every expectation of proceeding further if it were even possible, be it ever so late, that I should come that far. At every moment, Abraham can stop; he can repent of the whole thing as a spiritual trial; then he can speak out, and everybody will be able to understand him—but then he is no longer Abraham.

[61]Abraham *cannot* speak, because he cannot say that which would explain everything (that is, so it is understandable): that it is an ordeal such that, please note, the ethical is the temptation.[62] Anyone placed in such a position is an emigrant from the sphere of the universal. But even less can he say the next thing. To repeat what was sufficiently developed earlier, Abraham makes two movements. He makes the infinite movement of resignation and gives up Isaac, which no one can understand because it is a private venture; but next, at every moment, he makes the movement of faith. This is his consolation. In other words, he is saying: But it will not happen, or if it does, the Lord will give me a new Isaac, that is, by virtue of the absurd. The tragic hero, however, comes to the end of the story. Iphigenia submits to her father's resolve; she herself makes the infinite movement of resignation, and they now have a mutual understanding. She can understand Agamemnon, because the step he is taking expresses the universal. But if Agamemnon were to say to her, "Although the god demands you as a sacrifice, it is still possible that he would not demand it, that is, by virtue of the absurd"—then he would instantly be incomprehensible to Iphigenia. If he could say this by virtue of human reckoning, Iphigenia would very likely understand him, but as a result Agamemnon would not have made the infinite movement of resignation and thus would not be a hero; then the soothsayer's declaration is a sailor's yarn, and the whole event is a vaudeville.

III
161

[63]So Abraham did not speak. Just one word from him[64] has been preserved, his only reply to Isaac, ample evidence that he had not said anything before. Isaac asks Abraham where the lamb is for the burnt offering. "And Abraham

said: God himself will provide the lamb for the burnt offering, my son."

I shall now consider in more detail these last words by Abraham. Without these words, the whole event would lack something; if they were different words, everything perhaps would dissolve in confusion.

It has frequently been the subject of my pondering whether a tragic hero, culminating either in a suffering or in an action, ought to have last words. As far as I can see, it depends on the sphere of life to which he belongs, whether his life has intellectual significance, whether his suffering or action is related to spirit.[65]

It goes without saying that the tragic hero, like any other man who is not bereft of speech, can say a few words in his culminating moment, perhaps a few appropriate words,[66] but the question is how appropriate is it for him to say them. If the meaning of his life is in an external act, then he has nothing to say, then everything he says is essentially chatter, by which he only diminishes his impact, whereas the tragic conventions enjoin him to complete his task in silence, whether it consists in action or suffering. In order not to wander too far afield, I shall take the most pertinent example. If Agamemnon himself, not Calchas, should have drawn the knife to kill Iphigenia, he would only have demeaned himself if in the very last moment he had said a few words, for the meaning of his deed was, after all, obvious to everybody, the process of reverence, sympathy, emotion, and tears was completed, and then, too, his life had no relation to spirit— that is, he was not a teacher or a witness of the spirit. However, if the meaning of a hero's life is oriented to spirit, then the lack of a statement would diminish his impact. What he has to say is not a few appropriate words, a short declamatory piece. Instead, the significance of his statement is that he consummates himself in the decisive moment. An intellectual tragic hero like that ought to have and ought to retain the last word. He is required to have the same transfigured bearing proper to every tragic hero, but one word is still required. [67]If an intellectual tragic hero like this culminates in a suffering (in death), he becomes immortal through this last word before he dies, whereas the ordinary tragic hero does not become immortal until after his death.

Socrates can be used as an example. He was an intellectual tragic hero. His death sentence is announced to him. At that moment he dies, for anyone who does not understand that it takes the whole power of the spirit to die and that the hero always dies before he dies will not advance very far in his view of life. As a hero Socrates is now required to be calm and collected, but as an intellectual tragic hero he is required to have enough spiritual strength in the final moment to consummate himself. He cannot, as does the ordinary tragic hero, concentrate on self-control in the presence of death, but he must make this movement as quickly as possible so that he is instantly and consciously beyond this struggle and affirms himself. Thus, if Socrates had been silent in the crisis of death, he would have diminished the effect of his life and aroused a suspicion that the elasticity of irony in him was not a world power but a game, the resilience of which had to be used on an inverted scale in order to sustain* him in pathos at the crucial moment.

These brief suggestions are indeed not applicable to Abraham if one expects to be able to find by means of some analogy an appropriate final word for Abraham, but they do apply if one perceives the necessity for Abraham to consummate himself in the final moment, not to draw the knife silently but to have a word to say, since as the father of faith he has absolute significance oriented to spirit. I cannot form in advance any idea of what he is going to say; after he has said it, I presumably can understand it, perhaps in a certain

* There can be various opinions as to which of Socrates' statements may be regarded as decisive, inasmuch as Plato has poetically volatilized Socrates in so many ways. I suggest the following: the verdict of death is announced to him, and in that same moment he dies, in that same moment he triumphs over death and consummates himself in the celebrated response that he is surprised to have been condemned by a majority of three votes.[68] He could not have bantered more ironically with the idle talk in the marketplace or with the foolish comment of an idiot than with the death sentence that condemns him to death.

sense understand Abraham in what was said without thereby
coming any closer to him than in the preceding exposition.
If there were no final lines from Socrates, I could have imagined myself in his place and created some, and if I had been
unable to do so, a poet would have managed it, but no poet
can find his way to Abraham.

Before considering Abraham's final words more closely,
may I first point out the difficulty for Abraham to manage
to say anything at all. [69]As explained above, the distress and
anxiety in the paradox were due in particular to the silence:
Abraham cannot speak.* Thus it is a self-contradiction to
demand that he speak, unless one wishes him out of the paradox again, so that he suspends it in the decisive moment
and thereby ceases to be Abraham and nullifies all that preceded. Thus, if Abraham were to say to Isaac in the decisive
moment: You are the one intended—this would simply be a
weakness. For if he could speak at all, then he ought to have
spoken long before this, and the weakness then would be
that he had not had the spiritual maturity and concentration
to think through the whole agony beforehand but had shoved
something aside in such a way that the actual agony was
more than that in thought. Moreover, by speaking thus, he
would have turned away from the paradox, and [70]if he actually wished to speak with Isaac, he would have had to change
his position to one of spiritual trial, for otherwise he could
say nothing, and in that case he would not even be a tragic
hero.

But a final word by Abraham has been preserved, and insofar as I can understand the paradox, I can also understand
Abraham's total presence in that word. First and foremost,
he does not say anything, and in that form he says what he
has to say. His response to Isaac is in the form of irony, for
it is always irony when I say something and still do not say
anything. Isaac questions Abraham in the belief that Abra-

* If there is any analogy at all, it is one such as provided by the death
scene of Pythagoras, for in his final moment he had to consummate the
silence he had always maintained, and for this reason he *said*: It is better to
be killed than to speak. See Diogenes, VIII, para. 39.[71]

ham knows. Now, if Abraham had replied: I know nothing—he would have spoken an untruth. He cannot say anything, for what he knows he cannot say. Therefore he answers:
God himself will provide the lamb for the burnt offering,
my son! From this we see, as described previously, the double-movement in Abraham's soul. If Abraham in resignation[72]
had merely relinquished Isaac and done no more, he would
have spoken an untruth, for he does indeed know that God
demands Isaac as a sacrifice, and he knows that he himself in
this very moment is willing to sacrifice him. After having
made this movement, he has at every moment made the next
movement, has made the movement of faith by virtue of the
absurd. Thus he is not speaking an untruth, because by virtue of the absurd it is indeed possible that God could do
something entirely different. So he does not speak an untruth, but neither does he say anything, for he is speaking in
a strange tongue. This becomes still more evident when we
consider that it was Abraham himself who should sacrifice
Isaac. [73]If the task had been different, if the Lord had commanded Abraham to bring Isaac up to Mount Moriah so that
he could have his lightning strike Isaac and take him as a
sacrifice in that way, then Abraham plainly would have been
justified in speaking as enigmatically as he did, for then he
himself could not have known what was going to happen.
But given the task as assigned to Abraham, he himself has
to act; consequently, he has to know in the crucial moment
what he himself will do, and consequently, he has to know
that Isaac is going to be sacrificed. If he has not known this
for sure, he would not have made the infinite movement of
resignation; then his words certainly are not untruth, but he
is also very far from being Abraham, and he has less significance than a tragic hero—indeed, he is a man devoid of resolution who cannot make up his mind one way or the other
and for that reason always speaks in riddles. A vacillator like
that, however, is merely a parody of the knight of faith.

III
165

Here again it is apparent that one perhaps can understand
Abraham, but only in the way one understands the paradox.
I, for my part, perhaps can understand Abraham, but I also

realize that I do not have the courage to speak in this way, no more than I have the courage to act as Abraham did; but by no means do I therefore say that the act is of little importance, since, on the contrary, it is the one and only marvel.

And what was the contemporary age's verdict on the tragic hero? That he was great and that it admired him. And that honorable assembly of noble-minded men, the jury that every generation sets up to judge the past generation—it gave the same verdict. But there was no one who could understand Abraham. And yet what did he achieve? He remained true to his love. But anyone who loves God needs no tears, no admiration; he forgets the suffering in the love. Indeed, so completely has he forgotten it that there would not be the slightest trace of his suffering left if God himself did not remember it, for he sees in secret[74] and recognizes distress and counts the tears and forgets nothing.

Thus, either there is a paradox, that the single individual as the single individual stands in an absolute relation to the absolute, or Abraham is lost.

EPILOGUE[1]

Once when the price of spices in Holland fell, the merchants had a few cargoes sunk in the sea in order to jack up the price. This was an excusable, perhaps even necessary, deception. Do we need something similar in the world of the spirit? Are we so sure that we have achieved the highest, so that there is nothing left for us to do except piously to delude ourselves into thinking that we have not come that far, simply in order to have something to occupy our time? Is this the kind of self-deception the present generation needs? Should it be trained in a virtuosity along that line, or is it not, instead, adequately perfected in the art of deceiving itself? Or, rather, does it not need an honest earnestness that fearlessly and incorruptibly points to the tasks, an honest earnestness that lovingly maintains the tasks, that does not disquiet people into wanting to attain the highest too hastily but keeps the tasks young and beautiful and lovely to look at, inviting to all and yet also difficult and inspiring to the noble-minded (for the noble nature is inspired only by the difficult)? Whatever one generation learns from another, no generation learns the essentially human from a previous one. In this respect, each generation begins primitively, has no task other than what each previous generation had, nor does it advance further, insofar as the previous generations did not betray the task and deceive themselves. The essentially human is passion, in which one generation perfectly understands another and understands itself. For example, no generation has learned to love from another, no generation is able to begin at any other point than at the beginning, no later generation has a more abridged task than the previous one, and if someone desires to go further and not stop with loving as the previous generation did, this is foolish and idle talk.

But the highest passion in a person is faith, and here no generation begins at any other point than where the previous one did. Each generation begins all over again; the next generation advances no further than the previous one, that is, if that one was faithful to the task and did not leave it high and dry. That it should be fatiguing is, of course, something that one generation cannot say, for the generation does indeed have the task and has nothing to do with the fact that the previous generation had the same task, unless this particular generation, or the individuals in it, presumptuously assumes the place that belongs to the spirit who rules the world and who has the patience not to become weary. If the generation does that, it is wrong, and no wonder, then, that all existence seems wrong to it, for there surely is no one who found existence more wrong than the tailor who, according to the fairy story,[2] came to heaven while alive and contemplated the world from that vantage point. As long as the generation is concerned only about its task, which is the highest, it cannot become weary, for the task is always adequate for a person's lifetime. [3]When children on vacation have already played all the games before twelve o'clock and impatiently ask: Can't somebody think up a new game—does this show that these children are more developed and more advanced than the children in the contemporary or previous generation who make the well-known games last all day long? Or does it show instead that the first children lack what I would call the endearing earnestness belonging to play?

Faith is the highest passion in a person. There perhaps are many in every generation who do not come to faith, but no one goes further. Whether there also are many in our day who do not find it, I do not decide. I dare to refer only to myself, without concealing that he has a long way to go, without therefore wishing to deceive himself or what is great by making a trifle of it, a childhood disease one may wish to get over as soon as possible. But life has tasks enough also for the person who does not come to faith, and if he loves these honestly, his life will not be wasted, even if it is never comparable to the lives of those who perceived and grasped the highest. But the person who has come to faith (whether he is extraordinarily gifted or plain and simple does not matter) does not come to a standstill in faith. Indeed, he would be indignant if anyone said this to him, just as the lover would resent it if someone said that he came to a standstill in love; for, he would answer, I am by no means standing still. I have my whole life in it. Yet he does not go further, does not go on to something else, for when he finds this, then he has another explanation.

⁴"One must go further, one must go further." This urge to go further is an old story in the world. Heraclitus the obscure, who deposited his thoughts in his books and his books in Diana's temple⁵ (for his thoughts had been his armor in life, and therefore he hung it in the temple of the goddess), Heraclitus the obscure said: One cannot walk through the same river twice.* ⁶Heraclitus the obscure had a disciple who did not remain standing there but went further—and added: One cannot do it even once.** Poor Heraclitus, to have a disciple like that! By this improvement, the Heraclitean thesis was amended into an Eleatic thesis that denies motion, and yet that disciple wished only to be a disciple of Heraclitus who went further, not back to what Heraclitus had abandoned.

---

* Καὶ ποταμοῦ ῥοῇ ἀπεικάζων τὰ ὄντα λέγει ὡς δίς ἐς τὸν αὐτὸν ποταμὸν οὐκ ἐμβαίης [He compares being to the stream of a river and says that you cannot go into the same river twice].⁷ See Plato, *Cratylus*, 402. Ast., III, p. 158.

** Cf. Tennemann, *Gesch. d. Philos.*, I, p. 220.

REPETITION

A VENTURE IN
EXPERIMENTING PSYCHOLOGY

by Constantin Constantius

On wild trees the flowers are fragrant, on cultivated trees, the fruits. (See Flavius Philostratus the
Elder's *Hero Tales*.)

[PART ONE]

[REPORT BY CONSTANTIN CONSTANTIUS]

[1]When the Eleatics denied motion, Diogenes, as everyone knows, came forward as an opponent.[2] He literally did come forward, because he did not say a word but merely paced back and forth a few times, thereby assuming that he had sufficiently refuted them. When I was occupied for some time, at least on occasion, with the question of repetition[3]—whether or not it is possible, what importance it has, whether something gains or loses in being repeated—I suddenly had the thought: You can, after all, take a trip to Berlin; you have been there once before, and now you can prove to yourself whether a repetition is possible and what importance it has. At home I had been practically immobilized by this question. Say what you will, this question will play a very important role in modern philosophy, for *repetition* is a crucial expression for what "recollection" was to the Greeks.[4] Just as they taught that all knowing is a recollecting, modern philosophy will teach that all life is a repetition. The only modern philosopher who has had an intimation of this is Leibniz.[5] Repetition and recollection are the same movement, except in opposite directions, for what is recollected has been, is repeated backward, whereas genuine repetition is recollected forward. Repetition, therefore, if it is possible, makes a person happy, whereas recollection makes him unhappy—assuming, of course, that he gives himself time to live and does not promptly at birth find an excuse to sneak out of life again, for example, that he has forgotten something.

Recollection's love [*Kjærlighed*], an author has said,[6] is the only happy love. He is perfectly right in that, of course, provided one recollects that initially it makes a person unhappy. Repetition's love is in truth the only happy love. Like recollection's love, it does not have the restlessness of hope, the uneasy adventurousness of discovery, but neither does it have the sadness of recollection—it has the blissful security of the moment. Hope is a new garment, stiff and starched and lustrous, but it has never been tried on, and therefore one does not know how becoming it will be or how it will fit. Recollection is a discarded garment that does not fit, however beautiful it is, for one has outgrown it. Repetition is an indestructible garment that fits closely and tenderly, neither binds nor sags. Hope is a lovely maiden who slips away between one's fingers; recollection is a beautiful old woman with whom one is never satisfied at the moment; repetition is a beloved wife of whom one never wearies, for one becomes weary only of what is new. One never grows weary of the old, and when one has that, one is happy. He alone is truly happy who is not deluded into thinking that the repetition should be something new, for then one grows weary of it. It takes youthfulness to hope, youthfulness to recollect, but it takes courage to will repetition. He who will merely hope is cowardly; he who will merely recollect is voluptuous; he who wills repetition is a man, and the more emphatically he is able to realize it, the more profound a human being he is. But he who does not grasp that life is a repetition and that this is the beauty of life has pronounced his own verdict and deserves nothing better than what will happen to him anyway—he will perish. For hope is a beckoning fruit that does not satisfy; recollection is petty travel money that does not satisfy; but repetition is the daily bread that satisfies with blessing. When existence has been circumnavigated, it will be manifest whether one has the courage to understand that life is a repetition and has the desire to rejoice in it. The person who has not circumnavigated life before beginning to live will never live; the person who circumnavigated it but became satiated had a poor constitution; the person who chose repetition—he lives. He does not run about like a boy chasing butterflies or stand on tiptoe to look for the glories of the world, for he knows them. Neither does he sit like an old woman turning the spinning wheel of recollection but calmly goes his way, happy in repetition. Indeed, what would life be if there were no repetition? Who could want to be a tablet on which time writes something new every instant or to be a memorial volume of the past? Who could want to be susceptible to every fleeting thing, the novel, which always enervatingly diverts the soul anew? If God himself had not willed repetition, the world would not have come into existence. Either he would have followed the superficial plans of hope or he would have retracted everything and preserved it in recollection. This he did not do. Therefore, the world continues, and it continues because it is a repetition. Repetition—that is actuality and the earnestness of existence.[7] The person who wills repetition is mature in earnestness. This is my private opinion, and this also means that it is not the earnestness of life to sit on the sofa and grind one's teeth—and to be somebody, for example, a councilor—or to walk the streets sedately—and to be somebody, for example, His Reverence—any more than it is the earnestness of life to be a riding master. In my opinion, all such things are but jests, and sometimes rather poor ones at that.

Recollection's love is the only happy love, says an author[8] who, as far as I know him, is at times somewhat deceitful, not in the sense that he says one thing and means another but in the sense that he pushes the thought to extremes, so that if it is not grasped with the same energy, it reveals itself the next instant as something else. He advances that thesis in such a way that one is easily tempted to agree with him and then forgets that the thesis itself expresses the most profound melancholy, so that a deep depression concentrated in one single line could scarcely express it better.

About a year ago, I became very much aware of a young man (with whom I had already often been in contact), because his handsome appearance, the soulful expression of his eyes, had an almost alluring effect upon me. A certain toss of his head and flippant air convinced me that he had a deeper and more complex nature, while a certain hesitation in inflection suggested that he was at the captivating age in which spiritual maturity, just like physical maturity at a far earlier age, announces itself by a frequent breaking of the voice.

Through casual coffee-shop associations, I had already attracted him to me and taught him to regard me as a confidant whose conversation in many ways lured forth his melancholy in refracted form, since I, like a Farinelli,[9] enticed the deranged king out of his dark hiding place, something that could be done without using tongs, inasmuch as my friend was still young and pliant. Such was our relationship when, about a year ago, as I said, he came to me, quite beside himself. He appeared more vigorous and handsome than usual; his large glowing eyes were dilated—in short, he seemed to be transfigured. When he told me that he had fallen in love, I involuntarily thought that the girl who was loved in this way was indeed fortunate. He had been in love for some time now, concealing it even from me, but now the object of his desire was within reach; he had confessed his love and found love in return. Although as a rule I tend to relate to men as an observer, it was impossible to do that with him. Say what you will, a young man deeply in love is something so beautiful that one forgets observation out of joy at the sight. Usually all deeply human emotions disarm the observer in a person. One is inclined to observe only when they are lacking and there is an emptiness or when they are coquettishly concealed. Who could be so inhuman as to play the observer if he saw a person praying with his whole soul? Who would not rather be permeated by an emanation from the devotion of the person praying? But if one hears a clergyman declaim a learned sermon in which, unsolicited on the part of the congregation, he testifies several times in an artificial, grandiloquent, and affected passage that what he is saying is the simple faith that knows nothing of neatly turned phrases but through prayer provides what he, by his own account and probably for good reasons, sought in vain in poetry, art, and scholarship—then one calmly puts one's eye to the microscope, then one does not swallow everything one hears but closes the jalousie, the critic's screen that tests every sound and every word. The young man of whom I speak was deeply and fervently and beautifully and humbly in love. For a long time nothing had made me so happy as

III
176

to look at him, for it is often distressing to be an observer—
it has the same melancholy effect as being a police officer.
And when an observer fulfills his duties well, he is to be
regarded as a secret agent[10] in a higher service, for the observer's art is to expose what is hidden. The young man
talked about the girl with whom he was in love. He did not
use many words, and, unlike most lovers' eulogies, what he
said was not a vapid analysis. He was not self-important, as
if he were a cunning fellow to have caught such a girl; he
was not self-confident—his love was wholesome, pure, sound.
With a charming openness[11] he confided that the reason for
his visit to me was that he needed a confidant in whose presence he could talk aloud to himself, as well as the most immediate reason that he was afraid to sit all day with the girl
and thus be a nuisance to her. He had already gone to her
house several times but had forced himself to turn back. He
then asked me to go for a ride with him to divert him and
to help pass the time. And I was agreeable, for from the
moment he had taken me into his confidence, he could be
assured that I would be wholeheartedly at his service. I used
the half hour before the carriage arrived to write a few business letters, asked him to fill his pipe meanwhile or page
through an album that had been laid out. But he did not need
such occupation; he was sufficiently occupied with himself,
was too restless to sit down but paced swiftly back and forth.
His gait, his movement, his gestures—all were eloquent, and
he himself glowed with love. Just as a grape at the peak of
its perfection becomes transparent and clear, the juice trick-
ling from its delicate veins, just as the peel of a fruit breaks
when the fruit is fully ripe, just so love broke forth almost
visibly in his form. I could not resist stealing an almost enamored glance at him now and then, for a young man like
that is just as enchanting to the eye as a young girl.

Just as lovers frequently resort to the poet's words to let
the sweet distress of love break forth in blissful joy, so also
did he. As he paced back and forth, he repeated again and
again a verse from Poul Møller:

Then, to my easy chair,
Comes a dream from my youth.
To my easy chair.
A heartfelt longing comes over me for you,
Thou sun of women.[12]

III
178

His eyes filled with tears, he threw himself down on a chair, he repeated the verse again and again. I was shaken by the scene. Good God, I thought, never in my practice had I seen such melancholy as this. That he was melancholy, I knew very well—but that falling in love could affect him in this way! And yet, how consistent even an abnormal mental state is if it is normally present. People are always shouting that a melancholiac should fall in love, and then his melancholy would all vanish. If he actually is melancholy, how would it be possible for his soul not to become melancholically absorbed in what has come to be most important of all to him?

He was deeply and fervently in love, that was clear, and yet a few days later he was able to recollect his love. He was essentially through with the entire relationship. In beginning it, he took such a tremendous step that he leaped over life. If the girl dies tomorrow, it will make no essential difference; he will throw himself down again, his eyes will fill with tears again, he will repeat the poet's words again. What a curious dialectic! He longs for the girl, he has to do violence to himself to keep from hanging around her all day long, and yet in the very first moment he became an old man in regard to the entire relationship. Underneath it all, there must be a misunderstanding. For a long time nothing has affected me so powerfully as this scene. It was obvious enough that he was going to be unhappy; that the girl would also become unhappy was no less obvious, although it was not immediately possible to predict how it would happen. But so much is certain: if anyone can join in conversation about recollection's love, he can. Recollection has the great advantage that it begins with the loss; the reason it is safe and secure is that it has nothing to lose.

The carriage had arrived. We drove out along Strandveien[13] in order to return through the heavily forested areas later.

Since against my will I had taken an observational approach to him, I could not refrain from all kinds of attempts to log, as the sailor says, the momentum of his melancholy. I set the tone for possible erotic moods—none. I explored the influence of change in the environment—in vain. Neither the broad bold assurance of the sea nor the hushed silence of the forest nor the beckoning solitude of the evening could bring him out of the melancholy longing in which he not so much drew near to the beloved as withdrew from her. His mistake was incurable, and his mistake was that he stood at the end instead of at the beginning, but such a mistake is and remains a person's downfall.[14]

And yet I maintain that his mood was a genuine erotic mood; anyone who has not experienced this mood at the very beginning in his own love has never loved. But he must have a second mood alongside it. This intensified recollecting[15] is erotic love's [*Elskovens*] eternal expression at the beginning, is the sign of genuine erotic love. But on the other hand it takes an ironic resiliency to be able to use it. This he lacked; his soul was too compliant for that. It may be true that a person's life is over and done with in the first moment, but there must also be the vital force to slay this death and transform it to life. In the first dawning of erotic love, the present and the future contend with each other to find an eternal expression, and this recollecting is indeed eternity's flowing back into the present—that is, when this recollecting is sound.

III
179

We turned homeward; I took leave of him. But my sympathy had been aroused almost too powerfully, and I could not rid myself of the thought that very soon it would all have to eventuate in a dreadful explosion.

During the next two weeks, I saw him occasionally at my place. He began to grasp the misunderstanding himself; the adored young girl was already almost a vexation to him. And yet she was the beloved, the only one he had loved, the only one he would ever love. Nevertheless, he did not still love her, because he only longed for her. During all this, a remarkable change took place in him. A poetic creativity awakened in him on a scale I had never believed possible. Now I easily grasped the whole situation. The young girl was not his beloved: she was the occasion that awakened the poetic in him and made him a poet.[16] That was why he could love only her, never forget her, never want to love another, and yet continually only long for her. She was drawn into his whole being; the memory of her was forever alive. She had meant much to him; she had made him a poet—and precisely thereby had signed her own death sentence.

As time went on, his state became more and more anguished. His depression became more and more dominant, and his physical strength was devoured in mental struggles. He was aware that he had made her unhappy, and yet he was conscious of no guilt; but precisely this, in all innocence to become guilty of her unhappiness, was an offense to him and vehemently stirred his passion. He believed that to confess to her how things stood would hurt her deeply. It would indeed amount to telling her that she had become an imperfect being, that he had grown away from her, that he no longer needed that ladder rung by which he had climbed. And what would the result be? Since she knew that he would not love any other, she would become his grieving widow who lived only in the memory of him and their relationship. He could not make a confession; he was too proud on her behalf for that. His depression entrapped him more and more, and he decided to proceed with a fabrication. Now he used all his poetic originality in order to delight and amuse her; what he could have provided for many he now devoted entirely to her; she was and remained the beloved, the one and only adored, even though he was close to losing his mind in his anxiety over the monstrous falsehood, which only enthralled her all the more. In a sense, her existence or nonexistence was virtually meaningless to him, except that his melancholy found delight in making her life enchanting. It goes without saying that she was happy, for she suspected nothing, and the fare was only too appetizing. He did not want to be creative in a stricter sense, for then he would have to leave her; therefore, as he said, he kept his creativity under

III
180

the pruning shears and cut everything as a bouquet for her. She suspected nothing. This I do believe. Indeed, it would be shocking if a young girl could be so self-loving as to treat a man's depression with disregard. But that can happen, and once I was very close to discovering such a situation. There is nothing so captivating for a young girl as being loved by a poetic-melancholic nature. And if she only has enough self-love to delude herself that she loves him faithfully by clinging to him instead of by giving him up, then she has a very easy task in life, enjoying the honor and the good conscience of being faithful and at the same time also the very finest distilled erotic love. God keep each and every person from such faithfulness!

One day he came up to me; his dark passions had attained total dominance. In the wildest outburst, he cursed life, his love, the girl he loved. From that time on, he never visited me again. Presumably he could not forgive himself for having confessed to another person that the girl was a torment to him; now he had spoiled everything for himself, even the joy of maintaining her pride and making a goddess of her. When we met, he avoided me, and if we chanced to be together, he never spoke to me; at the same time, he obviously tried hard to appear happy and confident. I contemplated shadowing him at closer quarters and to that end began investigating subordinates around him. In dealing with a depressed person, one often learns most from his subordinates, because a depressed person often opens up more to a servant, a maid, an old unnoticed dependent in a family than to someone of similar culture and station. A depressed person I once knew went through life as a dancer and deceived everyone, myself included, until I came upon another clue through a barber. This barber was an older man who lived on slender means and tended his customers himself. Concern about the barber's indigence prompted the dancer to let his melancholy burst forth, and this barber knew what no one else ever suspected. The young man, however, spared me the inconvenience, for he approached me again, though firmly resolved never to set his foot inside my door again. He proposed that we meet in out-of-the-way places at specified times. I agreed and to that end bought two tickets to the fishery at the town moat. Here we met early in the morning. In the hour when day struggles with night, when even in midsummer a cold shudder goes through nature, we met down there in the clammy morning fog and the dew-damp grass, and the birds flew up in fright at his cry. In the hour when day has conquered, when all that lives rejoices in life, in the hour when the beloved young girl, whom he pampered with his pain, raised her head from the pillow and opened her eyes because the god of sleep who had sat beside her bed rose up, in the hour when the god of dreams laid his finger on her eyelids so that she once again dozed off briefly while he told her what she had never suspected and breathed it so softly that when she awoke she had forgotten everything—in that hour we parted again. And whatever the god of dreams confided to her, she still did not dream of what passed between us. No wonder the man grew pale! No wonder that I am the one who was his confidant and the confidant of several like him!

Once again some time passed. I actually suffered exceedingly with the young man, who wasted away day by day. And yet I by no means regretted sharing in his suffering, because in his love the idea was indeed in motion. (Occasionally one still sees such an erotic love in life—God be praised!—but seeks it in vain in novels and short stories.) Only when this is the case does erotic love have meaning, and if one is not enthusiastically convinced that the idea is the life-principle in erotic love and that, if necessary, one must sacrifice life for it, yes, what is more, sacrifice erotic love itself, even though actuality lavished it with favors— that person is excluded from poetry. But when erotic love is in the idea, every motion, even every fleeting emotion, is not without meaning, because the most important thing is always present: the poetic collision, which, as far as I know, can then be far more dreadful than the one I am describing here. But to want to serve the idea—which in regard to erotic love is not to serve two masters[17]—is in fact a strenuous service, for no beautiful woman can be as exacting as the idea, and no girl's disapproval can be as distressing as the wrath of the idea, which above all is impossible to forget.

If I were to elaborate on the young man's moods as I learned to know them, to say nothing of anecdotally including a host of irrelevant things—living rooms and wearing apparel, lovely localities, relatives and friends—this narrative could become an interminable story. That, however, I do not want. I like to eat lettuce, but I always eat only the heart; in my opinion the leaves are for the pigs. Along with Lessing, I prefer the delights of conception to the discomforts of childbirth.[18] If anyone has anything to say against this, go ahead—it is all the same to me.

Time passed. When possible, I attended this nightly vigil, where by his wild cries he gained momentum for the entire day, for he used the day to charm the girl. Just as Prometheus, bolted to the rock while the vulture pecked his liver, enthralled the gods with his prophesying,[19] so he enthralled his beloved. Each day everything was raised to a higher level, because each day was the last. But so it could not be. He bit the chain that bound him, but the more his passion seethed, the more ecstatic his song, the more tender his talk, the tighter the chain. It was impossible for him to create a real relationship out of this misunderstanding; it would, in fact, leave her at the mercy of a perpetual fraud. To explain this confusing error to her, that she was merely the visible form, while his thoughts, his soul, sought something else that he attributed to her—this would hurt her so deeply that his pride rose up in mutiny against it. It was a method he despised more intensely than anything else. And he was right in that. It is contemptible to delude and seduce a girl, but it is even more contemptible to forsake her in such a way that one does not even become a scoundrel but makes a brilliant retreat by palming her off with the explanation that she was not the ideal and by comforting her with the idea that she was one's muse. No doubt that can be done if one has any practice in cajoling a girl. If in the hour of need she does indeed accept that version, one gets out of it in fine shape,

III
183

becomes an honest man, even lovable—and later on she is fundamentally more deeply hurt than the one who *knows* herself deceived. Therefore, in any relationship of love that cannot be fulfilled even though begun, tactfulness is the most offensive of all, and he who has an erotic eye and is not cowardly readily perceives that to be tactless is the only means he has left to hold the girl in honor.

To put an end to these sufferings, if possible, I encouraged him to venture the utmost with vigor. Everything depended upon finding a point of unity. I then made the following proposal. Burn all your bridges. Transform yourself into a contemptible person whose only delight is to trick and deceive. If you can do that, a balance will be established, and there can no longer be a question of esthetic differences that gave you a higher right in comparison with her, something people are much too often inclined to grant to a so-called unusual individuality. She is the victor, she is absolutely right; you are absolutely wrong. But do not go about it all too suddenly, for that would only inflame her love. First of all, try, if possible, to be somewhat unpleasing to her. Do not tease her—that stimulates her. No! Be inconstant, nonsensical; do one thing one day and another the next, but without passion, in an utterly careless way that does not, however, degenerate into inattention, because, on the contrary, the external attentiveness must be just as great as ever but altered to a formal function lacking all inwardness. In place of all love's delight, show a certain cloying *quasi* love that is neither indifference nor desire; let your conduct be just as unpleasant as it is to watch a person drool. But do not begin if you do not have the power to carry it out; otherwise the jig is up, for there is no one so clever as a girl—that is, when it is a question of her being loved or not—and no operation is so difficult as extirpation if one is obliged to wield the instrument oneself, an instrument that ordinarily only time knows how to handle properly. When all this is in process, then just come to me, and I will take care of the rest. Spread the rumor that you are having a new love affair, *et quidem* [and moreover] one of a rather unpoetic nature, for otherwise you will merely egg her on. I know very well that such a thing could not occur to you, for we are both firmly convinced that she is the only one you love, even though it is impossible to translate the purely poetic relationship into real love. There must be some truth as the basis for the rumor, and I will take care of that. I will pick out a local girl and make an arrangement with her.

It was not merely concern for the young man that prompted me to work out this plan. I cannot deny that little by little I had begun to look askance at his beloved. That she should not notice anything at all, that she should not suspect his suffering and its probable cause, and, if she did notice it, that she did nothing at all, made no attempt to save him with that which he needed and which she could give him—namely, freedom, which would indeed save him only if it were she who gave it, for she would again have dominance over him through her generosity and would not be hurt! I can forgive a girl everything, but I can never forgive her if in her love she is wrong about the task of love. When a girl's love is not a sacrificing love, she is not feminine but masculine, and then I shall always give myself the pleasure of letting her incur revenge or laughter. What a subject for a writer of comedies to have: a lover who with her love has sucked her lover's blood until in distress and despair he breaks with her, a lover who steps forth as an Elvira,[20] a star in her role, wept over by commiserating relatives and friends, an Elvira who is prima donna in the singing society of the deceived, an Elvira who can talk with vim and vigor about the faithlessness of men, a faithlessness that obviously will cost her her life, an Elvira who does all this with such aplomb and assurance that never for a second does it occur to her that her faithfulness was better suited to take the life of her beloved. Great is feminine faithfulness, especially when it is declined; inscrutable and unfathomable is it at all times. The situation would be priceless if her lover, despite all his distress, had maintained sufficient humor not to waste an angry word on her but limited himself to a more subtle revenge, duping her and strengthening her in the illusion that he had shamefully deceived her.

If this is the case with her, and if the young man is able to carry out my plan, I promise her that revenge will hit her hard, and yet only with poetic justice. For he is determined to do the best he can, and yet this deception, if she is self-loving, will punish her the most severely. He treats her with all possible erotic solicitude, and yet his method will be most painful to her if she herself is self-loving.

He was willing and fully approved of my plan. In a fashion boutique I found what I was looking for, a very attractive girl, for whom I promised to provide in return for her going along with my plan. He was supposed to appear with her in public places, visit her at times, so there would be no doubt that he had an understanding with her. With that in mind, I got an apartment assigned to her in a building with hallway exits on two streets so that he needed only to walk through the building late in the evening and thereby give the maidservants etc. proof and set gossip in motion. When everything was in order, I would see to it that his beloved would not remain ignorant of the new connection. The seamstress was not bad-looking but otherwise of such a kind that his beloved, without being jealous in any way, could be amazed that such a girl was preferred to her. If I had had his beloved in my telescopic eye, the seamstress probably ought to have been of a different sort, but since I could be sure of nothing in that regard and, moreover, since I did not want to be crafty with the young man, I made my selection solely in the interest of his method.

The seamstress was engaged for one year; in order to fool the beloved completely, the relationship had to be maintained that long. During that time, he should also try to break through, if possible, his poet-existence. If he succeeded in that, a *redintegratio in statum pristinum* [reestablishment of the prior state] might be accomplished. During that year the young girl would also have the opportunity (which was of great importance) to extricate herself from the relationship; he had not honored her with any false expectations for the result of such an operation. If, when the moment of repetition ar-

rived, she had grown weary, well, he still would have acted
honorably.

Everything was organized in this way. I already had the
ropes in hand[21] and was unusually tense about the outcome.
But he stayed away; I did not see him any more. He had not
had the strength to carry out the plan.[22] His soul lacked the
elasticity of irony. He had not had the strength to make irony's vow of silence, had not had the strength to keep it.
Only he who is silent[23] will amount to anything. Only he
who actually can love, only he is a man; only he who can
give his love any expression whatsoever, only he is an artist.
In a certain sense, it may have been all right that he did not
make a beginning, for he would hardly have endured the
horrors of the adventure, and from the very first I was a little
afraid because he needed a confidant. He who knows how
to keep silent discovers an alphabet that has just as many
letters as the ordinary one; thus he can express everything in
his jargon, and no sigh is so deep that he does not have the
laughter that corresponds to it in his jargon, and no request
so obtrusive that he does not have the witticism to fulfill the
demand. For him there will come a moment when he will
feel as if he were losing his mind, but even though the experience is appalling, it is for just an instant. It is like a fever
a person gets between 11:30 and 12:00 at night; at 1:00 he
works more vigorously than ever. If one lasts out that madness, one will surely triumph.

But here I sit going on at great length about what was
mentioned just to show that in fact recollection's love makes
a man unhappy. My young friend did not understand repetition;[24] he did not believe in it and did not powerfully will
it. His predicament was that he actually loved the girl, but
in order actually to love her he first had to be disencumbered
of the poetic confusion he had gotten into. He could have
confessed this to the girl; if one wishes to end an affair with
a girl, this is, after all, a respectable thing to do. But this he
would not do. I was in full agreement with him that this was
not right. He would thereby have cut off the possibility for
her to exist autonomously in the meantime and would have

III
186

exempted himself from perhaps becoming an object of her contempt and from the mounting anxiety about whether he would ever manage to make up for what had been spoiled.

If the young man had believed in repetition, what great things might have come from him, what inwardness he might have achieved in this life!

But I have gone further along in time than I actually intended. My purpose was simply to describe the first time when it became clear that the young man was in the wide sense the sorrowful knight of recollection's only happy love. With the reader's permission, I shall once again consider the time he came to my room intoxicated with recollection, when his heart continuously *ging ihm über* [overflowed][25] in that verse by Poul Møller, when he confided that he had to deny himself lest he spend the whole day with the girl he loved. He repeated the same verse that evening when we parted. It will never be possible for me to forget that verse; indeed, I can more easily obliterate the recollection of his disappearance[26] than the memory of that moment, just as the news of his disappearance disturbed me far less than his situation that first day. So I am by nature: with the first shudder of presentiment, my soul has simultaneously run through all the consequences, which frequently take a long time to appear in actuality. Presentiment's concentration is never forgotten. I believe that an observer should be so constituted, but if he is so constituted, he is also sure to suffer exceedingly. The first moment may overwhelm him almost to the point of swooning, but as he turns pale the idea impregnates him, and from now on he has investigative rapport with actuality. If a person lacks this feminine quality so that the idea cannot establish the proper relation to him, which always means impregnation, then he is not qualified to be an observer, for he who does not discover the totality essentially discovers nothing.[27]

When we parted that evening and he once again thanked me for helping him to pass the time, which went far too slowly for his impatience, I thought to myself: Is he probably frank enough to tell the young girl everything and will

she then love him all the more? I wondered if he would do
that! If he had asked my advice, I would have dissuaded him.
I would have said to him, "Be adamant at first; from the
purely erotic point of view, that is the most judicious, unless
your soul is so earnest that you can lead the thought to something far more lofty." If he has told, he has not acted judi-
ciously.

Anyone who has had any opportunity to observe young
girls, to listen secretly to their conversation, has certainly
heard this kind of talk: "N. N. is a good person, but he is
boring; but F. F., he is so interesting and exciting." Every
time I hear these words in a little miss's mouth, I always
think, "You ought to be ashamed; isn't it sad for a young
girl to talk that way." If a man has gone astray in the interesting,[28] who is to save him if not a girl? And does she not
do wrong thereby? Either the person referred to is unable to
provide it, and then it is tactless to ask it, or he is able, and
then . . . . . For a young girl should be careful never to evoke
the interesting; the girl who does always loses as far as the
idea is concerned, for the interesting can never be repeated;
she who does not do it always triumphs.

III
188

Six years ago, while on a drive of about thirty miles out
into the country, I stopped to eat lunch at an inn. I had spent
a pleasant and delectable lunch hour and was in rather good
humor. I was standing with a cup of coffee and inhaling its
fragrance when just then a beautiful young girl, buoyant and
lovely, walked by the window and turned into the courtyard
belonging to the inn, leading me to conclude that she wanted
to go down into the garden. One is young—so I quickly
drank my coffee, lit a cigar, and was just about to pursue the
hint of fate and the girl's trail when there was a knock on
my door and in stepped—the young girl. She curtsied graciously, asked if it was not my carriage in the courtyard,
whether I was going to Copenhagen, and would I allow her
to ride along. The modest and yet genuinely dignified way
in which she did it was enough to make me instantly lose
sight of the interesting and exciting aspects. And yet to meet
a young girl in a garden is far less interesting than to drive

thirty-two miles alone with her in one's own carriage, with coachman and servant, and have her completely in one's power. All the same, I am convinced that even a more reckless man than I would not have felt tempted. The reliance with which she entrusted herself to my power is a better defense than all feminine cleverness and cunning. We drove together. She could not have driven more safely if she had driven with her brother or father. I kept silent and reserved and was complaisant only when it seemed that she wished to make a comment.

My coachman had orders to make good time. A stop of five minutes was requested at each station. I got out; with hat in hand, I asked if she would like some refreshments; my servant stood behind with hat in hand. When we approached the city, I had the coachman drive down a side road, where I got out and walked two miles to Copenhagen so that no encounter or the like would perturb her. I have never inquired about who she was, where she lived, what could have prompted her sudden journey; but to me she has always been a pleasant recollection, which I have not allowed myself to intrude upon by any curiosity, however innocent. —A girl who wishes for the interesting becomes a trap in which she herself is caught. A girl who does not wish for the interesting believes in repetition. Honor to the one who was such a person originally, honor to the one who became that in time.

But I must constantly repeat that I say all this in connection with repetition. Repetition is the new category that will be discovered. If one knows anything of modern philosophy and is not entirely ignorant of Greek philosophy, one will readily see that this category precisely explains the relation between the Eleatics and Heraclitus,[29] and that repetition proper is what has mistakenly been called mediation.[30] It is incredible how much flurry has been made in Hegelian philosophy over mediation and how much foolish talk has enjoyed honor and glory under this rubric. One should rather seek to think through mediation and then give a little credit to the Greeks. The Greek explanation of the theory of being and nothing, the explanation of "the moment,"[31] "non-being,"[32] etc. trumps Hegel. "Mediation" is a foreign word; "repetition" is a good Danish word, and I congratulate the Danish language on a philosophical term. There is no explanation in our age as to how mediation takes place, whether it results from the motion of the two factors and in what sense it is already contained in them, or whether it is something new that is added, and, if so, how. In this connection, the Greek view of the concept of κίνησις [motion, change][33] corresponds to the modern category "transition"[34] and should be given close attention. The dialectic of repetition is easy, for that which is repeated has been—otherwise it could not be repeated—but the very fact that it has been makes the repetition into something new. When the Greeks said that all knowing is recollecting,[35] they said that all existence, which is, has been; when one says that life is a repetition, one says: actuality, which has been, now comes into existence.[36] If one does not have the category of recollection or of repetition, all life dissolves into an empty, meaningless noise. Recollection is the ethical [*ethniske*] view of life,[37] repetition the modern; repetition is the *interest* [*Interesse*] of metaphysics, and also the interest upon which metaphysics comes to grief; repetition is the watchword [*Løsnet*] in every ethical view; repetition is *conditio sine qua non* [the indispensable condition] for every issue of dogmatics.[38]

Let everyone form his own judgment with respect to what is said here about repetition; let him also form his own judgment about my saying it here and in this manner, since I, following Hamann's example, mit mancherlei Zungen mich ausdrücke, und die Sprache der Sophisten, der Wortspiele, der Creter und Araber, Weiszen und Mohren und Creolen rede, Critik, Mythologie, *rebus* und Grundsätze durch einander schwatze, und bald κατ' ἄνθρωπον bald κατ' ἐξοχὴν argumentire [express myself in various tongues and speak the language of sophists, of puns, of Cretans and Arabians, of whites and Moors and Creoles, and babble a confusion of criticism, mythology, *rebus*, and axioms, and argue now in a human way and now in an extraordinary way].[39] Assuming that what I say is not a mere lie, I perhaps did right in sub-

III
190

mitting my aphorism to a systematic appraiser. Perhaps
something may come of it, a footnote in the system—great
idea! Then I would not have lived in vain!

With regard to the meaning that repetition has for something, much can be said without making oneself guilty of a
repetition. When Professor Ussing[40] once gave a speech at
the May 28 Society and a statement in the speech did not
meet with approval, what did he do, this professor who at
that time was always resolute and forceful—he pounded the
table and said: I repeat. What he meant at the time was that
what he said gained by repetition. Some years ago I heard a
pastor give the very same talk on two festive occasions. If
he had been of the same mind as the professor, the second
time he ascended the pulpit he would have pounded the pulpit and said: I repeat what I said last Sunday. He did not do
so and made no allusion whatsoever. He was not of the same
mind as Professor Ussing, and who knows, perhaps the professor himself no longer thinks that his speech would be of
benefit if it were repeated again. When the queen had finished telling a story at a court function and all the court of-
ficials, including a deaf minister, laughed at it, the latter stood
up, asked to be granted the favor of also being allowed to
tell a story, and then told the same story. Question: What
was his view of the meaning of repetition? When a school-
teacher says: For the second time I repeat that Jespersen is to
sit quietly—and the same Jespersen gets a mark for repeated
disturbance, then the meaning of repetition is the very opposite.

I shall not dwell any longer on such examples but shall
proceed to speak a little of the investigative journey I made
to test the possibility and meaning of repetition. Without
anyone's knowing about it (lest any gossip render me incapable of the experiment and in another way weary of repetition), I went by steamship to Stralsund and took a seat in
the *Schnellpost* [express coach] to Berlin. The learned disagree
on which seat is the most comfortable in a stagecoach; in my
Ansicht [opinion], they are all wretched, the whole lot. Last
time I had an end seat forward inside the carriage (some re-

gard this as the big prize) and after thirty-six hours was so jounced together with those sitting next to me that when I arrived in Hamburg I had lost not only my mind but my legs as well. During those thirty-six hours, we six people sitting inside the carriage were so worked together into one body that I got a notion of what happened to the Wise Men of Gotham,[41] who after having sat together a long time could not recognize their own legs. Hoping at least to remain a limb on a lesser body, I chose a seat in the forward compartment. That was a change. Everything, however, repeated itself. The postilion blew his horn. I shut my eyes, surrendered to despair, and thought the thoughts I usually think on such occasions: God knows if you can endure it, if you actually will get to Berlin, and in that case if you will ever be human again, able to disengage yourself in the singleness of isolation, or if you will carry a memory of your being a limb on a larger body.

So I arrived in Berlin. I hurried at once to my old lodgings[42] to ascertain whether a repetition is possible. May I assure any commiserating reader that the previous time I managed to get one of the most pleasant apartments in Berlin; may I now give even more emphatic assurance, inasmuch as I have seen many. Gensd'arme Square is certainly the most beautiful in Berlin; *das Schauspielhaus* [the theater] and the two churches[43] are superb, especially when viewed from a window by moonlight. The recollection of these things was an important factor in my taking the journey. One climbs the stairs to the first floor in a gas-illuminated building, opens a little door, and stands in the entry. To the left is a glass door leading to a room. Straight ahead is an anteroom. Beyond are two entirely identical rooms, identically furnished, so that one sees the room double in the mirror. The inner room is tastefully illuminated. A candelabra stands on a writing table; a gracefully designed armchair upholstered in red velvet stands before the desk. The first room is not illuminated. Here the pale light of the moon blends with the strong light from the inner room. Sitting in a chair by the window, one looks out on the great square, sees the shadows of passersby hurrying

III
192

along the walls; everything is transformed into a stage setting. A dream world glimmers in the background of the soul. One feels a desire to toss on a cape, to steal softly along the wall with a searching gaze, aware of every sound. One does not do this but merely sees a rejuvenated self doing it. Having smoked a cigar, one goes back to the inner room and begins to work. It is past midnight. One extinguishes the candles and lights a little night candle. Unmingled, the light of the moon is victorious. A single shadow appears even blacker; a single footstep takes a long time to disappear. The cloudless arch of heaven has a sad and pensive look as if the end of the world had already come and heaven, unperturbed, were occupied with itself. Once again one goes out into the hallway, into the entry, into that little room, and—if one is among the fortunate who are able to sleep—goes to sleep.

But here, alas, again no repetition was possible. My landlord, the druggist, *er hatte sich verändert*, in the pointed sense in which the German understands this phrase, and as far as I know "to change oneself" is similarly used in some of Copenhagen's streets—that is, he had married.[44] I wanted to congratulate him, but since I am not such a master of the German language that I know how to improvise in a pinch and did not have suitable idioms at hand for such an occasion, I limited myself to a gesture. I laid my hand on my heart and looked at him with tender sympathy legible on my face. He pressed my hand. After this show of mutual understanding, he went on to prove the esthetic validity of marriage.[45] He succeeded marvelously, just as well as he had the last time in proving the perfection of bachelorhood. When I speak German, I am the most accommodating man in the world.

My former landlord was only too glad to be of service to me and I only too glad to live with him; consequently, I took one room and the entry. When I came home the first evening and had lit the candles, I thought: Alas! Alas! Alas! Is this the repetition? I became completely out of tune, or, if you please, precisely in tune with the day, for fate had strangely contrived it so that I arrived in Berlin on the *allgemeine Busz-*

und Bettag [Universal Day of Penance and Prayer]. Berlin was prostrate. To be sure, they did not throw ashes into one another's eyes with the words: *Memento o homo! quod cinis es et in cinerem revertaris* [Remember, O man! that you are dust and to dust you will return].[46] But all the same, the whole city lay in one cloud of dust. At first I thought it was a government measure, but later I was convinced that the wind was responsible for this nuisance and without respect of persons followed its whim or its bad habit, for in Berlin at least every other day is Ash Wednesday. But this is of little concern to my project. This discovery had no connection with "repetition," for the last time I was in Berlin I had not noticed this phenomenon, presumably because it was winter.

When a fellow has settled himself cosily and comfortably in his quarters, when he has a fixed point like this from which he can rush out, a safe hiding place to which he can retreat and devour his booty in solitude—something I especially appreciate, since, like certain beasts of prey, I cannot eat when anyone is looking on—then he familiarizes himself with whatever notable sights there may be in the city. If he is a traveler *ex professo* [by trade], a courier who travels to smell what everybody has smelled or to write the names of notable sights in his journal, and in return gets his in the great autograph book of travelers, then he engages a *Lohndiener* [a temporary servant] and buys *das ganze Berlin* for four *Groschen*. This way he becomes an impartial observer whose utterances ought to have the credibility of any police record. But if on his journey he has no particular purpose, he lets matters take their course, occasionally sees things others do not see, disregards the most important, receives a random impression that is meaningful only to him. A careless wanderer like this usually does not have much to communicate to others, and if he does, he very easily runs the risk of weakening the good opinion good people might have regarding his morality and virtue. If a person has traveled abroad for some time and has never been on a train,[47] would he not be thrown out of all the better circles! What if a man had been in London and had never driven in the tunnel![48] What if a man went to Rome, fell in love with a little part of the city that was an inexhaustible source of joy to him, and left Rome without having seen one single notable sight!

Berlin has three theaters. The opera and ballet performances in the opera house[49] are supposed to be *groszartig* [magnificent]; performances in the theater are supposed to be instructive and refining, not only for entertainment.[50] I do not know. But I do know that Berlin has a theater called the Königstädter Theater. Professional travelers visit this theater seldom, though more frequently—which also has its own significance—than they visit the congenial, more out-of-the-way places of entertainment, where a Dane has the opportunity to refresh his memory of Lars Mathiesen and Kehlet.[51] When I came to Stralsund and read in the newspaper that *Der Talisman*[52] would be performed at that theater, I was in a good mood at once. The recollection of it awakened in my soul; the first time I was there, it seemed as if the first impression evoked in my soul only a recollection that pointed far back in time.

There is probably no young person with any imagination who has not at some time been enthralled by the magic of the theater and wished to be swept along into that artificial actuality in order like a double to see and hear himself and to split himself up into every possible variation of himself, and nevertheless in such a way that every variation is still himself. Such a wish, of course, expresses itself only at a very early age. Only the imagination is awakened to his dream about the personality; everything else is still fast asleep. In such a self-vision of the imagination, the individual is not an actual shape but a shadow, or, more correctly, the actual shape is invisibly present and therefore is not satisfied to cast one shadow, but the individual has a variety of shadows, all of which resemble him and which momentarily have equal status as being himself. As yet the personality is not discerned, and its energy is betokened only in the passion of possibility, for the same thing happens in the spiritual life as with many plants—the main shoot comes last. But this shadow-existence also demands satisfaction, and it is never beneficial to a person if this does not have time to live out its life, whereas on the other hand it is tragic or comic if the individual makes the mistake of living out his life in it. Such an individual's pretensions to being a genuine human being become just as doubtful as the claim to immortality by those who are not even capable of appearing in person on Judgment Day but are represented by a deputation of good intentions, twenty-four-hour resolutions, half-hour plans, etc. The main point is that everything takes place at the right time. Everything has its time in youth, and what has had its time then has it again in later life. And it is just as salutary for the adult to have something in his past life that he can laugh about as something past that draws his tears.

    In a mountain region where day in and day out one hears the wind relentlessly play the same invariable theme, one may be tempted for a moment to abstract from this imperfection and delight in this metaphor of the consistency and sureness of human freedom. One perhaps does not reflect that there was a time when the wind, which for many years has had its dwelling among these mountains, came as a stranger to this area, plunged wildly, absurdly through the canyons, down into the mountain caves, produced now a shriek almost startling to itself, then a hollow roar from which it itself fled, then a moan, the source of which it itself did not know, then from the abyss of anxiety a sigh so deep that the wind itself grew frightened and momentarily doubted that it dared reside in this region, then a gay lyrical waltz—until, having learned to know its instrument, it worked all of this into the melody it renders unaltered day after day. Similarly, the individual's possibility wanders about in its own possibility, discovering now one possibility, now another. But the individual's possibility does not want only to be heard; it is not like the mere passing of the wind. It is also *gestaltende* [configuring][53] and therefore wants to be visible at the same time. That is why each of its possibilities is an audible shadow. The cryptic individual believes as little in noisy, powerful feelings as in the wily whispering of evil, believes as little in the ecstatic jubilation of joy as in the endless sighing of sor-

row; the individual wants only to see and hear with pathos—
but, please note, to see and hear himself. But the individual
does not want actually to hear himself. That will not do. At
the very same moment the cock crows and the twilight shapes
vanish, the nocturnal voices fall silent. If they keep on, then
we are in an altogether different realm where all this takes
place under the disquieting supervision of responsibility, then
we approach the demonic. Then, in order not to gain an
impression of his actual self, the hidden individual needs an
environment as superficial and transient as the shapes, as the
frothing foam of words that sound without resonance.

III
196   The stage is that kind of setting, and therefore it is particularly suitable for the *Schattenspiel* [shadow play] of the hidden individual. Among the shadows in which he discovers
himself, there may be a robber captain whose voice is his
voice. He must recognize himself in this reflected image. The
robber's masculine form, his quick and yet penetrating glance,
the autograph of passion in the lines of his face—all must be
there. He must lie in wait in the mountain pass, he must
listen for the movements of the travelers, he must blow his
whistle; the robber band rushes out; his voice must drown
out the noise; he must be cruel, have everyone cut down,
and turn indifferently away; he must be chivalrous to the
frightened girl, etc., etc. A robber, after all, lives in the gloomy
forests. If that hero of the imagination were to be set down
in such a place, be furnished with all the trappings, and then
be asked just to keep quiet until one had put about ten miles
between them before he could then surrender completely to
his passionate raging—I believe he would become absolutely
tongue-tied. His experience would perhaps be like that of a
man who a few years ago honored me with his literary confidence. He came to me complaining that he was so overwhelmed by a wealth of ideas that it was impossible to get
something written down because he could not write quickly
enough. He asked me to take the trouble of being his secre-
tary and to write from dictation. I immediately suspected
mischief afoot and therefore consoled him by saying that I
could write in competition with a runaway horse, since I

merely wrote one letter of each word and yet guaranteed that
I could read everything I had written. My willingness to oblige
knew no limits. I had a large table set out, numbered several
large sheets of paper so that I would not even waste time
turning over the page, laid out a dozen mounted steel pens,
dipped the pen—and the man began his discourse thus: Well,
now, you see, gentlemen, what I really would like to say is
. . . . . When he had finished his discourse, I read it aloud to
him, and since then he has never asked me to be his secre-
tary.

That robber would presumably find the scale too large and
yet in another sense too small. No, paint him a stage set with
one tree and hang a lamp in front, making the lighting even
more singular, and this forest will nevertheless be larger than
the actual forest, larger than the virgin forests of North
America, and yet he can penetrate it with his voice without
getting hoarse. This is the sophistical inclination of imagination, to have the whole world in a nutshell this way, a
nutshell larger than the whole world and yet not too large
for the individual to fill.

Such a predilection for theatrical performing and expec-
torating [*expektoreren*][54] in no way indicates any call to theatrical art. Where there is such a thing, the talent immediately manifests itself as a capacity for detail, and even the
most abundant dawning talent does not have such a dimen-
sion. This predilection is simply the immaturity of imagination. However, it is something else when it is based on
vanity and a propensity to show off, for then the whole thing
has no deeper basis than vanity, a basis that regrettably can
be quite deep.

Even though this element in the individual's life vanishes,
it is nevertheless reproduced later at a more mature age, when
the soul has integrated itself in earnest. Yes, although the art
may not then be sufficiently earnest for the individual, he
may at times be disposed to return to that first state and
resume it in a mood. He desires the comic effect and wants
a relation to the theatrical performance that generates the

comic. Since tragedy, comedy, and light comedy fail to please him precisely because of their perfection, he turns to farce.[55]

The same phenomenon is repeated in other spheres. At times we see the more mature individuality who satiates himself on the strong food of actuality and is not really influenced by a well-executed painting. But he can be stirred by a Nürnberg print,[56] a picture of the kind found on the market not long ago. There one sees a landscape depicting a rural area in general. This abstraction cannot be artistically executed. Therefore the whole thing is achieved by contrast, namely, by an accidental concretion. And yet I ask everyone if from such a landscape he does not get the impression of a rural area in general, and if this category has not stayed with him from childhood. In the days of childhood, we had such enormous categories that they now almost make us dizzy, we clipped out of a piece of paper a man and a woman who were man and woman in general in a more rigorous sense than Adam and Eve were. A landscape artist, whether he strives for effect by faithful representation or by ideal reproduction, perhaps leaves the individual cold, whereas a print like that produces an indescribable effect, since we do not know whether to laugh or to cry, and the whole effect depends upon the observer's mood. There probably is no person who has not gone through a period when no richness of language, no passion of interjection was adequate, since no expression, no gesture sufficed, since nothing satisfied him other than breaking into the strangest leaps[57] and somersaults. Perhaps the same individual learned to dance. Perhaps he went frequently to the ballet and admired the art of the dancer.[58] Perhaps there came a time when ballet no longer stirred him, and yet he had moments when he could return to his room and, indulging himself, find indescribably humorous relief in standing on one leg in a picturesque pose or, giving not a damn for the world, settle everything with an *entrechat*.

Farce is performed at the Königstädter Theater, and quite naturally a varied audience goes there—yes, anyone wanting to make a pathological study of laughter at various social and temperamental levels ought not to neglect the opportunity offered by the performance of a farce. The cheers and shrieks of laughter in the second balcony and gallery are entirely different from the applause of a refined and critical audience; it is a sustained accompaniment without which farce simply could not be performed. Farce generally moves on the lower levels of society, and therefore the gallery and second balcony audiences recognize themselves immediately, and their noise and cheers are not an esthetic appraisal of the individual actor but a purely lyrical outburst of their feeling of well-being. They are not at all conscious of themselves as audience but want to be down there on the street or wherever the scene happens to be. But since this is out of the question because of distance, they behave like children who only get permission to look out of the window at the commotion on the street. The orchestra and first balcony audiences are also moved to laughter, although it is considerably different from that Cimbrian-Teutonic vulgar hooting, and even in this sphere the variation in the laughter is infinitely nuanced in a way quite distinct from what is found at the performance of the best comedy. Whether it is regarded as an excellence or a defect, the difference is nevertheless so. Every general esthetic category runs aground on farce; nor does farce succeed in producing a uniformity of mood in the more cultured audience. Because its impact depends largely on self-activity and the viewer's improvisation, the particular individuality comes to assert himself in a very individual way and in his enjoyment is emancipated from all esthetic obligations to admire, to laugh, to be moved, etc. in the traditional way. For a cultured person, seeing a farce is similar to playing the lottery, except that one does not have the annoyance of winning money. But that kind of uncertainty will not do for the general theater-going public, which therefore ignores farce or snobbishly disdains it, all the worse for itself. A proper theater public generally has a certain restricted earnestness; it wishes to be—or at least fancies that it is—ennobled and educated in the theater. It wishes to have had—or at least fancies that it has had—a rare artistic enjoyment; it wishes, as

III
199

soon as it has read the poster, to be able to know in advance
what is going to happen that evening. Such unanimity cannot be found at a farce, for the same farce can produce very
different impressions, and, strangely enough, it may so happen that the one time it made the least impression it was
performed best. Thus a person cannot rely on his neighbor
and the man across the street and statements in the newspaper to determine whether he has enjoyed himself or not. The
individual has to decide that matter for himself, and as yet
scant success has attended any reviewer's prescription of an
etiquette for a cultured theater public seeing a farce: here it
is impossible to establish a *bon ton* [proper style]. The otherwise so reassuring mutual respect between theater and audience is suspended. Seeing a farce can produce the most un-
predictable mood, and therefore a person can never be sure
whether he has conducted himself in the theater as a worthy
member of society who has laughed and cried at the appropriate places. One cannot, as a conscientious spectator does,
admire the fine character portrayal that a dramatic performance is supposed to have, for in a farce all of the characters
are portrayed according to the abstract criterion "in general." Situation, action, the lines—everything is according to
this criterion. Therefore one can just as well be made sad as
ecstatic from laughter.

No effect in farce is brought about by irony; everything is
naiveté. Therefore the viewer must be self-active solely as an
individual, for the naiveté of the farce is so illusory that it is
impossible for the cultured person to relate naively to it. But
the amusement consists largely in the viewer's self-relating
to the farce, something he himself must risk, whereas he
seeks in vain to the left or the right or in the newspapers for
a guarantee that he actually has enjoyed himself. Nevertheless, farce will perhaps have a very singular meaning for the
cultured person who also has sufficient unconstraint to dare
to enjoy himself entirely solo, sufficient self-confidence to
think for himself without consulting others as to whether he
has enjoyed himself or not. For him the farce will perhaps
have a very singular meaning, because his own mood will

be affected in different ways, at times by the copiousness of the abstract and then again by the interjection of a tangible actuality. Of course, he will not come with a firm and fixed mood and make everything have an effect in conformity with it, but he will have achieved perfection in mood and will maintain himself in the state in which not a single mood is present but a possibility of all.

III
200

Farce is performed at the Königstädter Theater, and in my opinion superbly. My view, of course, is entirely my own; I press it on no one and disapprove of any importuning. A completely successful performance of a farce requires a cast of special composition. It must include two, at most three, very talented actors or, more correctly, generative geniuses. They must be children of caprice, intoxicated with laughter, dancers of whimsy who, even though they are at other times like other people—yes, the very moment before—the instant they hear the stage manager's bell they are transformed and, like a thoroughbred Arabian horse, they begin to snort and puff, while their distended nostrils betoken the chafing of spirit because they want to be off, want to cavort wildly. They are not so much reflective artists who have studied laughter as they are lyricists who themselves plunged into the abyss of laughter and now let its volcanic power hurl them out on the stage. Thus they have not deliberated very much on what they will do but leave everything to the moment and the natural power of laughter. They have the courage to venture what the individual makes bold to do only when alone, what the mentally deranged do in the presence of everybody, what the genius knows how to do with the authority of genius, certain of laughter. They know that their hilarity has no limits, that their comic resources are inexhaustible, and they themselves are amazed at it practically every moment. They know that they are able to sustain laughter the whole evening without its costing them any more effort than it takes me to scribble this down on paper.

Two such geniuses are enough for a farce theater; three are the most that can be used advantageously, for otherwise the effect is diminished, just as a person dies of hypersthenia.

The rest of the cast need not be talented; it is not even good if they are. Nor do the rest of the cast need to be recruited according to standards of good looks; they should instead be brought together by chance. The rest of the cast may very well be just as accidental as the company that, according to a sketch by Chodowiecki,[59] founded Rome. No one needs to be excluded even for a physical abnormality; on the contrary, such an accidental feature would be a splendid contribution. Whether a person is bowlegged or knock-kneed, overgrown or stunted—in short, a defective example in one way or another—he can very well be used in farce and can have an incalculable effect. That is, the accidental is second only to the ideal. A wit has said that mankind can be divided into officers, servant girls, and chimney sweeps.[60] In my opinion, this remark is not only witty but also profound, and it would take great speculative talent to make a better classification. If a classification does not ideally exhaust its object, the accidental is preferable in every way, because it sets the imagination in motion. A somewhat true classification cannot satisfy the understanding, is nothing at all for the imagination, and for that reason it should be completely rejected, even though in daily use it enjoys great honor, because people for one thing are very stupid and for another have very little imagination. If there is to be a representation of a person in the theater, what is required is either a concrete creation thoroughgoingly portrayed in ideality or the accidental. The theaters that exist not only for entertainment should produce the first. But there people are satisfied if an actor is a handsome fellow with a prepossessing appearance and good stage presence and a good voice. This rarely satisfies me, for his performance *eo ipso* awakens the critic in me, and as soon as that is awake it is not easy for me to determine what it takes to be a human being, nor is it easy to fulfill the requirements of one. People will certainly agree that I am right in thinking this if they stop to consider that Socrates, who was particularly strong in the knowledge of human nature and in self-knowledge, "did not know for sure whether he was a human being or an even more changeable

III
201

animal than Typhon."[61] In farce, however, the minor characters have their effect through that abstract category "in
general" and achieve it by an accidental concretion. In this
way, one gets no further than actuality. Nor should one, but
the spectator is comically reconciled to watching this accidental concretion make a claim to be the ideal, which it does
by stepping onto the artificial world of the stage. If an exception should be made for any of the minor characters, then
it must be the sweetheart. She, of course, must in no way
be an artist, but in selecting her, one nevertheless might see
to it that she is winsome, that her appearance and actions on
stage are friendly and engaging, that she is pleasant to look
at, pleasant, so to speak, to have around.

III
202

I am rather well satisfied with the composition of the cast
at the Königstädter Theater. If I were to make an objection,
it would be with regard to the minor characters, for I have
not a word of criticism for Beckmann[62] and Grobecker.[63]
Beckmann is unquestionably a comic genius who purely lyrically frolics freely in the comic, one who does not distinguish himself by character portrayal but by ebullience of mood.
He is not great in the commensurables of the artistic but is
admirable in the incommensurables of the individual. He does
not need the support of interaction, of scenery and staging;
precisely because he is in an ebullient mood, he himself carries everything along. At the same time that he is being in-
ordinately funny, he himself is painting his own scenery as
well as a set painter. What Baggesen says of Sara Nickels,[64]
that she comes rushing on stage with a rustic scene in tow,
is true of B. in the positive sense, except that he comes walking. In an art theater proper, one rarely sees an actor who
can really walk and stand. As a matter of fact, I have seen
only one, but what B. is able to do, I have not seen before.
He is not only able to walk, but he is also able to *come walking*. To come walking is something very distinctive, and by
means of this genius he also improvises the whole scenic setting. He is able not only to portray an itinerant craftsman;
he is also able to come walking like one and in such a way
that one experiences everything, surveys the smiling hamlet

from the dusty highway, hears its quiet noise, sees the foot-path that goes down by the village pond when one turns off there by the blacksmith's—where one sees B. walking along with his little bundle on his back, his stick in his hand, untroubled and undaunted. He can come walking onto the stage followed by street urchins whom one does not see. Even Dr. Ryge[65] in *Kong Salomon og Jørgen Hattemager* could not produce this effect. Yes, Mr. B. is sheer economy for a theater, for when it has him, it needs neither street urchins nor stage scenery. But this workman is no character sketch; he is too casual in his truly masterly contours for that. He is an incognito in whom dwells the lunatic demon of comedy, who quickly extricates himself and carries everything away in sheer abandonment. In this respect, B.'s dance is incomparable. He has sung his couplet, and now the dance begins. What B. ventures here is neck-breaking, for he presumably does not trust himself to create an effect with his dance routines in the narrow sense. He is now completely beside himself. The sheer lunacy of his laughter can no longer be contained either in forms or in lines; the only way to convey the mood is to take himself by the scruff of the neck, as did Münchhausen,[66] and cavort in crazy capers. As stated before, the individual recognizes very well the relief in doing something like that,[67] but to do it on stage—that takes positive genius. That requires the authority of genius; otherwise it is most repellent.

Every burlesque comedian ought to have a voice recognizable at once from the wings, for then he is able to pave his own way. B. has an excellent voice, which of course is not identical with good vocal chords. Grobecker's voice is harsher, but one word from him in the wings has the same effect as three trumpet blasts at Dyrehavsbakken;[68] it creates receptivity for the ludicrous. In this respect I give him the advantage over B. The essential in B. is a certain untamable, frolicsome good sense, and through it he achieves lunacy. Grobecker, however, sometimes rises to lunacy by way of sentimentality and bathos. I remember seeing him in a farce in which he played an estate overseer who, because of his devotion to his master and mistress and his belief in the importance of festive

III 203

arrangements in embellishing life for their lordships, thinks of nothing but having a rustic festival in readiness for their lordships' very important arrival. Everything is ready. Grobecker has chosen to portray Mercury. He has not changed his overseer's uniform but has simply attached wings to his feet and put on a helmet. He takes up a picturesque pose on one leg and is about to begin his speech to the master and mistress. Grobecker certainly is not as great a lyricist as Beckmann, but he does have a lyrical understanding with laughter. He has a certain bent for correctness, and in this respect he often achieves a masterly performance, especially in dry comedy, but he is not the yeasty ingredient in the whole farce that B. is. But he is a genius, and a genius in farce.

III
204

One enters the Königstädter Theater and gets a place in the first balcony, for relatively few sit there, and in seeing a farce, one must sit comfortably and in no way feel hampered by the exaltation of art that makes people jam a theater to see a play as if it were a matter of salvation.[69] The air in the theater is also fairly pure, untainted by the sweat of a fervent empathizing audience or by the miasma of art enthusiasts. In the first balcony one can be quite sure of getting a box all to oneself. If not, however, may I recommend to the reader boxes five and six on the left so that he can still have some useful information from what I write. In a corner in the back there is a single seat where one has an unsurpassed position. So you are sitting alone in your box, and the theater is empty. The orchestra plays an overture, the music resounds in the hall a bit *unheimlich* [eerily] simply because the place is so deserted. You have gone to the theater not as a tourist, not as an esthete and critic but, if possible, as a nobody, and you are satisfied to sit as comfortably and well, almost as well, as in your own living room. The orchestra has finished, the curtain rises slowly, and then begins that second orchestra, which does not obey the conductor's baton but follows an inner drive, that second orchestra, the nature sound[70] in the gallery, which already has a presentiment that Beckmann is in the wings. As a rule, I sat far back in the box and therefore could not see the second balcony and gallery, which jutted out over my head like the visor of a cap. All the more magical is the effect of this noise. Everywhere I looked there was mainly emptiness. Before me the vast space of the theater changed into the belly of the whale in which Jonah sat; the noise in the gallery was like the motion of the monster's viscera. From the moment the gallery has begun to perform its music, no accompaniment is necessary, for B. stimulates it and it stimulates B.

My unforgettable nursemaid, you fleeting nymph who lived in the brook that ran past my father's farm and always helpfully shared our childish games, even if you just took care of yourself! You, my faithful comforter, you who preserved your innocent purity over the years, you who did not age as I grew older, you quiet nymph to whom I turned once again, weary of people, weary of myself, so weary that I needed an eternity to rest up, so melancholy that I needed an eternity to forget. You did not deny me what men want to deny me by making eternity just as busy and even more appalling than time.[71] Then I lay at your side and vanished from myself in the immensity of the sky above and forgot myself in your soothing murmur! You, my happier self, you fleeting life that lives in the brook running past my father's farm, where I lie stretched out as if my body were an abandoned hiking stick, but I am rescued and released in the plaintive purling! —Thus did I lie in my theater box, discarded like a swimmer's clothing, stretched out by the stream of laughter and unrestraint and applause that ceaselessly foamed by me. I could see nothing but the expanse of theater, hear nothing but the noise in which I resided. Only at intervals did I rise up, look at Beckmann, and laugh so hard that I sank back again in exhaustion alongside the foaming stream.

By itself this was blissful, and yet I lacked something. Then in the wilderness surrounding me I saw a figure that cheered me more than Friday cheered Robinson Crusoe.[72] In the third row of a box directly across from me sat a young girl, half hidden by an older gentleman and lady sitting in the first row. The young girl had hardly come to the theater to be seen, since in this theater one generally is spared these odious female exhibitions. She sat in the third row; her dress was simple and modest, almost domestic. She was not wrapped in sable and marten but in a voluminous scarf, and out of this sheath her humble head bowed, just as the highest bell on a lily-of-the-valley stem leans out from the sheath of the large leaf. When I had watched Beckmann and let myself be convulsed with laughter, when I sank back in exhaustion and let myself be carried away on the current of jubilation and hilarity and then climbed out of the pool and returned to myself again, my eyes sought her, and the sight of her refreshed my whole being with its friendly gentleness. Or when in the farce itself a feeling of greater pathos burst forth, I looked at her, and her presence helped me to yield to it, for she sat composed in the midst of it all, quietly smiling in childlike wonder. She came there, as did I, every evening. At times I wondered what could be the reasons for it, but these thoughts, too, were but moods that turned to her, so that momentarily it seemed as if she might be a girl who had suffered much and now wrapped herself tightly in her shawl and wanted nothing more to do with the world, until the expression on her face convinced me that she was a happy child who drew her scarf so tightly together in order to enjoy herself thoroughly. She did not suspect that she was being observed and even less that my eyes were upon her; it would have been a sin against her and, worst of all, for myself, for there is an innocence, an unawareness that even the purest thought can disturb. A person does not find this out by himself, but if his good guardian spirit confides to him where such primitive privacy hides, then he does not intrude upon it and does not grieve his guardian spirit. If she had even suspected my mute, half-infatuated delight, everything would have been spoiled beyond repair, even with all her love.

I know a place a few miles from Copenhagen where a young girl lives; I know the big shaded garden with its many trees and bushes. I know a bushy slope a short distance away, from which, concealed by the brush, one can look down into the garden. I have not divulged this to anyone; not even my

III
206

coachman knows it, for I deceive him by getting out some distance away and walking to the right instead of the left. When my mind is sleepless and the sight of my bed makes me more apprehensive than a torture machine does, even more than the operating table strikes fear in the sick person, then I drive all night long. Early in the morning, I lie in hiding in the shelter of the brush. When life begins to stir, when the sun opens its eye, when the bird shakes its wings, when the fox steals out of its cave, when the farmer stands in his doorway and gazes out over the fields, when the milk-maid walks with her pail down to the meadow, when the reaper makes his scythe ring and entertains himself with this prelude, which becomes the day's and the task's refrain— then the young girl also appears. Fortunate the one who can sleep! Fortunate the one who can sleep so lightly that sleep itself does not become a burden heavier than that of the day! Fortunate the one who can rise from his bed as if no one had rested there, so that the bed itself is cool and delicious and refreshing to look at, as if the sleeper had not rested upon it but only bent over it to straighten it out! Fortunate the one who can die in such a way that even one's deathbed, the instant one's body is removed, looks more inviting than if a solicitous mother had shaken and aired the covers so that the child might sleep more peacefully! Then the young girl appears and walks around in wonderment (who marvels most, the girl or the trees!), then she crouches and picks from the bushes, then skips lightly about, then stands still, lost in thought. What wonderful persuasion in all this! Then at last my mind finds repose. Happy girl! If a man ever wins your love, would that you might make him as happy by being everything to him as you make me by doing nothing for me.

III
207

    Der Talismann was to be performed in the Königstädter Theater. The recollection of it awakened in my soul; everything was as vivid for me as it was the time before. I hurried to the theater. No box was available for me alone, not even a seat in number five or six on the left. I had to take the right. There I encountered a group that was not sure whether it should be amused or be blasé, and one can be sure that such company is boring. There was scarcely a single empty box. The young girl was not to be found, or, if she was present, I was unable to recognize her because she was together with others. Beckmann could not make me laugh. I endured it for half an hour and then left the theater, thinking: There is no repetition at all. This made a deep impression on me. I am not so very young, am not altogether ignorant of life, and long before my previous trip to Berlin I had cured myself of calculating on the basis of uncertainties. I did believe, however, that the enjoyment I had known in that theater would be of a more durable nature, precisely because a person must have learned to let himself be trimmed by existence in many ways and yet learned to manage somehow until he actually got a sense of life—but then life also ought to be all the more secure. Should life [*Tilværelsen*] be even more deceitful than a bankrupt! He still gives 50 percent or 30 percent, at least something. After all, the least one can ask for is the comic—should not even that be capable of repetition!

With these thoughts in my mind, I went home. My desk was in place. The velvet armchair was still there, but when I saw it, I became so furious I almost smashed it to pieces, all the more so because everyone in the house had gone to bed and no one could take it away. Of what good is an armchair of velvet when the rest of the environment does not match; it is like a man going around naked and wearing a three-cornered hat. When I went to bed without having had one single rational thought, it was so light in the room that, half-awake, half-dreaming, I kept on seeing the armchair, until in the morning I got up and carried out my resolve to have it thrown into an out-of-the-way nook.

My home had become dismal to me simply because it was a repetition of the wrong kind. My mind was sterile, my troubled imagination constantly conjured up tantalizingly attractive recollections of how the ideas had presented themselves the last time, and the tares of these recollections choked out every thought at birth.[73] I went out to the café where I had gone every day the previous time to enjoy the beverage that, according to the poet's precept, when it is "pure and hot and strong and not misused,"[74] can always stand alongside that to which the poet compares it, namely, friendship. At any rate, I prize coffee. Perhaps the coffee was just as good as last time; one would almost expect it to be, but it was not to my liking. The sun through the café windows was hot and glaring; the room was just about as humid as the air in a saucepan, practically cooking. A draft, which like a small trade wind cut through everything, prohibited thoughts of any repetition, even if the opportunity had otherwise offered itself.

In the evening, I went to the restaurant I had frequented the previous time and, no doubt by force of habit, had even found satisfactory. Coming there every evening as I did, I was thoroughly familiar with everything: I knew when the early guests would leave, how they would greet the brotherhood whom they left, whether they put on their hats in the inner room or the outer or not until they opened the door or until they stepped outside. No one escaped my attention. Like Proserpine, I plucked a hair from every head,[75] even the bald ones. —It was just the same, the same witticisms, the same civilities, the same patronage; the place was absolutely the same—in short, the same sameness. Solomon says that a woman's nagging is like rain dripping from the roof;[76] I wonder what he would say about this still life. What an appalling thought—here a repetition was possible!

The next evening I went to the Königstädter Theater. The only repetition was the impossibility of a repetition. Unter den Linden was unbearably dusty; every attempt to mingle with people and thus take a human bath was extremely disappointing. No matter how I turned and shifted, all was futile. The little dancer who last time had enchanted me with her gracefulness, who, so to speak, was on the verge of a leap, had already made the leap. The blind man at the Brandenburger Tor, my harpist—for I probably was the only one who cared about him—had acquired a coat of mixed gray in place of the light green one for which I was pensively nostalgic and in which he looked like a weeping willow—he was lost to me and won for the universally human. The beadle's admired nose had become pallid; Professor A. A. had gotten a pair of new trousers with an almost military fit.— —

When this had repeated itself several days, I became so furious, so weary of the repetition, that I decided to return home. My discovery was not significant, and yet it was curious, for I had discovered that there simply is no repetition and had verified it by having it repeated in every possible way.

My hope lay in my home. Justinus Kerner[77] tells somewhere of a man who became bored with his home; he had his horse saddled so he could ride out into the wide, wide world. When he had ridden a little way, the horse threw him off. This turn of events became crucial for him, because as he turned to mount his horse, his eyes fell once again on the home he wanted to forsake. He gazed at it, and behold, it was so beautiful that he promptly turned back. I could be fairly certain of finding everything in my home prepared for repetition. I have always strongly mistrusted all upheavals, yes, to the extent that for this reason I even hate any sort of housecleaning, especially floor scrubbing with soap. I had left the strictest instructions that my conservative principles should be maintained also in my absence. But what happens. My faithful servant thought otherwise. When he began a shakeup very shortly after I left, he counted on its being finished well before my return, and he certainly was the man to get everything back in order very punctually. I arrive. I ring my doorbell. My servant opens the door. It was a moment eloquent with meaning. My servant turned as pale as a corpse. Through the door half-opened to the rooms beyond I saw the horror: everything was turned upside down. I was dumbfounded. In his perplexity, he did not know what to do; his bad conscience smote him—and he slammed the door in my face. That was too much. My desolation had reached its extremity, my principles had collapsed; I was obliged to fear the worst, to be treated like a ghost as was Grønmeyer, the business manager.[78] I perceived that there is no repetition, and my earlier conception of life was victorious.

How humiliated I was: I, who had been so brusque with that young man, had now been brought to the same point. Indeed, it seemed as if I were that young man myself, as if my great talk, which I now would not repeat at any price, were only a dream from which I awoke to have life unremittingly and treacherously *retake* everything it had given without providing a *repetition*.[79] And is it not the case that the older a person grows, the more and more of a swindle life proves to be, that the smarter he becomes and the more ways he learns to shift for himself, the bigger the mess he makes of life and the more he suffers! A little child is utterly helpless and always emerges unscathed. I recollect once seeing on the street a nursemaid pushing a baby carriage with two children. The one, scarcely a year old, had fallen asleep and lay there in the carriage dead to the world. The other was a little girl of about two years, husky, chubby, with sleevelets quite like a little lady. She had pushed herself to the front of the carriage and took up a good two-thirds of the space, and the smaller child lay at her side as if it were a parcel the lady had taken along in the carriage. With admirable egotism, the girl paid no attention whatsoever to anyone but herself or to anything anyone did, provided she could only have a good seat. When a cart came speeding along, the baby carriage was obviously in danger; people ran toward it, and with a swift turn the nursemaid pushed it into a doorway. All the bystanders were apprehensive, I among them. During all this, the little lady sat quite calm and passively kept on picking her nose. Presumably she thought: What does all this have to do with me; it's the nursemaid's business. Such heroism is sought in vain among adults.

The older a person grows, the more he understands life and the more he relishes the amenities and is able to appreciate them—in short, the more competent one becomes, the less satisfied one is. Satisfied, completely, absolutely satisfied in every way, this one never is, and to be more or less satisfied is not worth the trouble, so it is better to be completely dissatisfied. Anyone who has painstakingly pondered the matter will certainly agree with me that it has never been granted to a human being in his whole life, not even for as much as a half hour, to be absolutely satisfied in every conceivable way.[80] Certainly it is unnecessary for me to say that for this it takes something more than having food and clothes.

At one time I was very close to complete satisfaction. I got up feeling unusually well one morning. My sense of well-being increased incomparably until noon; at precisely one o'clock, I was at the peak and had a presentiment of the dizzy maximum found on no gauge of well-being, not even on a poetic thermometer. My body had lost its terrestrial gravity; it was as if I had no body simply because every function enjoyed total satisfaction, every nerve delighted in itself and in the whole, while every heartbeat, the restlessness of the living being, only memorialized and declared the pleasure of the moment. My walk was a floating, not like the flight of the bird that cuts through the air and leaves the earth behind, but like the undulating of the wind over a field of grain, like the longing rocking of the sea, like the dreaming drifting of clouds. My being was transparent, like the depths of the sea, like the self-satisfied silence of the night, like the soliloquizing stillness of midday. Every mood rested in my soul with melodic resonance. Every thought volunteered itself, and every thought volunteered itself jubilantly, the most foolish whim as well as the richest idea. I had a presentiment of every impression before it arrived and awakened within me. All existence seemed to have fallen in love with me, and everything quivered in fateful rapport with my being. Everything was prescient in me, and everything was enigmatically transfigured in my microcosmic bliss, which transfigured everything in itself, even the most disagreeable: the most boring remark, the most disgusting sight, the most calamitous conflict. As stated, it was one o'clock on the dot when I was at the peak and had presentiments of the highest of all; when suddenly something began to irritate one of my eyes, whether it was an eyelash, a speck of something, a bit of dust, I do not know, but this I do know—that in the same instant I was plunged down almost into the abyss of despair, something everyone will readily understand who has been as high up as

III
211

I was and while at that point has also pondered the theoretical question of whether absolute satisfaction is attainable at all. Since that time, I have abandoned every hope of ever feeling satisfied absolutely and in every way, abandoned the hope I had once nourished, perhaps not to be absolutely satisfied at all times but nevertheless at certain moments, even though all those instances of the moment were no more, as Shakespeare says, than "an alehouse keeper's arithmetic would be adequate to add up."[81]

That was how far I had come before I learned to know that young man. As soon as I asked myself or there was a question about perfect satisfaction for even a half hour, I always declared *renonce* [short suit]. It was then that time after time I turned to and became excited about the idea of repetition, and thereby I once again became the victim of my zeal for principles, for I am completely convinced that if I had not gone abroad with the idea of assuring myself of it, I would have amused myself immensely with the very same thing. Why is it that I cannot stay within the ordinary, that I insist on principles, that I cannot go around dressed like others, that I like to walk in stiff boots! Do not all agree—both ecclesiastical and secular speakers, both poets and prose writers, both skippers and undertakers, both heroes and cowards—do they not all agree that life is a stream. How can one get such a foolish idea, and, still more foolishly, how can one want to make a principle of it. My young friend thought: Let it pass—and he thereby would have been far better off than if he had wanted to begin with repetition. Then he probably would have gained the beloved again in the same way as the lover in the folk song who wanted repetition, as the nun with shorn hair and pale lips. He wanted repetition, and he got it all right, and the repetition killed him.

> Das Nönnlein kam gegangen
> In einem schneeweiszen Kleid;
> Ihr Häärl war abgeschnitten,
> Ihr rother Mund war bleich.

Der Knab, er setzt sich nieder,
Er sasz auf einem Stein:
Er weint die hellen Thränen,
Brach ihm sein Herz entzwei.*[82]

[The little nun came walking
And snow-white was her veil;
Her hair was shorn and taken,
Her red-red lips were pale.

The youth sat down so sadly,
He sat on a stone apart:
He wept his big bright tears,
Asunder broke his heart.]

Long live the stagecoach horn! It is the instrument for me
for many reasons, and chiefly because one can never be certain of wheedling the same notes from this horn. A coach
horn has infinite possibilities, and the person who puts it to
his mouth and puts his wisdom into it can never be guilty
of a repetition, and he who instead of giving an answer gives
his friend a coach horn to use as he pleases says nothing but
explains everything. Praised be the coach horn! It is my sym-
bol. Just as the ancient ascetics placed a skull on the table,
the contemplation of which constituted their view of life, so
the coach horn on my table always reminds me of the meaning of life. Long live the coach horn! But the journey is not
worth the trouble, for one need not stir from the spot to be
convinced that there is no repetition. No, one sits calmly in
one's living room; when all is vanity[83] and passes away, one
nevertheless speeds faster than on a train, even though sitting
still. Everything is to remind me of that; my servant will be
dressed as a postilion, and I myself will not drive to a dinner
party except by special coach. Farewell! Farewell! You exu-
berant hope of youth, what is your hurry? After all, what
you are hunting for does not exist, and the same goes for
you yourself! Farewell, you masculine vim and vigor! Why
are you stamping the ground so violently? What you are

III
213

* Herder, *Volkslieder*, ed. Falk. Leipzig, 1825. I, p. 57.

stepping on is an illusion! Farewell, you conquering resolve! You will reach your goal, all right, for you cannot take the deed along with you without turning around, and that you cannot do! Farewell, loveliness of the woods! When I wanted to behold you, you were withered! Travel on, you fugitive river! You are the only one who really knows what you want, for you want only to flow along and lose yourself in the sea, which is never filled! Move on, you drama of life—let no one call it a comedy, no one a tragedy, for no one saw the end! Move on, you drama of existence, where life is not given again any more than money is! Why has no one returned from the dead? Because life does not know how to captivate as death does, because life does not have the persuasiveness that death has. Yes, death is very persuasive if only one does not contradict it but lets it do the talking; then it is instantly convincing, so that no one has ever had an objection to make or has longed for the eloquence of life. O death! Great is your persuasiveness, and next to you there is no one who can speak as beautifully as the man whose eloquence gave him the name πεισιθάνατος [persuader to death],[84] because with his power of persuasion he talked about you!

[PART TWO]

[PART TWO]

REPETITION[1]

Some time went by. My servant, like a housewifely Eve, had remedied his earlier wrongdoing. A monotonous and unvarying order was established in my whole economy. Everything unable to move stood in its appointed place, and everything that moved went its calculated course: my clock, my servant, and I, myself, who with measured pace walked up and down the floor. Although I had convinced myself that there is no repetition, it nevertheless is always certain and true that by being inflexible and also by dulling one's powers of observation a person can achieve a sameness that has a far more anesthetic power than the most whimsical amusements and that, like a magical formulary, in the course of time also becomes more and more powerful. In the excavation of Herculaneum and Pompeii, everything was found in its place just as the respective owners left it. If I had lived at that time, the archeologists, perhaps to their amazement, would have come upon a man who walked with measured pace up and down the floor. To maintain this established and enduring order, I made use of every possible expedient. At certain times, like Emperor Domitian,[2] I even walked around the room armed with a flyswatter, pursuing every revolutionary fly. Three flies, however, were preserved to fly buzzing through the room at specified times. Thus did I live,[3] forgetting the world and, as I thought, forgotten,[4] when one day a letter arrived from my young friend. More followed, always spaced about a month apart, but from this I dared not draw any conclusion as to the distance of his place of residence. He himself divulges nothing, and he could very well be trying to perplex me by deliberately and carefully varying the intervals between five weeks and just a day over three weeks. He does not wish to trouble me with a correspondence, and even if I were willing to reciprocate or at

least to answer his letters, he does not care to receive anything like that—he simply wishes to pour himself out.

From his letter, I see what I knew before, that like any
melancholiac he is quite irritable and, despite this irritability
as well as because of it, is in a state of continual self-contradiction. He wants me to be his confidant, and yet he does
not want it—indeed, it bothers him that I am. He feels secure
in my so-called superiority, and yet it annoys him. He confides in me, and yet he does not want it—indeed, it bothers
him that I am. He feels secure in my so-called superiority,
and yet it annoys him. He confides in me and yet wants no
reply, indeed, will not see me. He demands silence of me,
unbroken silence, "by all that is holy," and yet he seems to
become furious at the thought that I have this power to be
silent. No one is to know that I am his confidant, not one
soul; therefore he himself does not want to know of it, and
I must not know of it. In order to account for this confusion
to our mutual satisfaction and amusement, he so much as
politely suggests that he actually regards me as mad. How
would I have the courage to express any thought on the im-
pudence of this interpretation! It would, after all, augment
substantiation of the charge—in my opinion—while in his
eyes my self-restraint would simply be a new sign of the
passionlessness and mental disorder that do not allow one to
be personally affected, not even to be insulted. This, then, is
the thanks one gets for having trained oneself every day for
years to have only an objective theoretical interest in people
and also, if possible, in everyone for whom the idea is in
motion! At one time, I tried to assist the idea in him; now I
am reaping the harvest, namely, I am supposed to be and
also not to be both being and nothing, entirely as he so pleases,
and not to receive the slightest appreciation for being able to
be that and thereby to help him out of the contradiction. If
he himself thought of how much indirect approval there is
in such a *Zumuthung* [encouragement], he would undoubtedly be furious all over again. To be his confidant is harder
than the hardest, and he completely forgets that with one
single word—for example, by declining correspondence with

him—I could deeply offend him. Punishment came not only
to him who betrayed the Eleusinian mysteries but also to
him who insulted this institution by refusing to be initiated.
According to a Greek author,[5] the latter was the case with a
man named Demonax,[6] who nevertheless by his brilliant defense got out of it with skin intact. My position as confidant
is even more critical, for he is even more chaste with his
mysteries; he becomes ever so angry when I do what he most
urgently requests—when I keep silent.

But if in the meantime he believes that I have completely
forgotten him, then he wrongs me once again. His sudden
disappearance actually made me fear that in his despair he
had done away with himself. As a rule, such an event does
not remain hidden very long; therefore, since I neither heard
nor read anything, I decided that he presumably must be
alive, wherever he was lurking. The girl he left in the lurch
knew nothing whatsoever. One day he did not show up and
sent no word at all. Her transition to pain was not sudden,
for at first the uneasy suspicion awakened little by little and
at first the pain consolidated itself little by little, so that she
slumbered sweetly in a dreamlike ambiguity about what had
happened and what it could mean. For me the girl was new
material for observation.[7] My friend was not one of those
who know how to squeeze everything out of the beloved
and then throw her away; on the contrary, his disappearance
left her in the most desirable state: healthy, in full bloom,
enriched by all his poetic yield, powerfully nourished by the
priceless cordial of poetic illusion. Rarely does one meet a
jilted girl in this state. When I saw her a few days later, she
was still as lively as a freshly caught fish; usually a girl like
that is likely to be as famished as a fish that has lived in a
tank. I was in all conscience convinced that he must be alive
and rejoiced that he had not seized the desperate means of
passing himself off as dead. It is unbelievable how confusing
an erotic relationship can be if one party wants to die of grief
or wants to die to get away from it all. According to her
own solemn declaration, a girl would die of grief[8] if her lover
was a deceiver.[9] But look, he was no deceiver and perhaps

had better intentions than she realized. Nevertheless, what he otherwise might eventually have done, he now could not resolve to do, just because she once had allowed herself to alarm him with that protestation, because she, as he said, resorted to an oratorical trick on him or in any case said what a girl ought never to say, whether or not she believes him a deceiver, for in that case she ought to be too proud, or she still has faith in him, for then she ought to perceive that she can only do him an abominable wrong. To want to die to get away from the whole thing[10] is the most wretched way imaginable and implies the most offensive insult to a girl. She thinks he is dead, she goes into mourning, she weeps and laments the dead one honestly and sincerely. Indeed, she must almost be nauseated by her own feelings once she discovers later that he is living and had never even considered death. Or, if it is in the next life that she first begins to have misgivings—not whether he actually is dead, for that is indisputable, but whether he was dead at the time he declared it and she grieved—a situation like that would be a task for an apocalyptic author[11] who has understood his Aristophanes (I mean the Greek, not the particular individuals who have been called that, like the *doctores cerei*[12] in the Middle Ages) and his Lucian. The mistake could be maintained for a long time, for dead he was and dead he would remain. The sorrowing girl would then wake up to begin where they left off, until she discovered that there was a little parenthetical clause.[13]

Recollection came alive in my soul when I received his letter, and by no means did I pick up his story dispassionately. When I came to the not inappropriate explanation in the letter that I was mad, it promptly occurred to me: Now he has indeed a most intimate secret, and this secret is guarded by a jealousy that has more than a hundred eyes. When I was seeing him personally, it did not escape me that before coming out with it all he very carefully insinuated the observation that I was "odd." Well! An observer has to be ready for that. He has to know how to offer the confessor a little guarantee. In making a confession, a girl always demands a pos-

III
218

itive guarantee, a man a negative one; this is due to feminine
devotedness and humbleness and masculine pride and will-
fulness. How comforting, then, that the one from whom one
seeks advice and explanation is—mad! Then there is no need
to be ashamed. Talking with a person like that, after all, is
like talking to a tree, "something one does merely out of
curiosity"—if anyone should ask about it. An observer knows
how to appear easygoing; otherwise no one opens up. Above
all, he guards against being ethically rigorous or portraying
himself as the morally upright man. There is a degenerate
man, one says, he has taken part, has had some wild experiences, *ergo*, I certainly can confide in him, I who am far
superior to him! Well, so be it. I ask nothing of men but the
substance of their consciousness. I scale it, and if it is weighty,
no price is too high for me.

It was clear to me merely in skimming the letter that his
love affair had made a far deeper impression than I had imagined. He must have concealed some moods from me. Obviously, for at that time I was merely "odd"; now I am mentally disordered, which is *was Andres* [another matter]. If this
is the way it is, then there is nothing left for him except to
make a religious movement. Thus does love lead a person
further and further. What I have so often affirmed, I affirm
once again here: "Life [*Tilværelsen*] is extremely profound,
and its governing power knows how to intrigue in a way
entirely different from that of all the poets *in uno* [put to-
gether]." The young man was so constituted and endowed
by nature that I would have wagered that he had not been
caught in the snare of erotic love. The fact is that there are
exceptions in this respect that cannot be declined into the
usual case forms. He had unusual mental powers, particularly imagination. As soon as his creativity was awakened,
he would have enough for his whole life, especially if he
understood himself properly and limited himself to a cozy
domestic diversion, together with mental activity and pas-
times of the imagination, which are the most perfect substitute for all erotic love, are not at all accompanied by the
inconveniences and disasters of erotic love, and have a defi-

nite similarity to what is most beautiful in the bliss of erotic love. Anyone with that nature does not need feminine love, something I usually account for by his having been a woman in a previous existence and his having retained a recollection of it now that he has become a man. To fall in love with a girl only disturbs him and always distorts his task, for he is almost able to take on her *partes* [role]. This is vexatious both to her and to him. On the other hand, he was by nature very melancholy. Just as the first factor would keep him from a more intimate relationship with any girl, the latter one would protect him if it so pleased some calculating, shrewd beauty to chase after him. A profound melancholy of a sympathetic nature is and remains a consummate humiliation to all feminine arts. If a girl succeeded in attracting him to her, the very moment she began revelling in her victory he would think: Do you not sin against her and wrong her by giving way to these feelings? Will you not simply be in her way? In that case, farewell, all feminine intrigues. Now his position has changed in a remarkable way: he has gone over to her side, he is exceedingly eager to see all her excellent points, knows how to set them forth perhaps even better than she does herself, admires them even more than she asks—but further than that she never gets him.

That he should get stuck in a love affair, I had never expected. But life is ingenious. What traps him is not the girl's lovableness at all but his regret over having wronged her by disorganizing her life. He has rashly approached her, he assures himself that the love cannot be actualized; he can be happy without her insofar as he can be happy at all, especially with the addition of this new element, and he breaks off. But now he cannot forget that he has committed a wrong, just as if it were wrong to break off when something cannot be accomplished. If he were untrammeled and if it were said, "Here is the girl, will you draw near to her, will you fall in love with her?" he would be fairly certain to answer: Not for the whole world; I once learned what comes of it—such things one does not forget. And this is the way the matter should be stated if he does not want to fool himself. He still firmly believes that, humanly speaking, his love cannot be realized. He has now come to the border of the marvelous;[14] consequently, if it is to take place at all, it must take place by virtue of the absurd.[15] The thought of any difficulty does not enter his head, or is my own ingenious head perhaps too inventive! Does he actually love the girl, or is she not once again simply the occasion that sets him in motion? Again, what preoccupies him is undoubtedly not possession in the stricter sense and the contents developing in the sphere of possession but rather the return in a purely formal sense. If she died tomorrow, that would not distress him further; he would not actually feel a loss, for his being was at rest. The split in him caused by his contact with her would be reconciled by his actually having returned to her. So once again the girl was not an actuality but a reflexion[16] of motions within him and an incitement of them. The girl has enormous importance, and he will never be able to forget her, but her importance lies not in herself but in her relation to him. She is, so to speak, the border of his being, but such a relation is not erotic. From a religious point of view, one could say it is as if God used this girl to capture him, and yet the girl herself is not an actuality but is like the lace-winged fly with which a hook is baited. I am completely convinced that he does not know the girl at all, although he has been attached to her and she probably has never been out of his thoughts since then. She is the girl—period. Whether, more concretely, she is this or that, the loveliness, the lovableness, the faithfulness, the sacrificial love for whose sake one risks everything and sets heaven and earth in motion—that never enters his head. If he wanted to give an account of the joy and the bliss he truly expects from an actual erotic relationship, he probably would not have a word to say. His main objective is achieved the moment it is possible for him to redeem his honor and his pride! As if it were not also a matter of honor and pride to keep at bay such childish, uneasy feelings! He perhaps even expects his own personality to be distorted, but that is nothing if he can only get revenge, as it were, on life, which has mocked him by making him guilty

III
221

where he was innocent, by making his relation to actuality
meaningless at this point, so that he has to reconcile himself
to being regarded as a deceiver by every genuine lover. What
a burden to carry! But perhaps I do not fully understand
him, perhaps he is hiding something. Maybe he does in truth
love after all. Then it will probably all end with his murder-
ing me in order to confide to me the holiest of the holy. It
is obvious that being an observer is a dangerous position.
Meanwhile, I wish merely for the sake of my own psychological interest that I could get the girl away for a time, get
him to think that she has married. I wager that I would find
some other explanation, for his sympathy is so melancholy
that I believe that he, in kindness to the girl, fancies that he
loves her.

The issue that brings him to a halt is nothing more nor
less than repetition. He is right not to seek clarification in
philosophy, either Greek or modern, for the Greeks make
the opposite movement,[17] and here a Greek would choose to
recollect without tormenting his conscience. Modern philosophy makes no movement; as a rule it makes only a commotion,[18] and if it makes any movement at all, it is always
within immanence, whereas repetition is and remains a transcendence.[19] It is fortunate that he does not seek any explanation from me, for I have abandoned my theory, I am adrift.
Then, too, repetition is too transcendent for me. I can cir-
cumnavigate myself, but I cannot rise above myself. I cannot
find the Archimedean point.[20] Fortunately, my friend is not
looking for clarification from any world-famous philosopher
or any *professor publicus ordinarius* [regularly appointed state
professor]; he turns to an unprofessional thinker who once
possessed the world's glories but later withdrew from life—
in other words, he falls back on Job,[21] who does not posture
on a rostrum and make reassuring gestures to vouch for the
truth of his propositions but sits on the hearth and scrapes
himself with a potsherd and without interrupting this activity casually drops clues and comments. He believes that here
he has found what he sought, and in his view truth sounds
more glorious and gratifying and true in this little circle of

Job and his wife and three friends than in a Greek symposium.

Even if he were still to seek my guidance, it would be futile. I am unable to make a religious movement; it is contrary to my nature. Yet I do not therefore deny the reality [*Realiteten*] of such a thing or that one can learn very much from a young man. If he succeeds, he will have no admirer more ardent than I. If he succeeds, he will be free of all the irritation in his relationship with me. But I cannot deny that the more I ponder the matter the more I have new misgivings about the girl, that in one way or another she has allowed herself to want to trap him in his melancholy. If so, I would rather not be in her shoes. It will end in disaster. Life always wreaks the severest revenge upon such conduct.

August 15

My Silent Confidant:

You perhaps will be surprised suddenly to receive a letter from the person who presumably for you has been dead for a long time and as good as forgotten, or forgotten and as good as dead. I dare not assume more surprise than that. I can imagine that you will promptly take out my case history, as it were, and say: Right! It's the fellow with the unhappy love affair. Where did we leave off? Well, well—then the symptoms must surely be these. Really, your calmness is appalling! When I think about it, my blood boils, and yet I cannot tear myself loose—you hold me captive with a strange power. There is something indescribably salutary and alleviating in talking with you, for it seems as if one were talking with oneself or with an idea. Then, upon finishing speaking and finding solace in this speaking out, when one suddenly looks at your impassive face and reflects that this is a human being standing before one, a prodigiously intelligent man with whom one has been speaking, one grows quite fearful. Good lord, after all, as a point of honor the sorrow-stricken person always has some self-esteem about his sorrow. He is not going to confide in everybody; he demands silence—something one can be sure of with you. And yet when one has thereby been reassured, one becomes anxious again, for your silence is more silent than the grave, and it no doubt holds many similar deposits. You know about everything, do not get mixed up; the very next second you can pull out another secret and begin where you left off. Then one regrets having confided in you. Good lord! As a point of honor the sorrow-stricken person has some self-esteem about his sorrow. He wants the person he initiates into it to feel all its weight and meaning. You do not disappoint one's expectations, for you grasp the finest nuances better than the person himself. The very next moment I despair over the superiority that inheres in knowing so much about everything that nothing is new or unfamiliar. If I were an autocrat over all men, then God help you! I would have you locked up in a cage with me so that you belonged to me alone. And then, by seeing you day after day, I very likely would be arranging for myself the most tormenting anxiety. You have a demonic power that can tempt a person to want to risk everything, to want to have powers that he does not otherwise have and that he does not otherwise crave—just as long as you are gazing at him—that can tempt him to appear to be what he is not just in order to buy this approving smile and its ineffable reward. I would like very much to gaze upon you all day long and listen to you all night, and yet if I were to take some action, I would not do it in your presence for anything. One word from you could confuse everything. I lack the courage to confess my weakness in your presence; if I ever did, I would be the chief of cowards, because I would think that I had lost everything. Thus do you hold me captive with an indescribable power, and this same power makes me anxious; thus do I admire you, and yet at times I believe that you are mentally disordered. Is it not, in fact, a kind of mental disorder to have subjugated to such a degree every passion, every emotion, every mood under the cold regimentation of reflection! Is it not mental disorder to be normal in this way—pure idea, not a human being like the rest of us, flexible and yielding, lost and being lost! Is it not mental disorder always to be alert like this, always conscious, never vague and dreamy! —Right now I do not dare to see you, and yet I cannot get along without you. That is why I write to you and beg you not to take the trouble of answering. For safety's sake, I enclose no address. That is the way I want it. Then it is good to write to you, then I am safe—and happy in you.[1]

Your plan was superb, indeed, matchless. At odd moments I can still reach like a child for the heroic figure you held up before my admiring gaze with the explanation that this was my future, the heroic figure that would have made

III
224

me a hero if I had had the power to play the part. At the
time, I was completely carried away by the force of the illusion into an intoxication of imagination. To conclude one's
whole life in this way for the sake of one single girl! To make
oneself out a scoundrel, a deceiver, simply and solely to prove
how highly she is esteemed, because a person does not sacrifice his honor for a triviality! To brand oneself, to throw
away one's life! To take on the task of revenge and fulfill it
in a way utterly different from what people are able to do
with their empty gossip! To be that kind of hero—not in the
eyes of the world but to oneself—to be able to appeal to
nothing in defense against men but to live imprisoned within
one's own personality, to have in oneself one's own witness,
one's own judge, one's own prosecuting attorney, and in
oneself the only one. To abandon one's future life to the
tangle of thoughts that inevitably follow such a step, thereby
in a way, humanly speaking, to renounce the understanding!
To do all this for the sake of a girl! And if it could be done
over again, then, as you said, to have paid a girl the most
chivalrous and most erotic compliment, surpassing even the
most fantastic exploit simply because one would have used
only oneself! This remark made a deep impression on me.
Of course, it was not said fanatically—you a fanatic! It was
spoken with calm and cold good sense, out of professional
knowledge, as if you had thoroughly studied all the literature
of chivalry solely for the sake of the affair. To make a discovery in the sphere of the erotic [*erotiske Omfang*] was for
me what it must be for a thinker to discover a new category.

Unfortunately, I was not the artist with the strength for
such a performance or the perseverance. Fortunately, I saw
you rarely and only in out-of-the-way places. If I had had
you at my side, if you could have sat in the room, even if it
were in a corner, reading, writing, pursuing irrelevant matters, and yet—that I know all too well—and yet aware of
everything, I believe I would have commenced. If that had
happened, it would have been terrible. Or is it not a terrible
thing day after day, calmly and coldly, to hex the beloved
into a lie! And suppose she had seized upon the resources at

her disposal—feminine supplications. Suppose she had tearfully pleaded with me, beseeched me by my honor, my conscience, my eternal salvation, my peace in life and death, my peace both here and in eternity![2] I shudder just to think of it.

I have not forgotten the specific hints you dropped, since I did not dare to raise any objections at all and was only all too enthralled. "If a girl in using these means is within her rights, then one should allow them to work their influence—yes, more than that, help her to use them. In relation to a girl, one should be chivalrous enough not merely to be oneself but also to be the prosecuting attorney on her behalf. If she is not within her rights, then it is all meaningless, and one lets them slip past." That is true, absolutely, perfectly true, but I do not have that good sense. "What foolish contradiction is often found in human cowardliness and courage. One fears to see something terrible but has the courage to do it. You abandon the girl; that is the terrible thing. For that you have courage, but you lack the courage to see her grow pale, to count her tears, to witness her distress. And yet, compared with the other, that is nothing. If you know what you want, why and how much, then you ought to inspect, you ought to respect, every argument and not sneak away from something in the hope that your imagination is duller than actuality. In doing so, you are also deceiving yourself, for when the time comes that you visualize her distress, your lively imagination will be stirred in quite another way than it will be if you have seen it and have helped her to make everything as anxious and dreadful for you as possible." It is true, every word is true, but it is a truth so very cold and logical, as if the world were dead. It does not convince me, it moves me not. I admit that I am weak, that I was weak, that I shall never be that strong or undaunted. Reflect on the whole matter, imagine yourself in my place, but do not forget that you actually love her as much as I loved her. I am convinced that you would win out, that you would carry it through, that you would surmount all the terrors, that you would delude her with your fraud. What would happen? If you were not lucky enough to have your

hair turn gray and to breathe your last within an hour after
the strain was all over, then, as entailed by your plan, you
would have to continue the fraud. I am convinced that you
would succeed in doing so. Are you not afraid of losing your
sanity? Are you not afraid of running headlong into a dreadful passion called contempt for men? To be in the right this
way, to be faithful, and yet to pass oneself off as a scoundrel,
and then in the deception to mock all the wretchedness that
so often struts and swaggers, but also to sneer at what is
superior in the world! What head could endure anything like
this! Do you not think that it would often become necessary
to get up in the night and drink a glass of cold water or sit
on the side of the bed and take stock! Suppose I had commenced—it would have been impossible to go on with it. I
chose another way: I quietly left Copenhagen and went to
Stockholm. According to your plans, this would have been
wrong. I should have gone openly. Think of her standing
near the customhouse—I shudder at the thought. Think of
me spotting her only after the machinery was set in motion.
I believe I would have gone mad. I have no doubt that you
would have had the strength to remain calm. If it had been
necessary, if you had expected her to appear at the customhouse, you would have taken the seamstress along and traveled with her. If it had been necessary, not only would you
have suborned a girl, but merely for the sake of aiding the
beloved, you would also have seduced a girl, actually seduced, ravaged, and pillaged, if necessary. But suppose at
some time you awakened suddenly in the night and were
unable to recognize yourself, had changed places with the
character you were using for your pious deception. This I
must admit: you certainly did not believe that one should
enter into anything like this rashly; yes, you even remarked
casually that it would never be urgently necessary to use this
method if the girl herself were not guilty, either of being
careless enough not to recognize the tokens of sympathy or
of being selfish enough to let them pass. But on this very
point, would there not come a moment when she would
realize what she should have done, when she would despair

III
227

over the consequences of her omission, which still was due
not so much to her insensitivity as to the other's whole personality. Would not her experience have been the same as
mine? She would not have suspected, would not have dreamed
what forces she was setting in motion, what passions she was
playing with. And thus she was in fact guilty of everything,
although innocent. Would this not be too rigorous toward
her! If I were to do anything here, I would prefer to quarrel,
become angry—but this silent, objective denunciation!

No! No! No! I could not, I cannot, I will not, I will not
do it for anything. No! No! No! I could despair over these
written symbols, standing there alongside each other cold
and like idle street-loafers, and the one "no" says no more
than the next. You should hear how my passion inflects them.
Would that I stood beside you, that I could tear myself from
you with the last "no" as Don Giovanni did from the Com-
mandatore, whose hand was no colder than the good sense
with which you irresistibly sweep me off my feet. And yet,
if I stood face to face with you, I would hardly say more
than one "no," because before I got any further you no doubt
would interrupt me with the cold response: Yes, yes.

What I did was very mediocre and clumsy. Go ahead and
laugh at me. When a swimmer, practiced in diving from the
ship's mast and in turning somersaults before touching water,
invites another person to follow his example, and this one
climbs down the ladder instead, sticking out one foot and
then the other, and finally flops in—then, well, then I do not
need to find out what the first one does. One day I stayed
away, and without having said a word to her, I boarded a
ship to Stockholm. I ran away and hid from everybody. God
in heaven help her to find her own explanation! Have you
seen her[3]—the girl whose name I never mention, whose name
I was not man enough to write, for my hand would shake
with terror. Have you seen her? Is she pale, or perhaps dead?
Does she grieve, or has she invented an explanation that con-
soles her? Does she still walk lightly, or is her head bowed
and is her demeanor troubled? Good lord, my imagination
is able to supply everything. Are her lips pale, those lips I

III
228

admired even though I permitted myself only to kiss her hand.[4] Is she weary and thoughtful, she who was as full of bliss as a child. Write, I beg you. No, do not write. I wish for no letter from you, I do not want to hear anything about her, I believe nothing. I believe no one, not even her herself. Were she to stand as large as life before me, gayer than ever before, I would not be happy, I would not believe her, I would think it a trick to mock me or to console me. Have you seen her? No! I hope that you have not ventured to see her or to become involved in my love story. If I happen to find that out! When a girl becomes unhappy, then along come all those ravenous monsters wanting to satiate their psychological hunger and thirst or to write novels. If only I dared to rush out and at least keep those blowflies from the fruit, which was sweeter to me than everything else, more delicate and tender to gaze upon than a peach in its prime, gloriously decked out in silk and velvet.

What am I doing at present? I begin from the beginning, and then I begin backwards. I avoid every external reminder of it all, while night and day, awake and in my dreams, I am constantly preoccupied with it. I never speak her name, and I thank fate for having acquired a false name by mistake. A name, my name—after all, it actually belongs to her. Would that I could get rid of it. My own name is enough to remind me of everything, and all life seems to contain only allusions to this past. The day before I left, I read in *Adresseavisen*[5] "that sixteen yards of heavy black silk cloth are for sale because of a change in plan." I wonder what the first plan could have been, perhaps a bridal dress! Would that I, too, could sell my name in the newspaper because of a change in plan. If a powerful spirit were to take away my name and offer it back to me resplendent with immortal honors, I would hurl it away, far away, and would beg for the most insignificant, the most commonplace name, to be called no. 14 like a blue boy.[6] Of what avail to me is a name that is not mine; of what avail to me is a glorious name, even if it were mine:

For what is the flattering voice of fame
To the sigh of love from a maiden's breast.[7]

What am I doing at present? I am walking in my sleep
during the day and lying awake at night. I am busy and
working hard, a model of domesticity and home industry. I
moisten my finger, I press my foot on the treadle, I stop the
wheel, I set the spindle in motion—I spin. But when I come
to put the spinning wheel away in the evening, nothing is
there, and what has happened to what I have spun only my
cat knows. I am active and clever, indefatigable, but what
comes of it all? Compared with me, the peatman performs
miracles. In short, if you want to understand, if you want to
have an idea of my fruitless efforts, then understand spiritually the pertinence of the poet's words to my thoughts; that
is everything I can say.

> Die Wolken treiben hin und her,
> Sie sind so matt, sie sind so schwer;
> Da stürzen rauschend sie herab,
> Der Schoos der Erde wird ihr Grab.[8]

> [The clouds are drifting to and fro,
> They are so sad and weary—lo,
> Then down they plunge, and, as they crave,
> The womb of earth will be their grave.]

Surely I need say no more to you, or, more correctly, I rather
would need you to be able to say more, to express clearly
and intelligently what my groping thoughts can only franti-
cally intimate.

If I were to relate everything fully, my letter would be
exceedingly long, at least as long as a bad year and as long
as the days of which it is said: I have no pleasure in them.[9]
But I do have one advantage: I can stop anywhere, just as I
can clip at any time the thread I am myself spinning. And
with this, God speed you! He who believes in existence
[*Tilværelsen*] is well insured; he will achieve everything, just

as surely as the man hides his feelings who holds a hat without a crown in front of his face when he prays.

Sir! I have the honor etc.

—Yes, whether I will or not,

I still remain,
Your
devoted, nameless friend[10]

September 19

My Silent Confidant:

Job! Job! O Job! Is that really all you said, those beautiful words: The Lord gave, and the Lord took away; blessed be the name of the Lord?[11] Did you say no more? In all your afflictions did you just keep on repeating them? Why were you silent for seven days and nights? What went on in your soul? When all existence collapsed upon you and lay like broken pottery around you, did you immediately have this suprahuman self-possession, did you immediately have this interpretation of love, this cheerful boldness of trust and faith? Is your door then shut to the grief-stricken person, can he hope for no other relief from you than what miserable worldly wisdom poorly affords, lecturing on the perfection of life? Do you know nothing more to say than that? Do you dare to say no more than what professional comforters scantily measure out to the individual, what professional comforters, like formal masters of ceremonies, lay down for the individual, that in the hour of need it is appropriate to say: The Lord gave, and the Lord took away; blessed be the name of the Lord—no more, no less, just as they say "God bless you" when one sneezes! No, you who in your prime were the sword of the oppressed,[12] the stave of the old, and the staff of the brokenhearted, you did not disappoint men when everything went to pieces—then you became the voice of the suffering, the cry of the grief-stricken, the shriek of the terrified, and a relief to all who bore their torment in silence, a faithful witness to all the affliction and laceration there can be in a heart, an unfailing spokesman who dared to lament "in bitterness of soul"[13] and to strive with God. Why is this kept secret? Woe to him who devours the widows and the fatherless and cheats them out of their inheritance,[14] but woe also to him who would cunningly cheat the sorrowing of sorrow's temporary comfort in airing its sorrow and "quarreling with God."[15] Or is there so much fear of God today that the sorrowing do not need what was customary in those days of old? Perhaps we do not dare to complain to God? Has the fear of God then increased—or fear and cowardliness? In our time it is thought that genuine expressions of grief, the despairing language of passion, must be assigned to the poets, who then like attorneys in a lower court plead the cause of the suffering before the tribunal of human compassion. No one dares to go further than that. Speak up, then, unforgettable Job, repeat everything you said, you powerful spokesman who, fearless as a roaring lion, appears before the tribunal of the Most High! Your speech is pithy, and in your heart is the fear of God even when you bring complaints, when you defend your despair to your friends who jump up like highwaymen to attack you with their speeches, even when you, provoked by your friends, crush their wisdom under foot and scorn their defense of the Lord as if it were the miserable shrewdness of a decrepit court functionary or a politically shrewd government official. I need you, a man who knows how to complain so loudly that he is heard in heaven, where God confers with Satan on drawing up plans against a man.[16] Complain—the Lord is not afraid, he can certainly defend himself. But how is he to defend himself when no one dares to complain as befits a man. Speak up, raise your voice, speak loudly. To be sure, God can speak louder—after all, he has the thunder[17]—but that, too, is a response, an explanation, trustworthy, faithful, original, a reply from God himself, which, even if it crushes a man, is more glorious than the gossip and rumors about the righteousness of Governance that are invented by human wisdom and spread by old women and fractional men.

My unforgettable benefactor, tormented Job! Do I dare to attach myself to your following, may I listen to you! Do not push me away; I do not stand fraudulently by your hearth, my tears are not false, even though I am able to do no more than to weep with you. Just as the joyful person seeks rejoicing, shares in it, even if what makes him most joyful is the joy residing within himself, so the sorrowing person seeks out sorrow. I have not owned the world, have not had seven sons and three daughters.[18] But one who owned very little may indeed also have lost everything; one who lost the beloved has in a sense lost sons and daughters, and one who

lost honor and pride and along with it the vitality and meaning of life—he, too, has in a sense been stricken with malig-
nant sores.[19]

Your
nameless friend

October 11

My Silent Confidant:

I am at the end of my rope. I am nauseated by life; it is insipid—without salt and meaning. If I were hungrier than Pierrot,[20] I would not choose to eat the explanation people offer. One sticks a finger into the ground to smell what country one is in; I stick my finger into the world—it has no smell. Where am I? What does it mean to say: the world? What is the meaning of that word? Who tricked me into this whole thing and leaves me standing here? Who am I? How did I get into the world? Why was I not asked about it, why was I not informed of the rules and regulations but just thrust into the ranks as if I had been bought from a peddling shanghaier[21] of human beings? How did I get involved in this big enterprise called actuality? Why should I be involved? Isn't it a matter of choice? And if I am compelled to be involved, where is the manager—I have something to say about this. Is there no manager? To whom shall I make my complaint? After all, life is a debate—may I ask that my observations be considered? If one has to take life as it is, would it not be best to find out how things go? What does it mean: a deceiver? Does not Cicero say that such a person can be exposed by asking: *cui bono* [to whose benefit]?[22] Anyone may ask me and I ask everyone whether I have benefited in any way by making myself and a girl unhappy. Guilt—what does it mean? Is it hexing? Is it not positively known how it comes about that a person is guilty? Will no one answer me? Is it not, then, of the utmost importance to all the gentlemen involved?

My mind is numb—or is it more correct to say I am losing it? One moment I am weak and weary, yes, practically dead with apathy; the next moment I am in a rage and in desperation rush from one end of the world to the other to find someone on whom I can vent my anger. My whole being screams in self-contradiction. [23]How did it happen that I became guilty? Or am I not guilty? Why, then, am I called that in every language? What kind of miserable invention is this human language, which says one thing and means another?

Has something happened to me, is not all this something that has befallen me? Could I anticipate that my whole being would undergo a change, that I would become another person? Can it be that something darkly hidden in my soul burst forth? But if it lay darkly hidden, how then could I anticipate it? But if I could not anticipate it, then I certainly am innocent. Would I also have been guilty if I had had a nervous breakdown? What kind of wretched jargon is this human speech called language, which is intelligible only to a clique? Are not the dumb animals wiser in never talking about such things? —Am I unfaithful? If she were to go on loving me and never loved anyone else, she would then certainly be faithful to me. If I go on wanting to love only her, am I then unfaithful? Indeed, we are both doing the same thing—how then do I become a deceiver because I manifest my faithfulness by deceiving? Why should she be in the right and I in the wrong? If both of us are faithful, why then is this expressed in human language in such a way that she is faithful and I am a deceiver?

Even if the whole world rose up against me, even if all the scholastics argued with me, even if it were a matter of life and death—I am still in the right. No one shall take that away from me, even if there is no language in which I can say it. I have acted rightly. My love cannot find expression in a marriage. If I do that, she is crushed. Perhaps the possibility appeared tempting to her. I cannot help it; it was that to me also. The moment it becomes a matter of actuality, all is lost, then it is too late. The actuality in which she is supposed to have her meaning remains but a shadow for me, a shadow that trots alongside my essential spiritual actuality, a shadow that sometimes makes me laugh and sometimes wants to enter disturbingly into my existence [*Existens*]. It would end with my fumbling for her as if I were grabbing at a shadow or as if I stretched out my hand after a shadow. Would not her life then be ruined? To me she is as if dead— yes, she could almost tempt me to wish her dead. Suppose, then, that I crush her, volatilize her in the very moment I want to make her an actuality, instead of the other alterna-

III
236

tive, that I keep her in a true, even though in another sense uneasy, actuality—what then? Then language declares me guilty, for I ought to have anticipated that.

What kind of power is it that wants to deprive me of my honor and my pride and do it in such a meaningless way? Have I been abandoned? Am I inevitably guilty, a deceiver, whatever I do, even if I do nothing?

Or have I perhaps gone mad? Then the best thing to do would be to lock me up, for people cravenly fear particularly the utterances of the insane and the dying. What does it mean: mad? What must I do to enjoy civic esteem, to be regarded as sensible? Why does no one answer? I offer a reasonable reward to anyone who invents a new word! I have set forth the alternatives. Is there anyone so clever that he knows more than two? But if he does not know more, then it certainly is nonsense that I am mad, unfaithful, and a deceiver, while the girl is faithful and reasonable and esteemed by people. Or am I to be blamed for making the first part as beautiful as possible? Thanks! When I saw her joy in being loved, I subordinated myself and everything she pointed to under the magic spell of erotic love. Is it blameworthy that I was able to do it or blameworthy that I did it?

Who is to blame but her and the third factor, from whence no one knows, which moved me with its stimulus and transformed me? After all, what I have done is praised in others. —Or is becoming a poet my compensation? I reject all compensation, I demand my rights—that is, my honor. I did not ask to become one, and I will not buy it at this price. —Or, if I am guilty, then I certainly should be able to repent of my guilt and make it good again. Tell me how. On top of that, must I perhaps repent that the world plays with me as a child plays with a beetle? —Or is it perhaps best to forget the whole thing? Forget—indeed, I shall have ceased to be if I forget it. Or what kind of life would it be if along with my beloved I have lost honor and pride and lost them in such a way that no one knows how it happened, for which reason I can never retrieve them again? Shall I allow myself to be shoved out in this manner? Why, then, was I shoved in? I never requested it.

Someone imprisoned on bread and water is better off than I am. Humanly speaking, my observations are the poorest diet imaginable, and yet I feel a satisfaction in carrying on at a scale as macrocosmic as possible in all my microcosmicness.

I do not converse with people, but in order not to break off all communication with them, as well as not to give them blather for their money, I have collected quite a few poems, pithy sayings, proverbs, and brief maxims from the immortal Greek and Roman writers who have been admired in every age. I have added to this anthology several superb quotations from Balle's catechism published under the license of the orphans' home. If anyone asks me anything, I have a ready answer. I quote the classics as well as Per Degn,[24] and as a bonus I quote Balle's catechism.[25] "Even if we have attained all desirable honor, we ought not to let ourselves be carried away by pride and haughtiness." Then I deceive no one. Indeed, how many are there who always utter a truth or a good comment. "As a rule, the word 'world' includes both heaven and earth and everything found therein."

What could be gained if I did say something—there is no one who understands me. My pain and my suffering are nameless, even as I myself am nameless, one who, although he has no name, nevertheless may always be something to you and in any case remains

Your devoted

III
238

November 15

My Silent Confidant:

   If I did not have Job! It is impossible to describe all the shades of meaning and how manifold the meaning is that he has for me. I do not read him as one reads another book, with the eyes, but I lay the book, as it were, on my heart and read it with the eyes of the heart, in a *clairvoyance* interpreting the specific points in the most diverse ways. Just as the child puts his schoolbook under his pillow to make sure he has not forgotten his lesson when he wakes up in the morning, so I take the book to bed with me at night. Every word by him is food and clothing and healing for my wretched soul. Now a word by him arouses me from my lethargy and awakens new restlessness; now it calms the sterile raging within me, stops the dreadfulness in the mute nausea of my passion. Have you really read Job? Read him, read him again and again. I do not even have the heart to write one single outcry from him in a letter to you, even though I find my joy in transcribing over and over everything he has said, sometimes in Danish script and sometimes in Latin script,[26] sometimes in one format and sometimes in another. Every transcription of this kind is laid upon my sick heart as a God's-hand-plaster.[27] Indeed, on whom did God lay his hand as on Job! But quote him—that I cannot do. That would be wanting to put in my own pittance, wanting to make his words my own in the presence of another. When I am alone, I do it, appropriate everything, but as soon as anyone comes, I know very well what a young man is supposed to do when the elderly are speaking.

III
239

   In the whole Old Testament there is no other figure one approaches with so much human confidence and boldness and trust as Job, simply because he is so human in every way, because he resides in a *confinium* touching on poetry.[28] Nowhere in the world has the passion of anguish found such expression. What are Philoctetes[29] and his laments, which remain continually earthbound and do not terrify the gods. What is Philoctetes' situation compared with Job's, where the idea is constantly in motion.

Forgive me for telling everything—after all, you are my confidant, and you are unable to answer. If anyone learned about this, I would be indescribably distressed. At night I can have all the lights burning, the whole house illuminated. Then I stand up and read in a loud voice, almost shouting, some passage by him. Or I open my window and cry out his words into the world. If Job is a poetic character, if there never was any man who spoke this way, then I make his words my own and take upon myself the responsibility. I cannot do more, for who has such eloquence as Job, who is able to improve upon anything he said?

Although I have read the book again and again, each word remains new to me. Every time I come to it, it is born anew as something original or becomes new and original in my soul. Like an inebriate, I imbibe all the intoxication of passion little by little, until by this prolonged sipping I become almost unconscious in drunkenness. But at the same time, I hasten to it with indescribable impatience. Half a word—and my soul rushes into his thought, into his outcry; more swiftly than the sounding-line sinker seeks the bottom of the sea, more swiftly than lightning seeks the conductor does my soul glide therein and remain there.

Other times I am more calm. Then I do not read, then I slump like an ancient ruin[30] and observe everything. Then it seems as if I were a little child who pokes around the room or sits in a corner with his toys. Then I get a curious feeling. I cannot understand what makes the adults so passionate, I cannot comprehend what they are disputing about, and yet I cannot quit listening. Then I think that it is evil men who have brought all this grief upon Job, that it is his friends, who now sit there barking at him. Then I weep aloud; a nameless anxiety about the world and life and men and everything crushes my soul.

Then I wake up and begin to read him aloud again with all my strength and all my heart. Then suddenly I am mute; I no longer hear anything, no longer see anything, and have only an intimation in dim outline of Job sitting at the hearth

III
240

and of his friends, but no one says a word.[31] Yet this silence hides all horrors within itself as a secret no one dares to name.

Then the silence is broken, and Job's tormented soul breaks forth in powerful cries. These I understand; these words I make my own. At the same time, I sense the contradiction and smile at myself as one smiles at a little child who has donned his father's clothes. Indeed, is it not something to smile at if anyone else but Job would say: Alas, if only a man could take God to court as a child of man does his fellow.[32] And yet anxiety comes over me, as if I still did not understand what someday I would come to understand, as if the horror I was reading about was waiting for me, as if by reading about it I brought it upon myself, just as one becomes ill with the sickness one reads about.[33]

December 14   III
241

My Silent Confidant:

Everything has its time;[34] the rage of fever is over, and I am like a convalescent.

The secret in Job, the vital force, the nerve, the idea, is that Job, despite everything, is in the right. On the basis of this position, he qualifies as an exception to all human observations, and his perseverance and power manifest authority and authorization. To him every human interpretation is only a misconception, and to him in relation to God all his troubles are but a sophism that he, to be sure, cannot solve, but he trusts that God can do it. Every *argumentum ad hominem* [argumentation based on the opponent's personal circumstances] is used against him, but he undauntedly upholds his conviction. He affirms that he is on good terms with God; he knows he is innocent and pure in the very core of his being, where he also knows it before the Lord, and yet all the world refutes him. Job's greatness is that freedom's passion in him is not smothered or quieted down by a wrong expression. In similar circumstances, this passion is often smothered in a person when faintheartedness and petty anxiety have allowed him to think he is suffering because of his sins, when that was not at all the case. His soul lacked the perseverance to carry through an idea when the world incessantly disagreed with him. It can be very becoming and true and humble if a person believes that misfortune has struck him because of his sins, but this belief may also be the case because he vaguely conceives of God as a tyrant, something he meaninglessly expresses by promptly placing him under ethical determinants. —Job did not become demonic, either. In such a case, for example, a person will admit that God is in the right, although he believes that he himself is. He wants, so to speak, to show that he loves God even when God is tempting [*frister*][35] the lover. Or, since God cannot remake the world for his sake, he will be sufficiently noble to go on loving him. This is an altogether demonic passion, which merits a separate psychological treatment, whether it humorously, so to speak, halts the dispute in order to avoid

III
242

any more disruption or culminates in an egotistical defiance on the strength of its feelings.

Job continues to take the position that he is in the right. He does it in such a way that he thereby witnesses to the noble, human, bold confidence that knows what a human being is, knows that despite his being frail, despite his swift withering away like the flower,[36] that in freedom he still has something of greatness, has a consciousness that even God cannot wrest from him even though he gave it to him.[37] Furthermore, Job maintains his position in such a way that in him are manifest the love and trust that are confident that God can surely explain everything if one can only speak with him.

The friends give Job enough to do; the conflict with them is a purgatory in which the thought that he nevertheless is in the right is purified. If he himself should lack the power and the ingenuity to disquiet his conscience and to terrify his soul, if he should lack the imagination to become afraid for himself because of the guilt and blame that might secretly dwell in his innermost being, then the friends help him with their obvious insinuations, with their offensive charges, which like envious divining rods might be able to call forth what lay in deepest concealment. Their main argument is his calamity, and thus everything is an established fact for them. Job could certainly be expected either to lose his senses or to collapse exhausted in his wretchedness and surrender unconditionally. Eliphas, Bildad, Zophar, and, most of all, Elihu, who rises up *integer* [with renewed vigor][38] when the others are tired out, present versions of the theme that his calamity is a punishment; he must repent, beg forgiveness, and then all will be well again.

Meanwhile, Job holds fast to his interpretation. His position is like a permit by which he departs from the world and men. It is a claim that men do not acknowledge, but still Job does not renounce it. He uses every means to influence his friends. He tries to move them to compassion ("Have pity on me"[39]); his voice shocks them ("You are weaving lies"[40]).

In vain. His cry of anguish becomes more and more intense as his friends' opposition drives his thoughts even deeper into his sufferings. But this does not influence his friends, and this is not the central issue. They willingly concede that he suffers and has reason to cry out that "the wild ass does not bray when it has grass,"[41] but they insist that he must see punishment in this.

How, then, is Job's position to be explained? The explanation is this: the whole thing is an *ordeal* [*Prøvelse*].[42] But this explanation leaves a new difficulty, which I have tried to clarify for myself in the following manner. It is true that science and scholarship consider and interpret life and man's relationship to God in this life. But what science is of such a nature that it has room for a relationship that is defined as an ordeal, which viewed infinitely does not exist at all but exists only for the individual? Such a science does not and cannot possibly exist. Moreover, the question arises: How does the individual discover that it is an ordeal? The individual who has any notion at all of an existence [*Existents*] in thought and consciousness of being easily perceives that this is more quickly said than done, more quickly said than finished, or more quickly said than maintained. First of all, the event must be cleared of its cosmic associations and get a religious baptism and a religious name, then one must appear before ethics for examination, and then comes the expression: an ordeal. Before this, the individual obviously does not exist by virtue of thought. Any explanation is possible, and the maelstrom of passion begins to spin. Only those with no conception or a low conception of living by virtue of spirit are quickly finished in this respect; they have a half hour of reading ready for consolation, just as many philosophical neophytes have a hasty, superficial conclusion to offer.

Job's greatness, then, is not even that he said: The Lord gave, and the Lord took away; blessed be the name of the Lord[43]—something he in fact said at the beginning and did

III
244

not repeat later. Rather, Job's significance is that the disputes
at the boundaries of faith are fought out in him, that the
colossal revolt of the wild and aggressive powers of passion
is presented here.

For this reason Job does not bring composure as does a
hero of faith,[44] but he does give temporary alleviation. Job
is, so to speak, the whole weighty defense plea on man's
behalf in the great case between God and man, the lengthy
and appalling trial that started with Satan's creation of dis-
cord between God and Job and ends with the whole thing
having been an ordeal.

This category, ordeal, is not esthetic, ethical, or dog-
matic—it is altogether transcendent. Only as knowledge about
an ordeal, that it is an ordeal, would it be included in a dogmatics. But as soon as the knowledge enters, the resilience
of the ordeal is impaired, and the category is actually another
category. This category is absolutely transcendent and places
a person in a purely personal relationship of opposition to
God, in a relationship such that he cannot allow himself to
be satisfied with any explanation at second hand.

That there are many who promptly have this category handy
for every occasion, even when the oatmeal burns, simply
proves that they have not grasped it. The person with a mature awareness of the world has an extremely long, round-
about way before he reaches it. This is the situation with Job,
who proves the dimensions of his world view by the stead-
fastness with which he knows how to avoid all cunning ethical evasions and wily devices.[45] Job is not a hero of faith; he
gives birth to the category of "ordeal" with excruciating anguish precisely because he is so developed that he does not
possess it in childlike immediacy.

That this category could tend to cancel out and suspend
all actuality by defining it as an ordeal in relation to eternity,
I readily perceive. But this doubt has not gained the upper
hand over me, because, inasmuch as ordeal is a *temporary*
category,[46] it *eo ipso* is defined in relation to time and therefore must be annulled in time.

This is the extent of my understanding now, and as I have let myself initiate you into everything, I write this also to you on my own. From you, as you know, I ask nothing, save that I may be permitted to remain

Your devoted

My Silent Confidant:

The storms have spent their fury—the thunderstorm[47] is over—Job has been censured before the face of humankind—the Lord and Job have come to an understanding, they are reconciled, "the confidence of the Lord dwells again in the tents of Job as in former days"[48]—men have come to understand Job. *Now* they come to him and eat bread with him and are sorry for him and console him; his brothers and sisters, each one of them, give him a farthing and a gold ring—Job is blessed and has received everything *double*.[49] —This is called a *repetition*.

How beneficent a thunderstorm is! How blessed it is to be rebuked by God! As a rule, a person very easily becomes defiant when censured; when God judges, then he subsides, and, surrounded by the love that wishes to educate him, he forgets the pain.

Who could have imagined this ending? Yet no other ending is thinkable, and not this one, either. When everything has stalled, when thought is immobilized, when language is silent, when explanation returns home in despair—then there has to be a thunderstorm. Who can understand this? And yet who can conceive of anything else?

Was Job proved to be in the wrong? Yes, eternally, for there is no higher court than the one that judged him. Was Job proved to be in the right? Yes, eternally, by being proved to be in the wrong *before God*.[50]

So there is a repetition, after all. When does it occur? Well, that is hard to say in any human language. When did it occur for Job? When every *thinkable* human certainty and probability were impossible. Bit by bit he loses everything, and hope thereby gradually vanishes, inasmuch as actuality, far from being placated, rather lodges stronger and stronger allegations against him. From the point of view of immediacy, everything is lost. His friends, especially Bildad,[51] know but one way out, that by submitting to the punishment he may dare to hope for a repetition to the point of overflowing. Job will not have it. With that the knot and the entanglement are tightened and can be untied only by a thunderstorm.

For me this story is an ineffable comfort. Was it not fortunate that I did not go through with your ingenious, admirable plan. Humanly speaking, it may have been cowardliness on my part, but perhaps now Governance can all the more easily help me.

My only regret is that I did not ask the girl to give me my freedom. I am sure that she would have done it.[52] Indeed, who can grasp the generosity of a girl? And yet I cannot really regret it, for I know that I did what I did because I was too proud on her behalf.

If I had not had Job! I say no more lest I burden you with my everlasting refrain.

Your devoted

February 17

My Silent Confidant:

I am inside. With clean hands—as the thieves usually say—
or at the king's pleasure?[53] I do not know. All I know is that
I am inside here and that I do not stir from the spot. Here I
stand. On my head or on my feet? I do not know. All I
know is that I am standing and have been standing *suspenso
gradu* [immobilized] for a whole month now, without moving a foot or making one single movement.

I am waiting for a thunderstorm[54]—and for repetition.[55]
And yet I would be happy and indescribably blessed if the
thunderstorm would only come, even if my sentence were
that no repetition is possible.

What will be the effect of this thunderstorm? It will make
me fit to be a husband. It will shatter my whole personality—I am prepared. It will render me almost unrecognizable
to myself—I am unwavering even though I am standing on
one foot. My honor will be saved, my pride will be redeemed, and no matter how it transforms me, I nevertheless
hope that the recollection of it will remain with me as an
unfailing consolation, will remain when I have experienced
what I in a certain sense dread more than suicide, because it
will play havoc with me on quite another scale. If the thunderstorm does not come, then I will become crafty. I will
not die, not at all, but I will pretend to be dead so that my
relatives and friends may bury me. When they lay me in my
coffin, I will in all secrecy hide my expectancy. No one will
get to know it, for people would take care not to bury someone in whom there is still some life.

In other respects, I am doing my best to make myself into
a husband. I sit and clip myself, take away everything that
is incommensurable in order to become commensurable. Every
morning I discard all the impatience and infinite striving of
my soul—but it does not help, for the next moment it is
there again. Every morning I shave off the beard of all my
ludicrousness—but it does not help, for the next morning
my beard is just as long again. I *recall* myself, just as the
bank calls in its paper money in order to put new money in

circulation—but it does not work. I convert my whole wealth of ideas, my mortgages, into matrimonial pocket money— alas! alas! in that kind of coin my wealth amounts to very little.

But I will be brief; my position and my situation do not permit me to use many words.

Your devoted[56]

[INCIDENTAL OBSERVATIONS BY CONSTANTIN CONSTANTIUS]

Although I forsook the world long ago and renounced all theorizing, I nevertheless cannot deny that because of my interest in the young man he set me off my pendulum beat somewhat. It is easy to see that he is caught in a total misunderstanding. He is suffering from a misplaced melancholy high-mindedness that belongs nowhere except in a poet's brain. He is waiting for a thunderstorm that is supposed to make him into a husband, a nervous breakdown perhaps. It is completely the reverse. In fact, he is one of those who say: Battalion, about-face![1]—instead of turning around himself. This can be expressed in another way: the girl must go. If I myself were not so old, I would give myself the pleasure of taking her simply to help the man.

He rejoices over not having carried out my "ingenious" plan. That is just like him. Even now he does not see that it would have been the only right thing to do! It is impossible to get involved with him, and thus it is fortunate that he does not wish for a reply, because to correspond with a man who holds a trump card such as a thunderstorm in his hand would be ludicrous. If he only had my sagacity. I say nothing else. It is his own business if he would want to give a religious expression to his expectancy if it is fulfilled—I have no objection to that. But it is always good to have done everything human sagacity can prescribe. I should have been the one—I would have been more helpful to the girl. Now it perhaps will be far more difficult for her to forget him. The trouble is that she did not reach the point of screaming. There must be screaming; it is beneficial, like bleeding with a bruise. A girl must be allowed to scream; then she has nothing to scream about later but quickly forgets.[2]

He did not take my advice, and now most likely she is grieving. I can well understand that this must be a real calamity for him. If there were a girl who would remain unmarried and be faithful to me, I would fear her more than anything else in all the world, I would fear her more than liberals fear a tyrant. She would trouble me; at every moment she would be in my consciousness like an aching tooth. She would trouble me because she would be ideal, and I am too proud, when it comes right down to that, of my feelings to put up with one single person's having stronger and more enduring feelings than I have. If she remained on that ideal pinnacle, I would have to accept my life as being *in pausa* [in a state of rest] instead of going forward.[3] There might be someone who could not tolerate the painful admiration she extorted from him and would become so envious of her that he would use every means to get her dislodged, i.e., married.

If she were to say—as has so often been said and written and printed and read and forgotten and repeated—"I have loved you, now I confess it" ("*now*," although she probably has said it a hundred times before), "I have loved you more than I loved God" (that is not saying a little . . . . . and yet not very much, either, in our God-fearing times when fear of God would probably be an even rarer phenomenon)— then this probably would not upset him.[4] The ideal is not to perish of grief but to keep healthy and happy if possible and yet to save one's feelings. To be able to take another is not something great. It is a weakness, a very simple and plebian[5] virtuosity for which only the bourgeois give the call to arms. Anyone with an artistic eye for life readily sees that it is an error[6] that cannot be rectified, not even by marrying seven times.

Moreover, if he repents of not asking her for his freedom, he might as well save himself the trouble, for it would not have helped much. In all human probability he simply would have supplied her with more ammunition against him, because actually to ask for freedom is quite different from doing a girl the favor of explaining that she was his muse. Here again we see that he is a poet. A poet seems to be born to be a fool for the girls.[7] If a girl made a fool of him to his face, he would think it generous of her. He may instead consider himself fortunate that he did not start anything like that.[8] Then she presumably would have gone about things in earnest.[9] She would have tried her hand not only with the little multiplication table of erotic love, which would be permissible and she would be within her rights, but also with the big multiplication table[10] of marriage. She would have had God vouch for her, called on everything that is holy, impounded every precious memory that could reside in his soul.[11] In this sphere, when the occasion arises, many a girl[12] quite unabashedly uses a deceit that not even a seducer[13] allows himself. One who moves in the realm of the erotic by the help of God or wants to be loved for God's sake ceases to be himself and tries to be stronger than heaven and more important than an individual's eternal salvation.[14] Suppose the girl had taken him to task this way—he perhaps would never have forgotten it or recovered from it, since he presumably would have been sufficiently chivalrous not to listen to any reasonable advice from me but would have taken every outcry of hers to be bona fide and preserved it as an eternal truth. Suppose that later it had proved to be an extravagance, a little lyrical impromptu, an emotional excursion[15]—well, maybe his idea[16] of generosity would have helped him here, too.[17]

My friend is a poet, and this romantic faith in women is intrinsic to a poet. With all due respect, I say that I am a prose writer. As far as the other sex is concerned, I have my own opinion, or, more correctly, I have none at all,[18] for I have rarely seen a girl whose life could be comprehended in a category. She usually lacks the consistency required for admiring or scorning a person. Before a woman deceives another, she first deceives herself, and therefore there is no criterion at all.[19]

Eventually my young friend will come to understand. I do not have much confidence in his thunderstorm; I believe he would not have acted amiss if he had followed my advice. The idea was in motion in the young man's love, and therefore he engrossed me. The plan I suggested had the idea as its criterion. That is the most reliable in the world. If a per-

son pays attention to that in his life, anyone who wants to
deceive him is made a fool. The idea was worked out—in
my opinion he owed that to his beloved and to himself. If
she had been able to live in that manner—for which unusual
capacities other than inwardness are not needed—she would
have said to herself the minute he left her, "Whether he is a
deceiver or not, whether he comes back or not, I will have
no more to do with him; what I keep is the ideality of my
own love, and that I will certainly know how to hold in
honor." If she had done that, my friend's position would
have been painful enough, for then he would have continued
in sympathetic pain and distress. But who would not endure
that if in the midst of all his grief he had the joy of admiring
the beloved? His life would have come to a stop just as hers,
but it would have stopped just as the tide, enchanted by the
power of music, comes to a stop. If she were unable to use
the idea as the regulator of her life, then the point would be
that by his pain he would not have interfered with her use
of another mode of advance.

III
252

May 31[1]

My Silent Confidant:

She is married—to whom I do not know, for when I read it in the newspaper I was so stunned that I dropped the paper and have not had the patience since then to check in detail. I am myself again. Here I have repetition; I understand everything, and life seems more beautiful to me than ever. It did indeed come like a thunderstorm,[2] although I am indebted to her generosity for its coming. Whoever it is she has chosen—I will not even say preferred, because in the capacity of a husband any one is preferable to me—she has certainly shown generosity toward me. Even if he were the handsomest man in the world, the epitome of charm, capable of enchanting any woman, even if she drove her whole sex to despair by giving him her "yes," she still acted generously, if in no other way than by completely forgetting me. Indeed, what is as beautiful as feminine generosity. Let the earthly beauty fade, let her eyes grow dull, let her erect form bend with the years, let her curly locks lose their alluring power when they are concealed by the modest hood, let her regal glance that ruled the world simply embrace and watch with motherly love over the little circle she safeguards—a girl who has been so generous never grows old. Let existence [*Tilværelsen*] reward her as it has, let it give her what she loved more; it also gave me what I loved more—myself, and gave it to me through her generosity.

I am myself again. This "self" that someone else would not pick up off the street I have once again. The split that was in my being is healed; I am unified again. The anxieties of sympathy that were sustained and nourished by my pride are no longer there to disintegrate and disrupt.

Is there not, then, a repetition? Did I not get everything double? Did I not get myself again and precisely in such a way that I might have a double sense of its meaning? Compared with such a repetition, what is a repetition of worldly possessions, which is indifferent toward the qualification of the spirit? Only his children did Job not receive double again,[3] for a human life cannot be redoubled that way. Here only repetition of the spirit is possible, even though it is never so perfect in time as in eternity, which is the true repetition.[4]

I am myself again; the machinery has been set in motion. The inveiglements in which I was entrapped have been rent asunder; the magic formula that hexed me so that I could not come back to myself has been broken. There is no longer anyone who raises his hand against me. My emancipation is assured; I am born to myself, for as long as Ilithyia[5] folds her hands, the one who is in labor cannot give birth.

It is over, my skiff is afloat. In a minute I shall be there where my soul longs to be, there where ideas spume with elemental fury, where thoughts arise uproariously like nations in migration,[6] there where at other times there is a stillness like the deep silence of the Pacific Ocean, a stillness in which one hears oneself speak even though the movement takes place only in one's interior being, there where each moment one is staking one's life, each moment losing it and finding it again.

I belong to the idea. When it beckons to me, I follow; when it makes an appointment, I wait for it day and night; no one calls me to dinner, no one expects me for supper. When the idea calls, I abandon everything, or, more correctly, I have nothing to abandon. I defraud no one, I sadden no one by being loyal to it; my spirit is not saddened by my having to make another sad. When I come home, no one reads my face, no one questions my demeanor. No one coaxes out of my being an explanation that not even I myself can give to another, whether I am beatific in joy or dejected in desolation, whether I have won life or lost it.

The beaker of inebriation is again offered to me, and already I am inhaling its fragrance, already I am aware of its bubbling music—but first a libation to her who saved a soul who sat in the solitude of despair: Praised be feminine generosity! Three cheers for the flight of thought, three cheers for the perils of life in service to the idea, three cheers for the hardships of battle, three cheers for the festive jubilation of victory, three cheers for the dance in the vortex of the infinite, three cheers for the cresting waves that hide me in the abyss, three cheers for the cresting waves that fling me above the stars!

To

Mr. X, Esq.
the real reader of this book

[CONCLUDING LETTER BY CONSTANTIN CONSTANTIUS]

Copenhagen, August[1] 1843

My dear Reader!

Forgive me for addressing you so familiarly, but we are, after all, *unter uns* [by ourselves]. Although you are indeed fictional, you are by no means a plurality to me but only one, and therefore we are just you and I.

If it is assumed that anyone who reads a book for one or another superficial reason unrelated to the book is not a genuine reader, then there perhaps are not many genuine readers left even for authors with a large reading public. Who in our day thinks of wasting any time on the curious idea that it is an art to be a good reader, not to mention spending time to become that? Of course, this deplorable state has its effect on an author who, in my opinion, very properly joins Clement of Alexandria in writing in such a way that the heretics are unable to understand it.[2]

An inquisitive female reader who reads the end of every book she finds on her bedside table to see if the lovers get each other will be disappointed, for surely the two lovers do get each other, but my friend, who also is indeed a male, gets no one. Since it is also apparent that this outcome is not due to a negligible coincidence, it becomes a grave matter for marriageable, man-hunting girls, who see their prospects diminished just by having to cross off one single male. —A concerned family man will perhaps fear that his son will go the same way as my friend and therefore thinks the book leaves a jarring impression, inasmuch as it is not a ready-made uniform that fits every musketeer. —A temporary genius will perhaps find that the exception creates too many difficulties for himself and takes the matter too seriously. — A convivial family friend will look in vain for a transfiguration of parlor trivialites or a glorification of tea-time gossip. —A vigorous champion of actuality will perhaps think the whole thing revolves around nothing. —An experienced matchmaking woman will consider the book a failure, since her main interest would be to find out what a girl must be like "to make such a man happy," for she satisfies herself in a way very pleasant to her that there must be, or at least must have been, such a girl. —His Reverence will assert that there is too much philosophy in the book; His Right Reverence's mental eye will seek in vain for what the congregation, especially in our day, needs so very much, the genuinely speculative. —My dear reader, we certainly may speak this way about these matters *unter uns*, for you no doubt realize that I do not believe all these opinions will actually be advanced, since the book will not have many readers.

The book may provide an ordinary reviewer the desired opportunity to elucidate in detail that it is not a comedy, tragedy, novel, short story, epic, or epigram. He will also find it inexcusable that one tries in vain to say 1, 2, 3.[3] He will also find it difficult to understand the movement in the book, for it is inverse; nor will the aim of the book appeal to him, either, for as a rule reviewers explain existence in such a way that both the universal and the particular are annihilated.[4] Above all, it is asking too much of an ordinary reviewer to be interested in the dialectical battle in which the exception arises in the midst of the universal, the protracted and very complicated procedure in which the exception battles his way through and affirms himself as justified, for the unjustified exception is recognized precisely by his wanting to bypass the universal. This battle is very dialectical and infinitely nuanced; it presupposes as a condition an absolute promptitude in the dialectic of the universal, demands speed in imitating the movements—in a word, it is just as difficult as to kill a man and let him live. On the one side stands the exception, on the other the universal, and the struggle itself is a strange conflict between the rage and impatience of the universal over the disturbance the exception causes and its infatuated partiality for the exception, for after all is said and done, just as heaven rejoices more over a sinner who repents

than over ninety-nine righteous,[5] so does the universal rejoice over an exception. On the other side battles the insub-
ordination and defiance of the exception, his weakness and
infirmity. The whole thing is a wrestling match in which the
universal breaks with the exception, wrestles with him in
conflict, and strengthens him through this wrestling. If the
exception cannot endure the distress, the universal does not
help him any more than heaven helps a sinner who cannot
endure the pain of repentance. The vigorous and determined
exception, who although he is in conflict with the universal
still is an offshoot of it, sustains himself. The relation is as
follows. The exception also thinks the universal in that he
thinks himself through; he works for the universal in that he
works himself through; he explains the universal in that he
explains himself. Consequently, the exception explains the
universal and himself, and if one really wants to study the
universal, one only needs to look around for a legitimate
exception; he discloses everything far more clearly than the
universal itself. The legitimate exception is reconciled in the
universal; basically, the universal is polemical toward the exception, and it will not betray its partiality before the exception forces it, as it were, to acknowledge it. If the exception
does not have this power, he is not legitimized, and for that
reason it is very sagacious of the universal not to allow anything to be noticed prematurely. If heaven loves one sinner
more than ninety-nine who are righteous, the sinner, of course,
does not know this from the beginning; on the contrary, he
is aware only of heaven's wrath until he finally, as it were,
forces heaven to speak out.

Eventually one grows weary of the incessant chatter about
the universal and the universal repeated to the point of the
most boring insipidity. There are exceptions. If they cannot
be explained, then the universal cannot be explained, either.
Generally, the difficulty is not noticed because one thinks the
universal not with passion but with a comfortable superficiality. The exception, however, thinks the universal with
intense passion.

When one does this, a new order of rank results, and the

poor exception, if he has any competence at all, once again, like the girl spurned by the stepmother in the fairy tale, enjoys favor and honor.

Such an exception is a poet, who constitutes the transition to the truly aristocratic exceptions, to the religious exceptions. A poet is ordinarily an exception. People are usually pleased with someone like that and with his compositions. I thought, therefore, that for me it might be well worth the trouble to bring someone like that into being. The young man I have brought into being is a poet. I can do no more, for the most I can do is to imagine a poet and to produce him by my thought. I myself cannot become a poet, and in any case my interest lies elsewhere. My task has engaged me purely esthetically and psychologically. I have put myself into it, but if you look more carefully, my dear reader, you will readily see that I am only a ministering spirit and that I am far from being what the young man fears—indifferent toward him. This was a misunderstanding that I prompted as another way of drawing him out. Every move I have made is merely to throw light on him; I have had him constantly *in mente* [in mind]; every word of mine is either ventriloquism or is said in connection with him. Even where jesting and flippancy seem to play inconsiderately, there is consideration for him; even where everything ends in gloom, there is a hint about him, of his state of mind. For that reason all the movements are purely lyrical, and what I say is to be understood as obscurely pertaining to him or as helping to understand him better. In this way I have done what I could for him, just as I now try to help you, dear reader, by once again taking another role.[6]

A poet's life begins in conflict with all life. The point is to find reassurance or legitimation, for he must always lose the first conflict, and if he wants to win immediately, then he is unjustified. My poet now finds legitimation precisely in being absolved by life the moment he in a sense wants to destroy himself. His soul now gains a religious resonance. This is what actually sustains him, although it never attains a breakthrough. His dithyrambic joy in the last letter is an example of this, for beyond a doubt this joy is grounded in a religious mood, which remains something inward, however. He keeps a religious mood as a secret he cannot explain, while at the same time this secret helps him poetically to explain actuality. He explains the universal as repetition, and yet he himself understands repetition in another way, for although actuality becomes the repetition, for him the repetition is the raising of his consciousness to the second power. He has had what belongs essentially to a poet, a love affair, but a very ambivalent one: happy, unhappy, comic, tragic. With respect to the girl, everything may be construed as comic, for inasmuch as he was moved primarily by sympathy, his suffering was to a great extent a consequence of the beloved's suffering. If on that point he was mistaken, the comic becomes pronounced. If he looks to himself, then the tragic emerges, just as when he in another sense regards the beloved ideally. He has kept the whole love affair in its ideality, to which he can give any expression whatsoever, but always as mood, because he has no facticity. He has, then, a fact of consciousness, or, more correctly, he has no fact of consciousness but rather a dialectical resiliency that will make him productive of mood. While this productivity becomes his external aspect, he is sustained by something inexpressibly religious. In the earlier letters, especially in some of them, the movement was much closer to a genuinely religious resolution, but the moment the temporary suspension is terminated, he gains himself again, but as a poet, and the religious founders, that is, becomes a kind of inexpressible substratum.

If he had had a deeper religious background, he would not have become a poet. Then everything would have gained religious meaning. The situation in which he was trapped would then have gained meaning for him, but the collision would have come from higher levels, and he would also have had a quite different authority, even though it would have been purchased with still more painful suffering. Then he would have acted with an entirely different iron consistency and imperturbability, then he would have won a fact of con-

III
263

sciousness to which he could constantly hold, one that would never become ambivalent for him but would be pure earnestness because it was established by him on the basis of a God-relationship.[7] Immediately the whole question of finitude would have become a matter of indifference; in the more profound sense, actuality itself would make no difference to him. Then he would have religiously emptied that situation of all its frightful consequences. He would not be essentially changed if actuality manifested itself some other way, no more than he would be more terrified than he already had been if the very worst were to happen. Then with religious fear and trembling, but also with faith and trust, he would understand what he had done from the very beginning and what as a consequence of this he was obligated to do later, even though this obligation would have strange results. It is characteristic of the young man, however, precisely as a poet, that he can never really grasp what he has done, simply because he both wants to see it and does not want to see it in the external and visible, or wants to see it in the external and visible, and therefore both wants to see it and does not want to see it. A religious individual, however, is composed within himself and rejects all the childish pranks of actuality.

My dear reader, you will now understand that the interest focuses on the young man, whereas I am a vanishing person, just like a midwife in relation to the child she has delivered. And that is indeed the case, for I have, so to speak, delivered him, and therefore as the elder I act as spokesman. My personality is a presupposition of consciousness that must be present in order to force him out, but my personality will never be able to attain what he attains, for the primitivity in which he comes forward is the other factor. So he has been in good hands from the very beginning, even though I frequently had to tease him so that he himself could emerge. At first sight, I perceived that he was a poet—if for no other reason I saw it in the fact that a situation that would have been taken easily in stride by a lesser mortal expanded into a world event for him.

Although I frequently do the talking, you, my dear reader

(for you understand the interior psychic states and emotions, and that is why I call you "dear"), will nevertheless be reading about him on every page. You will understand the variety of the transitions, and even if now and then you wonder a bit at suddenly getting a shower bath of moods, you nevertheless will subsequently realize how everything is variously adapted, the one mood to the other, so that the particular mood is fairly correct, which is a primary point here where the lyrical is so important. At times you may be distracted by an apparently pointless witticism or an idle defiance, but later you perhaps will be reconciled to those things.[8]

Your devoted,
CONSTANTIN CONSTANTIUS

SUPPLEMENT

Marginal references alongside the text are to volume and page [I 100] in *Søren Kierkegaards Samlede Værker*, I–XIV, edited by A. B. Drachman, J. L. Heiberg, and H. O. Lange (1 ed., Copenhagen: Gyldendal, 1901-06). The same marginal references are used in Sören Kierkegaard, *Gesammelte Werke*, Abt. 1-36 (Düsseldorf: Diederichs Verlag, 1952-69).

References to Kierkegaard's works in English are to this edition, *Kierkegaard's Writings* [*KW*], I–XXV (Princeton: Princeton University Press, 1978-). Specific references to the *Writings* are given by English title and the standard Danish pagination referred to above [*Either/Or*, I, *KW* III (*SV* I 100)].

References to the *Papirer* [*Pap.* I A 100; note the differentiating letter A, B, or C, used only in references to the *Papirer*] are to *Søren Kierkegaards Papirer*, I–XI³, edited by P. A. Heiberg, V. Kuhr, and E. Torsting (1 ed., Copenhagen: Gyldendal, 1909-48), and 2 ed., photo-offset with two supplemental volumes, I–XIII, edited by Niels Thulstrup (Copenhagen: Gyldendal, 1968-70), and with index, XIV–XVI (1975-78), edited by N. J. Cappelørn. References to the *Papirer* in English [*JP* II 1500] are to the volume and serial entry number in *Søren Kierkegaard's Journals and Papers*, I–VII, edited and translated by Howard V. Hong and Edna H. Hong, assisted by Gregor Malantschuk (Bloomington: Indiana University Press, 1967-78).

References to correspondence are to the serial numbers in *Breve og Aktstykker vedrørende Søren Kierkegaard*, I–II, edited by Niels Thulstrup (Copenhagen: Munksgaard, 1953-54), and to the corresponding serial numbers in *Kierkegaard: Letters and Documents*, translated by Henrik Rosenmeier, *Kierkegaard's Writings*, XXV [*Letters, KW* XXV, Letter 100].

References to books in Kierkegaard's own library [*ASKB* 100] are based on the serial numbering system of *Auktions-*

protokol over Søren Kierkegaards Bogsamling (Auction-catalog of Søren Kierkegaard's Book-collection), edited by H. P. Rohde (Copenhagen: Royal Library, 1967).

In the Supplement, references to page and lines in the text are given as: 100:1-10.

In the notes, internal references to the present work are given as: p. 100.

Three periods indicate an omission by the editors; five periods indicate a hiatus or fragmentariness in the text.

Frygt og Bæven.

Dialektisk Lyrik

af

Johannes de silentio.

Kjøbenhavn.

Faaes hos C. A. Reitzel.

Trykt i Bianco Lunos Bogtrykkeri.

1843.

FEAR AND TREMBLING.

Dialectical Lyric

by

Johannes de silentio.

Copenhagen.
Available at C. A. Reitzel's.
Printed by Bianco Luno Press.
1843.

SELECTED ENTRIES FROM
KIERKEGAARD'S JOURNALS AND PAPERS
PERTAINING TO
FEAR AND TREMBLING

Fear and trembling (see Philippians 2:12) is not the *primus motor* in the Christian life, for it is love; but it is what the oscillating *balance wheel* is to the clock—it is the oscillating *balance wheel* of the Christian life.—*JP* III 2383 (*Pap.* II A 370) February 16, 1839

We read:[1] And God tempted [*fristede*][2] Abraham, and he said to him: Abraham—and Abraham answered: Here I am. We ought to note in particular the trusting and God-devoted disposition, the bold confidence in confronting the test, in freely and undauntedly answering: Here I am. Is it like that with us, or are we not rather eager to evade the severe trials when we see them coming, wish for a remote corner of the world in which to hide, wish that the mountains would conceal us, or impatiently try to roll the burden off our shoulders and onto others; or even those who do not try to flee—how slowly, how reluctantly they drag their feet. Not so with Abraham; he answers undauntedly: Here I am. He does not trouble anyone with his suffering, neither Sarah, who he knew very well would be grief-stricken over losing Isaac, nor Eliezer, the faithful servant in his house, with whom, if with anyone, he certainly might have sought consolation. We read: He arose early in the morning. He hurried as if to a jubilant festival, and by daybreak he was at Moriah, the place designated by the Lord. And he cut the wood for the fire, and he bound Isaac, and he lighted the fire, and he drew the knife. My listener, there was many a father in Israel who believed that to lose his child was to lose everything that was

dear to him, to be robbed of every hope for the future, but
there was no one who was the child of promise in the sense
Isaac was to Abraham. There was many a father who had
had that loss, but since it was always, after all, God's almighty and inscrutable governance, since it was God who
personally obliterated, as it were, the promise given, he was
obliged to say with Job: The Lord gave, the Lord took away.
Not so with Abraham—he was commanded to do it with his
own hand. The fate of Isaac was laid in Abraham's hand
together with the knife. And here he stood on the mountain
early in the morning, the old man with his one and only
hope. But he did not doubt; he looked neither to the right
nor to the left; he did not challenge heaven with his complaints. He knew it was the weightiest sacrifice God could
ask, but he also knew that nothing was too great for God.
Of course, we all know the outcome of the story. Perhaps it
does not amaze us anymore, because we have known it from
our earliest childhood, but then in truth the fault does not
really lie in the story, but in ourselves, because we are too
lukewarm genuinely to feel with Abraham and to suffer with
him. He went home happy, confident, trusting in God, for
he had not wavered, he had nothing for which to reproach
himself. If we imagine that Abraham, by anxiously and des-
perately looking around, discovered the ram that would save
his son, would he not then have gone home in disgrace,
without confidence in the future, without the self-assurance
that he was prepared to bring to God any sacrifice whatsoever, without the divine voice from heaven in his heart that
proclaimed to him God's grace and love.

Nor did Abraham say: Now I have become an old man,
my youth is gone, my dream has not been fulfilled; I became
a man and what I yearned for you denied me, and now that
I am an old man you fulfilled everything in a wonderful way.
Grant me now a quiet evening; do not summon me to new
battles; let me rejoice in what you gave me, in the consolation of my old age.—*JP* V 5485 (*Pap.* III C 4) *n.d.*, 1840-41

OUTLINE[3]

Let us assume (something neither the Old Testament nor the Koran reports) that Isaac knew the purpose of the journey he was going to make with his father to Mt. Moriah, that he was going to be sacrificed—if the present age had a poet, he would be able to relate what these two men talked about along the way.* I imagine that Abraham first of all looked at him with all his fatherly love, and his crushed heart and venerable countenance made what he said more urgent; he admonished Isaac to bear his fate patiently, he vaguely led him to understand that as a father he was suffering even more because of it. —But it did not help. I imagine that then Abraham turned away from him for a moment and when he turned back to him again he was unrecognizable to Isaac—his eyes were wild, his expression chilling, his venerable locks bristled like furies upon his head. He grabbed Isaac by the chest, drew his knife, and said, "You thought I was going to do this because of God, but you are wrong, I am an idolater, and this passion has again stirred in my soul—I want to murder you, this is my desire; I am worse than a cannibal. Despair, you foolish boy who fancied that I was your father; I am your murderer, and this is my desire." And Isaac fell on his knees and cried to heaven, "Merciful God, have mercy on me." But then Abraham whispered softly to himself, "So must it be, for it is better that he believes I am a monster, that he curses me and the fact that I was his father, and still better, that he prays to God—than that he should know that it was God who imposed the test, for then he would lose his mind and perhaps curse God."

—But where indeed is the contemporary poet who has intimations of such conflicts? And yet Abraham's conduct was genuinely poetic, noble, more noble than anything I have read in tragedies. —When the child is to be weaned, the mother blackens her breast, but her eyes rest just as lovingly on the child. The child believes that it is the breast that has changed, but the mother is unchanged. And why does she

IV
A 76
28

IV
A 76
29

blacken her breast? Because, she says, it would be a shame for the breast to appear attractive when the child must not have it. —This collision is easily resolved, for the breast is only a part of the mother herself. Fortunate is he who has never experienced more dreadful collisions, who did not need to blacken himself, who did not need to journey to hell to find out what the devil looks like so that he could make himself look like him and in this way possibly save another human being, at least in that person's God-relationship. This would be Abraham's collision.

—He who has explained this riddle has explained my life. But who of my contemporaries has understood this?—*JP* V 5640 (*Pap.* IV A 76) *n.d.,* 1843

In margin of Pap. IV A 76:

* One could also have Abraham's previous life be not devoid of guilt and have him secretly ruminate on the thought that this was God's punishment, perhaps even have him get the melancholy thought that he must help God to make the punishment as severe as possible.—*JP* V 5641 (*Pap.* IV A 77) *n.d.*

I have thought of adapting [the legend of] Agnes and the merman[4] from an angle that has not occurred to any poet. The merman is a seducer, but when he has won Agnes's love he is so moved by it that he wants to belong to her entirely. —But this, you see, he cannot do, since he must initiate her into his whole tragic existence, that he is a monster at certain times etc., that the Church cannot give its blessing to them. He despairs and in his despair plunges to the bottom of the sea and remains there, but leads Agnes to believe that he only wanted to deceive her.

But this is poetry, not that wretched, miserable trash in which everything revolves around ridiculousness and nonsense.

Such a complication can be resolved only by the religious (which has its name because it resolves all witchcraft); if the merman could believe, his faith perhaps could transform him into a human being.—*JP* V 5668 (*Pap.* IV A 113) *n.d.*, 1843

From draft; see title page and 54, 68, 82:

Problemata
by
S. Kierkegaard
—*JP* V 5658 (*Pap.* IV B 60) *n.d.*, 1843

From draft; see title page:

Between Each Other [*][5]
by
Simon Stylita[6]
Solo Dancer and Private Individual

---

edited
by
S. Kierkegaard

[*] *In margin:* Movements and Positions[7]
—*JP* V 5659 (*Pap.* IV B 78) *n.d.*, 1843

From draft, in margin of Pap. IV B 78; see title page:

FEAR AND TREMBLING
dialectical lyric
by
Johannes de silentio
a poetic person[8] who exists
only among poets.
—*JP* V 5660 (*Pap.* IV B 79) *n.d.*, 1843

Deleted from final copy; see 3:

"Write."—"For whom?"—"Write for the dead, for those in the past whom you love."—"Will they read me?"—"Yes, for they come back as posterity."[9]

An old saying.

"Write."—"For whom?"—"Write for the dead, for those in the past whom you love."—"Will they read me?"—"No!"[10]

An old saying slightly altered.

rebus und Grundsätze durcheinander.

Hamann, I.[11]

—*JP* II 1550 (*Pap.* IV B 96:1 a–c) *n.d.,* 1843

From draft of Preface; see 7:25–8:22:

IV
B 80:3
235
IV
B 80:3
236

The present author is by no means a philosopher; he* is a poor supplementary clerk in Danish literature,** who prefers to lock his door and speak cryptically and entirely according to circumstances now dances to the honor of the deity, now begs at his door, and once in a while does not hesitate to become the modest occasion for the revelation of more profound wisdom even though he himself may be disgraced.†

This does not trouble him; he does not consider himself as one who is condemned from life but condemned for life, and a prisoner for life can certainly easily put up with rasping[12] work—his life is lost anyway.

He acquiesces in the verdict given, because he was not condemned from life but for life.

Respectfully
Joh. d. silentio
formerly poetic person

IV
B 80:3
235

In margin: * *poetice et eleganter* [in a poetic and refined way] and his whole existence is nothing but poetry.

In margin: ** who easily envisions his fate in an age that has crossed out passion in order to serve science,‡ and who at most can hope that some anemic abstracter or other, a gobbler of paragraphs, will reduce it to a few sentences.[§] I beseech every systematic snooper: this is not the system, it does not have the least thing to do with the system. I invoke everything good for the system and the shareholders in this omnibus; I wish every participant success and good fortune.

‡ who foresees the dreadful fate of being totally ignored; I dread the even more dreadful fate

§ that in order to save taste he will do to it what Trop is willing to do with the destruction of the human race: cut it down the middle and then cut it up into paragraphs according to a specific norm that uses three pages for every paragraph—just like the man who in order to serve orthography placed a period after every thirty words.

In margin: †which is natural, since he is not writing the system§§ but some scribbles and doodles between each other [*mellem hverandre*].¹³

§§ and does not pledge himself to it by promises

—*Pap.* IV B 80:3 n.d., 1843

IV
B 80:3
236

Addition, later deleted from final draft; see 7:37–8:5:

for to be an author is just as humiliating in our day as it was to be a student in the time when the academic citizens went around and sang at the door.—*Pap.* IV B 89:1 *n.d.*, 1843

From final draft; see 61:1, 61:19-22:

1. (προοίμια [proem].) Exordium.
2. His craving was not¹⁴ to go along on the three-day journey when Abraham rode, not as that old pagan¹⁵ did, on horseback through life with sorrow behind him, but with sorrow before him, with Mount Moriah before his eyes, and with Isaac beside him. He wished to be present only in that hour . . . . .—*Pap.* IV B 81 *n.d.*, 1843

From final draft; see 12:17-20:

In margin: When the child has grown big and is to be weaned, the mother hides her breast, and then the child believes that the breast is no longer there, but the mother keeps it. —How fortunate the one who needed only this innocent deceit to wean the child.

When the child is to be weaned, the mother virginally hides her breast—then the child no longer has a mother.—*Pap.* IV B 83 *n.d.*, 1843

In margin of final draft; see 66:17-23:

When the child is to be weaned, the mother, too, is not without sorrow,* because the child who lay under her heart, who rested on her breast, will no longer be so close to her. So they grieve together the brief sorrow. —How fortunate the one who did not have to thrust the child away further.

* because they are more and more separated, estranged from each other, because the child who first lay under her heart, who thereafter rested on her breast, will never more be so close to her,—*Pap.* IV B 84 *n.d.*, 1843

In margin of final draft; see 14:17-19:

When the child is to be weaned, the mother feeds it with stronger sustenance—How fortunate the one who did not need to wean the child so that it perishes.—*Pap.* IV B 85 *n.d.*, 1843

From draft; see 14:20-24:

Thus and in many similar ways he thought about that event. He could never grow weary of it, and every time[*] he finished, he folded his hands and said: No one was as great as Abraham; whoever is able to understand him is great just because of that. Now and then he wondered whether it would

IV
B 66
230

have been more burdensome if Abraham had had something for which to reproach himself, if in his innermost being he had had certain elements that allowed him to read the divine script otherwise. Yet he could understand that Abraham's ordeal [Prøvelse] was the most difficult, because, insofar as doubt arose in his soul, it was only about God's love—but that one who has called down wrath upon himself is not tried but is punished, even though it would be a terrible punishment to have to sacrifice one's own child, to destroy one's most cherished, and to be doomed to consume these torments throughout a long life. —But these two spiritual trials [Anfægtelser][16] were of equal degree or of the same intensity; nevertheless, whenever he began to be confused by these thoughts, because he wanted to hold firmly to the idea that in this sense God tried a person, he consoled himself with the simpler explanation that he had rashly plunged into something that he could not carry through.

[*] *In margin*: every time he had been out to M[oriah] and returned home, he sank down exhausted

he could never grow weary of this journey to Mount Moriah.

—*Pap.* IV B 66 *n.d.*, 1843

In margin of Pap. IV B 66:

The point in the whole story lies in Abraham's being genuinely assured that he loves Isaac more than himself. This doubt is dreadful; who decides it; assurances to the Cherethites and Pelethites[17] are of no use; here it is a question of the God-consciousness in an individual, since the outward manifestation itself, the deed, is in contradiction to it. If Abraham does it and then becomes uncertain about himself, he can be certain that no one will understand him, that he either will go mad or will win God-consciousness within himself again. If he sacrifices him because of duty, it is less significant, for placed in the context of duty his son has the position of a single human being (in the same way as when that Roman allowed his son to be executed because he had committed an offense); but if he violates duty and the whole thing appears in the context of an ordeal, then it is of extreme importance. He who denies himself, sacrifices himself out of duty, and gives up the finite in order to grasp the infinite is safe enough, and he must always be understood within the universal, for duty is the universal; but the one who gives up duty in order to grasp something still higher, if he is in error, what salvation is there for him?*—The terrifying thing in the collision is this—that it is not a collision between God's command and man's command but between God's command and God's command.—*JP* I 908 (*Pap.* IV B 67) *n.d.*, 1843

Addition to Pap. IV B 67:

* He destroys his happiness in the world in order to have his happiness with God—and now if he has misunderstood God—where shall he turn?

A eulogy on Shakespeare,[18] regretting that he has never depicted this final torment.—*Pap.* IV B 68 *n.d.*, 1843

From final draft; see 14:20-24:

. . . . . the one who is able to understand him is already great.—*Pap.* IV B 86 *n.d.*, 1843

From draft; see 15:

Eulogy on Abraham

If Abraham had doubted and consequently been prudent, he perhaps would have remained silent, gone out and sacrificed himself[19] on Mount Moriah, and that would indeed have been noble, and yet Abraham would have been a doubter. But then he would not have been out in the stream but would have waded; he would not have given up human calculation

but would have been noble according to human calculation.—*Pap.* IV B 72 *n.d.*, 1843

From draft, addition to Pap. IV B 72; *see 17:*

Abraham was great not because he sacrificed Isaac but because he had faith, because he was cheerful and willing. That
is what is accentuated in the four *Problemata*,[20] for in each
case he does it, but not in faith.—*Pap.* IV B 73 *n.d.*, 1843

In margin of final draft; see 21:9:

"Now I am an old man; my youth has passed, my man-
hood; then you finally fulfilled my wish—grant now a quiet
evening to me."—*Pap.* IV B 87:1 *n.d.*, 1843

In margin of final draft; see 23:21:

[faith.*] *not as the content of a concept but as a form of
the will.—*Pap.* IV B 87:2 *n.d.*, 1843

Section epigraph deleted from final copy; see 25:

Ein Laye und Ungläubiger kann meine Schreibart nicht
anders als für Unsinn erklären, weil ich mit mancherley
Zungen mich ausdrücke, und die Sprache der Sophisten,
der Wortspiele, der Creter und Araber, Weissen und Mohren und Creolen rede, Critik, Mythologie, rebus und
Grundsätze durch einander schwatze, und bald κατ' ἄνθρωπον bald κατ' ἐξοχὴν argumentire.

Hamann.[21]

[A layman and unbeliever can explain my manner of
writing in no other way than as nonsense, since I express
myself in various tongues and speak the language of sophists, of puns, of Cretans and Arabians, of whites and Moors
and Creoles, and babble a confusion of criticism, mythol-

ogy, rebus, and axioms, and argue now in a human way
and now in an extraordinary way.]

Hamann.
—*JP* II 1551 (*Pap.* IV B 96:4) *n.d.,* 1843

From final draft; see 27:1:

Changed from: Introduction
—*Pap.* IV B 88:1 *n.d.,* 1843

From final draft; see 29:20-32:

for in our generation faith has come to be nil and nought,
and if it is removed, then Abraham is a murderer.* The situation of the sinner, however, is very tragic. His fate is easy
to foresee; he is

In margin: *and there is nothing remaining but the brutal
fact that Abraham was going to murder Isaac, which is easy
enough for anyone to copy, especially for someone who does
not have faith, does not have the faith that makes it hard for
him.

—*Pap.* IV B 88:2 *n.d.,* 1843

From final draft; see 32:24-31:

so they [listeners] would not say: He has faith to such a degree[*] that all we have to do is to allow ourselves to be
influenced by him a little, because, after all, there is something in what he says. Then I would say: I do not have faith
at all. By nature I am very shrewd, my plans have rarely
gone awry, but I nevertheless have grasped that faith is higher
than everything else.**

[*] *In margin*: if we can only grab his coattails.
                    enough to hang on to his coattails.

In margin: **and per se I cannot attribute any worth to the fact that it is more difficult for me to make the movement than for many others.

—*Pap.* IV B 88:4 *n.d.*, 1843

From draft; see 53:31, 67:5, 81:12, 120:19:

All *Problemata* should end as follows:

This is the paradox of faith, a paradox that no reasoning is able to master—and yet it is so, or we must obliterate the story of Abraham.—*JP* III 3079 (*Pap.* IV B 75) *n.d.*, 1843

From draft; see 59:16–60:3:

Abraham did not sacrifice Isaac for the universal. On the contrary, it must be said that all Israel, which, so to speak, was hidden in Isaac, pleaded for his life, and thus the universal demands specifically that Abraham should refrain from it. It was a purely personal ordeal [*Prøvelse*] for Abraham.
—*Pap.* IV B 74 *n.d.*, 1843

Deleted from final copy; see 79:20:

Anyone who takes the paradoxical isolation of faith in vain is, of course, not a knight of faith but a Simon Magus[22] who wants a bargain. Distress, pain, anxiety—this is the verification, but it is also the saving factor that will discourage people from beginning rashly. And anyone who begins rashly will crush himself. One may therefore quite calmly abandon the silly officiousness that keeps people so busy getting such an unfortunate person crushed before their eyes; if he is crushed within himself, then their punishment is nothing but child's play. There is an oriental tale about a deposed sultan who sat in his prison thinking only of escaping with the help of a fantastic bird about which he had heard marvelous things. The bird comes to his window, takes a muslin band from his turban, and changes it into a magnificent carriage in which the sultan can sit. He goes to the window, is already standing with one foot in the carriage, when the bird says, "Get in, but repeat these words loudly and clearly: In the name of the great Kokopilesobeh, the one god, I wish to travel from here to Herak." "What are you saying?" shouted Ali-Ben-Giad in horror. "There is only one God and Mohammed is his prophet." Instantly, the carriage vanished, and he dropped dead. —See, he had not reckoned correctly.

In margin: Cf. *Blaue Bibliothek*,[23] VI, p. 269.

—*Pap.* IV B 96:5 *n.d.*, 1843

Deleted from final copy; replaced with 84:31-32:

I shall make it brief, and inasmuch as I move for a moment in the sphere of esthetics, I shall throw a lighter cloak about me, the ironical incognito,[24] in which irony prefers to appear when it participates in the exercises of esthetics. But first a more ordinary observation.—*Pap.* IV B 96:8 *n.d.*, 1843

Deleted from margin of final copy; see 89:8-9:

if he would dip it, as did the brothers with Joseph's coat,[25] in the blood of mood and now hold it up before sorrowing Jacob's eyes, would he not recognize it?—*Pap.* IV B 96:10 *n.d.*, 1843

From draft; see 94:18:

1. [sea]—who explains this mystery, for the one who captures is captive and the one who is captive captures . . . . . —*Pap.* IV B 91:1 *n.d.*, 1843

In margin of draft; see 96:30-97:4:

3. If he does this, and Agnes is not exactly as I have described her, then he will have a living impression of purgatory. The more selfish Agnes is, the more dreadful is her

resistance. She will not modestly conceal her suffering from him out of shame for him and for herself; she will be gazing at herself too much to be disturbed at any time by the thought that he is suffering under this. Her loyalty will know no limit; she will use the last resource—she will die before his eyes and make him a murderer.—*Pap.* IV B 91:3 *n.d.*, 1843

From draft; see 111:8:

There is nothing so contemptible as cowardly treachery, and a temple raider is far from being as contemptible as those who carry on trade in the temple.—*Pap.* IV B 91:13 *n.d.*, 1843

Deleted from final copy; see 112:4:

One of the gospels tells the parable of two sons,[26] one of whom always promised to do his father's will but did not do it, and the other always said "No" but did it. The latter is also a form of irony, and yet the gospel commends this son. The gospel does not let repentance enter in,[27] either, that he repented of having said "No." By no means. This suggests that it is a kind of modesty that keeps the son from saying that he will do it. A man of any depth cannot be unacquainted with this modesty. It has its basis partly in a noble distrust of oneself, for as long as a person has not done what is demanded, it is still possible for him to be weak enough not to do it, and for that reason he will not promise anything.—*JP* II 1740 (*Pap.* IV B 96:13) *n.d.*, 1843

From draft; see 113:12:

This paradox cannot be mediated, the one knight of faith cannot understand the other, and there can be no question of any universal clue by which the individual can determine whether he is in the paradox or is involved in a spiritual trial [*Anfægtelse*].—*Pap.* IV B 91:15 *n.d.*, 1843

Marginal addition, later deleted from draft; see 114:15:

In the play by Euripides,[28] Iphigenia is allowed to weep for a moment and, in place of other signs of interceding, is allowed to wind herself like an olive branch about his knee. She really ought to have been granted more time; like Jephthah's daughter, she ought to have had at least two months in which to weep, not in solitude, but under the father's special supervision.—*Pap.* IV B 91:16 *n.d.*, 1843

In margin of draft; see 115:8-34:

There is also another reason why Abraham cannot speak, for in silence he is continually making the movement of faith; this [if he were to speak] they could understand even less, since he would thereby contradict himself.—*Pap.* IV B 91:17 *n.d.*, 1843

From sketch; see 115:35–119:35:

1. it does not consist in his saying a few appropriate words; insofar as he is a hero, the poet will certainly be interested in him; insofar as he is not a hero, he can have the family make arrangements with the priest for a funeral sermon—but it consists in his carrying out his standpoint.

2. for this reason the intellectual tragic hero becomes immortal before he dies—whereas the tragic hero, whose life-meaning lies in action, who belongs to the external world, becomes immortal after his death.

3. Abraham's distress consists in silence (death of Pythagoras);[29] how then can he speak.

　　if he says anything to Isaac in the crucial moment, he drops beneath a tragic hero

4. Abraham's words are not simply resignation*:
　　but faith also
The Lord himself *must* select
The Lord himself *has* selected

5. *because then he has expressed himself incorrectly, because he must indeed know whether Isaac is going to die or not, since he himself is the one who is going to sacrifice him—and he expresses himself as if the task were something different, that he, for example, should take Isaac to Mount Moriah and then the lightning would kill him, for then in a certain sense he cannot know it before the lightning has struck.

6. the believing ἐποχή [suspension][30]—*Pap.* IV B 93:1-6 *n.d.*, 1843

Deleted from final copy; see 116:12:

If his life culminates in suffering, in dying, then of course the tragic hero, like any other person who is not deprived of speech, can say a few words, perhaps say a few appropriate words, but the question is whether it is appropriate for him to say them, whether he does not weaken the impression of his life, inasmuch as he becomes untrue to his character in the last moment, becomes an after-dinner speaker.—*Pap.* IV B 96:14 *n.d.*, 1843

From draft; see 116:

Perhaps even one more move could be made—let Sarah get to know about it and let her make an objection, at which point Abraham's despair would find expression in this way: Wretched woman, Isaac is in fact not our child; were not both of us old when he was born; did you yourself not laugh when it was announced.[31]—*Pap.* IV B 69 *n.d.*, 1843

From draft; addition to Pap. IV B 69:

Abraham said this to Sarah. She became terrified and would dissuade him, but Abraham said: Wretched woman, how did you know it is our child; was it not in your old age that you had him; were not both of us decrepit. It is not our child but a phantom.—*Pap.* IV B 70 *n.d.*, 1843

From draft; addition to Pap. IV B 69:

Abraham wanted to be divorced from Sarah; he maintained that her barrenness was to blame for everything. —*Pap.* IV B 71 *n.d.*, 1843

From draft; see 121:1–123:20:

Epilogue

let us love and strengthen ourselves in existence
1. one who in stillness does his work
2. the tragic hero
3. faith

—*Pap.* IV B 92 *n.d.*, 1843

From sketch; see 121:1–123:20:

The children who play and are finished before midday.

Aeschylus,[32] who is supposed to be declared incompetent.

One cannot stop with faith but must go further.

—But in days of old, faith accomplished wonders in the world—no doubt it has accomplished this in the individual, who must have it since he goes further. Will he then forget this. —when Aeschylus grew old, his sons could not slay him, could not conceal his debility—they accused him—*Pap.* IV B 94 *n.d.*, 1843

From draft; see 121:1–123:20:

When the price of cloves[*] became erratic in Holland, several shiploads were burned—it was a pious fraud; is a pious fraud really needed in our time?**

Let us check the market in order to make sure that faith is something other than a bit of worldly wisdom, that it is a power of which few, perhaps, have any idea. Let us run through its dialectic and not talk loosely, as if sacrificing Isaac were merely a poetic expression for sacrificing the best. How many are there who have really tried themselves in such a struggle, and yet people in our day want to go further, as if it were an easy matter to bring about a more unbelieving, more correctly, a less believing, age than our own, whose insipid rationality has pumped all passion out of life.

It is the same for the great ones as for the little people—first one creeps, then one walks in a walker, then one walks holding on to a person's hand, then one walks alone.

The two examples from ancient times of going further are Apollonius[33] and the disciple of Heraclitus.[34]

[*] *Written above*: spices
** Or rather a frank truthfulness that could discipline a no less than pious fraud that has preceded.
—*JP* II 1109 (*Pap*. IV B 76) *n.d.*, 1843

From final draft; see 123:8-14:

3. One cannot stop with faith; must one go further? One must go further. This urge to go further is not reserved for our generation alone.

4. This is a very profound thought, and in this form Heraclitus has beautifully and multifariously commented on what approaches a whole view of life for anyone who immerses himself in it.—*Pap*. IV B 95:3, 4 *n.d.*, 1843

Oh, once I am dead, *Fear and Trembling* alone will be enough for an imperishable name as an author. Then it will be read, translated into foreign languages as well. The reader will almost shrink from the frightful pathos in the book. But when it was written, when the person thought to be the author was going about in the incognito of an idler, appearing to be flippancy, wittiness, and irresponsibility personified, no one was able to grasp its earnestness. O you fools, the book was never as earnest as then. Precisely that was the authentic expression of the horror.

For the author to appear earnest would have diminished

the horror. The reduplication is what is monstrous in the horror.

But when I am dead, an imaginary character will be conjured up for me, a dark, somber figure—and then the book will be terrifying.

But in calling attention to the difference between the poet and the hero,[35] a truth has already been said. There is a predominating poetic strain in me, and yet the real hoax was that *Fear and Trembling* actually reproduced my own life. This aspect of the book was intimated in the first hint[36] about it in the oldest journal, the one in octavo, that is, the oldest journal from the time of my literary activity.—*JP* VI 6491 (*Pap.* X² A 15) *n.d.*, 1849

X²
A 594
424

AN OBSERVATION ABOUT SOMETHING IN "FEAR AND TREMBLING"

Johannes de Silentio is right in saying that in order to show the various psychological stages a passionate concentration is needed.

So it is with the decision whether or not I shall assume that this or that is, humanly speaking, impossible for me. I am not thinking here even of the highest collisions, where the expected is altogether opposed to the order of nature (for example, that Sarah gets a child although far beyond the natural age to bear children). That is why Johannes de Silentio constantly repeats that he cannot understand Abraham, since in addition the collision here is so high that the ethical is spiritual trial [*Anfægtelsen*].

No, in lesser situations, there are many people, surely by far the majority, who are able to live without any real consciousness penetrating their lives. For them it is certainly possible that they never come in passionate concentration to the decision whether they should cling expectantly to this possibility or give it up; they live on this way in unclarity.

It is otherwise with the individualities whose nature is consciousness. They can very well give up this or that, even if it is their dearest wish, but they must have clarity on whether they should expect or not.

It is forever impossible to make this comprehensible to immediately spontaneous or half-reflective natures. Therefore they never come to distinguish between resignation [*Resignation*] and faith.

This is precisely what Johannes de Silentio has again and again enjoined. Everything, he says, depends upon passionate concentration.

X²
A 594
425

Thus when someone comes and wants to correct him by taking the matter back into ordinary intellectual unclarity (which undeniably is common among men)—then, yes, then he of course succeeds in being understood by many.

So it goes always when that which an authentic thinker has pushed to its logical conclusion is corrected with the help of that "which he rejected before he ever began."—*JP* III 3130 (*Pap.* X² A 594) *n.d.*, 1850

[*] Reply to Theophilus Nicolaus,[37] author of a book entitled:

X⁶
B 68
72

The reply is your own words on p. 178, as well as other portions.

"If we categorically assume the dogmas of the *Church*, then we will readily believe that ultimately there is no other alternative left than to establish the principle of absurdity as the principle of *faith*, for to every thinking and also religious spirit these dogmas certainly must seem to contain very much that is absurd and paradoxical (at variance with the understanding as well as reason)."**

[*] Note. Since there is no literary journal in Denmark, I have requested space for these lines in this paper[38] and must therefore request—so much the worse for me—the pardon of the majority of subscribers, because in a way they get no paper tonight, since my article will scarcely be of interest to them.

** Note. The italics in the quotation are the author's own italics, and this will be the case throughout this article wherever italics are used in quotations from the book.

So, basically, you are taking it upon yourself to defend my thesis of the paradox and in addition—what more could I ask—throughout the whole book to hit out very stalwartly and violently at speculative dogmatics and speculation, fatal if the blows make contact—one alone would be enough if it makes contact. I would appeal to you if there were not other difficulties involved in doing so.

N.B. [*In margin: To typesetter:* N.B. one line space between.]

The new and curious turn you give to the matter is this, then. You throw out all of Christianity and thereupon, with an exultant look, say something like this: Where now is the paradox? More correctly, you should say: Where now is Christianity? Incidentally, an amazing situation! I, Johannes Climacus, say that I "by no means make out that I am a Christian" (see *Concluding Postscript*),[39] but I let Christianity stand. You throw out all of Christianity—and then continue to be a Christian and, furthermore, in the capacity of a Christian make no petty distinctions between (see title page) "Jews, Christians, and Mohammedans."[†]

N.B. [*In margin: To typesetter:* N.B. one line space between.]

As far as Abraham's faith is concerned, which you maintain in particular, you do not entirely avoid the absurd here, for the absurd is also present in Abraham's faith. Abraham is called the father of faith because he has the formal qualifications of faith, believing against the understanding, although it has never occurred to the Christian Church that Abraham's faith had the content of Christian faith, which relates essentially to a later historical event. This [I say] with

X⁶
B 68
73

[†] Note. You presumably are referring to yourself when you mention on p. 205 "*someone who, possibly motivated by pure piety, rejects all the distinctive doctrines of Christianity.*" What is distinctive, then, about you is that you then go on being a Christian. Yet this is your distinctiveness, which I least of all shall deny to you. But you certainly have no right to hint darkly (pp. 204–05) that the world-famous Royal Councilor Ørsted[40] secretly is in that situation: possibly out of pure piety rejecting all the characteristic doctrines of Christianity.

X⁶
B68
73

respect to the difficulties you make for yourself in order to point out a contradiction between two different authors, one of whom is concerned "lyrically dialectically" with Abraham and the other "existentially" with the problem "of becoming a Christian": Johannes de Silentio, who, moreover, does not claim to be a believer but himself says, "I do not have faith,"[41] and the undersigned, who does not claim to be a Christian, and what he himself says he does not do.

N.B. [*In margin: To typesetter:* N.B. one line space between.]

And now for this oddity! You, a declared rationalist, who want to do away with everything called the absurd, the paradox, etc., you get rid of it in the following manner, among others, and for a rationalist this is a strange way: you assume—and this is quite clear in your book—that direct communications from God, higher intimations, visions, revelations, etc., that all these are entirely natural and in order, something the really religious person—thus very likely you yourself, in any case your brother—knows from experience, just as the rest of us know everyday things. Understand me correctly—what surprises me is that the writer is a rationalist who wants to get rid of the supernatural in this—well, certainly not rationalistic—way.

X⁶
B 68
74

N.B. [*In margin: To typesetter:* N.B. one line space between.]

Finally a word about your scholarly essay, which stands approximately *au niveau* with Magnus Eiríksson's *Tro, Overtro, Vantro*. According to your interpretation, what we pseudonymous writers, who, please note, say of ourselves that "we do not claim to have faith," call the absurd, the paradox, is according to your explanation by no means the absurd but rather "the higher rationality," although not in the speculative sense. No, speculation, the speculatives (Prof. Martensen etc.) are scoffed down into the deepest abyss, so far down that Johannes de Silentio, according to your declaration, stands infinitely higher, and yet down lower with the speculatives, since you most likely stand infinitely higher than Johannes de Silentio. In truth this may be expected to

be something rather high. Consequently, "the higher rationality." But pay attention to the definition; if the absurd is
not the negative sign and predicate that dialectically makes
sure that the scope of "the purely human" is qualitatively
terminated, then you actually have no sign of your higher
reason; you are taking the chance that your "higher reason"
does not lie on that side of "the human," in the heavenly
regions of the divine, of revelation, but on this side, and
somewhat farther down, in the underground territory of
misunderstanding. The absurd is the negative sign. "I," says
the believer, "I really cannot be satisfied with having only
rhetorical predicates for determining where I have my life,
where, from the spiritual point of view, I am, so to speak.
But the absurd is a category, and a category that can exercise
a restraining influence. When I believe, then assuredly neither faith nor the content of faith is absurd. Oh, no, no—
but I understand very well that for the person who does not
believe, faith and the content of faith are absurd, and I also
understand that as soon as I myself am not in the faith, am
weak, when doubt perhaps begins to stir, then faith and the
content of faith gradually begin to become absurd for me.
But this may have been the divine will: in order that faith—
whether a man will have faith or not—could be the test, the
examination, faith was bound up with the absurd, and the
absurd formed and composed in such a way that only one
force can prevail over it—the passion of faith—its humility
sharpened by the pain of sin-consciousness."

N.B. [*In margin: To typesetter:* N.B. one line space between.]

You conclude with the invitation to Climacus to reconsider—as a consequence of your book—the subject of the
paradox. The same invitation is directed to "the gentlemen
who seem to agree most with me (Climacus)" and finally to
"all thinking persons," but presumably only in these king-
doms and countries. What a frightful clamor! I for my part
do not feel called upon by your book to reconsider the paradox. On the contrary, as I see it, if you are going to hold
forth on Christianity in the future, whether you let your

X⁶
B 68
75

summons on that subject be sent out to "all thinking persons" or not, it is necessary for you first of all to take up
Christianity, which, probably without even noticing it, you
lost in your zeal to prove that there is no paradox in Christianity, which, as stated before, you did superbly well: both
the paradox and Christianity, jointly and separately, vanished completely.

Postscript

Your endeavor is indeed well meant, honest, disinterested,
of that I have no doubt; to that extent it may also be called
religious in the ordinary sense, may actually have some moral
value, especially compared with the orthodox gangrenous
tissue in Christendom. It is this conception of you that made
me decide to reply. But with respect to Christianity you are
in basic error, and as a thinker you are not, as Johannes de
Silentio is, in "fear and trembling," but very cavalier in your
copious unclarity.

X⁶
B 68
76

You have misinterpreted *Fear and Trembling* to such an extent that I do not recognize it at all. Johannes de Silentio's
supreme concern (thus "the problems," which are the thought-
categories of the book, read: "Is there a teleological suspension of the ethical?"[42] "Is there an absolute duty to God?"[43]),
all this, that is to say, the heart of the matter, also the subject
of Abraham and Isaac, you have completely overlooked or
forgotten, but on the other hand, with an almost infatuated
prejudice, you have devoted yourself solely (making it the
chief substance of your book) to the story of the princess, a
minor illustration, an approximation, used by Johannes de
Silentio merely to illuminate Abraham, not to explain Abraham directly, for after all he cannot understand Abraham.
[*Addition with reference markings on the back of the sheet:* while
you so forget the point, which is to illuminate Abraham, and
so forget Abraham, that you create for yourself a new prototype for the knight of faith: Captain Jessen[44] of the navy.
See p. 94, note.]

And even the instance of the princess you have made completely unrecognizable. Johannes de Silentio proceeds on the assumption that, humanly speaking, it is *impossible* for the lover to get the princess. This is the assumption. And for reasonable people, especially for thinking persons, it is a rule that the assumption must remain fixed. It is the same with Johannes de Silentio; if it were not, it would not be feasible to point out the slightest difference between resignation and faith. Now read your version of the story. To you the "knight of faith" is preoccupied with understanding that it is not *impossible* to get the princess,[45] yes, that for many reasons it is "*possible*," which becomes especially clear to "the knight of faith" when he—and this possibility certainly is what we call, humanly speaking, the possible—"*contemplates himself, his own personality*" (see p. 92), "since with respect to his own inner worth the knight of faith does not stand on a *lower* level than the nobility," and therefore the union is by no means a mis-alliance. Ye gods, what is this! The story does not resemble in the least that little illustration in *Fear and Trembling*. With you it actually is a kind of defense for falling in love with a princess, showing that, humanly speaking, it is very well possible (the assumption was that, humanly speaking, this was impossible) to get the princess, which demonstrates that it is by no means *absurd* when a man, perhaps of lowly extraction, if only he is a knight of faith, falls in love with a princess: humanly speaking, the two may very well get each other. And just as the nobility usually send their portraits to the beloved, so you provide a kind of portrait of the knight of faith (somewhat more plump but otherwise much like the pagans' description of "the wise"), presumably intended for the princess. Consequently, to repeat, with you it is *possible*, humanly speaking, for the lover to get the princess, something he is very sure of, especially when he "contemplates himself, his own personality," its high inner value, which makes him perfectly equal in rank to the nobility, yes, even places him above "*kings and princes*" (p. 105). With Johannes de Silentio the assumption was that, humanly speaking, it was *impossible*; and least of all did he think that her being a

X⁶
B 68
77

princess would be taken so seriously. Johannes de Silentio is by no means that aristocratic; he could just as well, absolutely just as well, have used a commoner, a maidservant. The only important thing to him was the assumption that the lover is totally in love and, humanly speaking, cannot possibly get her. On the basis of this assumption, if it is firmly maintained, the difference between resignation and faith can be elucidated, as is done in *Fear and Trembling*—and is totally undone with the help of your princess.

Respectfully,
Johannes Climacus
—*JP* VI 6598 (*Pap.* X⁶ B 68) *n.d.*, 1850

Addition to Pap. X⁶ B 68:

[*] Reply to Theophilus Nicolaus, author of a book entitled: *Er Troen et Paradox og "i Kraft af det Absurde" et Spørgsmaal foranledigt ved "Frygt og Bæven, af Johannes de silentio," besvaret ved Hjælp af en Troes-Ridders fortrolige Meddelelser, til fælles Opbyggelse for Jøder, Christne og Muhamedanere, af bemeldte Troes-Ridders Broder Theophilus Nicolaus* [Is faith a Paradox and "by Virtue of the Absurd" a Question occasioned by "Fear and Trembling, by Johannes de silentio," answered with the Help of the Confidential Communications of a Knight of Faith, for the mutual Upbuilding of Jews, Christians, and Mohammedans, by Theophilus Nicolaus, Brother of the aforesaid Knight of Faith].—*JP* VI 6599 (*Pap.* X⁶ B 69) *n.d.*, 1850

Regarding Theophilus Nicolaus.

> If there is to be a reply, it might be a few words by me, and then the remainder a little information by Anti-Climacus,[46] but personally I must give no information. The few words by me are found in this packet,[47] together with the basic material for Anti-Climacus's reply.—*JP* VI 6600 (*Pap.* X⁶ B 77) *n.d.*, 1850

Addition to Pap. X⁶ B 77:

If there is to be any explanation, perhaps it is right to use a pseudonym: Anti-Climacus.

With reference to Theophilus Nicolaus[48]

If I were to congratulate myself on any one thing, it would be the deliberateness with which I—while the poetic characters, the pseudonyms, were doing their utmost to present the ideal or the idealities—the deliberateness with which I, throughout a whole authorship, soberly and unreservedly have taken care and have employed safeguards in every way (also by being willing to sacrifice myself), lest confusion arise and I be mistaken for the ideal.

From the book at hand[49] it has become clear—as some other books bearing the author's name already have made clear—that there lives a man among us who is very willing (if only we are willing) to be the ideal himself: "the apostle" who reforms all the established, "God's friend and confidant," whose life is guided and led by "special orders." On that I can have no opinion.

Just one thing. If Theophilus Nicolaus is the person I think the author to be, it strikes me that he writes far better now than before. [*In penciled parentheses*: But the misunderstanding is so great that neither Johannes de Silentio nor I can get involved with him. If Johannes de Silentio gets involved with him, it would have to be in jest, but I do not feel I ought to give my consent to that.] But the misunderstanding is so great that there is scarcely any hope of an understanding.

Incidentally, I would be glad to have another pseudonym—one who does not like Johannes de Silentio say he does not have faith[50] but plainly, positively says he has faith—Anti-Climacus—repeat what, as a matter of fact, is stated in the pseudonymous writings.—*JP* VI 6601 (*Pap.* X⁶ B 82) *n.d.*, 1850

Abraham is an eternal prototype [*Forbillede*] of the religious man. Just as he had to leave the land of his fathers for a strange land, so the religious man must willingly leave, that is, forsake a whole generation of his contemporaries even though he remains among them, but isolated, *alien* to them. To be an alien, to be in exile, is precisely the characteristic suffering of the religious man—*JP* IV 4650 (*Pap.* X³ A 114) *n.d.*, 1850

FEAR AND TREMBLING
ABRAHAM

X⁴
A 338
193

. . . . . And he split the firewood; and he bound Isaac; and he lit the fire; and he drew the knife—and thrust it into Isaac!

The very same moment Jehovah stands visible beside Abraham and says: What have you done, you poor old man! That was not required of you at all; you were my friend, and I merely wanted to test your faith! And I also shouted to you in the last moment, I shouted: Abraham, Abraham, stop!

Then, in a voice faint with the solemn low tones of adoration, faint also with the broken feebleness of a deranged mind, Abraham answered, "O Lord, I did not hear it; yet now that you speak of it, it seems to me that I did hear such a voice. Oh, when it is you, my God, who commands, when it is you who commands a father to murder his own son, one is somewhat overstrained at such a moment—therefore I did not hear the voice. If I had heard it, how would I have dared believe that it was yours? When you command me to sacrifice my child—and at the critical moment a voice is heard that says, "Stop," I am obliged to think it is the tempter's voice that wants to keep me from carrying out your will. One of two alternatives: either I had to assume that the voice that told me to sacrifice Isaac was the tempter's voice, and then I would not have set out——. But since I was convinced that it was your voice, I had to conclude that the other voice was the voice of the tempter."

X⁴
A 338
194

Then Abraham set off for home. And the Lord gave him a new Isaac. But Abraham did not look at him with joy; when he saw him, he shook his head and said: This is not Isaac.

But to Sarah he said, "It was a strange business! It is certain, eternally certain, that God asked me to sacrifice Isaac; God himself cannot deny that—and yet when I carried it out, it was a mistake on my part, it was not God's will!"

But not so with the father of faith, Abraham! Obedience consists precisely in obeying promptly in the unconditional, the crucial moment. When one has come so far as to say A, one is, humanly speaking, very prone to say B and to act. Even more difficult than setting out for Moriah to offer Isaac is the capacity, when one has already drawn the knife, in unconditional obedience to be willing to understand: It is not required. With respect to decisions such as to sacrifice one's own child and to spare him, to maintain even in the final moment the same obedient, if I dare say so, agile willingness, like that of a servant who is already practically at the goal and then has to run back again and consequently had run in vain—oh, this is greatness. "No one was as great as Abraham; who can comprehend him?"—*JP* III 3020 (*Pap.* X⁴ A 338) *n.d.*, 1851

X⁴
A 338
195

X⁴
A 357
208

FEAR AND TREMBLING

. . . . . Abraham sacrificed the ram and went home with Isaac, whom he spared.

But, Abraham said to himself, the whole experience has made me forever at variance with what it is to be human. If it had pleased you, O Lord, to let me be changed into the form of a horse, yet remaining human, I would be no more at variance with what it is to be man than I have become through what has just happened; having a dissimilar form is not as great a difference as not to have common concepts, and then to have them infinitely opposite at the most crucial points. —I cannot discuss this with Sarah; she must regard this journey to Moriah as the most horrible crime against her, against her beloved child, against you, O Lord. Maybe a time will come when her wrath will subside and she will forgive me. And then I must thank her for this loving forgiveness. The same with Isaac; the time will come when he

X⁴
A 357
209

will feel strongly about what has happened—and he will hate me, until the moment arrives when he will forgive me, for which I must thank him. O Lord, my heart's sufferings when I brought myself to sacrifice Isaac has its compensation in this—the forgiveness of my crime, and I am humbly grateful for this loving forgiveness. And if I were to tell someone that this was your ordeal [*Prøvelse*] for me (something I would not do, lest I defile my relationship to you by initiating others into it)—O Lord, just to have such a relationship to you still sets me at variance with what it is to be man, more at variance than if I were changed into the shape of a horse.

But not so with Abraham, the father of faith. For to begin thinking such thoughts is to approach the boundaries of faith, even if one thought these reflections would help keep him inside the boundaries of faith: ah, reflections merely help one over the boundary. But Abraham, the father of faith, continues in faith, far from the boundary, from the boundary where faith vanishes in reflection.—*JP* III 3714 (*Pap.* X⁴ A 357) *n.d.,* 1851

ABRAHAM
NEW "FEAR AND TREMBLING"

[*In margin:* In journal NB²⁴ or NB²³ (from the summer or spring of 1851) there is a draft⁵¹ relating to this.]

The mood here should more decidedly border on madness. The point should be that Abraham had not been able to keep himself *in suspenso* at the apex of faith until the end—and therefore had sacrificed Isaac.

Exordium

There was once a man who as a child had learned the story of Abraham, and, as usual, knew his lesson brilliantly, inside and out.

The years went by, and as happens to much of what is learned in childhood, so also here, he found no use for it—and it faded into oblivion.

In the meantime, his life underwent a change; he had severe trials and was involved in a singular conflict that all at once or with one blow placed his life in abeyance, and just that alone gave him plenty to think about.

This preoccupied him from morning until night, awake and in his dreams, and he became old before his time.

Fifteen years went by. Then one morning as he woke up the thought suddenly struck him: What you are experiencing is similar to the story of Abraham.

And now he began to read. He read and read, he read aloud, he delineated the whole story; he cut it out in paper silhouettes;[52] he did nothing else—but he did not understand Abraham or himself.—*JP* VI 6791 (*Pap.* X⁴ A 458) *n.d.*, 1852

NEW "FEAR AND TREMBLING"

X⁵
A 132
140

[*In margin:* This is related to something in one of the journals[53] from the time I lived on Østerbro.]

. . . . . And Abraham climbed Mount Moriah with Isaac. He resolved to speak to Isaac—and he succeeded in inspiring Isaac—since it is God's will, Isaac is willing to become the sacrifice.

X⁵
A 132
141

And he cut the wood and he bound Isaac and he lighted the fire—he kissed Isaac once again; now they are not related to each other as father and son, no, as friend to friend, both like obedient children before Jehovah.

— —And he drew his knife— —and he thrust it into Isaac.

At that moment Jehovah in visible form stood beside Abraham and said: Old man, old man, what have you done? Did you not hear what I said; did you not hear me cry out: Abraham, Abraham, stop!

But Abraham replied in a voice half subservient, half confused: No, Lord, I did not hear it. Great was my grief—you know that best, for you know how to give the best and you know how to claim the best—yet my grief is tempered by Isaac's having understood me, and in my joy over being in accord with him I did not hear your voice at all, but obediently, as I thought, I thrust the knife into the obedient sacrifice.

Then Jehovah brought Isaac back to life. But in quiet sorrow Abraham thought to himself: But it is not the same Isaac; and in a certain sense it was not, for by having understood what he had understood on Mount Moriah, that he had been selected by God for the sacrifice, he had in a sense become an old man, just as old as Abraham. It was not the same Isaac, and they were properly suited to each other only for eternity. The Lord God Jehovah foresaw this and he had mercy upon Abraham and as always restored everything, infinitely better than if the mistake had not occurred. There is, he said to Abraham, an eternity; soon you will be united eternally with Isaac, and you will be in harmony for eternity. Had you heard my voice and had stopped short—you would have gotten Isaac back for this life, but that which concerns eternity would not have become clear to you. You went too far, you ruined everything—yet I am making it even better than if you had not gone too far—there is an eternity.

This is the relationship between Judaism and Christianity. In the Christian view Isaac actually is sacrificed—but then eternity. In Judaism it is only an ordeal [*Prøvelse*] and Abraham keeps Isaac, but then the whole episode still remains essentially within this life.—*JP* II 2223 (*Pap.* X^5 A 132) *n.d.*, 1853

X^5
A 132
141

Gjentagelsen.

Et Forsøg i den experimenterende Psychologi

af

Constantin Constantius.

Kjøbenhavn.

Faaes hos C. A. Reitzel.

Trykt i Bianco Lunos Bogtrykkeri.

1843.

REPETITION.

A Venture in Experimenting Psychology

by

Constantin Constantius.

Copenhagen.

Available at C. A. Reitzel's.
Printed by Bianco Luno Press.
1843.

From sketch of Johannes Climacus, or De omnibus dubitandum est:[1]

IV
B 1
149-50

3. *Repetition*

here doubt could be broken off—one assumes that there is no repetition. But it cannot be done without positing a repetition.

IV
B 1
145-47

4. *The Actuality [Virkelighed] of Repetition*

Illusion

IV
B 1
149-50

8. The first expression for the relationship between immediacy and mediacy is *REpetition.*

In immediacy there is no repetition; it may be thought to depend on the dissimilarity of things; not at all, if everything in the world were absolutely identical there still would be no repetition.

IV
B 1
134-37

9. But when the possibility of repetition is posited, then the question of its actuality arises: is it actually a repetition.

Illusion

—*JP* III 3792 (*Pap.* IV B 10:3, 4, 8, 9) *n.d.,* 1842-43

From draft of Johannes Climacus, or De omnibus dubitandum est:

IV
B 1
149

Consciousness, then, is the relation, a relation whose form is contradiction. But how does consciousness discover the contradiction? If that fallacy discussed above[2] could remain, that ideality and reality[3] in all naiveté communicated with one another, consciousness would never emerge, for consciousness emerges precisely through the collision, just as it presupposes the collision. Immediately there is no collision, but mediately it is present. As soon as the question of a *repetition* arises, the collision is present, for only a repetition of what has been before is conceivable.

In reality as such, there is no repetition. This is not because everything is different, not at all. If everything in the world were completely identical, in reality there would be no repetition, because reality is only in the moment.[4] If the world, instead of being beauty, were nothing but equally large unvariegated boulders, there would still be no repetition. Throughout all eternity, in every moment I would see a boulder, but there would be no question as to whether or not it was the same one I had seen before. In ideality alone there is no repetition, for the idea is and remains the same and as such cannot be repeated. When ideality and reality touch each other, then repetition occurs. When, for example, I see something in the moment, ideality enters in and will explain that it is a repetition. Here is the contradiction, for that which is is also in another mode. That the external is, that I see, but in the same instant I bring it into relation with something that also is, something that is the same and that also will explain that the other is the same. Here is a redoubling; here it is a matter of a repetition. Ideality and reality therefore collide—in what medium? In time? That is indeed an impossibility. In what, then? In eternity? That is indeed an impossibility. In what, then? In consciousness—there is the contradiction. The question is not disinterested, as if one asked whether all the world is not an image of the idea and to that extent whether visible existence is not, in a certain volatilized sense, a repetition. Here the question is more specifically one of a repetition in consciousness, consequently of recollection. Recollection involves the same contradiction. Recollection is not ideality; it is ideality that has been. It is not reality; it is reality that has been—which again is a double contradiction, for ideality, according to its concept, cannot have been, and the same holds true of reality according to its concept.—*Pap.* IV B 1, pp. 149-50 *n.d.*, 1842-43

IV
B 1
150

Revised in final copy; see title page:

REPETITION[5]
[*deleted*: A Fruitless Venture
A Venture of Discovery]
[*deleted*: A Fruitless Venture
A Venture in Experimental Philosophy]
A Venture in Experimenting [*deleted*: Philosophy] [*added*:]
Psychology
by
[*deleted*: Victorinus Constantinus de bona speranza]
[*added*:] Constantin [*deleted*: Walter] [*added*:] Constantius
—*Pap.* IV B 97:1 *n.d.*, 1843

Revised in final copy; see 127:

[*deleted*: Drink water from your own well.
Proverbs 5:15]

On wild trees the flowers are fragrant, on cultivated trees,
the fruit (see Flavius Philostratus the Elder's *Hero-tales*)[6] [*deleted*: ; but the fruits of the spirit are love. (See Galatians
5:22.)]—*Pap.* IV B 97:2 *n.d.*, 1843

Deleted from final copy; see 131 above first line:

Berlin May 1843.
—*Pap.* IV B 97:3 *n.d.*, 1843

Deleted from final copy; see 135:11:

(which I do not misuse, because he is dead)[7]
—*Pap.* IV B 97:4 *n.d.*, 1843

Revised in final copy; see 145:6:

[*Deleted*: he shot himself.]
[*Added in margin*:] he had disappeared.[8]
—*Pap.* IV B 97:5 *n.d.*, 1843

Revised in final copy; see 146:18:

[*Deleted*: death]
[*Added in margin*:] disappearance[9]
                        —*Pap*. IV B 97:6 *n.d.*, 1843

Deleted from margin of final copy; see 181:23:

What especially amazed me was that she could have had such great significance for him, for there was no trace of anything really stirring, enrapturing, creative. With him it was as is usually the case with melancholy persons—they trap themselves. He idealized her, and now he believed that she was that.—*Pap*. IV B 97:8 *n.d.*, 1843

Revised in final copy; (see 182:21-22) from:

for the particular individuals who have been called Aristophaneses by a reviewer, like the *doctores cerei* in the Middle Ages, do not have great significance; calling someone a German, Danish, Spanish, Jutland Aristophanes is like calling someone the Jutland Mrs. Heiberg[10] . . . . .—*Pap*. IV B 97:9 *n.d.*, 1843

Deleted from final copy; see 189:34:

It is with me as with a girl I have known, who admired the beloved so much that she was completely happy only when he shut his eyes and promised her to let his face be so apathetic that there was not even the possibility of its signifying what it otherwise so frequently signified.—*Pap*. IV B 97:10 *n.d.*, 1843

Deleted from margin of final copy; see 194:2:

this kiss that flowered upon them, whose sweetness I imbibed more passionately than Thor when he drank the ocean of the world,[11] this kiss that in the next moment blushed even more deeply, although I seemed to have drawn the blood out of her whole being.—*Pap.* IV B 97:11 *n.d.*, 1843

Revised in final copy (see 196:7) from:

Alphons.

—*Pap.* IV B 97:12 *n.d.*, 1843

Revised in final copy (see 216:32-33) from:

scream herself empty, must be incited to scream so that she forgets more quickly. [*Deleted*: If that has been done, then all one has to do is to strike while the iron is hot. At no moment is a girl more inclined to embrace a new love affair than when she escapes one that would cost her life. Then if one sees to it that a man is thrust into her arms, she will take him, even though he has been purchased at the hardware store.]—*Pap.* IV B 97:13 *n.d.*, 1843

Deleted from margin of final copy; see 217:11-14:

I was crushed. Therefore I would not hesitate to use every means to get her dislodged, that is, married. Then I would have peace.—*Pap.* IV B 97:14 *n.d.*, 1843

Revised in final copy (see 217:22) from:

this would not disturb me.

—*Pap.* IV B 97:15 *n.d.*, 1843

Revised in final copy (see 217:25) from:

a bestial

—*Pap.* IV B 97:16 *n.d.*, 1843

Revised in final copy (see 217:28) from:

false step

—*Pap.* IV B 97:17 *n.d.*, 1843

Deleted from final copy; see 217:37:

as reparation and compensation for those who make fools of the girls
                              —*Pap.* IV B 97:18 *n.d.*, 1843

Deleted from final copy; see 218:2:

for I think she has been like other girls
                              —*Pap.* IV B 97:19 *n.d.*, 1843

Revised in final copy (see 218:4) from:

in a feminine way would have permitted herself everything
                              —*Pap.* IV B 97:20 *n.d.*, 1843

Deleted from final copy; see 218:9:

If a girl could have the indescribable gratification, which satisfies in the long run, of having done much for a man, to have given a person himself again—only a rare exception chooses that. Usually a girl chooses essentially to devastate a person, and then she is noble enough to console him with her embrace and a flock of children.—*Pap.* IV B 97:21 *n.d.*, 1843

Revised in final copy (see 218:9) from:

a girl
                              —*Pap.* IV B 97:22 *n.d.*, 1843

Revised in final copy (see 218:10) from:

the most wretched seducer
                              —*Pap.* IV B 97:23 *n.d.*, 1843

Deleted from final copy; see 218:14:

For a young person's sake, such a girl ought not to be recognizable by a black tooth only;[12] no, her whole face should be green. But that is perhaps too much to ask. Then there would be many green girls.—*Pap.* IV B 97:24 *n.d.,* 1843

Revised in final copy (see 218:21) from:

wind

—*Pap.* IV B 97:25 *n.d.,* 1843

Revised in final copy (see 218:22) from:

fixed-[idea]

—*Pap.* IV B 97:26 *n.d.,* 1843

Deleted from final copy; see 218:23:

and saved him from having his life in the tragic-comic contradiction of owing another person very much, precisely because that other person had power enough to wrong him thoroughly.—*Pap.* IV B 97:27 *n.d.,* 1843

Revised in final copy (see 218:27) from:

view. In large part I have abandoned it

—*Pap.* IV B 97:28 *n.d.,* 1843

Revised in final copy (see 218:32) from:

[therefore] one cannot even have contempt for her.
[*Deleted:* If I were to catch myself as a liar, a murderer, yes, as a hypocrite, I still would not sink in despair, for I would continue to hope for repentance, but if I became comical to myself, if I discovered that the substance of my feelings was so much blather, I believe I would blush so violently that I would die from it. If I meet a hypocrite in ordinary

life, then I do as the poet says of that strong man who steps on a snake—I have contempt.[13] But I do have contempt, and that is sound. However, when I see a girl who is not a hypocrite but believes and with the most sacred vows vouches for her faith and then in the next moment believes something else—the effect upon me is like that of having a mouthful of freshly churned butter to which someone has forgotten to add salt.]—*Pap.* IV B 97:29 *n.d.*, 1843

Revised in final copy (see 225:4) from:

July

—*Pap.* IV B 97:30 *n.d.*, 1843

Revised in final copy (see 228:29-30) from:

see how everything refers to him about whom the discourse speaks everywhere

—*Pap.* IV B 97:32 *n.d.*, 1843

Basically, I now see that Prof. Heiberg and I agree that he is right on the main point, namely, that he has satisfied the demand of the times with his gilded New Year's gift.[14] The only difference between us is in regard to our understanding of what the times demand.[15] Prof. H. believes that it is astronomy.[16] This I doubt. In my opinion the times demand a very sleek and elegant book in gilded binding with as little as possible on the pages, or, to say it more clearly, the demand of the times is: to be taken by the nose.* Understood thus, the demand of the times has been completely satisfied by Prof. H. All things considered, then, I now see that Prof. H. and I agree that Prof. H. is right on the main point—that he has satisfied the demand of the times with his gilded New Year's gift.

* There are numberless examples to prove that this actually is the constant demand of the times, whereas the professor is the only one who has discovered that it was astronomy the times demanded.—*Pap.* IV B 101 *n.d.*, 1843-44

Every time I think of Prof. Heiberg sitting in his astrological observatory[17] I cannot help thinking of Hoffmann's
character Herr von Sabelthau[18] sitting in the observatory with
his long beard.

See Hoffmann's *Collected Works*, IV, p. 267.

—*Pap.* IV B 102 *n.d.*, 1843-44

Heiberg has continually contradicted himself.[19] Even in the
dispute with Hauch,[20] in which H. simply wanted to work
for the times, even in that he tried with all sorts of pompous
phrases and circumlocutions to prove that the dispute itself
was extremely important, inasmuch as it had to do with an
esthetic issue, which must always be of concern.—*Pap.* IV B
103 *n.d.*, 1843-44

It seems that Prof. Heiberg has been surprised once again,
as he was by *Either/Or* ("a lightning bolt out of a clear sky").[21]
It is inconceivable that it can happen to the professor, who,
after all, is an astrologer and an expert on stars.—*Pap.* IV B
104 *n.d.*, 1843-44

Prof. H[eiberg]. perhaps believes that Christianity is a theme
for a vaudeville play.—*Pap.* IV B 105 *n.d.*, 1843-44

Notations on folder containing Pap. IV B 109-24:

Unused.
Polemica in connection with Heiberg's "Repetition" in the
New Year's gift.[22]—*Pap.* IV B 108 *n.d.*, 1843-44

Included in Pap. IV B 108:

N.B. Since I wrote that little book[23] "so that the heretics
would not be able to understand it,"[24] it would be stepping
out of character to explain it in somewhat greater detail.
Moreover, all that nonsense of Heiberg's[25] is sheer triviality.

I ought not to waste my time and to let myself be dragged down into the ephemeral spheres. People will get polemics enough in my books—no polemics that could appeal to a gaping, inquisitive, lascivious public.—*Pap.* IV B 109 *n.d.,* 1843-44

OPEN LETTER
TO
PROFESSOR HEIBERG, KNIGHT OF DANEBROG
FROM
CONSTANTIN CONSTANTIUS[26]

IV
B 110
258

HONORABLE PROFESSOR!

Since I myself have published a little book[27] positing belief in repetition, I would, yes, I certainly would have to be star-crazed not to accept with joy a significant substantiation when it is offered in a manner flattering to me.[28] Would not even a person of lesser belief be won to a belief in repetition by seeing how that which was said by an obscure underling in a modest, yes, almost poorly clad book is gained by being repeated by the famous Professor Heiberg in an extremely sleek and elegant New Year's gift,[29] how it is also elevated to the loftiest sphere, for the starry heavens are indeed highest of all, to which all agree, and only Arv and Jesper Ridefoged[30] suppose that the crystalline heaven is still higher? And how could I fail to feel flattered to see my poor thoughts sparkling like stars in your heaven! Indeed, I confess that when I saw them printed in those fine letters in all that distinguished company, I could not recognize them at first, and when I did recognize them, I was moved in the way indigent parents are moved when they see their children become prominent, but, like indigent parents, I also was hesitant about daring to permit myself my old familiarity toward them.

IV
B 110
259

But the significance of repetition manifests itself in a more profound sense on this occasion in that what I expressed more obscurely[*] was made lucid by your correction,[31] Professor, because what I had said, already beautiful and appropriate[32] in a way, truly became very beautiful and appropriate through the correction it received in your elaboration. I do not know a more appropriate way to describe how beautiful the whole thing is.

In a discussion of repetition, the treatise "The Starry Heaven,"[33] with which you have embellished your elegant New Year's gift, contains the above-mentioned correction of what I have said about repetition. The treatise itself has a more comprehensive scope, but fortunately only a minor portion of it concerns me,[34] and fortunately I am able to comprehend this minor portion and fortunately dare to feel somewhat confident of being able to say a word about it. I say "fortunately," for I certainly would cut a sorry figure if I in any way were to take up the first part, the sixty pages of tables.[35] When I purchased the book and opened it up and saw page 1, Table, and turned the page and saw page 2, Table, and continued to turn the pages, I got no further than page 30 before fainting at the sight[**] of this infinite number and also at the thought of how learned you must be, Professor. I have never been very good at numbers, and insofar as there may be a little understanding in that respect, it does not reach very far. But this much I realized (something that my barber, who was summoned on the occasion of my fainting, also thought): what we have here is not *regula Detri* [the rule of three],[36] whether or not it is *regula Petri*, or whatever it is. I say "fortunately," for, with respect to the last part of the treatise, it is more comprehensible, but nevertheless to grasp it, to say nothing of replying to it, presupposes such a multifarious knowledge of astronomy that a student like me, who got only a C-plus in astronomy in the general studies examination and never concerned myself with this science later, knows only enough to be able to realize how little he knows about it. So I am able to read it and, if I take pains,

IV
B 110
260

[*] *In margin*: and erroneously[37]
[**] *In margin*: the repeated sight

understand it fairly well, but I can never be sure of having understood it, to say nothing of being foolhardy enough to think myself capable of having an opinion about it. Fortunately, in connection with all this, I do not need to be more than a reader, as I *pro virili* [according to my capacity] have tried hard to be. Just as in my earlier days,[38] when I believed I was capable of understanding your achievements, Professor, I had the pleasure of understanding and then, after the strain of it, relaxed in the arms of admiration; so now my admiration for your later achievements is no less but different, indefinable, feminine, and enthusiastic, which I very likely share with many of my contemporaries, who, like me, look forward to your conclusions with eager expectation, even if they, as do I, modestly leave it up to the experts in the field to judge whether your more recent astronomical, astrological, chiromantic, necromantic, talismanistic, chronological, horoscopical, metascopical studies will benefit science and mankind.

[Leave it up to the experts on the subject] to judge how successful, by means of all these arts and sciences, you might be in healing the mental depression[39] of the times.

how successful you might be, after having found the congregation sought in your latest poem,[40] in turning its gaze heavenward, while you yourself, like that heavenly councilor,[41] set a good example for the congregation.—*Pap.* IV B 110 *n.d.*, 1843-44

Continuation of Pap. IV B 110:

But I proceed to the subject, to the correction[42] that in your treatise has fallen to the lot of what I have said. So that everything may be clear and indisputable, I will first of all state your formulation of repetition[*] as it is in itself, together with the consideration it gives to mine, and after that

IV
B 111
261

[*] *In margin*: as it is explained with respect to nature and "adequately intimated with respect to spirit" (p. 98,[43] line 1)

I will state my formulation as it appears printed in my little book.

ask the reader to excuse the prolixity.

A. Your Formulation

Repetition belongs to the world of natural phenomena, and it is a mistake to transfer it to the world of spirit. "I have the category of nature especially in view and perhaps without being aware of it have stretched the validity of the concept beyond its legitimate boundaries."*

Repetition belongs to the world of natural phenomena and proclaims itself there as a law—a view that is the ideal view of repetition. If a more explicit explanation is requested as to how the finite spirit is and can be involved in this repetition, such an explanation is essentially the main content of your treatise. As far as I understood you, its intention is to open people's eyes and senses to repetition in natural phenomena, to make their hearts sensitive and sympathetic to it. All the credit in that respect belongs exclusively to you; I did not say a word about this in my little book,[44] and certainly there is no one who is more pleased than I with your total and unabridged service to mankind. Insofar as my eyes and also my heart are ever opened to such heavenly observations and my soul in truth grasps this beautiful enthusiasm in the bosom of nature and up in the heavens, I have no doubt but that your treatise was the first to awaken all this in me.

In the domain of the spirit, however, there is no repetition. There we should see the development that is implicit in repetition and that in a way annuls repetition as such.** "While no such development is found in nature,† in the world of the spirit, on the other hand, each new generation goes beyond the previous one and uses its achievements for genuinely new beginnings, that is, for those that lead to something genuinely new."††

IV
B 111
262

* See pp. 97 and 98.
** p. 97, top.
† p. 94, middle.
†† p. 95, top.

From the domain of nature, one proceeds to the domain of the spirit. This is entirely proper. But does the domain of the spirit then mean nothing but the world-historical process, concerning which it is rather *wohlfeilt* [cheap], especially today, to explain* that the one generation goes beyond the other and begins where the other left off? Is there not a spiritual existence [*Existents*] that belongs to individuals? Should not repetition become an issue here as well, but, please note, not such that repetition is not[45] outside the individual in the natural order and that the individual conducts himself contemplatively, essentially unconcerned about something with which he cannot interfere essentially, and sensitive at most only to the possibility of passing away the time? Should it not be important to illuminate this very point when helping an author who ventures into experimenting psychology?[46]

You see, there is very little about this in your adequate intimation[47] of the importance of repetition in the domain of the spirit, and the little that is there is very far from adequate if one desires an explanation from you, Professor, and not a pronouncement.

It is really at this point that the difficulty lies and the misinterpretation originates. Your observations are always superb, whether they are about the heavens or about world history. Suppose the individual has learned from you how he is to observe the heavens.** Credit where credit is due, but apart from the heavens and world history, there is still a history called the individual's history. This does not seem to concern you very much. If this fact were not adequately apparent, albeit somewhat unclearly, in the little you say about it, it would be clearly evident from your main observation in the treatise. You say that the age is mentally depressed,[48] is in labor—on that point you may not doubt for a moment that I agree with you since you are of the opinion that I have written books besides this little *Repetition* and, for example,

IV
B 111
263

In margin: * as, indeed, any poor wretch who fails the comprehensive examination can tell you

In margin: ** which is by no means a matter of freedom but is either sentimentality or arbitrariness

Or, the second part of
go on to say that you
ive birth; the thing to
d in your opinion it is
the times be the times;
even expel the fetus—
ls? If there is nothing
individuals are indeed
dom.

luals in their freedom,
declares oneself a psy-
in reserve, as soon as
ind away from all this
he heavens and world
ible and blessed object
hat meaning does rep-
irit, for indeed, every
, is qualified as spirit,

uestion becomes: What
More particularly, the
lom to the phenomena
h the individual lives,
ntinuity with his own
inding him. Here the
ithin the boundaries of
rvey all world history
ation begins where the
is on a grandiose scale;
light and insignificant.
ofessor has overlooked
ain and again, insofar
akes a beginning many
hether each individual
through his initial be-
gh his initial beginning
al does not relate con-
phenomena in which

it appears are phenomena of the spirit, but he relates to them in freedom, and thus the question becomes a different one and, in my opinion, a far more difficult but also far more significant one. But it is only of this that I spoke in my little book, which readily follows from my being a psychologist.

This question of the relation of repetition for the individuality qualified as free spirit is scarcely intimated at all in your "adequate" intimation.[49] When you speak about the individuality, you always conceive of him only as contemplating or as esthetically ambiguous. That there is repetition always remains certain, and what preoccupies you is assisting the individual to gain a feeling for repetition. But the first issue of freedom—whether there is repetition—is not touched on at all. And yet it is essentially about this that I have written, and that is why my book was titled *Repetition*. Apart from this, it follows as a matter of course that if the individual is conceived of esthetically ambiguously, there can be an occasion to say one thing and another, this and that, about repetition; but if this has been overlooked, nothing but confusion results—even when something good is said.

The misunderstanding you have occasioned is best seen by considering the "golden words of Goethe"[50] that you quoted but that by being quoted in such a manner have perhaps become the gold in which freedom perishes. In order to enjoin beautiful sympathy with nature, you quote Goethe's words.[51] The quotation is fairly long. Initially, it does in fact deal with sympathy with nature, where repetition is present, but without touching on freedom in the individual, where the point is—if one wants to have anything to do with it—to develop sympathy. But the quotation continues. And look, suddenly the quotation is about something entirely different. At its climax, the quotation declares that just as there is a repetition in nature, so "the continuous recurrence of our errors makes the sensitive youth anxious, for how late we learn to perceive that as we train our virtues we cultivate our errors."[*]

IV
B 111
265

[*] *In margin*: p. 106.

Thus there is repetition in the phenomena of nature and in the phenomena of the spirit, and there repetition means the repetition of our errors and of our virtues, one with the other. But there is repetition, and the question is merely how would the individual learn to become sensitive to this repetition.

This kind of observation scarcely considers the individual according to his freedom, and yet it is directly from this quotation that you develop the dialectic of repetition that you find in these golden words, after you have first of all drawn attention to the fact that Goethe himself attributes that lack of sympathy with nature and that hypochondria to the reading of English authors.[52] It is easy to see that the hypochondria was the result of that sensitive youth's being made *anxious* because his errors were repeated. If only he had been initiated into the dialectic of repetition and had comprehended that there is repetition in the world of spirit in the very same sense as in nature, that good and evil repeat themselves just as day and night, and that the individual's highest task is to sympathize with these alternations and to become sensitive—then he would not have become hypochondriacal.

Thus there is repetition in the phenomena of the spirit as well as in the phenomena of nature. The individual is not defined as spirit according to his freedom but is defined esthetically ambiguously in relation to repetition, finitely defined in relation to his object, which is not his to change. Indeed, the individual forbears changing the repetition in nature, and repetition in the phenomena of the spirit is to be treated entirely in the same way. Consequently, as you very accurately formulate it, everything depends upon thought, therefore the individual.[53] In the world of the spirit, then, the significance of repetition consists in what repetition carries along with it or in what the individual himself makes of it.[*] The repetition of good and evil is to be treated in the same way as the repetition of the orbits of the stars. Repetition is—and for the contemplating finite spirit there actually

IV
B 111
266

[*] *In margin*: p. 102, top. p. 101, top: "The allurement of repetition is not itself but what a person makes of it."

is no difference between its meaning in the existence [*Existents*] of the individual spirit and its presence in nature. This is clearly seen also in the fact that immediately after the above quotation this passage follows: "The same is true of our observation of nature, and especially of the natural and astronomical year. Nature always speaks the universal language of repetition . . .. What nature gives us is nothing other than repetition; what we do with it, so that it can continually be something new for us, depends upon us."[*] Consequently, it is here a matter of individual inventiveness in mood. Likewise, it is a matter of the relation of the individual spirit to the repetition of the phenomena of the spirit—indeed, the more alternation the better. Once the repetition is there, it is only a matter of becoming at times sentimental, at times witty, at times roguish, at times agitated, at times frivolous, at times depressed, etc. But there is no question of wanting to annul repetition.

Only once does another observation appear, rather oddly, in the whole discussion. We are told (p. 110) that what should teach us to see the year's repetitions in a varying light is especially "the superiority with which our self-conscious free will makes those uniform epochs into milestones on the road of our spiritual development."** If this is to be taken more seriously and is not to dissolve into a kind of philandering, as the following suggests—"no day should pass without having communicated some yield or other, be it ever so meager, from the sphere either of art or of science or of social intercourse or of inner development"[†]†† —then I believe the in-

IV
B 111
267

---

[*] *In margin*: p. 102.

In margin: ** in a higher sense the motto *nulla dies sine linea* [not a day without a line] holds true here.[54]

[†] *In margin*: p. 110.

†† If by the development of the individual you have not in the strictest sense understood a continuous producing but a development in which the individual remains within himself, then there arises the difficulty that he himself must communicate to himself something from the sphere of his inner development in the same sense as from the spheres of art, science, and social intercourse, although the appropriation is indeed precisely his inner development, and if in the strictest sense it is to be understood as a contin-

dividual will have enough to do with this development of
his self-conscious free will and little time to waste on sympathetic feelings for nature. The very moment the individual
realizes this, your suggestion about using astronomy as an
intermediary becomes superfluous, for in that very moment
he has more than enough to do. But in that very moment
the issue that preoccupies me arises. If the point is the spiritual development of a self-conscious free will, then repetition cannot be left nebulous this way, then it is a quesion of
nullifying the repetition in which evil recurs and of bringing
forth the repetition in which the good recurs. The issue, then,
IV
B 111
268
is not one of relating to repetition; rather, the question is
whether it can be generated in such a way that it is in the
interest of the development of the self-conscious free spirit.

I look in vain for a more detailed explanation of this [in
your treatise].

In your entire discussion, then, what remains firm is that
repetition unceasingly is. That is settled.

There is repetition in the sphere of nature. The essential
thing, then, is that the finite spirit contemplatively abandons
itself in sympathy with its repetitive movement. You are
preoccupied principally by this thought in the entire treatise.
What you with all your astronomical knowledge have said
about that, I cannot judge, but from a more general point of
view I make bold to have an opinion on what you have said
in general. You enjoin a sympathetic relation to nature, which,
as far as I understand it, must be defined as a sentimental
relation. In my view, this is one-sidedness. Only in freedom's relation to the task of freedom is there earnestness;
wherever else spirit relates to its other in such a way that this
other is not freedom, comic observation is just as legitimate,
just exactly as legitimate, as the sentimental. As a rule, the
person in whom the passion of freedom has awakened is
concerned very little with nature and regards it as a matter
of indifference. That is why, as I have already remarked, it

---

uous producing (with pen and ink), then there is no perception of the profound meaning which that motto, *nulla dies sine linea,* acquires here by being
"taken in a higher sense."

was curious to see, in a treatise that specifically recommends
the beneficial influence of the observation of nature on the
mind, the rather isolated remark about the self-conscious free
will that has so much to do on the road of its development
that the motto *nulla dies sine linea* applies here in a higher
sense. That is why it was so strange to see this isolated statement in a treatise that does not abandon time and is intended
only to pass away the time or to be a means for healing the
age's mental depression, which borders on insanity.[55]

There is, then, repetition in the phenomena of spirit. For
the individuality defined only esthetically ambiguously, the
task is to get along with it, to be reconciled to it, and to
bring something new out of it. There are several comments
along this line in my little book (to be interpreted in more
detail later). As soon as the matter is construed this way,
sagacity reigns supreme and tries to help as well as it can
while experience speaks *pro und contra* on this matter. As an
example of the instruction of such sagacity, I cite what you
say about me, that I should not have gone to Berlin because
the fact that many pleasant experiences make a far weaker
impression the second time than the first is generally acknowledged in the saying that one should never return to a
place where he once has been.[*] Here experience can just as
well say the opposite. In fact, generally it is only gypsies and
transient trapeze artists or bandits who say, as indeed the
leader of the gypsies in the play *Pretiosa*[56] says: Never return
to a place where you once have been,[57] because very likely
the next time people will watch their money and property
more carefully, or because the next time there will be nothing to pilfer. In that way you are right, Professor. But, on
the other hand, it is commonly said that going to a place the
second time is more pleasant than the first, because the resistance to the new that often frustrates enjoyment the first
time and is only gradually overcome is as good as overcome
at the very beginning the second time. Moreover, if the attraction of repetition is not the repetition itself "but what a

IV
B 111
269

[*] *In margin*: p. 101.

person makes of it," then one does not need to be very perceptive to see that the person who takes a trip to convince himself of repetition has already changed it into something else. One can go on dialecticizing in this manner. I do it here only to show what will be shown even better later—that what was a jest with me, because I had a far more profound issue in mind, was treated by you very seriously.

You continue: "On the other hand, the repetition of the reading of a book, of the enjoyment of a work of art, can heighten and in a way surpass the first impression, because one thereby immerses oneself more deeply in the object and appropriates it more inwardly."[*] Well, then, a large city like Berlin may also be compared with and stand alongside a book and a work of art.[**] If so, then it is reasonable to speak of a heightened enjoyment through repetition, and if that happens, one need not be tempted in observing the size of the city and the variety of its urban life to think that it is the result of one's having read or observed carelessly the first time. Here again one can go on dialecticizing in this manner. That is the amusing aspect of repetition, which one should never take seriously, something I do not do in my little book, whereas for you everything in the observation of repetition is equally serious.

The repeated reading of a book or enjoyment of a work of art can by no means be regarded as a repetition in the pregnant sense, for it is still liable to the dialectical ambiguity, to the jest in repetition, something I was particularly aware of because I was aware of the earnestness. There is but one pregnant repetition, and that is the individuality's own repetition raised to a new power. You do not mention this repetition at all, despite its being repetition *sensu eminentiori* [in the highest sense] and freedom's deepest interest. Only twice is repetition declared to exist, both times by the young man whom I have made the subject of my discussion. When he tells how Job got everything back double, he exclaims

IV
B 111
270

[*] *In margin*: p. 101.
[**] *In margin*: especially when even the enjoyment of a play is to be repeated.

that this is called a repetition.* The other time is when he himself, by the help of Governance, is freed from the entanglement of his unhappy love and exclaims: Is there not, then, a repetition? Did I not get everything double? Did I not get myself again and precisely in such a way that I might have a double sense of its meaning?[**] In my accompanying letter, I say that the young man explains repetition with reference to himself as his consciousness raised to the second power.[58] Only in the latter section of my little book—which is marked as a section by having the heading "Repetition" again[59]— only there is the authentic statement about repetition.[†] You do not have one single quotation from this part. Your quotations do not go beyond p. 40.[††60] If it were not you, Professor, I would think that you had not read the latter part of the book. On the basis of such an assumption, I would certainly be able to explain everything. Only the person who reads the whole book through, only he can understand it just as it should be understood; however, if read in snatches, it probably can always be understood, but one will understand something different from what I have understood. Now if this situation occurs with a man like Prof. H., he is gracious enough, in view of the beauty[61] of particular statements, to want to help the author out of the misunderstanding he himself has created for him. No author can ask for more. That is true, yet I am unreasonable enough to spurn help and merely ask that the book be read all the way through. However, I dare not think you could read a book any other way. And yet only this hypothesis explains everything. It explains to me how you can give the reading of a book, in contrast to my journey to Berlin, as an example of a potentiated repetition, although the second part of my little book gives the one and only pregnant example, the repetition of the indi-

IV
B 111
271

In margin: * *Repetition*, p. 130 [*i.e.*, *SV* III 245].

[**] *In margin*: p. 142 [*i.e.*, *SV* III 254].

[†] *In margin*: whereas I myself end the first part [*i.e. SV* III 213] by doubting the possibility of a repetition.

In margin: †† where nothing is said about repetition except in jest or in despair of its possibility.

viduality. It explains how you, prompted by my little book, can exclaim in a passage such as this: "Who could wish to repeat his life utterly unchanged . . . indeed, one would rather not repeat unchanged even joy or good fortune"[*]—although my second part says: Compared with such a repetition (that is, the repetition of the individuality to the second power), what is a repetition of worldly possessions, which is indifferent toward the qualification of the spirit?** It explains to me how you wish to teach me about the something more that repetition involves in the development of spirit, although in my second part there is a much more definite expression than in all you have said.

But let us now forget the second part and pretend that none of us has read it and with your help try to understand better the quotations that appear in your New Year's gift. The correction is that what I have said has its place in relation to repetition in nature and that understood in this way the sentences are very beautiful and striking.[62] As stated previously, I feel about these quoted words of mine as indigent parents feel about their very distinguished children: I do not know whether I dare to permit myself the old familiarity.[63] In the old days, we understood each other, but now the words have become so distinguished that I cannot understand them. In order not to weary the reader by scrutinizing every quotation, I shall take the first one—mindful of the unfortunateness of my position in having to thank Prof. Heiberg for the assistance provided and also in causing the reader new impediments to finding the meaning of what perhaps once appeared also to him to have meaning. "Repetition is a crucial expression for what recollection was to the Greeks. Just as they taught that all knowing is a recollecting, modern philosophy will teach that all life is a repetition."[†][64] Under the auspices of Prof. Heiberg, let us now apply these words to the observation of the repetition of natural phenomena and try to find the meaning. After all, what significance is there

IV
B 111
272

[*] *In margin:* p. 101.
In margin: ** *Repetition,* p. 142 [*i.e., SV* III 254].
[†] *In margin:* see *Repetition,* p. 91, bottom [*i.e., SV* III 221].

supposed to be in making the distinction between the ancient
and the modern world in the observation of repetition in
natural phenomena. In the same section of his treatise,[65] Prof.
H. specifically commends the Greeks' observation of repetition in natural phenomena. Nowhere in the whole book did
I discuss the observation of repetition in natural phenomena.
I spoke about repetition in the issues of freedom. The meaning, then, is that with the Greeks freedom is not posited as
freedom. Therefore, the first expression is recollecting: only
in recollection did it possess eternal life. The modern view,
however, must be to express freedom forwards, and herein
lies repetition.

What happened to that quotation happened to several
others—by being summoned by the Rector of Literature, Prof.
H., corrected, *et encomio publico ornati* [and honored with public
praise]—they became meaningless. But one example must
suffice. I do not wish either to be the death of the reader or
to do away with myself, which would surely result from
making several separate statements of mine, which to me are
simple, natural, and devoid of all pretension, the object of
protracted deliberation solely because it so pleased Prof. H.
to want to correct them and on his own to make what was
very natural into something extraordinary. If it were conceivable that quotations could walk by themselves and if I
suspected that they, seduced and infatuated by worldly pleasure, had made some attempt to ingratiate themselves with
Prof. H. in order to get into his gilded New Year's gift, then
I would regard them as prodigal sons. But since I know that
they are innocent, I forgive them and also beg the reader of
my book to forgive them if he, just as I, should meet them
in their eminence, no longer modest and unassuming as before but, despite their present eminence, meaningless.

Let us now look at the outcome of Prof. Heiberg's exposition,[66] the answer. We learn that there is repetition in nature, that repetition is the process in world history. Of the
significance of repetition in the world of spiritual freedom
we learn nothing, find only a few scattered comments. Fi-

IV
B 111
273

IV
B 111
274

nally, we learn that after the professor's correction[67] I also
said something beautiful and striking.[*][68] This is the *summa
summarum* [sum total]. If Prof. H. had not written it, we
would naturally take it for granted that he, like any other
educated person, knew this and a little more about repetition, whereas we are now tempted to believe that this is the
maximum of his knowledge into which it is important to
initiate the reading public. When I ventured to publish a little
book about repetition, I went about it a bit differently. It
was not my business to publish an exceedingly sleek and
elegant book intended for children and Christmas trees, one
especially useful as a gift in good taste. I therefore presupposed in every reader all the knowledge that Prof. H. propounds and uses even to correct what I say. At the same
time, I perceived that repetition in the sphere of individual
life has a far deeper meaning. This thought prompted me to
write. The other knowledge about and reflection upon repetition I reduced to a jest and thereby avoided becoming ridiculous in the eyes of my reader by earnestly wanting to
instruct him in what everyone knows. I concealed the main
idea in order to exclude the heretics from understanding the
book in that conceptual jest,[70] and thus I published the book
devoid of any importance or pretension whatsoever. As to
the reader's situation, I thought that he would discover the
main idea and, whether he considered it correct or crazy, that
he would nevertheless admit that previously he had not
thought it in this way and consequently would consider it an
appropriate subject to be written about. He would understand the jest and be amused by it, and he would understand
the courtesy of my not permitting myself to write trivialities
in a didactic tone but showing by the very act of entrusting
it to a jest that I presupposed that it is entirely familiar.—
Pap. IV B 111 *n.d.*, 1843-44

[*] *In margin*: and how important this knowledge is in the professor's eyes
we learn from his opinion that with this knowledge he has corrected what
I said and has helped me to say something beautiful and true.[69]

A LITTLE CONTRIBUTION
BY
CONSTANTIN CONSTANTIUS
AUTHOR OF *REPETITION* . . .

—Pap. IV B 112 *n.d.,* 1843-44

Continuation of Pap. IV B 112, *which with some variations is a version of the latter two-thirds of Pap.* IV B 110:

Once when Socrates had gone outside the gates of Athens, it was apparent that he was unfamiliar with the region. When Phaedrus expressed his amazement at having to act as a guide to this singular man (ἀτοπωτατός) as if he were a stranger, Socrates said to him, "Oh, forgive me, dear friend, I am very desirous of knowledge, but landscapes and trees teach me nothing, whereas men in the city do."* I have tried to bear this statement in mind and to fulfill it in the way an inferior is able to fulfill what a superior spirit (in the most beautiful sense of the word) has said. Therefore it has been a joy for me, in relation to every human being, to regard myself as an apprentice. But even though I thereby broaden the concept of apprentice, it does not follow that I would not know how to use it again in a stricter sense, and if it is a question of being an apprentice in a stricter sense, who would not wish to be an apprentice to Prof. Heiberg?[71] But even though this has been my burning desire, it has been difficult for me of late, because his gaze embraces things so grandiose that I shall never succeed in following him. Of late he has turned his gaze to the far-flung yonder, where, staring prophetically ahead like a brooding genius, he beheld the system, the realization of long contemplated plans.** But in

IV
B 116
278

* See Plato's *Phaedrus*, Ast's edition, I, p. 132.[72]
** See preface to the 23 logical ¶¶ in *Perseus:*[73] "The author ventures to submit hereby the first contribution to the carrying out of a long cherished plan, namely, to present the logical system . . . . . —By means of the present exposition and its sequel, he further intends to pave the way for the esthetics, which it has long been his wish to produce but which he cannot send

ward to celestial things,[74]
ars,[†] and replies to him
conclusion that there is
n other planets there are
owment of wings.[*] And
oment toward earth, he
ividuals, not the conti-
, and from such an eva-
great soul to have cour-
the statement "that also
kes a highly respectable
rations are so grand that
to learn something from
far; it is bound not only
lso to the single individ-
on the streets and roads
less than a philosopher,
and consideration. That
rive to understand better
erfection by that Greek
en he perceived that the
ur concern (τὴν φυσικὴν
n to philosophize in the
oout ethical matters" (see
pter 5, para. 21, on
43-44

d by a letter to "the real
om this letter that I, "like

---

logical support to which it can

those distant planets,
uestion arises whether we may
ings on other planets. The an-
de this idea."

Clement of Alexandria, have tried to write in such a way
that the heretics are unable to understand it."*[79]

When applied in the sphere of individual freedom, the concept of repetition has a history, inasmuch as freedom passes
through several stages in order to attain itself. (a) Freedom
is first qualified as desire [Lyst] or as being in desire. What it
now fears is repetition, for it seems as if repetition has a
magic power to keep freedom captive once it has tricked it
into its power. But despite all of desire's ingenuity, repetition appears. Freedom in desire despairs. Simultaneously
freedom appears in a higher form. (b) Freedom qualified as
sagacity. As yet, freedom has only a finite relation to its object and is qualified only esthetically ambiguously. Repetition is assumed to exist, but freedom's task in sagacity is
continually to gain a new aspect of repetition. This stage has

IV
B 117
281

---

* Note. See *Repetition*, p. 147 [i.e., SV III 259].

It may very well seem curious for an author to decide to write in this
manner, but it can be explained. Although literature today demonstrates
that practically nothing is being done (except for the contribution of a single, solitary man,[80] who presumably belongs to Denmark, inasmuch as he
is its pride and honor, but sometimes even by writing in a foreign language
does what he is entitled to do, establish a European criterion for his work),
one can scarcely hear a word because of the promises, trumpet blasts, sub-
scription hawking, toasts, announcements, assurances, compliments, etc. In
this simulated motion, the year marches on. At Christmas time, there is a
commotion in literature, because several very sleek and elegant New Year's
gifts,[81] intended for children and Christmas trees and especially useful as
gifts in good taste, compete with each other in *Adresseavisen* in order, after
creating a furor for fourteen days, to be assigned by a courteous critic to a
place in some anthology as inspiring models for all writers of esthetic literature in fine style. Esthetic fine style—that is the watchword. And esthetic
fine style is a deadly earnest matter for which one trains oneself by abandoning ideas and thinking. In such a literary milieu it is not inexplicable
that an author wishes to avoid public opinion and to let a little book, in
calm consciousness of itself, go out as unnoticed and as self-contained as
possible. In this respect, the long Trinity season is a very good time of the
year if one wishes to be exempted from being whirled about in the New
Year's rush[82] of literary beggars, and if one, carefree and unconcerned, renounces the throngs of both shoppers and readers and infinitely prefers this
to a very sleek and elegant cardboard-bound book to be palmed off on
people at New Year's time.

been given expression in—to mention a more recent work—
"Rotation of Crops" (in *Either/Or*).[83] "Rotation of Crops"
was a part of *Either/Or*, and therefore this view also appears
in its unwarrantability. People who in freedom do not stand
in any higher relation to the idea usually embellish this standpoint as the highest wisdom. But since freedom qualified as
sagacity is only finitely qualified, repetition must appear again,
namely, repetition of the trickery by which sagacity wants
to fool repetition and make it into something else. Sagacity
despairs. (c) Now freedom breaks forth in its highest form,
in which it is qualified in relation to itself. Here everything
is reversed, and the very opposite of the first standpoint ap-

IV
B 117
282

pears. Now freedom's supreme interest is precisely to bring
about repetition, and its only fear is that variation would
have the power to disturb its eternal nature. Here emerges
the issue: *Is repetition possible?* Freedom itself is now the repetition. [84]If it were the case that freedom in the individuality
related to the surrounding world could become so immersed, so to speak, in the result that it cannot take itself
back again (repeat itself), then everything is lost. Consequently, what freedom fears here is not repetition but variation; what it wants is not variation but repetition. If this will
to repetition is stoicism, then it contradicts itself and thereby
ends in destroying itself in order to affirm repetition in that
way, which is the same as throwing a thing away in order
to hide it most securely. When stoicism has stepped aside,
only the religious movement remains as the true expression
for repetition and with the passionate eloquence of concerned
freedom proclaims its presence in the conflict.

What is developed under (c) [*i.e., Pap.* IV B 117, pp. 281–
82] was what I wanted to set forth in *Repetition*, but not in a
scientific-scholarly way, still less in a scientific-scholarly way
in the sense that every teller in our philosophical bank could
count 1, 2, 3.[85] I wanted to depict and make visible psychologically and esthetically; in the Greek sense, I wanted to let
the concept come into being in the individuality and the situation, working itself forward through all sorts of misunderstandings. In order that their inclusion would be admis-
sible, these misunderstandings had to legitimize themselves

as either witty or intriguing situations, or as nuanced moods, or as ironic oddities. I believed that I owed it to my reader and myself to save my soul from giving instruction, seriously and with the pomposity of a parish clerk, on what everyone must be presumed to know. Thus repetition (a) and (b) constantly make fun of repetition (c). [86]Just as it sometimes happens in life that an alehouse keeper, for example, strikingly resembles the king or some other world-historical person and that on seeing the alehouse keeper one is deceived and then smiles at the deception, just so one is deceived by repetition (a) and (b) with respect to repetition (c). Just as on the street one hears the minutest portion of a solitary flute player's performance, and almost instantly the rattle of the carriages and the noise of traffic make it necessary even for the Amager hawker to shout loudly so that the madame standing there can hear the price of her kale, and then for a brief instant it is quiet and one again hears the flute player, just so in the first part repetition (c) is continually interrupted by the noise of life. Just as a man who knows how to conceal a more profound observation of life in one simple word sits in the living room conversing with various people who all use the same word, and he now sees on a young girl's lips what she really wants to say with this word and then says it for her, to her joy, although she knows that it is a misunderstanding and behind the experienced man's ear sees what he means and allows it to come forth, although she knows it is a misunderstanding, and then on occasion he intersperses one word out of his own deeper reflection—in like manner repetition (c) develops in the first part through parlor prattle. I myself play the stoic in order to stand a little higher than (a) and (b), in order to suggest *in abstracto* what cannot be realized [*realisere*] *in abstracto*, and in the meantime I maieutically arrange everything properly for the young man who is supposed to discover actually what appears defined in the second part: repetition (c). Just as the young man is himself an exception* in life, so also is repetition (c), which like him has to battle its way through misunderstandings.

IV
B 117
283

* See *Repetition*, pp. 151 and 152 [*i.e.*, *SV* III 262 and 263].

ler *repetition is possible.*
1 advance by undertak-
etition is possible. The
interior problem of the
externally, as if repeti-
found outside the indi-
1 within the individual,
oes indeed do just the
lly. The consequence of
ossibility and step aside
f his religious primitiv-
ep by step, educated by
his distress, it seems to
n because he received
appeals to him in Job
1g revolves around that.
t him become guilty. If
onger take himself back
o it is not a question of
but of the repetition of
the thunderstorm would
re that no repetition is
n is supposed to prove
providence steps in to
ment, and he exclaims,
not get everything dou-
precisely in such a way
its meaning? Compared
petition of worldly pos-
the qualification of the
I say, "The young man
his consciousness to the

out repetition is in the
on page 79 [*i.e., SV* III

214], and to arouse the reader's attention it is again entitled "Repetition."†† Whatever is said before is always either a jest or only relatively true, adequately illustrated by the fact that I who said it despair of the possibility,[89] and page 92 [*i.e.*, *SV* III 221-22] reads, "I am unable to make a religious movement; it is contrary to my nature." Yet I do not therefore deny the reality [*Realiteten*] of such a thing or that one can learn very much from a young man. Furthermore, it says in the letter "that in relation to the young man I am a vanishing person,"* "every move I have made was merely to throw light on him,"** "he has been in good hands from the very beginning, even though I frequently had to tease him so that he himself could emerge."†

IV
B 117
285

If one wishes to illustrate that the meaning of repetition in the world of the individuality is different from its meaning in the world of nature and in a simple repetition, I do not think one can do it more definitely. When repetition is defined in that way, it is: transcendent, a religious movement by virtue of the absurd—when the borderline of the wondrous is reached, eternity is the true repetition. Therefore I believe that I have expressed myself fairly intelligibly for the book's real reader, [90]whom I beg—as I almost beg the book— to forgive me if I distort its individuality by revealing what it preferred to hide within itself and only wished to entrust to the real reader as the meaning of the jest by making it more clear to the eyes of a chance outsider, although it wished to go on living as inconspicuously as possible in the public eye, but also wished to be saved by its insignificance from the self-importance of corrections.[91]

Let us now turn to Prof. Heiberg and his gilded New Year's gift,[92] but let us not forget that his quotations do not go beyond p. 40 [*i.e.*, *SV* III 192] and that he does not discuss the rest in one single word. Since my little book is now

†† The explanatory letter therefore says "that the movement of the book is inverse." P. 149 [*i.e.*, *SV* III 260].

* P. 156 [*i.e.*, *SV* III 264].

** P. 152 [*i.e.*, *SV* III 262].

† P. 156 [*i.e.*, *SV* III 264].

IV
B 117
286
unfortunate enough to take on such importance that it can
become the object of correction, then this must be applied
to the latter part of the book, where repetition is propounded
for the first time, whereas everything earlier is only jest or
relative statements, some of which may be true but still are
true only completely *in abstracto* and therefore, with respect
to realization [*Realisationen*], have to be retracted, which is
illustrated by my despair.[93] But let these various statements
be what they will—nowhere, in either the first or the latter
part, is there mention of the observation of repetition in nature.[94] I have spoken only of the significance of repetition for
the individual free spirit, which is quite appropriate when
one, as the title says, ventures into experimenting [*experimenterende*: imaginatively constructing] psychology.[95]

IN PROF. HEIBERG'S FORMULATION[96] REPETITION IS CONTINUOUS

There is repetition in nature, and here it proclaims itself as
law, the observation of which is the more ideal observation
of repetition. If a more explicit explanation is requested as to
how the finite spirit is and can be involved in this repetition,
the development of this point is the main content of the professor's treatise. As far as I understand it, its intention is to
open a person's eyes and senses to repetition in natural phenomena, to make his heart sensitive to it and sympathetic
with it. All the credit in that respect—at present incalculable
as to its greatness or smallness, something I do not venture
to have any opinion about—belongs exclusively to Prof.
Heiberg. Not a word is said about it in my little book, and
certainly no one can strive more honestly and painstakingly
than I to let the professor's positive service to mankind remain whole and unabridged. Should my own eyes and heart
ever be opened to these heavenly observations, ah, I shall
have no doubt but that this treatise initially awoke in me
what would need time to reveal itself more clearly. —Until
IV
B 117
287
this moment, I have comprehended only this much: only in
freedom's relation to the task of freedom is there earnestness;
wherever else the spirit relates to something in such a way
that it is not freedom, comic observation is just as legitimate

as the sentimental, precisely as legitimate.[97] Therefore nothing provides such a severe but also sure critique of the elasticity of an individuality as finding out by observation or by
some other means coming to know to which phenomenon
he relates in earnest.

Repetition is in the realm of spirit. But here it means more,
since "we should see the development that accompanies repetition and that in a way annuls repetition per se."* Consequently, repetition is in the realm of spirit, but it is a development. Now we have arrived at the correction. This I am
supposed to have overlooked, and those words of the professor—which, to be sure, are not golden like Goethe's[98] but
at least are found in a gilded book—also contain the correction. Only a thoughtless person can have read *Repetition*
through and not discovered that precisely this is definitely
propounded, illustrated, and expressed there. But for the sake
of order I have already quoted some passages to which I refer
anyone who may have forgotten the total and definitive aim
of *Repetition*, which is much more than a few stray remarks.
In the explanatory letter it says, "The young man explains it
as the raising of his consciousness to the second power."[99]
This certainly ought to be the most definite expression of the
fact that I conceive of repetition as a development, for consciousness raised to its second power is indeed no meaningless repetition, but a repetition of such a nature that the new
has absolute significance in relation to what has gone before,
is qualitatively different from it. I wonder whom the Professor wanted to benefit by his correction? It can be of no interest to the many who have not read the book, and the few
who have read it do not need it. Or was I the one, perhaps,
whom the professor wished to benefit. If so, the professor
has gotten the idea that I am guilty of the error of not distinguishing between the meaning of repetition in nature (of which
I did not speak at all) and its meaning in the realm of the
spirit (of which I just as definitely said the same thing as he
and illustrated it). Now if Professor Heiberg has grabbed

IV
B 117
288

*See New Year's gift, p. 97.[100]

that opinion out of the air, then he ought to be told that he should not stop with having said it but should go on and explain how that which did not occur at all happened to occur. [101]Like the estates of certain counts, this matter that has to be explained lies on the moon—no wonder, then, that the explanation aspires thither where the professor's longing is! The professor attributes my mistake to my actually having had the categories of nature in mind in my eulogy over repetition,* and the fact that I did so "seems to be evident from his having applied it (the concept of repetition) to a concept from natural philosophy, namely, *movement*."** Now, if what the professor himself propounds is fixed and firm, that repetition belongs in the sphere of spirit as well as in the sphere of nature, even if it means one thing in the former and something else in the latter, then it follows *eo ipso* that movement also belongs in the sphere of spirit. [102]In our day some have gone so far that they have even wanted to have movement in logic.[103] There they have called repetition "mediation."[104] But movement is a concept that logic simply cannot support. Mediation, therefore, must be understood in relation to immanence. Thus understood, mediation may not again be used at all in the sphere of freedom, where the subsequent always emerges—by virtue not of an immanence but of a transcendence. Therefore, the word "mediation" has contributed to a misunderstanding in logic, because it allowed a concept of movement to be attached to it. In the sphere of freedom, the word "mediation" has again done damage, because, coming from logic, it helped to make the transcendence of movement illusory. In order to prevent this error or this dubious compromise between the logical and freedom, I have thought that "repetition" could be used in the sphere of freedom.[105] That it presupposes movement is quite in order and essen-

IV
B 117
289

---

* Note. The reader will please [note] that the professor has found this eulogy on pages 2 and 3 [*i.e., SV* III 4-5, second and third text pages] and in part on p. 34 [*i.e., SV* III 189], but not a single word of the last part has been allowed to be included in the eulogy the professor is so good as to let me deliver.

** See New Year's gift, p. 98.[106]

tially is admitted by Prof. Heiberg when he himself declares
that repetition in the sphere of the spirit means something
different from what it does in the sphere of nature and consequently, as noted above, declares that it is present in both
areas. But I say this merely to argue for a moment *e concessis*
[from premises admitted]. If the professor should choose to
disclaim having said it, that does not matter to me; my little
bit of philosophical thought has the good characteristic of
neither standing nor falling with Prof. Heiberg, no more than
what he says in general is qualified to stop the development
of one who has not neglected to familiarize himself with
German philosophy, in order to learn from the masters what
one preferably and most profitably learns from them. Movement is dialectical, not only with respect to space (in which
sense it occupied Heraclitus and the Eleatics and later was so
much used and misused by the Sceptics), but also with respect to time. The dialectic in both respects is the same, for
the point and the moment correspond to each other. Since I
could not name two schools in which the dialectic of motion
with respect to time is expressed as explicitly as Heraclitus
and the Eleatics express it with respect to space, I named
them.[107] In that way, I also managed to cast a comic light
over the journey I took to Berlin, because movement thereby
became a pun. All such things are permissible in a book that
does not at all claim to be a scientific work and whose author, revolted by the unscientific manner in which scientif-
icity is trumpeted, prefers to remain outside this hullabaloo
and, far from pontificating trivialities, has his joy in presupposing that the reader has the greatest possible knowledge.
When movement is allowed in relation to repetition in the
sphere of freedom, then the development becomes different
from the logical development in that the *transition becomes*
[*vorder*]. In logic, transition is movement's silence, whereas
in the sphere of freedom it becomes. Thus, in logic, when
possibility, by means of the immanence of thought, has determined itself as actuality, one only disturbs the silent self-
inclosure of the logical process by talking about movement
and transition. In the sphere of freedom, however, possibil-

IV
B 117
290

ity remains and actuality emerges as a transcendence. Therefore, when Aristotle long ago said that the transition from
possibility to actuality is a κίνησις [motion, change],[108] he
was not speaking of logical possibility and actuality but of
freedom's, and therefore he properly posits movement. In all
of Schelling's philosophy, movement likewise plays a major
role, not only in the philosophy of nature (*stricte sic dicta* [in
the strict sense]), but also in the philosophy of spirit, in his
whole conception of freedom. What gives him the greatest
trouble is precisely this, to include movement. But it is also
to his credit that he wanted to include it, not in the ingenious
sense in which it later gained a place in logic in Hegelian
philosophy and then from logic added to the confusion by
signifying too much in logic and too little outside of it. But
I do readily admit that there are very many problems remaining here, and I gratefully accept any correction that does
not, please note, correct by reconstructing trivialities and above
all does not talk in such a way about the meaning of repetition in the world of spirit that the words themselves contradict one another, since the "more"[*][109] that almost annuls
repetition and makes it into something else is neither visible
nor audible.

To a degree, the professor finds it probable that I had primarily the categories of nature in mind, inasmuch as what I
"tend toward is what is called a *philosophy of life*, but in
something like that a sympathetic association with nature
would be an essential factor."** That may very well be.[110] It
would have to be a very inexperienced person who would
deny this to Prof. Heiberg's face if it is not more explicitly
determined whether by a life-view philosopher he means a
Chaldean shepherd who looks at the stars† or he means
something else by it. The only world-historical life-view
philosopher who has ever lived is Socrates. It is common

IV
B 117
291

[*] *In margin*: which the professor says one ought to see
** [P. 98].[111]

In margin: † or a fantasizing young pup who wants to reintroduce the
nomad's way of life, or a monster, a troglodyte, or a pensioned functionary
who stays in the country and sympathizes with nature.

knowledge that he was completely indifferent to sympathy with nature.[112] When an author "ventures into experimenting [*experimenterende*: imaginatively constructing] psychology,"[113] there is no probability that what will preoccupy him will be sympathy with the phenomena of nature.[114] But this improbability is just as suitable as is the "probable" proof[115] for that which is to be explained and demonstrated, or for the correction, and just as this is neither here nor there, so also the explanation and the proof are neither here nor there.

Repetition *is* in the realm of spirit (according to Prof. Heiberg). But the expression "realm of spirit" has various meanings. It can mean world-spirit and individual spirit.

Repetition *is* in the realm of world-spirit. In order to clarify the distinction between repetition in this sphere and that in the phenomena of nature, the professor says: Although no such process is found in nature, in the realm of spirit each new generation goes beyond the previous one and uses its achievements for genuinely new beginnings, that is, for that which leads to something genuinely new.* [116]In the pregnant sense, this wisdom has the remarkable characteristic of always coming afterward and of benefiting all the generations that have passed on to their eternal bliss, whereas in connection with the issues of freedom it explains absolutely nothing. Moreover, the thesis, precisely so worded, is as familiar as a nursery rhyme even to the very youngest students; it is something that even a poor wretch who fails the comprehensive examination can recite by heart even if he does not know a thing otherwise, something that tutors tell only to their very youngest pupils and include in even the very shortest single-drachma course.** Thus, without making oneself guilty of culpable superficiality, one dares to presuppose this as common knowledge and, without laying oneself open to the charge of superstitious trust in humanity, dares to assume that the person who occasionally writes about philosophical

IV
B 117
292

* See New Year's gift, p. 95.[117]
** See Plato's *Cratylus*,[118] an expression by Socrates.

things is not ignorant of it and thus is not to be corrected by a meaningless repetition of a phrase.

But truly there is also a realm of spirit, and this is a realm of individuals. Should not repetition become an issue here also, please note, one that emerges when repetition[119] is outside the individual in the phenomena of nature[120] or the phenomena of events and when the individual is essentially unconcerned about something with which he cannot interfere essentially but to which he at most is only able to be sensitive in order to pass away the time. Should it not be important to illuminate this very point as one corrects an author "who ventures into experimenting [*experimenterende*: imaginatively constructing] psychology"?

According to Prof. H., there *is* repetition in the world of individual spirit. Here, as everywhere, it exists only for the contemplating spirit, not as a task for freedom. Here, clearly apparent, is the confusion that the professor has caused by wanting to correct what he probably—quite contrary to my expectation—did not have time to read through, even if he was sufficiently munificent to spend a moment to correct a book that more than any other book in Danish literature has refrained from forcing or obtruding itself upon anyone as if it had any significance. For Prof. H. the question of repetition is the question of its significance for contemplation. It *is* everywhere, signifies something more in the realm of spirit than in the realm of nature. If it is temporarily absent, the individual must wait until it comes, [121]and then he once again [sees] the "more" implicit in repetition. The "more" into which subjectivity makes repetition is always a "more" of observation, either in such a way that this more is in the repetition and observation "wants to see it" or does see it, or in such a way that it is rather an expression of individual observation in its arbitrariness, an expression of the individuality only esthetically ambiguously qualified in his relation to the object. But as soon as the individual is viewed in his freedom, the question becomes a different one: Can repetition be realized? It is repetition in this pregnant sense as a task for freedom and as freedom that gives the title to my

IV
B 117
293

little book and that in my little book has come into being
depicted and made visible in the individuality and in the situation, which is the main point to the psychologist, and one
is justified in looking for it and demanding that it be esthetically depicted by one who, unlike the scientific psychologist, has very scrupulously designated himself as "experimenting" [*experimenterende*: imaginatively constructing]. Not
one word about repetition understood in this way is found
in Prof. H. [122]In my interpretation, the issue of repetition is
formulated in a completely different way; in its striving it
points toward the religious, which in so many ways is intimated and adequately expressed.[123] If in my book I had not
wanted to maintain merely a psychological and an esthetic
relation and only covertly had wanted to play a secret piece
of intelligence into the hand of the reader, in whom, as I
have always had the pleasure of doing with respect to my
reader, I have presumed just as much familiarity with both
modern and ancient philosophy and the religious issues as I
myself may have, then I easily would have worked out how
repetition progresses along this path until it signifies atonement,[124] which is the most profound expression of repetition. Precisely because I had this in mind, I took care not to
confuse mediation and repetition, because mediation is within
immanence and therefore can never have before it the transcendence of a religious movement (the dialectical at this point
is only in the direction of fate and providence), to say nothing of the actuality of sin, which is not to be nullified by any
mediation. That I had this in mind is clear from my characterizations of repetition, as already cited, that it is transcendent, religious, the movement by virtue of the absurd that
commences when one has reached the border of the wondrous—all of which statements are cues to the person who,
as I always take pleasure in presuming in my reader, knows
the formulation of philosophical issues in the various areas.

[125]How far Prof. H. is from being willing to comprehend
repetition as a task for freedom is very obvious in the way
in which he quotes Goethe's "golden words."[126] Quoted in
that way, they are at most to be regarded as gilded. These

IV
B 117
294

words are used to enjoin beautiful sympathy with repetition
in nature. The quotation is fairly long. At first it actually
does treat of sympathy with nature. But the quotation continues. And look! Suddenly the quotation is about something
different and among other things says, "What also makes the
sensitive youth anxious is the continuous recurrence of our
errors, for how late we learn to perceive that as we train our
virtues we cultivate our errors."[127] Consequently, here, too
(in the phenomena of freedom—that is, there is no freedom),
repetition *is*, just as it *is* in nature. The only question is what
meaning it can have for one who ponders repetition, all according to how one lives into it. But this observation does
not regard the individual according to his freedom, and yet
it is directly after this quotation that the professor, who first
reminded us that Goethe himself attributes the lack of sympathy with nature and the hypochondria to the generally
widespread reading of English authors[128]—and yet it is directly after this quotation that the professor expounds the
dialectic of repetition. So it is easy to see that the hypochondria was the result of that sensitive youth's anxiety that his
error would be repeated; if he had been initiated into the
dialectic of repetition, he would have known how to sympathize with repetition.*

IV
B 117
295

To interpret repetition as I have**[129] by illuminating it in
the contrast of jest and despair never occurred to the professor, but to correct my conception[130] certainly did. As soon
as we think of freedom, all the professor's serious knowledge
about repetition vanishes as a jest. Although reluctant to forsake the realm of individuals, I nevertheless will—in view of
the professor's once again deporting himself in this discussion as the savior of and physician to the whole age[131]—take
an example from a larger order of things in order to show
the extent of the professor's range and ability to help any
age. If the Greek nation were to wake up out of its lethargy
right now, were to rub the sleep out of its eyes and ponder

---

* Note. On p. 110 the professor seems to speak somewhat differently.
In margin: ** depicted and illustrated, audibly in the pathos of passion

that godlike time when the whole population of the world
was divided into two extremely unequal parts, into Greeks
and barbarians, [132]when the little country of Greece possessed
everything that was beautiful and glorious and thereby proved
the justice of the division, when the little country of Greece
knew how to guard its property by making the narrow
mountain pass of Thermopylae even narrower than it was
by nature, knew how to prove with the sword what was
already decided by the mighty evidences of the spirit, that
the division was just—and it now became a question of repetition—what then? Then the professor would instruct us that
in the world of spirit [133]repetition means something more
than in the world of nature;[134] the point here is to perceive
the development, inasmuch as the one generation begins where
the other stopped. Consequently, if repetition is realized, in
observing it one will perceive the more that must be present
in relation to what Greece once was—should we thereupon
take the opportunity to go out and look at the stars so that
our poets someday may be able to report the exact location
of the stars in the sky in the hour when Greece was regen-
erated and not indicate it by a simple phrase, that it was once
again as it was in the old days, only one heaven and only
one Greece? The question, however, is whether by looking
at the stars one redeems repetition, just as in the game of
forfeits one thereby redeems his forfeit. But this is only as a
larger example. In the individual, then, repetition appears as
a task for freedom, in which the question becomes that of
saving one's personality from being volatilized and, so to
speak, in pawn to events. The moment it is apparent that the
individual can lose himself in events, fate, lose himself in
such a way that he therefore by no means stops contemplating but loses himself in such a way that freedom is taken up
completely in life's fractions without leaving a remainder,
then the issue becomes manifest, not to contemplation's aristocratic indolence, but to freedom's concerned passion. Precisely here is a task for the psychological depiction and illustration that do not propound *in abstracto*—some thesis or other:
that freedom is the *übergreifende* [encompassing], and never-

IV
B 117
296

theless Professor Heiberg has not done even this—but *in concreto*, in the conflicts of passion, which he understands who observes repetition in such a way that he earnestly places it in relation to movement and in turn does not think that movement is a trick included in the single-drachma course[135] *zum Gebrauch* [for use] by one or another decrepit *writer* of fine literature.[136]

Since the correction with which Prof. Heiberg has graciously favored my exposition is such as indicated above, it is easy to see what a strange light now falls upon the quotations from my book, which after having renounced the former error and having undergone the chastening of correction now* have found a place of honor in the gilded New Year's gift. The human heart is weak and vain, especially an author's heart. To see his name enrolled, if not in the book of life, nevertheless in the gilded New Year's gift, to be quoted here as one who has almost said something very beautiful and striking—what more does an author want? [137]And now if the one whose kindness is responsible for this glory also allows himself an innocent little liberty in being just as unconstrained in understanding as in correcting, would one not be stupid not to be able to overlook this in view of being taken up among the beatified and then to profit by the praise. Does not Basilio declare that Figaro is stupid not to see that the count's relation to Susanna can be of inestimable advantage to him,[138] which is entirely comparable to what an author is able to attain when he is fortunate enough to have a very distinguished man tempt his innocent and insignificant thoughts to become something great in a nonchalant and diffuse relation.

But to the quotations. The correction in fact amounts to this: what I have said has its place in relation to repetition in nature, and understood in that way the sentences are very beautiful and appropriate. In the old days, the words and I

IV
B 117
297

In margin: * since they also are placed under the instructive restriction of a special police surveillance[139]

understood each other; now they have become so distinguished that I cannot understand them.[140] In order not to
weary the reader by scrutinizing every quotation, I shall take
the first one and surrender to my unfortunate fate of being
obliged to thank Prof. Heiberg for the correction and the
honor and of being obliged to cause the reader new inconvenience with what I myself have always regarded and represented as insignificant. "Repetition is a crucial expression
for what recollection was to the Greeks. Just as they taught
that all knowing is a recollecting, modern philosophy will
teach that all life is a repetition."[141] Under the auspices of the
professor, let us now try to find some meaning in these words
about the observation of repetition in natural phenomena.
After all, what does it mean to make this distinction between
the ancient and the modern observation of repetition in nature? Later in his treatise the professor specifically commends
the Greeks' observation, their sympathy for repetition in nature. In the past, the words had another, or at least some,
meaning. In my little book, I always spoke about the issues
of freedom for the life of the individual. The Greek mentality
was in one sense happy, but if this happiness ceased, recollection manifested itself as freedom's consolation; only in
recollection and by moving backward into it did freedom
possess its eternal life. The modern view, on the other hand,
must seek freedom forward, so that here eternity opens up
for him as the true repetition forward. For the Greek out-
look, eternity, regarded from the point of view of the moment, appears through the past; the modern view must look
at eternity, regarded from the point of view of the moment,
through the future. Here again, this means that when happiness ceases, when the crisis comes, freedom must press forward, not retreat. That this is the meaning truly needs no
proof, and yet there is something like that in the book if one
reads as far as p. 91 [*i.e., SV* III 221], where there is a reference to this thesis. The young man's life has come to a
standstill, the crisis has come, he has run up against the issue
of repetition. I, however, in despair have relinquished my

IV
B 117
298

theory of repetition, because my position also lies within immanence, but now I merely make the comment about him that he does well not to seek enlightenment instead in Greek philosophy, "for the Greeks make the opposite movement, and here a Greek would choose to recollect." When he seeks guidance and help in Job, repetition has to that extent already been discovered long ago, which it certainly has never been my intention to deny, since Job is indeed presented, but for this reason it can still be absolutely correct that repetition in relation to a modern philosophy is to be discovered by one more recent. That is why it says in a continuation of what was quoted (p. 91), "Modern philosophy makes no movement; as a rule it makes only a commotion, and if it makes any movement at all, it is always within immanence, whereas repetition is and remains a transcendence."[142] If one now takes the thought contained here without wanting to censure me for being constantly careful in an esthetic and psychological portrayal that the particular things said are also the speech of an individuality, then everything is, I believe, fairly clear. If one speaks of freedom in the qualifications of immanence, then crisis and everything related are only illusory, which is why it is also so easy to get them annulled. But as soon as this is grasped with the interest of actuality, then the distinction will readily appear between the Greek recollecting and repetition, which enters in after the whole movement of the crisis has started, but enters in precisely by pressing forward. Such a pressing forward is described in Job, particularly in his maintaining that he is right, for this passionate sleeplessness of freedom is a spiritual thrust, and of a physical thrust there is no question.

What happened to that quotation happened to most of them: by being summoned by the Rector of Literature, Prof. H., and corrected by him *et encomio publico ornati* [and honored with public praise], they became meaningless. But one example must suffice. I do not wish to be the death of the reader or of myself or of the poor quotations by such a death-dealing boredom.

My little book had scarcely hoped to be touched by fate in this way. I had presumed the reader to have fairly well-grounded knowledge in the various spheres of philosophy. With the modesty whereby one advances such things in order not to become disgusting to oneself and ridiculous in the eyes of the reader, I had clothed in lightness and jest what must be assumed to be entirely familiar to everyone. I had construed the whole thing humorously and therefore saw to it that there was also a more profound idea. But neither by word nor by gesture did I intimate that I wanted to instruct. My task was to portray and illustrate, and that I did. As to the reader's situation, I thought that he would discover the main idea and, whether he considered it to be true or not, would nevertheless admit that previously he had not thought of it in this way and insofar would consider it appropriate that I wrote about it. He would understand the jest and be amused by it, and he would understand the courtesy whereby I did not permit myself to write trivialities in a didactic tone but relinquished the familiar to jest in the same sense as two philologists would say to each other only in jest that *amo* is a form of the verb *amavi, amatum, amare*,[143] although it is in fact true and is said quite earnestly to pupils in school. He would understand the courtesy whereby I was so decorously dubious about instructing even with respect to the more significant matters in the book that I never for a moment wrote in such a way that the reader feels a trace of the didactic. That is the way I wrote; I was convinced and still am that here and there would be found one single reader who, while approving of the book, would approve even more of my writing this way, whereby I saved my soul from the inhuman self-importance with which instruction is now given in trivialities. I claim no more, and even if actuality protests, which it has not as yet done in any way of which I am aware, it makes no difference to the matter, for I shall continue and continue* to believe in repetition.

In margin: * not contemplating but acting, to be convinced that I am right and

IV
B 117
300

—*Pap.* IV B 117 *n.d.*, 1843-44

From preliminary draft of a portion of Pap. IV B 117:

Deleted from margin; see 302:15-29:

1. If freedom here [in repetition as a religious movement] now discovers an obstacle [*Anstød*], then it must lie in freedom itself. Freedom now shows itself not to be in its perfection in man but to be disturbed. This disturbance, however, must be attributed to freedom itself, for otherwise there would be no freedom at all, or the disturbance would be a matter of chance that freedom could remove. The disturbance that is attributed to freedom itself is sin. If it gets the right to rule, then freedom disperses itself and is never in a position to realize repetition. Then freedom despairs of itself but still never forgets repetition. But in the moment of despair a change takes place with regard to repetition, and freedom takes on a religious expression, by which repetition appears as atonement,[144] which is repetition *sensu eminentiori* [in the highest sense] and something different from mediation, which always merely describes the nodal points of oscillation in the progress of immanence.

See 303:6-30:

2. Just as it sometimes happens in life that a man of lowly birth may strikingly resemble, for example, the king and that on seeing him one is momentarily deceived by the likeness and then smiles at the mistake, just so repetition's two caricatures (a and b) constantly run around in the book and create confusion.

In margin; see 305:4:

3. I actually am a Stoic; it is the highest form of b adjacent to c. I am sagacious enough to have grasped the issue to some extent; therefore part of the first may be quite true, but I have not grasped that it is a religious [issue]; this I see later but declare that I cannot do it.

and in the letter I say that the movement in the book is inverse.

See 305:22-29:

4. . . . . . for everyone who has read the whole book and has not let himself be fooled by the first part and above all is not fooled* into showing up with a didactic correction.
In margin: *by himself.

See 306:33–307:5:

5. Should I have an opinion
        sentimental-comic
        only freedom earnestness
    A person must be careful about where he becomes earnest.

See 308:4-6:

6. I wonder whom the professor wants to benefit by this entertainment? Presumably those light creatures who inhabit other planets, for example, the moon, where lies that which is to be explained, as do the estates of certain counts, and to which the explanation naturally aspires. Since it is fixed and firm for the professor and on the moon that I have overlooked the distinction between repetition in nature and in the sphere of spirit, all that remains is to explain how this happened.

See 308:16–310:22:

7. Although in our age movement, under the name of mediation, has even been taken into logic, where everything nevertheless lies within immanence and where now again under the name of mediation movements in the sphere of the spirit are changed to mere immanences, the main point is to see that movement belongs specifically in the world of spirit, where repetition means more than mediation precisely because it always has a transcendence behind it, which is definitely and clearly indicated in the characterizations used in the essential discussion of repetition in my book: that it is transcendent, religious, a movement by virtue of the absurd. Moreover, for the very reason that movement is dialectical

with respect to the category of time, it has been assigned a place in the philosophy of spirit in both ancient and modern philosophy, but, please note, has been mistakenly applied to logic only by Hegel.

Thus Aristotle declares that the transition from possibility to actuality is a κίνησις [motion, change]. Thus movement plays a major role in the whole Schellingian philosophy,[145] not only in his philosophy of nature (in the stricter sense), but also in his philosophy of spirit. So, also, in his treatise on freedom,[146] where, moving partly in Jacob Böhme's expressions and partly in his self-made paraphrases, he constantly struggles to include movement. Consequently, on the ground that I have placed repetition in relation to movement, the professor (in view of his own statements and also of what is obvious to anyone who knows anything about philosophy) cannot conclude that in my book I discuss only repetition in nature—about which I did not say a word—and pay no attention to repetition in the sphere of spirit, about which I most definitely have said that which could not be said more definitely.

See 310:27–311:2:

8. That may very well be, but the main task of a philosophy of life is to devote itself to the phenomena of the individual spirit.

See 311:5:

9. . . . . . the observation of the phenomena of nature, about which there is not one word, even though in one place I do indicate, not didactically but in a situation, my sympathy for nature's repetition.[147] The preoccupation of such an author is, of course, repetition in the sphere of the individual spirit, and everything that is solid in the book can be reduced to the classification I set forth previously.[148]

See 311:20–312:2:

10. We shall make a present of this thesis to the professor; it is something that any poor wretch who fails the compre-

hensive examination can recount, something of which only theological tutors presume their tutees to be ignorant.

In margin: Something like that always comes afterwards and does not help freedom.

See 312:27-35:

11. . . . . . and then he can once again say what meaning repetition now has.

In margin: the more is for observation.

See 313:9:

12. Be it right or wrong, in any case the idea as I have presented it is new.

See 313:35-37:

14. Prof. Heiberg is so far from grasping the meaning of repetition as a task that he is even guilty of teaching an ethical indolence.

See 315:12-23:

16. . . . . . the significance of repetition in the world of spirit is that a more is added; consequently, repetition, as soon as it comes, will here be something higher. But it would never occur to him that repetition is a task for freedom. Presumably he would know how to gaze at the stars in the meantime . . . . .

See 316:18-31:

18. . . . . . some who see my protest may be sufficiently sagacious to say of me what Basilio in *Figaro* says of Figaro, that instead of deriving advantage from the count's relationship to Susanna, he will disturb it, since the liberty Prof. H. takes with me is still so innocent and in part the fruit of an illusion (in which he may be allowed to remain if there is any advantage in it) that he is the great philosophical master of our accumulated literature. But to the quotations.

—*Pap.* IV B 118 *n.d.*, 1843-44

Included in Pap. IV B 108:

IV
B 120
306

My dear Reader:

Repetition was insignificant, without any philosophical pre-tension, a droll little book, dashed off as an oddity, and, curiously enough, written in such a way that, if possible, the heretics would not be able to understand it.[149] . . . That rep-etition not only *is* for contemplation but that it is a task for freedom, that it signifies freedom itself, consciousness raised to the second power, that it is the *interest* of metaphysics and also the interest upon which metaphysics comes to grief, the watchword in every ethical view, *conditio sine qua non* [the indispensable condition] for every issue of dogmatics,[150] that the true repetition is eternity; however, that repetition (by being psychologically pursued so far that it vanishes for psy-chology as transcendent, as a religious movement by virtue of the absurd, which commences when a person has come to the border of the wondrous), as soon as the issue is posed dogmatically, will come to mean atonement, which cannot be qualified by mediation borrowed from immanence any more than a religious movement, which is still dialectical only with respect to fate and providence—all this and every-thing related to this, my dear reader, are misunderstandings that can occur only to a person who did not know the inter-pretation of repetition that we owe to Prof. H., and that is just as profound as it is original. . . .

IV
B 120
308

IV
B 120
309

Your Const. Const.
—*Pap.* IV B 120 *n.d.*, 1843

IV
B 120
310

Included in Pap. IV B 108:

[151]*Urania* is really not astronomical any more (in execu-tion).

Hired waiters presumably are not needed. —Yet all is not thereby past—Heiberg himself is a diplomat, before that miracle in Hamburg,[152] where through a miracle he gained an understanding of and became an adherent of a philosophy that (remarkably enough) does not accept miracles. —Ulysses says to Chilian: Listen, Chilian, you must never make sport of the emissaries of foreign nations[153] . . . . . that is, distant people versed in astronomy will demand that he be given up. —We all defend him. We all love you, Prof. H. The scene is now here at home. When a man has been shown to be insolvent in one direction, everybody comes.

The scene à la that in *Den politiske Kandestøber*[154] in which a messenger comes and asks about the plate, the dish—or in *Den pantsatte Bondedreng.*[155]

1. Messenger from the system, the logical.
2. Messenger from the esthetic system.
3. Messenger from linguistic science.
4. A person who does not know from whom he is to bring greetings, whether from one or many, from the big books H. has always collected (see his *Intelligensbladene*).
5. Messenger from many families in the capital city and the provinces with regard to the mirage that was predicted in *Urania* and did not occur. Whether the Herr Professor, together with Carstensen, could not arrange a mirage in Tivoli.

The History of Astronomy in Denmark since Heiberg Became an Astronomer.

In that way a course will be given in the mutual system of instruction: On the history of mutual instruction in Denmark.—*Pap*. IV B 124 (in XI³, Supplement, pp. xxxviii-ix) *n.d.*, 1843-44

Instead of the plot in *Repetition*, I could imagine something like this. A young man with imagination and a lot more, but who hitherto has been otherwise occupied, falls in love with a young girl—to use an experienced coquette here is not very interesting psychologically except from another angle. This young girl is of course pure and innocent but very imaginative in an erotic way. He comes with his simple ideas. She develops him. Just when she is really delighted with him, it becomes apparent that he cannot remain with her. A prodigious desire for multiplicity is awakened, and she must be set aside. In a way, she herself had made a seducer of him, a seducer with the limitation that he can never seduce her. Incidentally, it could be very interesting to have him sometime later, at the peak of his powers, improved by experience, proceed to seduce her as well, "because he owed her so much."—*JP* V 5694 (*Pap.* IV A 153) *n.d.*, 1843

Repetition comes again everywhere. (1) When I am going to act, my action has existed in my consciousness in conception and thought—otherwise I act thoughtlessly—that is, I do not act. (2) Inasmuch as I am going to act, I presuppose that I am in an original integral state. Now comes the problem of sin, which is the second repetition,[156] for now I must return to myself again. (3) The real paradox by which I become the single individual, for if I remain in sin, understood as the universal, there is only repetition no. 2.

One may at this point compare the Aristotelian categories: *Das—Was—war—sein.* See Marbach, *Geschichte der Philosophie des Mittelalters*, para. 128, pp. 4-5, and para. 102 in his *Geschichte der griechischen Philosophie.*[157]—*JP* III 3793 (*Pap.* IV A 156) *n.d.*, 1843

"Repetition" is and remains a religious category.[158] Constantin Constantius therefore cannot proceed further. He is clever, an ironist, battles the interesting[159]—but is not aware that he himself is caught in it. The first form of the interesting is to love change; the second is to want repetition,[160] but still in *Selbstgenugsamkeit* [self-sufficiency], with no suffering—therefore Constantin is wrecked on what he himself has discovered, and the young man goes further.—*JP* III 3794 (*Pap.* IV A 169) *n.d.*, 1844

Constantin Constantius's journey to Berlin[161] is not something accidental. He generates in particular the mood for the *Posse* [farce] and here reaches the extreme point of the humorous.—*JP* V 5704 (*Pap.* IV A 178) *n.d.*, 1844

From draft of The Concept of Anxiety:

The comic is a category that belongs specifically to the temporal. The comic always lies in contradiction (*Wiederspruch*).[162] But in eternity all contradictions are canceled, and the comic[*] is consequently excluded.[163] *Eternity is indeed the true repetition,***[164] in which history comes to an end and all things are explained.

[*] *Along the margin*: Perhaps no one knows better what the times want than I do.
** Note. See *Repetition*, p. 142 [*i.e.*, *SV* III 254].
                              —*Pap.* V B 60, p. 137 *n.d.*, 1844

From sketch of The Concept of Anxiety:

Earnestness is acquired originality.[165]
        Different from habit[166]—which is the disappearance
        of self-awareness. (See Rosenkrantz, *Psych.*)[167]
Therefore genuine repetition is—earnestness.[168]—*JP* III 3795
(*Pap.* V B 69) *n.d.*, 1844

From notes for Concluding Unscientific Postscript:

. . . (2) (a) Objectivity[169] stresses: what is said; the summary of thought-determinants.
        (b) Subjectivity[170] stresses: *how* it is said; infinite passion is crucial, not its content, for its content is in fact itself.

* This is also dialectical with respect to time,[171] continual repetition that is just as difficult as the first appropriation.[172] This is because man is a synthesis of the temporal and of the eternal, every moment out upon "70,000 fathoms."[173]
        In the moment of decision it appears as if the decision were in the present moment, and with that it changes into a striving. For example, prayer[174]—it was quite right once to sink into God and then re-

main there, but since man is a finite being, to pray
means continual striving to achieve the true inwardness of prayer.—*JP* V 5791, 5792 (*Pap.* VI B 17,
18) *n.d.*, 1844-45

Deleted from final copy of Postscript: -

That the discourse on Job[175] is different from the others*
is clear enough, and it is always a joy to see a judge like
Kts,[176] who strikes home with sureness. The basis of the distinction the Magister himself has related to me.[177] In the book
Repetition, the use of Job was so caught up in passion that it
could easily have a disturbing effect on one or another reader
accustomed to something more quietly upbuilding in a consideration of the devout man.** Therefore he immediately
decided to do his best to keep Job as a religious prototype
also for one who is not tried in the extremities of the passions
or who would not want this presented as imaginary construction [*experimenterende*].[178] Therefore the upbuilding discourse also appeared a few weeks after *Repetition*.[179]

In margin: *without its therefore being a sermon.

In margin: ** , even though the psychological and poetic
use of Job in that work must be upheld.—*Pap.* VI B 98:52 *n.d.*,
1845

William Afham's part (in *Stages*)[180] is so deceptively contrived that it is praise and high distinction to have stupid
fussbudgets pass trivial judgment on it and say that it is the
same old thing. Yes, that is just the trick. I never forget the
anxiety I myself felt about not being able to achieve what I
had once accomplished, and yet it would have been so very
easy to choose other names. This is also the reason Afham
states that Constantius said that never again would he arrange a banquet,[181] and Victor Eremita, that he would never
again speak admiringly of Don Giovanni. But the Judge declares that he will keep on repeating.*[182] As the author him-

self suggested, wherever it is possible and wherever it is not possible.

> * "That only thieves and gypsies say that one must never return where he has once been."—*JP* V 5823 (*Pap.* VI A 78) *n.d.*, 1845

. . . A pastor, for example, who conducts ten funerals every day, twenty marriages every Sunday, baptizes babies by the dozen, in short, never takes off his robe.

Therefore a good measure of the ethical earnestness of a pastor is the pathos with which he is able to invest each of these repetitious ceremonies.[183] This is the case with Bishop Mynster[184] and this really makes him far greater than all his eloquence. . . .—*JP* VI 6318 (*Pap.* X¹ A 58, p. 45) *n.d.*, 1849

Yes, "Either/Or"—that is where the battle is, and therefore my first words are: Either/Or. And that which is in *Either/Or* I can say of myself: I am an enigmatical being on whose brow stands Either/Or.[185]

But how this is to be understood could not be seen at once; much had to be arranged first. For this an entire productivity *uno tenore* [without interruption], an entire productivity nevertheless related to a repetition [*Gjentagelse*]: all must be taken up again. Therefore the work was under so much pressure, was so hasty—which local sagacity regarded as very foolish—because all pointed to a repetition, as it therefore stands in the little book *Repetition*:[186] Repetition is the category about which it will revolve. . . .—*Pap.* X⁶ B 236 *n.d.*, 1853

What It Means To Repeat

XI³
B 122
198

April '55

One of my pseudonyms[187] has written a little book called *Repetition*, in which he denies that there is repetition.[188]

Without being quite in disagreement with him in the deeper sense, I may very well be of the opinion that there nevertheless is a repetition, yes, that it is the true happiness, that there is a repetition, since there are situations and circumstances in which repetition is so extremely needed.

When something is said to people that they do not want to hear, something true, the usual way they use in seeking to avoid what is in essential opposition to them, to avoid letting the truth decisively exercise its power over them and over conditions—the usual way is to treat the discourse on the truth as daily news and then say: We have heard that once—as if it were the day's news they were listening to when it was said for the first time and now they want to be done with it, just as one ignores the day's news, which cannot stand a second hearing. . . .

XI³
B 122
199
Consequently, in relation to the day's news etc., repetition is more intolerable with each repetition. In relation to earnestness, repetition is all the more needed every time what is said is not received for appropriate action, has one more reason than previously. . . .—*Pap.* XI³ B 122 *n.d.*, April 1855

EDITORIAL APPENDIX

ACKNOWLEDGMENTS

Preparation of manuscripts for *Kierkegaard's Writings* is supported by a genuinely enabling grant from the National Endowment for the Humanities. The grant includes gifts from the Danish Ministry of Cultural Affairs, the Konsul George Jorck og Hustru Emma Jorcks Fond, and the A. P. Møller og Hustru Chastine McKinney Møllers Fond.

The translators–editors are indebted to the late Gregor Malantschuk and Grethe Kjær for their knowledgeable observations on crucial concepts and terminology. Many will join us in paying grateful tribute to Gregor Malantschuk (d. August 20, 1978) for his comprehensive and penetrating Kierkegaard studies and his stimulating association with other students of Kierkegaard's thought.

John Elrod, Per Lønning, and Sophia Scopetéa, members of the International Advisory Board for *Kierkegaard's Writings*, have given valuable criticism of the manuscript on the whole and in detail. Jack Schwandt, Pamela Schwandt, Michael Daugherty, Steven Knudson, Craig Mason, and Julia Watkin have helpfully scrutinized the manuscript. Niels Thulstrup has given useful suggestions regarding the notes. The index was prepared by Craig Mason and Rune Engebretsen.

Acknowledgment is made to Gyldendals Forlag for permission to absorb notes to *Søren Kierkegaards Samlede Værker*.

Inclusion in the Supplement of entries from *Søren Kierkegaard's Journals and Papers* is by arrangement with Indiana University Press.

The book collection and the microfilm collection of the Kierkegaard Library, St. Olaf College, have been used in preparation of the text, Supplement, and Editorial Appendix.

The manuscript, typed by Dorothy Bolton, has been guided through the press by Sanford Thatcher and Gretchen Oberfranc.

COLLATION OF *FEAR AND TREMBLING* IN THE DANISH EDITIONS OF KIERKEGAARD'S COLLECTED WORKS

Vol. III Ed. 1 Pg.	*Vol. III* Ed. 2 Pg.	*Vol. 5* Ed. 3 Pg.	*Vol. III* Ed. 1 Pg.	*Vol. III* Ed. 2 Pg.	*Vol. 5* Ed. 3 Pg.
56	66	8	113	126	59
57	67	9	114	127	60
58	68	9	115	128	60
59	69	10	116	130	61
60	70	11	117	131	63
61	71	13	118	132	63
62	72	13	119	133	64
63	73	14	120	134	65
64	73	14	121	135	66
65	75	15	122	136	67
66	76	15	123	137	68
67	77	16	124	138	69
68	78	17	125	140	70
69	79	17	126	141	71
70	80	18	127	142	72
71	81	19	128	143	73
72	82	20	129	144	74
73	83	21	130	145	75
74	84	22	131	146	75
75	86	23	132	147	76
79	89	27	133	148	77
80	89	27	134	149	78
81	91	28	135	150	79
82	92	29	136	151	80
83	93	30	137	152	81
84	94	31	138	153	82
85	95	32	139	154	83
86	96	33	140	156	84
87	98	34	141	157	85
88	99	35	142	158	86
89	100	36	143	159	87
90	101	37	144	160	87
91	102	38	145	161	88

Vol. III Ed. 1 Pg.	Vol. III Ed. 2 Pg.	Vol. 5 Ed. 3 Pg.	Vol. III Ed. 1 Pg.	Vol. III Ed. 2 Pg.	Vol. 5 Ed. 3 Pg.
92	103	39	146	162	89
93	105	40	147	163	90
94	106	41	148	165	91
95	107	42	149	166	92
96	108	43	150	167	93
97	109	44	151	168	94
98	110	45	152	169	95
99	111	46	153	170	96
100	113	47	154	171	97
101	114	48	155	172	98
102	115	49	156	173	99
103	116	50	157	174	99
104	117	51	158	175	100
105	118	51	159	176	101
106	119	52	160	178	102
107	120	53	161	179	103
108	121	54	162	180	104
109	122	55	163	181	105
110	123	56	164	182	106
111	124	57	165	183	107
112	125	58	166	185	108
			167	186	109
			168	187	110

COLLATION OF *REPETITION*
IN THE DANISH EDITIONS OF KIERKEGAARD'S
COLLECTED WORKS

Vol. III Ed. 1 Pg.	*Vol. III* Ed. 2 Pg.	*Vol. 5* Ed. 3 Pg.	*Vol. III* Ed. 1 Pg.	*Vol. III* Ed. 2 Pg.	*Vol. 5* Ed. 3 Pg.
172	192	114	217	243	157
173	193	115	218	244	158
174	193	115	219	245	159
175	195	116	220	246	160
176	196	117	221	247	161
177	197	118	222	248	162
178	198	119	223	249	162
179	199	120	224	250	163
180	201	121	225	251	164
181	202	122	226	252	165
182	203	123	227	253	166
183	204	124	228	254	167
184	205	125	229	256	168
185	207	126	230	257	169
186	208	127	231	258	169
187	209	128	232	259	170
188	210	129	233	260	171
189	211	130	234	261	171
190	212	131	235	261	171
191	213	132	236	263	172
192	214	133	237	264	173
193	216	134	238	266	174
194	217	135	239	267	175
195	218	136	240	268	176
196	219	137	241	269	176
197	220	138	242	269	177
198	222	139	243	271	178
199	223	140	244	272	279
200	224	141	245	274	180
201	225	142	246	275	180
202	226	143	247	276	181
203	227	144	248	276	181
204	228	145	249	278	182
205	229	145	250	279	183

Vol. III	*Vol. III*	*Vol. 5*	*Vol. III*	*Vol. III*	*Vol. 5*
Ed. 1	*Ed. 2*	*Ed. 3*	*Ed. 1*	*Ed. 2*	*Ed. 3*
Pg.	*Pg.*	*Pg.*	*Pg.*	*Pg.*	*Pg.*
206	231	146	251	280	184
207	232	148	252	281	184
208	233	149	253	282	185
209	234	149	254	283	185
210	235	150	255	284	186
211	236	151	257	285	187
212	238	152	259	287	189
213	239	153	260	287	189
214	240	155	261	290	191
215	240	155	262	290	191
216	242	156	263	291	192
			264	292	193

NOTES

FEAR AND TREMBLING

TITLE PAGE AND OVERLEAF

TITLE. See Philippians 2:12-13. See Supplement, p. 243 (*Pap.* IV B 60, 78, 79).

SUBTITLE. See Historical Introduction, pp. xxv-xxvi. See p. 90 and note 21.

AUTHOR. For a discussion of the pseudonymous author, see Historical Introduction, pp. xvii, xxv-xxvi. See p. 90 and note 21.

EPIGRAPH. Johann Georg Hamann, letter to Johannes Gotthelf Lindner, Riga, March 29, 1763, *Hamann's Schriften*, I–VIII[1-2], ed. Friedrich Roth (Berlin: 1821-43; *ASKB* 536-44), III, p. 190. When the son of Tarquinius Superbus had craftily gotten Gabii in his power, he sent a messenger to his father asking what he should do with the city. Tarquinius, not trusting the messenger, gave no reply but took him into the garden, where with his cane he cut off the flowers of the tallest poppies. The son understood from this that he should eliminate the leading men of the city. See Valerius Maximus, VII, 4, 2; *Valerius Maximus Sammlung merkwürdiger Reden und Thaten*, I–V (Stuttgart: 1829; *ASKB* 1296), III, pp. 455-56. A similar story about Periander is found in Aristotle, *Politics*, 1284 a; *Aristoteles graece*, I–IV, ed. Immanuel Bekker (Berlin: 1831; *ASKB* 1074-75), II, p. 1284; *The Works of Aristotle*, I–XII, ed. J. A. Smith and W. D. Ross (Oxford: Clarendon Press, 1908-52), X.

The epigraph is discussed by G. E. Lessing in *Abhandlungen über die Äsopische Fabel, Gotthold Ephraim Lessing's sämmtliche Schriften*, I–XXXII (Berlin: 1825-28; *ASKB* 1747-62), XVIII, pp. 164-65. Lessing's treatise (1759) antedates the Hamann source by four years. Kierkegaard was a reader of Lessing's works (see *JP* III 2369-79; VII, p. 56) also in the years 1842-1843, when he was writing *Fear and Trembling*. A later entry (*Pap*: X[1] A 363) indicates that Kierkegaard was familiar with Lessing's essay on the fable. It is therefore not unlikely that he drew on Lessing's allegorical interpretation of the Tarquinius story in this essay.

Originally the epigraph was to have been a quotation from Herder. See Supplement, pp. 244, 249-50 (*Pap.* IV B 96:1 a-c, 96:4); *JP* V 5560, 5674 (*Pap.* III A 203; IV A 126). See *Works of Love, KW* XVI (*SV* IX 343).

PREFACE

1. The references are most likely to Danish Hegelians, notably Johan Ludvig Heiberg (1791-1860) and Hans Lassen Martensen (1808-1884). Heiberg had published *Om Philosophiens Betydning for den nuværende Tid* (1833) and *Perseus, Journal for den speculative Idee*, I–II (1837-38). See *Prefaces, KW* IX (*SV* V 37-38, 51-55, 60-62); *Concluding Unscientific Postscript, KW* XII (*SV* VII 153); *Intelligensblade*, no. 1-48 (1842-44). See also Martensen's review of Heiberg's *Indlednings Foredrag til det i Novbr. 1834 begyndte logiske Kursus, Maanedsskrift for Litteratur*, XVI (1836), pp. 515-28. During a two-year European study tour (1832-1834), Martensen read Hegel's works and studied with the foremost Hegelian speculative theologian, Carl Daub. "Going further" refers to the system building attempted by Hegelians along the lines of Hegel's *Encyclopädie der philosophischen Wissenschaften*, titled *System der Philosophie* after the third edition. See *Philosophical Fragments, KW* VII (*SV* IV 190, 193).

2. René Descartes (1596-1650), French philosopher, the so-called father of modern European philosophy. Descartes is mentioned in the article by Martensen referred to in note 1 above. See *JP* I 736 (*Pap.* IV C 14).

3. Renati Descartes, *Opera philosophica* (Amsterdam: 1685; *ASKB* 473), pp. 8, 23; *The Philosophical Works of Descartes*, I–II, tr. Elizabeth S. Haldane and G.R.T. Ross (Cambridge: Cambridge University Press, 1931), I, pp. 231, 253.

4. Descartes, *Opera; Philosophical Works*, I, p. 83. The phrase "sc. juventutis," i.e., of youth, is an addition to Descartes's text.

5. See, for example, *Fragments, KW* VII (*SV* IV 246-47); *Postscript, KW* XII (*SV* VII 290 fn., 307).

6. See II Timothy 4:7.

7. With reference to the following paragraph, see Supplement, p. 245 (*Pap.* IV B 80:3).

8. See p. 90 and note 21.

9. In Danish the nouns "passion" and "science" rhyme: *Lidenskab, Videnskab*.

10. With reference to the remainder of the sentence, see Supplement, p. 245 (*Pap.* IV B 89:1).

11. See *JP* V 5647 (*Pap.* IV A 88).

12. The writer of a tragedy, "The Destruction of the Human Race," in Johan Ludvig Heiberg, *Recensenten og Dyret*, sc. 7. In that scene, Trop tears his manuscript into two equal pieces, saying, "If it does not cost more to save good taste, why should we not do it?"

13. Approximately three years before the publication of *Fear and Trembling* (1843), the first omnibuses (horse-drawn) were put into use in Copenhagen.

14. Presumably an allusion to Luke 14:28-30. See p. 72.

EXORDIUM

1. See Supplement, p. 245 (*Pap.* IV B 81); *JP* V 5651 (*Pap.* IV A 93).

2. Throughout the work, four related basic terms are used: "to tempt," "temptation" (*friste, Fristelse*); "to test," "test," (*prøve, Prøve*); "to try" (*forsøge*); "ordeal" (*Prøvelse*). All have essentially the same meaning: to try by way of a test or an ordeal. "To tempt," however, is used in two senses in the work. (1) Whenever a version of the Biblical report is given, as on pp. 9, 63, the term means "to test" (as in the Revised Standard Version) and is used because it is the terminology of the Danish Bible of that time. Sometimes "test" and "temptation" are used together as synonyms, as on pp. 60, 71, 123. (2) Later, however, as on pp. 60, 115, Johannes de Silentio uses "temptation" in the ordinary sense of the attraction of the lower in relation to the higher. Therefore, the ethical as the universal in relation to an absolute duty toward God may be a temptation. The meaning of the three other terms—"to test," "to try," and "ordeal"—is synonymous with the first meaning of "to tempt" ("to test," "test"). For a discussion of "spiritual trial" (*Anfægtelse*), see p. 31 and note 14. See *Repetition*, p. 209, *KW* VI (*SV* III 243); *Postscript, KW* XII (*SV* VII 226, 399); *JP* II 2222 (*Pap.* X⁴ A 572).

3. See Genesis 22.

4. With reference to the following sentence, see Supplement, p. 245 (*Pap.* IV B 81).

5. See p. 90 and note 21.

6. See Supplement, p. 249 (*Pap.* IV B 73).

7. See p. 9 and note 2.

8. A free, but essentially accurate, rendition of Genesis 22:1-2 in the contemporary Danish translation of the Bible. See p. 9 and note 2.

9. See Judith 10:11: "and the men of the city watched her until she had gone down the mountain and passed through the valley and they could no longer see her." See also *Postscript, KW* XII (*SV* VII 291); *JP* III 3822 (*Pap.* III A 197).

10. See Supplement, pp. 241-42 (*Pap.* IV A 76).

11. See Supplement, pp. 255-56 (*Pap.* IV B 69-71).

12. For the promise to Abraham and Sarah, see Genesis 12:1-3, 17:2-21.

13. With reference to the following paragraph, see Supplement, p. 246 (*Pap.* IV B 83).

14. See Genesis 16, 21:9-21, for the story of Hagar, Sarah's Egyptian maid, and Ishmael, Hagar's son by Abraham. See p. 77.

15. With reference to the following paragraph, see Supplement, p. 246 (*Pap.* IV B 84).

16. The childless Abraham regarded Eliezer of Damascus as his heir. See Genesis 15:2.

17. With reference to the following paragraph, see Supplement, p. 246 (*Pap.* IV B 85).

18. With reference to the following paragraph, see Supplement, pp. 245-48 (*Pap.* IV B 66-68).

19. See Supplement, p. 248 (*Pap.* IV B 86).

EULOGY ON ABRAHAM

1. See Supplement, pp. 248-49 (*Pap.* IV B 72).

2. Here for the first time in the pseudonymous writings the expression "eternal consciousness" and variants are used. See, for example, *Philosophical Fragments, KW* VII (*SV* IV 173, 224, 271); *The Concept of Anxiety*, p. 153, *KW* VIII (*SV* IV 418); *Stages on Life's Way, KW* XI (*SV* VI 91); *Postscript, KW* XII (*SV* VII 6, 122, 483, 500); *Upbuilding Discourses in Various Spirits, KW* XV (*SV* VIII 226); *The Sickness unto Death*, pp. 70-71, 79, 113, *KW* XIX (*SV* XI 182, 191, 223). In brief, it signifies consciousness of selfhood, particularly in the context of recollection (as in Plato) and ultimately before God.

3. See Homer, *Iliad*, VI, 146-48.

4. See ibid., III, 381, where Paris is carried away in a cloud.

5. See Hebrews 11:8-19.

6. Presumably the Roman poet Ovid (43 B.C.–A.D. 17?), who in A.D. 8 was banished by Caesar Augustus to Tomi on the Black Sea. See his *Tristia* and *Ex Ponto, P. Ovidii Nasonis opera quae extant*, ed. A. Richter (Leipzig: 1828; *ASKB* 1265); *Tristia [and] Ex Ponto*, tr. A. L. Wheeler (Loeb Classics, New York: Putnam, 1924).

7. See p. 12 and note 12.

8. See note 6.

9. See Numbers 20:11.

10. See p. 9 and note 2.

11. See p. 9 and note 2.

12. See Genesis 18:12. See also Genesis 17:17; Supplement, p. 255 (*Pap.* IV B 69).

13. See note 27.

14. See p. 9 and note 2.

15. See Genesis 12:2.

16. See p. 9 and note 2.

17. See Genesis 22:2.

18. Joseph. See Genesis 35:22-23, 37:3.

19. See Supplement, pp. 248-49 (*Pap.* IV B 72).

20. See Genesis 18:23.

21. Genesis 22:1-3. See Supplement, pp. 239-40 (*Pap.* III C 4). See p. 9 and note 2.

22. See Luke 23:30; Supplement, pp. 248-49 (*Pap.* IV B 72).

23. See p. 14, note 16.

24. A free rendition of Genesis 22:3, 9-10.

25. See Genesis 8:4. Ararat: a high or holy place.

26. Plato, *Phaedrus*, 244–45 c, 265 b; *Platonis quae exstant opera*, I–XI, ed. Fridericus Astius (Leipzig: 1819-32; *ASKB* 1144-54), I, pp. 164-67, 216-17; *The Collected Dialogues of Plato*, ed. Edith Hamilton and Huntington Cairns (Princeton: Princeton University Press, 1963), pp. 491-92, 511.

27. Since Abraham was 100 years old at the time of Isaac's birth, Isaac's age is placed here at 30. Kierkegaard was 30 years old at the time *Fear and Trembling* was written.

28. See Supplement, p. 249 (*Pap.* IV B 87:2).

Preliminary Expectoration

1. See Supplement, p. 243 (*Pap.* IV B 60). For deleted epigraph, see Supplement, pp. 249-50 (*Pap.* IV B 96:4).

2. From the Latin *ex + pectus* (from + heart, breast), an outpouring of the heart, in line with the subtitle, "Dialectical Lyric." In the final draft (Supplement, p. 250; *Pap.* IV B 88:1), the heading was changed from "Introduction." See *Repetition*, p. 157, *KW* VI (*SV* III 196).

3. See II Thessalonians 3:10.

4. Nourredin had control of both a ring and a lamp.

5. The symbolic figure of darkness in contrast to Aladdin in Oehlenschläger's *Aladdin, Adam Oehlenschlägers Poetiske Skrifter*, I–II (Copenhagen: 1805; *ASKB* 1597-98), II, pp. 75ff.

6. See Matthew 5:45.

7. See Plato, *Symposium*, 179 d; *Platonis opera*, III, p. 447; *Udvalgte Dialoger af Platon*, I–III, tr. C. J. Heise, (Copenhagen: 1830-38; *ASKB* 1164-66), II, p. 17; *Collected Dialogues*, pp. 533-34.

8. See Matthew 3:9.

9. Isaiah 26:18.

10. Themistocles. See Plutarch, *Lives*, "Themistocles," III, 3; *Plutarchs Levnetsbeskrivelser*, I–IV, tr. Stephan Tetens (Copenhagen: 1800-11; *ASKB* 1197-2000), I, p. 7; *Plutarch's Lives*, I–X, tr. Bernadotte Perrin (Loeb Classics, New York: Macmillan, 1914), II, p. 11.

11. See Matthew 19:16-22.

12. On June 17, 1845, nine months after the publication of *Fear and Trembling*, *The Concept of Anxiety*, by Vigilius Haufniensis, was published.

13. Three lines and marginal addition in the final draft were replaced by the following two sentences. See Supplement, p. 250 (*Pap.* IV B 88:2).

14. See p. 9 and note 2. "Spiritual trial," in contrast to "temptation" and in relation to "test," is the struggle and the anguish involved in venturing out beyond one's assumed capacities or generally approved expectations. For journal entries on this important category, see *JP* IV 4364-84 and pp. 692-94; VII, p. 90. See also, for example, *Either/Or*, II, *KW* IV (*SV* II 112-14, 126, 289, 298); *Anxiety*, pp. 117, 120, 143, *KW* VIII (*SV* IV 385, 388,

408-09); *Postscript, KW* XII (*SV* VII 12, 15, 18, 32-33, 109-10, 112, 226, 399-400).

15. With reference to the remainder of the paragraph, see Supplement, p. 251 (*Pap.* IV B 88:4).

16. See p. 5 and note 1.

17. *Nam tua res agitur, paries cum proximus ardet.* Horace, *Epistles,* I, 18, 84; Q. *Horatii Flacci opera* (Leipzig: 1828; *ASKB* 1248), p. 606; *Satires, Epistles and Ars Poetica,* tr. H. Rushton Fairclough (Loeb Classics, New York: Putnam, 1929), p. 375: "'Tis your own safety that's at stake when your neighbor's wall is in flames . . . ."

18. As a special expression, the phrase "the absurd" appears in the works for the first time in *Fear and Trembling* and, like its correlative, "the paradox," recurs only in the pseudonymous writings (almost exclusively in *Fragments, Postscript,* and *Practice in Christianity*) and the journals and papers. See *Fragments, KW* VII (*SV* IV 218, 227, 266, 291); *Stages, KW* XI (*SV* VI 156); *Postscript, KW* XII (*SV* VII 20, 80, 156, 171-72, 176-84, 222, 250, 327, 333, 347, 372, 375, 464, 470, 486-87, 490, 495-96, 504-05, 532); *Sickness unto Death,* pp. 71, 83, 87, *KW* XIX (*SV* XI 182, 195, 198). On this theme in the journals and papers, see *JP* I 5-12 and pp. 497-98; VII, p. 3.

19. "Resignation" [*Resignation*] and "resign" [*resignere*] here and later in this section denote an act, a movement (not apathetic acquiescence), presupposing a concentration of the person in an integrating choice of an encompassing goal or purpose. See, for example, pp. 42-43; Supplement, p. 254 (*Pap.* IV B 93:4).

20. See pp. 36, 41, 42, 170; *JP* III 2343 (*Pap.* V B 49:14). For other journal entries on this important category, see *JP* III 2338-59 and p. 794; VII, p. 56. See also, for example, *The Concept of Irony, KW* II (*SV* XIII 124); *Either/Or,* II, *KW* IV (*SV* II 20); *Fragments, KW* VII (*SV* IV 210-11); *Anxiety,* index, *KW* VIII (*SV* IV 289, 303-05, 309-12, 314, 318-19, 320, 323, 325, 331-33, 345-46, 348, 354, 361-63, 379-81, 390, 398-99); *Postscript, KW* XII (*SV* VII 3, 27, 78-85, 94, 102, 123, 218, 222, 253, 293, 296-97, 330, 333). The concept of the leap pertains to qualitative transitions, which cannot be accounted for by quantitative changes or by the continuity of mediation (see p. 42 fn.).

21. See Matthew 18:21-22.

22. See John 2:1-10.

23. See I Corinthians 10:12.

24. Before the development of electrical telegraphy, a system of mirrors (optical or fractional telegraphy) was used.

25. I.e., Frederiksberg, a castle and surrounding wooded park west of Copenhagen, a favorite outing place for Copenhageners, including Johannes Climacus and Kierkegaard, who also mentions Josty's café in the park. See *Postscript, KW* XII (*SV* VII 154-56); *JP* I 419; V 5756 (*Pap.* I A 172; V A 111).

26. See p. 8 and note 13.

27. The Øresund, between the Danish island Sjælland and the mainland of Sweden. Strandveien is the Øresund road running north from Copenhagen.

28. A rix-dollar (worth about $5.00 in 1973 money) contained 16 marks or 96 shillings, each worth about a nickel.

29. See Genesis 25:29-34.

30. An allusion to the death of Socrates, described by Plato at the end of *Phaedo*.

31. See *Repetition*, p. 148, *KW* VI (*SV* III 189), and note 30.

32. See *Apology*, 21 d; *Platonis opera*, VIII, p. 108; *Collected Dialogues*, p. 8. For the epigraph of *Anxiety* (1844), p. 3, *KW* VIII (*SV* IV 276), Vigilius Haufniensis uses this idea in a quotation from Hamann.

33. The source of this line has not been located. It may, however, be from Jacob Böhme, who is quoted in journal entry *JP* IV 5010 (*Pap.* VIII¹ A 105). The work cited, Moriz Carriere, *Die philosophische Weltanschauung der Reformationszeit* (Stuttgart, Tübingen: 1847; *ASKB* 458), also quotes Böhme's last words, which are in the same vein as the line in *Fear and Trembling*: "Nun fahre ich ins Paradies" (p. 620). Kierkegaard owned four works by Böhme: *Beschreibung der drey Principien Göttliches Wesens* (Amsterdam: 1660; *ASKB* 451); *Hohe und tiefe Gründe von dem dreyfachen Leben des Menschen* (Amsterdam: 1660; *ASKB* 452); *Mysterium Magnum* (Amsterdam: 1682; *ASKB* 453); *Christosophia oder Weg zu Christo* (Amsterdam: 1731; *ASKB* 454). See *JP* VI 6382 (*Pap.* X¹ A 247).

34. See *Repetition*, pp. 135-36, *KW* VI (*SV* III 177-78).

35. See *"Ridder Stig og Findal eller Runernes Magt,"* V, 62: "She sleeps every night by the side of Knight Stig Hvide." *Udvalgte danske Viser fra Middelalderen*, I-IV, ed. W. H. Abrahamson, R. Nyerup, and K. L. Rahbek (Copenhagen: 1812-14; *ASKB* 1477-81), I, p. 301 (ed. tr.).

36. Gottfried Wilhelm Leibniz's (1646-1716) hypothesis of preestablished harmony: each substance develops according to its own nature and is in harmony with other substances. See *Monadology*, para. 78-80, 86-87; *Guili Leibnitii opera philosophica . . .*, I-II, ed. J. E. Erdmann (Berlin: 1839-40; *ASKB* 620), II, pp. 711, 712; *Leibniz: The Monadology and Other Philosophical Writings*, tr. Robert Latta (London: Oxford University Press, 1965), pp. 262-64, 267-68.

37. See J. N. Mailáth, "Erzi die Spinnerin," *Magyarische Sagen, Märchen und Erzählungen*, I-II (Stuttgart, Tübingen: 1837; *ASKB* 1411), II, p. 18. See *JP* I 870 (*Pap.* II A 449).

38. Horace, *Odes*, III, 24, 6; *Carminum, Opera*, p. 218.

39. See, for example, *Either/Or*, II, *KW* IV (*SV* II 188-93).

40. See Matthew 19:26; Mark 10:27, 14:36; Luke 8:27.

41. See Matthew 17:20.

42. See Luke 18:18-23.

43. "So als Schildwacht, zur Nachtzeit auf einsamen Posten, etwa an einem Pulvermagazin, hat man Gedanken die auszerdem ganz unmöglich sind

[So like a sentry, at his lonely post at night, near a powder magazine, one has thoughts that otherwise are altogether impossible]." Karl Rosenkranz, *Erinnerungen an Karl Daub* (Berlin: 1837; *ASKB* 743), p. 24 (ed. tr.). See *JP* I 899 (*Pap.* IV A 92).

44. Kierkegaard's doctoral dissertation (1841) was *The Concept of Irony (KW* II [*SV* XIII]), on irony and humor. See, for example, numerous sections and passages in *Postscript, KW* XII (*SV* VII 229-32, 248-50, 434-58, 481-84, 524-25).

45. See Supplement, p. 251 (*Pap.* IV B 75).

Problema I

1. See, for example, G.W.F. Hegel, *Grundlinien der Philosophie des Rechts,* para. 104, 139, 142-57, *Georg Wilhelm Friedrich Hegel's Werke. Vollständige Ausgabe,* I–XVIII, ed. Philipp Marheineke et al. (Berlin: 1832-41; *ASKB* 549-65), VIII, pp. 210-21; *Jubiläumsausgabe [J.A.],* I–XXVI, ed. Hermann Glockner (Stuttgart: 1927-40), VII, pp. 226-37; *Hegel's Philosophy of Right* (tr. of *Philosophie des Rechts,* 1. ed., 1821; Kierkegaard had 2 ed., 1833), tr. T. M. Knox (Oxford: Clarendon Press, 1962), pp. 108-10.

2. On the important categories "individual" and "the single individual," see *JP* II 1964-2086 and pp. 597-99; *JP* VII, pp. 49-50. See also, for example, *Eighteen Upbuilding Discourses, KW* V (*SV* IV 152-53); *Fragments, KW* VII (*SV* IV 263-64); *Anxiety,* pp. 111-13, *KW* VIII (*SV* IV 379-81); *Postscript, KW* XII (*SV* VII 179-80); *Two Ages,* pp. 84-96, *KW* XIV (*SV* VIII 79-89); *Discourses in Various Spirits, KW* XV (*SV* VIII 219-42); *Sickness unto Death,* pp. 119-24, *KW* XIX (*SV* XI 228-34); *Practice, KW* XX (*SV* XII 85-89); *Armed Neutrality, KW* XXII (*SV* XIII 439-40); *On My Work as an Author, KW* XXII (*SV* XIII 507-09); *The Point of View for My Work as an Author, KW* XXII (*SV* XIII 599-610).

3. See p. 31 and note 14.

4. Hegel, *Werke,* VIII, pp. 171-209; *J.A.,* VII, pp. 187-225; *Philosophy of Right,* pp. 86-103 (*aufgehoben* is translated as "annulled," para. 139, 141).

5. Hegel, *Werke,* VIII, p. xix; *J.A.,* VII, p. 16 (ed. tr.). "Moral Forms of Evil. Hypocrisy, Probabilism, Good Intentions, Conviction, Irony, Note to para. 140." The rubrics are omitted in the table of contents of *Philosophy of Right;* see note 1 above.

6. See, for example, Hegel, *Encyclopädie der philosophischen Wissenschaften, Erster Theil, Die Logik,* para. 63, *Werke,* VI, p. 128; *J.A.,* VIII, p. 166; *Hegel's Logic* (tr. of *Encyclopädie,* 3 ed., 1830; the text of the edition Kierkegaard had was of the 3 ed.), tr. William Wallace (Oxford: Clarendon Press, 1975), p. 97: "But, seeing that derivative knowledge is restricted to the compass of facts, Reason is knowledge underivative, or Faith." See p. 69 and note 6.

7. Danish *det sædelige* or *Sædelighed,* corresponding to the German *Sittlichkeit,* is here translated as "social morality," whereas the translation of *Sittlichkeit* in Hegel is usually "ethical life." See, for example, Hegel, *Philosophie*

des Rechts, para. 141, *Werke*, VIII, p. 207; *J.A.*, VII, p. 223, *Philosophy of Right*, p. 103:

Transition from Morality to Ethical Life

141. For the good as the substantial universal of freedom, but as something still abstract, there are therefore required determinate characteristics of some sort and the principle for determining them, though a principle identical with the good itself. For conscience similarly, as the purely abstract principle of determination, it is required that its decisions shall be universal and objective. If good and conscience are each kept abstract and thereby elevated to independent totalities, then both become the indeterminate which ought to be determined.—But the integration of these two relative totalities into an absolute identity has already been implicitly achieved in that this very subjectivity of pure self-certainty, aware in its vacuity of its gradual evaporation, is identical with the abstract universality of the good. The identity of the good with the subjective will, an identity which therefore is concrete and the truth of them both, is Ethical Life.

On morality and the ethical in Kierkegaard's thought, see *JP* I, pp. 530-32.

8. Boileau, *L'Art poétique*, I, 232, *Œuvres de Boileau*, I–IV (Paris: 1830), II, p. 190; *The Art of Poetry*, tr. Albert S. Cook (Boston: Ginn, 1892), p. 172: "And in all times a forward scribbling fop / Has found some greater fool to cry him up."

9. See p. 31 and note 14.

10. The Trojan War.

11. Euripides, *Iphigenia in Aulis*, ll. 446-48; *Euripides*, tr. Christian Wilster (Copenhagen: 1840; *ASKB* 1115), p. 116; *The Complete Greek Tragedies*, I–IV, ed. David Grene and Richard Lattimore (Chicago: University of Chicago Press, 1958-60), IV, p. 316 (tr. Charles R. Walker):

> [*Agamemnon speaking*]
> O fortunate men of mean,
> Ignoble birth, freely you may weep and
> Empty out your hearts, but the highborn—
> Decorum rules our lives . . . .

12. Menelaus, Calchas, and Ulysses, ibid., l. 107; *Euripides*, tr. Wilster, p. 104; *Greek Tragedies*, IV, p. 301.

13. Line reference to *Iphigenia in Aulis, Euripides*, tr. Wilster, p. 125.

14. Jephthah. See Judges 11:30-40.

15. Brutus (Junius) had led the Romans in expelling the Tarquins after the rape of Lucrece. He then executed his sons for plotting a Tarquinian restoration. See Livy, *From the Founding of a City (History of Rome)*, II, 3-5; T. Livii Patavini, *Historiarum libri, quæ supersunt omnia*, I–V, ed. Augusto Guil. Ernesti (Leipzig: n.d.; *ASKB* 1251-55), I, pp. 75-77; *Livy*, I–XIV, tr.

B. O. Foster (Loeb Classics, Cambridge: Harvard University Press, 1939-59), I, pp. 227-35.

16. See Hegel, *Philosophie des Rechts*, para. 150, *Werke*, VIII, pp. 214-16; *J.A.*, VII, pp. 230-32; *Philosophy of Right*, pp. 107-08.

17. See Supplement, p. 251 (*Pap.* IV B 74).

18. For a clarification of "temptation" and "ordeal" and of the shifting relational meaning of "temptation" in the work, see p. 9 and note 2.

19. See Problema III, pp. 82-120.

20. See Exodus 19:12.

21. See Supplement, p. 248 (*Pap.* IV B 68).

22. See Mark 3:15-22.

23. See W. G. Tennemann, *Geschichte der Philosophie*, I–XI (Leipzig: 1798-1819; *ASKB* 815-26), I, p. 106. The Pythagoreans gave a number of reasons, not wholly satisfying, for this distinction. Odd numbers added successively to the number one give square numbers; even numbers added to the number two give "oblong" numbers. The whole universe is identified with the number one. Even numbers are "unlimited" and therefore are endless (no τέλος) and incomplete. See *JP* V 5616 (*Pap.* IV A 56).

24. *Docenter* (pl.) literally means tutors in the university setting of the time, university teachers who assisted the professors in the teaching of the discipline. The root *docere* (Latin and Danish) emphasizes the didactic. Here Johannes de Silentio uses the term broadly to include specifically the professors with their detached objectivity, their pontifical evaluations of the past, and their lifetime appointments. See *Point of View*, *KW* XXII (*SV* XIII 300).

25. The Virgin Mary is celebrated also in other writings. See, for example, *Irony*, *KW* II (*SV* XIII 181); *Either/Or*, I, *KW* III (*SV* I 173, 288, 303); *Eighteen Discourses*, *KW* V (*SV* 97, 159); *Fragments*, *KW* VII (*SV* IV 201); *Postscript*, *KW* XII (*SV* VII 220); *Discourses in Various Spirits*, *KW* XV (*SV* VIII 190, 339); *Christian Discourses*, *KW* XVII (*SV* X 47); *Practice*, *KW* XX (*SV* XII 157); *An Upbuilding Discourse*, in *Without Authority*, *KW* XVIII (*SV* XII 249); *Judge for Yourselves!*, *KW* XXI (*SV* XII 433); *The Moment and Late Writings*, *KW* XXIII (*SV* XIV 35). See also *JP* III 2669-74 and p. 814; VII, p. 60.

26. See Genesis 18:11.

27. See Luke 1:38.

28. See Luke 23:28.

29. On the theme of contemporaneity, see especially *Fragments*, *KW* VII (*SV* IV 221-34, 247-71).

30. *Auszüge aus Lessing's Antheil an den Litteratur-briefen*, Letter 81, *Schriften*, XXX, pp. 221-23 (ed.tr.).

Problema II

1. See Immanuel Kant, *Grundlegung zur Metaphysik der Sitten* (2 ed., Riga: 1786), for example, pp. 29, 73-74, 85-86; *Kant's gesammelte Schriften*, I–XXIII

(Berlin: 1902-55), IV, pp. 409-10, 433-34, 439; *Foundations of the Metaphysics of Morals*, tr. Lewis White Beck (Indianapolis: Bobbs-Merrill, 1969), pp. 25, 51, 58:

> Even the Holy One of the Gospel must be compared with our ideal of moral perfection before He is recognized as such; even He says of Himself, "Why call ye Me (whom you see) good? None is good (the archetype of the good) except God only (whom you do not see)." But whence do we have the concept of God as the highest Good? Solely from the idea of moral perfection which reason formulates a priori and which it inseparably connects with the concept of a free will.

> If we now look back upon all previous attempts which have ever been undertaken to discover the principle of morality, it is not to be wondered at that they all had to fail. Man was seen to be bound to laws by his duty, but it was not seen that he is subject only to his own, yet universal, legislation, and that he is only bound to act in accordance with his own will, which is, however, designed by nature to be a will giving universal laws. For if one thought of him as subject only to a law (whatever it may be), this necessarily implied some interest as a stimulus or compulsion to obedience because the law did not arise from his will. Rather, his will was constrained by something else according to a law to act in a certain way. By this strictly necessary consequence, however, all the labor of finding a supreme ground for duty was irrevocably lost, and one never arrived at duty but only at the necessity of action from a certain interest. This might be his own interest or that of another, but in either case the imperative always had to be conditional and could not at all serve as a moral command. This principle I will call the principle of *autonomy* of the will in contrast to all other principles which I accordingly count under *heteronomy*.

> The essence of things is not changed by their external relations, and without reference to these relations a man must be judged only by what constitutes his absolute worth; and this is true whoever his judge is, even if it be the Supreme Being. Morality is thus the relation of actions to the autonomy of the will, i.e., to possible universal lawgiving by maxims of the will. The action which can be compatible with the autonomy of the will is permitted; that which does not agree with it is prohibited. The will whose maxims necessarily are in harmony with the laws of autonomy is a holy will or an absolutely good will.

Kant's denial of an absolute duty to God transcending rational morality (or a conflation of divine will and the autonomy of man's rational will) is shared with variations by Fichte, Schleiermacher, and Hegel. In raising the question, Johannes de Silentio runs counter to the dominant ethical thought of the time.

2. See p. 54 and note 1.

3. The source has not been located.

4. See Hegel, *Wissenschaft der Logik, Erster Theil, Die objective Logik, Zweites Buch*, II, 3, C, *Werke*, IV, pp. 177-83; *J.A.*, IV, pp. 655-61; *Hegel's Science of Logic* (tr. of *W.L.*, Lasson ed., 1923), tr. A. V. Miller (New York: Humanities Press, 1969), pp. 523-28; Hegel, *Encyclopädie, Logik*, para. 140, *Werke*, VI, pp. 275-81; *J.A.*, VIII, pp. 313-19; *Hegel's Logic*, pp. 197-200. See *Either/Or*, I, *KW* III (*SV* I, pp. v-vi).

5. See p. 62 and note 23.

6. See faith as second immediacy (spontaneity), immediacy after reflection, in *Stages*, *KW* XI (*SV* VI 372); *Postscript*, *KW* XII (*SV* VII 301 fn.); *Works of Love*, *KW* XVI (*SV* IX 342-43); *JP* II 1123 (*Pap.* VIII¹ A 469) and pp. 594-95; VII, pp. 48-49, 90.

7. See Hegel, *Encyclopädie, Logik*, para. 63, *Werke*, VI, pp. 128-31; *J.A.*, VIII, pp. 166-69; *Hegel's Logic*, pp. 97-99, especially, p. 99: "With what is here called faith or immediate knowledge must also be identified inspiration, the heart's revelations, the truths implanted in man by nature, and also in particular, healthy reason or Common Sense, as it is called. All these forms agree in adopting as their leading principle the immediacy, or self-evident way in which a fact or body of truths is presented in consciousness." See also Hegel, *Philosophische Propädeutik*, para. 72, *Werke*, XVIII, p. 75; *J.A.*, III, p. 97. See *JP* I 49; II 1096 (*Pap.* V A 28; I A 273); the latter includes a reference to Hegel. See p. 55 and note 6.

8. See p. 9 and note 2.

9. See John 6:60.

10. See C. G. Bretschneider, *Lexicon Manuale Graeco-Latinum in Libros Novi Testamenti*, I–II (Leipzig: 1829; *ASKB* 73-74), II, p. 87.

11. The reference is to the practice of standing for the reading of the Gospel text for the day.

12. See Genesis 4:2-16.

13. See p. 9 and note 2.

14. Johannes de Silentio reckons that Abraham was married at the age of thirty and that Isaac was born when Abraham was one hundred. See p. 23 and note 27.

15. See p. 31 and note 14.

16. The allusion is to certain Hebrew consonants that can serve also to indicate certain vowel sounds. Kierkegaard, following Jacob Christian Lindberg, *Hovedreglerne af den hebraiske Grammatik* (2 ed., Copenhagen: 1835; *ASKB* 989), pp. 8, 17-18, and the interpretation given in Ludvig Beatus Meyer, *Fremmed Ordbog* (Copenhagen: 1837), uses metaphorically the Danish version of *matres lectionis* or *literae quiescibiles: Hvile-Bogstaver*. According to Lindberg and Meyer, such a consonant may be sounded as a consonant, or, quiescent, it may "rest" [*hvile*] in the vowel indicated while it remains unsounded as a consonant. Here Johannes de Silentio seems to have inverted the relationship. See *Either/Or*, I, *KW* III (*SV* I 6); *JP* II 2263; V 5378 (*Pap.* II A 404, 406).

17. Fabius Maximus (d. 203 B.C.), who in 217 B.C. fought against Hannibal and was named Cunctator (Latin: delayer) because of his deliberate tactic of harassing Hannibal's troops but never joining battle.

18. Danish *Du*, the familiar second-person singular pronoun, used (as in German) in addressing family members and close friends. In English, "thou" is a relic of the same form, but current ecclesiastical usage endows it with the distance and solemnity of the old formal second-person plural form.

19. See Matthew 6:34.

20. For the deleted remainder of this paragraph, see Supplement, pp. 251-52 (*Pap.* IV B 96:5).

21. Christian Olufsen, *Gulddaasen*, II, 10 (Copenhagen: 1793), p. 64.

22. Deuteronomy 13:6-7, 33:9; Matthew 10:37, 19:29. The final copy has I Corinthians 7:11 in parentheses.

Problema III

1. See p. 54 and note 1.

2. See p. 69 and note 6.

3. See *JP* I 899 (*Pap.* IV A 92).

4. See pp. 82-83. On this many-leveled theme, the *interesting* and *interest*, see, for example, *Either/Or*, I, *KW* III (*SV* I 80, 89, 306, 310, 321-22, 337, 341), II, *KW* IV (*SV* II 75, 209-10); *Repetition*, pp. 147-49, *KW* VI (*SV* III 187-89); *Anxiety*, pp. 18, 21-22, *KW* VIII (*SV* IV 291, 293-94); *Postscript*, *KW* XII (*SV* VII 7, 11, 16, 40-41, 114, 116, 132, 144, 161, 172, 221, 269-75, 338, 533); *JP* II 2105-09 and p. 603; VII, p. 51.

5. *Poetics*, ch. 12, 1452 b; *Aristotelis opera omnia graece*, I–V, ed. Johannes Theophilus (Gottlieb) Buhle (Zweibrücken: 1791-97; *ASKB* 1069-73), V, p. 224; *Aristoteles Dichtkunst*, tr. Michael Conrad Curtius (Hannover: 1753; *ASKB* 1094), p. 24 (the end of chapter 11 in this edition); *Works*, XI. "Peripety" denotes the part of a drama in which the plot is brought to a conclusion, the denouement. In the Curtius translation (which Kierkegaard most likely used, according to the reference to chapter 11), ἀναγνώρισις is given as *Wiedererkenntnisz*. Therefore the Greek and the Danish *Gjenkendelse* are rendered as "recognition."

6. Oedipus in *Oedipus Rex* by Sophocles.

7. Iphigenia in *Iphigenia in Tauris* by Euripides.

8. For an extended discussion of modern tragedy against the background of Greek tragedy, see *Either/Or*, I, *KW* III (*SV* I 115-41).

9. *Natural History*, 541 a, 27-30, 560 b, 11-17; *Aristoteles*, ed. Bekker, pp. 541, 560; *Works*, IV. See *JP* V 5611 (*Pap.* IV A 36).

10. The preceding sentence replaced two sentences in the final copy. See Supplement, p. 252 (*Pap.* IV B 96:8).

11. Lines 855-96; *Euripides*, tr. Wilster, pp. 132-35; *Complete Greek Tragedies*, IV, pp. 340-44.

12. See Mark 1:11.

13. See Judges 11:38.

14. *Euripides*, tr. Wilster, p. 145. In *Complete Greek Tragedies*, IV, p. 359, instead of having the figure of the olive branch (in Greece, the sign of a suppliant) as Wilster does, the text has "My body is a suppliant's, tight clinging / To your knees."

15. See L. Apuleii, "*Fabula de Psyche et Cupidine*," *Metamorphoseon*, V, 11; *Opera omnia*, ed. G. F. Hildebrand, I–II (Leipzig: 1842; *ASKB* 1215 [*editio minor* 1843]), I, p. 337; Joseph Kehrein, *Amor und Psyche* [free metrical version] (Giessen: 1834; *ASKB* 1216), p. 40; Apuleius, *The Golden Ass* (Loeb Classics, New York: Macmillan, 1915), p. 217. See *Either/Or*, I, *KW* III (*SV* I 16); *Pap.* III B 179:42; *JP* IV 3978 (*Pap.* IV A 28).

16. See Supplement, p. 243 (*Pap.* IV B 78).

17. No. I–II, *Schriften*, XXIV, pp. 11-25; G. E. Lessing, *Hamburg Dramaturgy*, tr. Helen Zimmern (New York: Dover, 1962), esp. pp. 4-8. The particular reference is to Tasso's *Olindo and Sophronia*.

18. An older distinction in theology between *theologia viatorum* (theology of wayfarers) and *theologia beatorum* (theology of the blessed), analogous to the concepts of "the Church militant" and "the Church triumphant."

19. *Politics*, V, 4, 1303 b–1304 a; *Aristoteles*, ed. Bekker, II, pp. 1303-04; *Die Politik des Aristoteles*, tr. Christian Garve (Breslau: 1799; *ASKB* 1088-89), pp. 407-08; *Works*, X.

20. For the remainder of this sentence, deleted from the final copy, see Supplement, p. 252 (*Pap.* IV B 96:10).

21. The subtitle of the work is "Dialectical Lyric." Nevertheless, Johannes de Silentio seems alternately to claim and to deny that he is either a poet or a dialectician (philosopher). See pp. 15-16 on the task of the poet, which he does carry out; p. 90, where he says that he is not a poet but is only a dialectician; and pp. 7, 9, where he disclaims being a philosopher. Despite Johannes's disclaimers, which are akin to Socratic disclaimers of knowledge, he poetically celebrates Abraham and the knight of faith, and as a philosopher (if not a contributor to the system) he does think a thought through dialectically.

22. See *Repetition*, p. 146, *KW* VI (*SV* III 187), where this alternative is changed to flight.

23. Adam Oehlenschläger, *Axel og Valborg, Oehlenschlägers Tragødier*, I–X (Copenhagen: 1841-49; *ASKB* 1601-05), V, pp. 4-111. Axel and Valborg were close relatives and therefore were forbidden by the Church to marry until they received papal dispensation. Then, however, it was learned that they were baptismal brother and sister (baptized on the same day in the same church), which was an additional hindrance to their marriage (see pp. 9 and 49).

24. See Lessing, *Hamburgische Dramaturgie*, no. XXII; *Schriften*, XXIV, pp. 163-65; *Hamburg Dramaturgy*, pp. 57-58.

25. See, for example, "*Agnete og Havmanden*," in Christian Molbech, *Et Hundrede udvalgte danske Viser* (Copenhagen: 1847), pp. 313-15. See Supplement, pp. 242-43 (*Pap.* IV A 113).

26. One of the interpretations had been by Hans Christian Andersen in a dramatic piece, *Agnete og Havmanden*, which was written in 1834 and performed in Copenhagen on April 20 and May 2, 1843.

27. For a portion deleted from the draft, see Supplement, p. 252 (*Pap.* IV B 91:1).

28. See p. 82 and note 4.

29. This is not in the legend of Agnes and the merman (see note 25), but it is found, for example, in *"Deiligheden og Uhyret"* ("Beauty and the Beast"). See Christian Molbech, *Udvalgte Eventyr og Fortællinger* (Copenhagen: 1843), no. 8, pp. 25-41.

30. See *Stages, KW* XI (*SV* VI 191-93).

31. A past life as a human being before his becoming a merman, not an eternal preexistence as in Plato.

32. For a marginal draft additon to the remainder of this paragraph, see Supplement, pp. 252-53 (*Pap.* IV B 91:3).

33. Cf. Hegel, *Encyclopädie, Logik*, para. 24, *Zusatz* 3, *Werke*, VI, pp. 55-59; *J.A.*, VIII, pp. 92-97; *Hegel's Logic*, tr. Wallace, pp. 42-45: "We all know the theological dogma that man's nature is evil, tainted with what is called Original Sin. Now while we accept the dogma, we must give up the setting of incident which represents original sin as consequent upon an accidental act of the first man. For the very notion of spirit is enough to show that man is evil by nature, and it is an error to imagine that he could ever be otherwise. To such extent as man is and acts like a creature of nature, his whole behavior is what it ought not to be. For the spirit it is a duty to be free and to realize itself by its own act. Nature is for man only the starting-point which he has to transform" (p. 44).

34. See p. 69 and note 6.

35. In a Danish game called *Gnavspil* (also *Vexel-Spil*), one is fooled by the figure of the fool, one among various figures drawn from a bag and passed around secretly according to certain rules. See *Fragments, KW* VII (*SV* IV 191).

36. See, for example, [Ludwig Feuerbach], *Gedanken über Tod und Unsterblichkeit* (Nürnberg: 1830).

37. See Plato, *Phaedrus*, 230 a; *Platonis opera*, I, pp. 130-31; *Collected Dialogues*, p. 478: "If our skeptic, with his somewhat crude silence, means to reduce every one of them to the standard of probability, he'll need a deal of time for it. I myself have certainly no time for the business, and I'll tell you why, my friend. I can't as yet 'know myself,' as the inscription at Delphi enjoins, and so long as that ignorance remains it seems to me ridiculous to inquire into extraneous matters. Consequently I don't bother about such things, but accept the current beliefs about them, and direct my inquiries, as I have just said, rather to myself, to discover whether I really am a more complex creature and more puffed up with pride than Typhon, or a simpler, gentler being whom heaven has blessed with a quiet, un-Typhonic nature." See *Fragments, KW* VII (*SV* IV 204).

38. The Apocrypha, Tobit 6-8.

39. Friedrich von Schiller, "*Resignation*," st. 2, l. 3; *Schillers sämmtliche Werke*, I–XII (Stuttgart, Tübingen: 1838; *ASKB* 1804-15), I, p. 95; *The Poems of Schiller*, tr. Edgar A. Bowring (New York: Hurst, 1851), p. 77: "Take, then, these Joy-Credentials back from me."

40. Longus, *Daphnis and Chloe*, Introduction, para. 2; *Longi Pastoralia græce & latine*, ed. Ernest Edward Seiler (Leipzig: 1843; *ASKB* 1128), p. 4; *Daphnis & Chloe*, tr. George Thornley, rev. J. M. Edmonds (New York: Putnam, 1916), p. 9.

41. See Tobit 8:1-3. The smoke and odor from the heart and liver on the embers of incense drove the demon away to the remotest parts of Egypt, the traditional home of magic and witchcraft.

42. *King Richard the Third*, I, 1; *Shakespeare's dramatische Werke*, I–XII, tr. August Wilhelm v. Schlegel and Ludwig Tieck (Berlin: 1839-40; *ASKB* 1883-88), III, pp. 235-36.

43. The central figure in Richard Cumberland's *The Jew*, published in Danish translation (*Jøden*) in 1796. The play was presented in Copenhagen at various times between 1795 and 1834.

44. Jens Baggesen, "*Kirkegaarden i Sobradise*," *Danske Værker*, I–XII (Copenhagen: 1827-32; *ASKB* 1509-20), I, p. 282.

45. See Seneca, *On Tranquillity of Mind*, 17, 10; *L. Annae Senecae Opera*, I–V (Leipzig: 1832; *ASKB* 1275-79), IV, p. 102; *Seneca: Moral Essays*, I–III, tr. John W. Basore (Loeb Classics, Cambridge, Mass.: Harvard University Press, 1935), II, p. 285.

46. Legendary German teller of fanciful, incredible adventures.

47. Tamerlane or Timur (1370-1405), a Mongolian king with a reputation of being a cruel conqueror.

48. In 356 B.C., Herostratus burned the temple of Artemis in Ephesus in order to gain enduring fame.

49. Augustinian monk (?-1358), professor at the University of Paris.

50. The contrast here is between "my Faust" and Goethe's representation of Faust. See Goethe, *Faust*, I, ll. 2074-2110; *Goethe's Werke. Vollständige Ausgabe aus letzter Hand*, I–LV (Stuttgart, Tübingen: 1828; *ASKB* 1641-68), XII, pp. 124-25; *Faust*, tr. Bayard Taylor (New York: Modern Library, 1950), p. 89:

FAUST

(who during all this time has been standing before
a mirror, now approaching and now retreating from it).
What do I see? What heavenly from revealed
Shows through the glass from Magic's fair dominions!
O lend me, Love, the swiftest of thy pinions,
And bear me to her beauteous field!
Ah, if I leave this spot with fond designing,
If I attempt to venture near,
Dim, as through gathering mist, her charms appear!—

A woman's form, in beauty shining!
Can woman, then, so lovely be?
And must I find her body, there reclining,
Of all the heavens the bright epitome?
Can Earth with such a thing be mated?

51. See Ludvig Holberg, *Erasmus Montanus*, I, 3 (ed. tr.): "Do you want fine sand or just plain dirt?" *Den Danske Skue-Plads*, I–VII (Copenhagen: 1798; *ASKB* 1566-67), V (unpaginated).

52. For a following sentence omitted from the draft, see Supplement, p. 253 (*Pap.* IV B 91:13).

53. See Matthew 6.

54. See Hegel, *Philosophie des Rechts*, para. 140, *Werke*, VIII, pp. 200-04; *J.A.*, VII, pp. 216-20; *Philosophy of Right*, pp. 101-03; *Æsthetik*, Introduction, 7, iii, *Werke*, X¹, pp. 84-90; *J.A.*, XIII, pp. 100-06; *Hegel's Aesthetics* (tr. of *A.*, 2 ed., 1842; Kierkegaard had 1 ed., T. M. Knox (Oxford: Clarendon Press, 1975), I, pp. 64-68; *Vorlesungen über die Geschichte der Philosophie*, II, pt. 1, sec. 1, ch. 2, B, 1, *Werke*, XIV, pp. 60-64; *J.A.*, XVIII, pp. 60-64; *Hegel's Lectures on the History of Philosophy* (tr. of *G.P.*, 2 ed., 1840; Kierkegaard had 1 ed., 1833), I–III, tr. E. S. Haldane (New York: Humanities Press, 1955), I, pp. 398-402; *Ueber "Solger's nachgelassene Schriften und Briefwechsel," Vermischte Schriften*, IV, 4, *Werke*, XVI, pp. 486-94; *J.A.*, XX, pp. 182-90.

55. Matthew 6:17-18.

56. For a following paragraph, deleted from the final copy, see Supplement, p. 253 (*Pap.* IV B 96:13).

57. For the sentence that followed but was omitted from the draft, see Supplement, p. 253 (*Pap.* IV B 91:15).

58. Shakespeare, *King Richard the Third, Shakspeare's dramatische Werke*, Schlegel and Tieck, III, p. 278. Johannes de Silentio changed *hiesz* to *bat* in the second line, a change that is closer to the English.

59. For an addition at this point in the margin of the draft, see Supplement, p. 254 (*Pap.* IV B 91:16).

60. See I Corinthians 12-14.

61. For a sentence in the margin of the draft of the following paragraph, see Supplement, p. 254 (*Pap.* IV B 91:17).

62. For the two meanings of temptation [*Fristelse*] in the work, see p. 9 and note 2.

63. For a sketch of the following portion up to 119:35, see Supplement, pp. 254-55 (*Pap.* IV B 93:1-6).

64. See Genesis 22:8.

65. For a following paragraph, deleted from the final copy, see Supplement, p. 255 (*Pap.* IV B 96:14).

66. See Supplement, p. 254 (*Pap.* IV B 93:1).

67. With reference to the following sentence, see Supplement, p. 254 (*Pap.* IV B 93:2).

68. Plato, *Apology*, 36 a; *Platonis opera*, VIII, p. 142; *Collected Dialogues*, p. 21. *Platons Werke*, I–III, tr. F. Schleiermacher (Berlin: 1817-28; *ASKB* 1158-63), I², p. 219, also has "three votes" (*drei Stimmen*). Now the reading is more commonly "thirty votes."

69. With reference to the following sentence, see Supplement, p. 254 (*Pap.* IV B 93:3).

70. With reference to the remainder of this sentence, see Supplement, p. 254 (*Pap.* IV B 93:3).

71. Diogenes Laertius; *Vitis*, II, p. 106; Loeb, II, p. 355.

72. See Supplement, p. 254 (*Pap.* IV B 93:4).

73. With reference to the following sentence, see Supplement, p. 255 (*Pap.* IV B 93:6).

74. See Matthew 6:6.

Epilogue

1. For sketches of pp. 121-23, see Supplement, pp. 256-57 (*Pap.* IV B 92, 94, 76).

2. "*Der Schneider im Himmel*," no. 35, *Kinder- und Haus-Märchen gesammelt durch die Brüder Grimm*, I–III (2 ed., Berlin: 1819-22; *ASKB* 1425-27), I, pp. 177-79; *The Complete Grimm's Fairy Tales*, tr. Padraic Colum (New York: Pantheon, 1972), pp. 175-77.

3. With reference to the following sentence, see Supplement, p. 256 (*Pap.* IV B 94).

4. For a draft of the following two sentences, see Supplement, p. 257 (*Pap.* IV B 95:3).

5. See *JP* II 2285 (*Pap.* IV A 58).

6. For a draft of the following sentence, see Supplement, p. 257 (*Pap.* IV B 95:4).

7. *Collected Dialogues*, p. 439.

REPETITION

TITLE PAGE. For various changes in the title page, see Supplement, p. 276 (*Pap.* IV B 97:1). For recurrence of the theme of repetition in the works, see: *Either/Or*, I, *KW* III (*SV* I 38), II, *KW* IV (*SV* II 128-29, 217); *Johannes Climacus, or De omnibus dubitandum est, KW* VII (*Pap.* IV B 1, pp. 149-50); *Eighteen Upbuilding Discourses, KW* V (*SV* IV 46, 63); *The Concept of Anxiety*, index, *KW* VIII (*SV* IV 289-91, 296, 360, 363, 373, 375, 381, 414-15, 417); *Three Discourses on Imagined Occasions, KW* X (*SV* V 186); *Concluding Unscientific Postscript, KW* XII (*SV* VII 99, 132, 268); *Works of Love, KW* XVI (*SV* IX 364-65); *Practice in Christianity, KW* XX (*SV* XII 178). Although an important concept, repetition as a term rarely appears in the journals and papers. See *JP* III 3791-95 and pp. 920-21; VII, p. 81.

SUBTITLE. The Danish *experimenterende* refers not so much to Constantin's journey to Berlin in order to test his theory about repetition as it does to an *experiential* mode of depicting the concept of repetition in the person of the young man: hence, "Experimenting" or "Imaginatively Constructing." Therefore, the work approaches the form of a short novel, as Aage Henriksen calls *Repetition* and parts of other works ("The Seducer's Diary" in *Either/Or*, I, and " 'Guilty?'/'Not Guilty?' " in *Stages*) in his *Kierkegaards Romaner* [Kierkegaard's novels] (Copenhagen: Gyldendal, 1969). See Historical Introduction, pp. xxi-xxvi. For various forms of the term in other works and in the journals and papers and for its relation to indirect communication, see for example: *JP* I 3846 (*Pap.* I C 69, October 1835: Schleiermacher's *Vertraute Briefe über Schlegel's Lucinde* is "an example of how such a thing can be most productive, in that he constructs a host of personalities out of the book itself and through them illuminates the work and also illuminates their individuality, so that instead of being faced by the reviewer with various points of view, we get instead many personalities who represent these various points of view. But they are complete beings, so that it is possible to get a glance into the individuality of the single individual and through numerous merely relatively true judgments to draw up our own final judgment. Thus it is a true masterpiece"); *JP* III 2799 (*Pap.* I A 300; 1836: "Just as the poetic is the subjunctive but does not claim to be more (poetic actuality), mythology, on the other hand, is a hypothetical statement in the indicative"); *JP* III 2310 (*Pap.* II A 156, 1837: "The indicative thinks something as actual (the identity of thinking and actuality). The subjunctive thinks something as thinkable"); *JP* III 2314 (*Pap.* II A 160, 1837: "It should be possible to write a whole novel in which the present subjunctive is the invisible soul, is what lighting is for painting"); *JP* III 2315 (*Pap.* II A 161, 1837: "This is why it may legitimately be said that the subjunctive, which

occurs as a glimmer of the individuality of the person in question, is a
dramatic retort in which the narrator steps aside as it were and makes the
remark as true of the individuality (that is, poetically true), not as factually
so and not even as if it may be that, but it is presented under the illumination
of subjectivity"); *JP* II 1974 (*Pap.* II A 652, 1837: "The hero in a novel is
just about to make a remark when the author takes it out of his mouth,
whereupon the hero becomes angry and says that it belongs to him and he
shows that this remark is appropriate only to his individuality, and 'if things
are going to be like this, I just won't be hero any more' "); *JP* V 5303 (*Pap.*
II A 210, 1838: "This morning I saw a half dozen wild geese fly away . . .
at last they separated into two flocks, like two eyebrows over my eyes,
which now gazed into the land of poetry"); *The Concept of Irony, KW* II
(*SV* XIII 171, 228, 307: "a curious hypothesis [*Experiment*]"; "vacuous
imaginary constructions [*Experimenter*]"; "imaginatively constructed virtues
[*experimenterende Dyder*]"); *Either/Or,* II, *KW* IV (*SV* II 14, 96, 128, 227:
"You do not want to act at all, you want to construct imaginatively"; "a
little trip into the kingdom of fantasy . . . little imaginary constructions";
"Your imaginary construction [*Experiment*] . . . visible symbols . . . symbols
and 'gesticulations' "; "as soon as the ethical person's gymnastics become
an imaginative constructing [*Experimenteren*], he has ceased to live ethically.
Any such imaginary gymnastic constructions are equivalent to sophistry in
the realm of knowledge"); *Pap.* III B 181:7, 1841-42 ("continually to want
to construct imaginatively leads to nothing"); *Pap.* IV B 117, pp. 282, 293,
1843-44 ("I wanted to describe and illustrate psychologically and esthetically; in the Greek sense, I wanted to let the concept come into existence in
the individuality and the situation, working itself forward through all sorts
of misunderstandings"; "an author 'who tries his hand at imaginatively constructing psychology [*experimenterende Psychologie*]' "); *Philosophical Fragments, KW* VII (*SV* IV 242: "to construct imaginatively [experimentere] *in
concreto*"); *Anxiety,* pp. 40, 54, *KW* VIII (*SV* IV 311, 325: "an imaginatively
constructed relation"; "true psychological-poetic authority"); *JP* V 5714 (*Pap.*
V A 102, 1844: "*Vocalizations / to / the Concept of Anxiety / loquere ut videam
te* [speak so that I may see you]"); *Pap.* V B 148:36, 39, 1844 [from draft of
Stages on Life's Way] ("Moreover, the forgiveness of sins is a difficult problem. Earnest men have spoken well and competently in order to show that
it is present, but how this expresses itself, . . . how an individual exists by
virtue of it . . .. Here many existential details are needed"; "Imaginatively-
constructing [*Experimenterende*], I have here again prepared everything for
the religious: the forgiveness of sins"); *JP* I 633 (*Pap.* VI B 40:45, 1845:
"Later I again found illumination of the meaning of imaginary construction
[*Experiment*] as the form of communication. If existence is the essential and
truth is inwardness, . . . it is also good that it be said in the right way. But
this right way is precisely the art that makes being such an author very
difficult . . .. If this is communicated in a direct form, then the point is
missed"); *Stages, KW* XI (*SV* VI 374, 401, 407, 409, 434-35: "give my

imaginatively constructed character flesh and blood"; "my imaginatively constructed personality"; "the Aristotelian dictum that the poet is a greater philosopher than the historian because he shows how it is supposed to be and not how it is"; "In order to grasp the ideality, I must be able to dissolve the historical into the ideality"; "the historical is always raw material which the person who acquires it knows how to dissolve in a *posse* and assimilate as an *esse*"; "I have become aware of this in fashioning the story of suffering that I have developed as an imaginary construction"; "in my imaginative constructing I merely set the categories in motion in order to observe quite unconcernedly what they require without caring who has done it or can do it"; "anyone who otherwise has the desire and the aptitude to work imaginatively-constructively [*experimenterende*] without needing pageantry, scenery, many characters"); "The Activity of a Traveling Esthetician," *The Corsair Affair*, p. 39, *KW* XIII (*SV* XIII 423: "I shall imaginatively construct a character [*jeg vil experimentere en Figur*]"—note the transitive verb and the absence of the preposition *med* or *paa*, "with" or "on"; "The imaginative constructor himself says that the point of view of the imaginatively constructed character [*Experimenterede*] is a deviation but adds that he is doing the whole imaginary construction [*Experiment*] in order to study normality by means of the passion of deviation"); *Postscript, KW* XII (*SV* VII 61, 223-24, 273, 435, 447, [546]: "In order to make this clear in the form of an imaginary construction [*Experimentets*], without determining whether someone actually existing has himself been conscious of this or not, . . . I will suggest the existential situation"; "that this was a doubly reflected communication form was immediately clear to me. By taking place in the form of an imaginary construction, the communication creates for itself an opposition, and the imaginary construction establishes a chasmic gap between reader and author and fixes the separation of inwardness between them . . . . the imaginary construction is the conscious, teasing recall of the communication"; "This form won my complete approval, and I believed I had also found that in it the pseudonymous authors continually aimed at existing"; "the form of the imaginary construction is a good exploratory means"; "Aristotle remarks in his *Poetics* that poetry is superior to history, because history presents only what has occurred, poetry what could and ought to have occurred, i.e., poetry has possibility at its disposal"; "Frater Taciturnus . . . transforms his observation into a psychological-poetic production"; "In the story of suffering . . . I am just as remote from being the *Quidam* of the imaginary construction as from being the imaginary constructor, just as remote, since the imaginary constructor is a poetic-actual subjective thinker and what is imaginatively constructed is his psychologically consistent production"); *The Book on Adler, KW* XXIV (*Pap.* VII² B 235, pp. 5, 14-15: "Here there is no poet who poetically rounds off a whole, no philosophical anthropologist [*Psycholog*] who orders the particular and the individual in a total view, no dialectician who assigns a place within the life view at his disposal"; "The art in all communication is to come as close as possible to actuality, to contemporaries in the role of readers, and yet at the same time to have the distance of a point of view, the reassuring, infinite distance of ideality from them. Permit me to illustrate this by an example from a later work. In the imaginary psychological construction [*psychologiske Experiment*] " 'Guilty?'/'Not Guilty?' " (in *Stages on Life's Way*), there is depicted a character in tension in the most extreme mortal danger of the spirit to the point of despair, and the whole thing is done as though it could have oc-curred yesterday. In this respect, the production is placed as close as possible to actuality . . .. If the imaginary construction [*Experiment*] has made any impression, it might be like that which happens when the wing strokes of the wild bird, in being heard overhead by the tame birds of the same kind who live securely in the certainty of actuality, prompt these to beat their wings, because those wing strokes simultaneously are unsettling and yet have something that fascinates. But now comes what is reassuring, that the whole thing is an imaginary construction and that an imaginary constructor [*Experimentator*] stands by. . . . an imaginary constructor is along . . . who very quietly shows how the whole thing hangs together, theoretically educes a life view that he completes and rounds out, while he points interpretively to the imaginatively constructed character in order to indicate how he makes the movements according to the drawing of the strings. If this were not an imaginary construction, if no imaginary constructor were along, if no life view were represented . . .."); *JP* I 691 (*Pap.* IX A 95, 1848: "Out with history. In with the situation of contemporaneity. . . . This is why I use imaginary constructions instead of *actual* histories"); *Two Ethical-Religious Essays, KW* XVIII (*SV* XI 91: "a poetic venture"); *The Sickness unto Death,* pp. 68-70, *KW* XIX (*SV* XI 180-81: "it constantly relates itself to itself only by way of imaginary constructions"; "that it becomes an imaginatively con-structed god"; "Consequently, the self in despair is always building only castles in the air, is only shadowboxing. All these imaginatively constructed virtues make it look splendid"; "it wants to have the honor of this poetic, masterly construction"; "But it does not succeed, its proficiency in imagi-natively constructing does not stretch that far, even though its proficiency in abstracting does"); *JP* VI 6440 (*Pap.* X^1 A 531, 1849: "So it became my task to create author-personalities and let them enter into the actuality of life in order to get men a bit accustomed to hearing discourse in the first person"); *JP* I 1059 (*Pap.* X^2 A 439, 1850: "Art, science, poetry, etc. deal only with possibility, that is, possibility not in the sense of an idle hypoth-esis [*Hypothese*] but possibility in the sense of ideal actuality"); *JP* I 188 (*Pap.* X^2 A 396, 1850: "Real self-redoubling without a restraining third factor . . . makes such existing into an illusion or into an imaginative constructing [*Experimenteren*] . . . an illusion, imaginative constructing . . . illusion and make-believe and imaginative constructing"); *JP* VI 6870 (*Pap.* XI^1 A 131, 1854: "That was why I turned the relation around and concealed what in substance was from actual life by always using the phrase: imaginary psychological construction [*Experiment*]").

The various formulations of the subtitle eventuate in the use of the term "psychology" rather than "philosophy." Here, as in *Anxiety* and *Sickness unto Death*, the term "psychology" might more accurately, but perhaps too freely in a translation, be rendered as "philosophical anthropology" or "phenomenology." To Constantius-Kierkegaard, psychology pertains to the imaginatively depicted stages in the actualization of human possibilities rather than to an empirical description of behavior. See Historical Introduction, p. xxix. For uses of the term in other works and in journals and papers, see: *Anxiety*, pp. 23, 54-56, *KW* VIII (*SV* IV 295, 325-26: "Ethics . . . does not waste time on such deliberations. Psychology, on the other hand, loves these, and as it sits and traces the contours and calculates the angles of possibility, it does not allow itself to be disturbed any more than did Archimedes"; "Often the examples . . . lack true psychological-poetic authority . . . construct his example, which even though it lacks factual authority nevertheless has an authority of a different kind . . . a poetic originality in his soul so as to be able at once to create both the totality and the invariable . . . he can fashion at once . . . the quality of freshness and the interest of actuality . . . fictitiously invents"); *Stages, KW* XI (*SV* VI 181, 447: "imaginative psychological constructions . . . create an individuality from its private knowledge"; "Statistics are of no use to an imaginatively constructing psychologist; but then he does not need an immense crowd of people, either. Once again in an imaginary construction [*Experiment*]"); *Postscript, KW* XII (*SV* VII 48, 217, 228, 291, 300, 332, 429, 435, [545-46]: "It pertains not to Lessing as poet, not to his mastery in constructing the dramatic line, not to his psychological authority in poetically making manifest"; "The poet has no τέλος other than psychological truth and the art of presentation"; "But it is the misfortune of our age that it has come to know too much, has forgotten what it means to exist; therefore it was important that sin not be conceived in abstract categories . . . because it stands in an essential relation to existing. Therefore it was good that the work [*Anxiety*] was a psychological inquiry, which in itself makes clear that sin . . . [is] essentially related to existing"; "great mastery in psychological depiction is required to produce by concretion such a great effect as this abstract 'until,' which evokes the imagination"; "In a scientific-scholarly way it may indeed be quite proper—and perhaps so masterly that I am far from assuming to be a judge— it may be quite proper to ascend abstractly-dialectically in psychological [*psychologiske*] categories from the psychical-somatic to the psychical, to the pneumatic . . . with respect to existence thought is not at all superior to imagination and feeling but coordinate"; "existence communication. Therefore it introduces psychologically, not world-historically, by evoking an awareness of how much must be lived"; "But I have kept this rather abstract and now will have it take place as if it were today . . . as I attend to the psychological states in imaginary construction"; "Frater Taciturnus seems already to have been aware of this dialectical difficulty, for he has avoided this irregularity by means of the form of an imaginary construction. He is not in an observational relation to the Quidam of the imaginary construction but transforms his observation into a psychological-poetic production and then draws this as close as possible to actuality by using the form of the imaginary construction and the proportions of actuality rather than the fore-shortened perspective"; "My pseudonymity or polyonymity has not had an *accidental* basis in my *person* . . . but an essential basis in the production itself, which, for the sake of the lines, of the diversity of the psychologically varied individualities, poetically required an indiscriminateness with regard to good and evil, brokenheartedness and gaiety, despair and overconfidence, suffering and elation, etc., which is ideally limited only by psychological consistency, which again no factually actual person dares to allow himself or can want to allow himself in the moral limitations of actuality. What has been written, then, is mine, but only insofar as I, by means of audible lines, have placed the life view of the creative, poetically actual individuality in his mouth, for my relation is even more remote than that of a poet, who *poetizes* characters and yet in the preface is himself the author"); *JP* I 119 (*Pap.* I A 86, 1835: "does not seem right that they stop with the historical themes already given"); *JP* IV 3846 (*Pap.* I C 69, 1835: "constructs a host of personalities out of the book itself and through them illuminates the work and also illuminates their individuality"); *JP* IV 4400 (*Pap.* II A 163, 1837: "It would be interesting to follow the development of human nature (in the individual man—that is, at various ages) by depicting what one laughs at on the different age levels, in part by making these imaginary constructions [*Experimenter*] with one and the same author, for example, our literary foun-tainhead, Holberg, and in part by way of the different kinds of comedy. It would—together with research and imaginary constructions concerning the age level at which tragedy is most appreciated and with other psychological observations about the relation between comedy and tragedy, why, for ex-ample, one reads tragedy alone by himself and comedy together with others—contribute to the work I believe ought to be written—namely, the history of the human soul (as it is in an ordinary human being) in the continuity of the state of the soul (not of the concept) consolidating itself in particular mountain clusters (that is, noteworthy world-historical representatives of life views)").

EPIGRAPH. Flavius Philostratus des Ædtern, *Heldengeschichten, Werke*, I–V, tr. Friedrich Jakobs (Stuttgart: 1828-32; *ASKB* 1143), I, p. 20. For changes in this page, see Supplement, p. 276 (*Pap.* IV B 97:2). In *JP* I 451 (*Pap.* IV A 27), there is an interpretation of the epigraph: "The lines found in Philo-stratus the Elder's *Hero-tales* (in [German] translation, p. 20) could be a little epigram on the relation between paganism and Christianity: On wild trees the flowers are fragrant, on cultivated trees, the fruits."

PART ONE

[Report by Constantin Constantius]

1. Originally, the printing manuscript opened with the line: Berlin in May 1843. See Supplement, p. 276 (*Pap.* IV B 97:3).

2. Parmenides and Zeno, of Elea, maintained that the concepts of motion and change involved logical contradictions and that sense experience is therefore illusory. The anecdote about Diogenes of Sinope is found in Diogenes Laertius, *Lives of Eminent Philosophers*, VI, 2, 39; *De vitis philosophorum*, I–II (Leipzig: 1833; *ASKB* 1109), I, p. 266; *Diogen Laertses filosofiske Historie*, I–II, tr. Børge Riisbrigh (Copenhagen: 1811-12; *ASKB* 1110-11), I, p. 246; *Diogenes Laertius*, I–II, tr. R. D. Hicks (Loeb Classics, New York: Putnam, 1925), II, p. 41. In his version of the incident, Hegel uses the expression *stillschweigend*, which corresponds to "he did not say a word." See *Geschichte der Philosophie, Georg Wilhelm Friedrich Hegel's Werke. Vollständige Ausgabe*, I–XVIII, ed. Philipp Marheineke et al. (Berlin: 1832-45; *ASKB* 549-65), XIII, p. 314; *Jubiläumsausgabe [J.A.]*, I–XXVI, ed. Hermann Glockner (Stuttgart: 1927-40), XVII, p. 330; *Hegel's Lectures on the History of Philosophy* (tr. of *G.P.*, 2 ed., 1840; Kierkegaard had 1 ed., 1833), I–III, tr. E. S. Haldane and Frances H. Simson (New York: Humanities Press, 1955), I, p. 267. See *Kierkegaard: Letters and Documents*, Letter 150, *KW* XXV.

3. For earlier references to repetition in Kierkegaard's writings, see note to title page, p. 357.

4. See Plato, *Phaedrus*, 250, 275 a; *Phaedo*, 73-76, 92; *Meno*, 85-86. *Platonis quae exstant opera*, I–IX, ed. Fredricus Astius (Leipzig: 1819-32; *ASKB* 1144-54), I, pp. 178-81, 240-41; V, pp. 510-21, 556-59; IX, pp. 234-41; *The Collected Dialogues of Plato*, ed. Edith Hamilton and Huntington Cairns (Princeton: Princeton University Press, 1963), pp. 497-98, 520, 55-60, 73-74, 369-71. See *Fragments, KW* VII (*SV* IV 179-90); *Stages, KW* XI (*SV* VI 15-21); *Postscript, KW* XII (*SV* VII 172-73).

5. See, for example, Gottfried Wilhelm Leibniz, *Theodicy*, para. 360; *Theodicee* (Hannover, Leipzig: 1763; *ASKB* 610); *Guil. Leibnitii Opera philosophica*, ed. Johann Eduard Erdmann, I–II (Berlin: 1839-40; *ASKB* 620), II, p. 608; *Theodicy*, ed. A. Farrar, tr. E. M. Huggard (New Haven: Yale University Press, 1952), p. 341: "*The present is big with the future.*" In *Nouveaux Essais*, I, 1 (*Opera*, I, pp. 208-09), Leibniz discusses Platonic recollection.

6. See *Either/Or*, I, *KW* III (*SV* I 28). The quotation is not quite exact. With respect to the remainder of the paragraph, see *JP* I 1030 (*Pap.* IV A 188).

7. See *Anxiety*, p. 149, *KW* VIII (*SV* IV 415).

8. See note 6. Constantin Constantius's observations on A of *Either/Or*, I, are part of the explicit aspect of the internal dialectic of Kierkegaard's pseudonymous authorship. The comments on writing and reading in the

remainder of the paragraph constitute a significant compact instruction on the way to approach Kierkegaard's writings. See also, for example, Johannes Climacus's observations on the pseudonymous works in "Appendix. A Glance at a Contemporary Effort in Danish Literature," *Postscript, KW* XII (*SV* VII 212-57).

9. *Farinelli*, III, 12. Created by Saint Georges and Leuren, translated by J. L. Heiberg, the opera *Farinelli* was produced at the Royal Theater from 1837; *Kongelige Theaters Repertoire*, IV, no. 94. Farinelli (1705-1782), male soprano, lived in the Spanish court from 1737 to 1759, where he was the only one who could divert the melancholy of Philip V. Kierkegaard sometimes used this name in letters to his friend Emil Boesen. See *Letters, KW* XXV, Letters 54, 86.

10. The expressions "secret agent," "police agent," and "spy" appear in a number of Kierkegaard's works. See, for example, *Irony, KW* II (*SV* XIII 143, 178); *Fragments, KW* VII (*SV* IV 225, 287); *Anxiety*, pp. 55, 155, *KW* VIII (*SV* IV 326, 422); *Stages, KW* XI (*SV* VI 333, 433); *Postscript, KW* XII (*SV* VII 353); *The Point of View, KW* XXII (*SV* XIII 571, 608). For entries in the journals and papers, see *JP* VII, pp. 74, 85, especially *JP* VI 6192 (*Pap.* IX A 142).

11. See Supplement, p. 276 (*Pap.* IV B 97:4), for a deletion made necessary because of a change in the ending of *Repetition*. See Historical Introduction, p. xx.

12. "Da kommer en Drøm fra min Ungdomsvaar / Til min Lænestol, / Efter Dig jeg en inderlig Længsel faaer, / Du Qvindernes Sol!" Poul Martin Møller, "Den gamle Elsker," *Efterladte Skrifter*, I–III (Copenhagen: 1839-42; *ASKB* 1574-76), I, p. 12 (ed. tr.). See *JP* I 804 (*Pap.* III A 95) for an earlier reference to the Møller stanza. *The Concept of Anxiety* is dedicated to Møller, Kierkegaard's favorite professor at the University of Copenhagen.

13. The coastal road running north from Copenhagen.

14. This suggestion of the original tragic ending was not removed from the manuscript as some others were. See note 11.

15. See *Either/Or*, II, *KW* IV (*SV* II 24, 28).

16. This conflation of love and poetry is not an autobiographical reference but is a view drawn from the romantic poets.

17. See Matthew 6:24.

18. See Gotthold Ephraim Lessing, *Fabeln, Vorrede, Sämmtliche Schriften*, I–XXXII (Berlin: 1825-28; *ASKB* 1747-62), XVIII, p. 96.

19. Prometheus alone knew the prophecy that Thetis's son would be stronger than Zeus, who could avert fulfillment of the prophecy if he heeded it by avoiding a relationship with Thetis. Prometheus revealed the prophecy to Zeus, who in return released Prometheus from his chains. See Aeschylus, *Prometheus Bound*. Kierkegaard owned *Aeschylos' Werke*, tr. Johann Gustav Droysen (2 ed., Berlin: 1842; *ASKB* 1046), and later *Æschylos's Tragedier*, I–II, tr. Niels Vinding Dorph (Copenhagen: 1854; *ASKB* 1047-48). See also

Wilhelm Vollmer, *Vollständiges Wörterbuch der Mythologie* (Stuttgart: 1836; *ASKB* 1942-43), pp. 1363-64.

20. In Mozart's *Don Giovanni*, Elvira is "Don Giovanni's epic fate"; *Either/Or*, I, *KW* III (*SV* I 167). For a discussion of Elvira, see ibid. (*SV* I 167-79). See *JP* V 5541 (*Pap*. III A 190).

21. The metaphor refers to the ropes on a stage curtain.

22. For changes in the manuscript, see Supplement, p. 276 (*Pap*. IV B 97:5); Historical Introduction, pp. xx-xxi. Cf. *Fear and Trembling*, p. 91, *KW* VI (*SV* III 139).

23. See *Either/Or*, I, *KW* III (*SV* I 16); *Fear and Trembling*, "Problema III."

24. On the concept of repetition, see Historical Introduction, p. xiii-xiv fn., xxxiii-xxxiv.

25. See *"die Augen gingen ihm über"* in Margaret's song, Goethe; *Faust*, I, 8, l. 2409 *Goethe's Werke*, I–LV (Stuttgart: 1828-33; *ASKB* 1641-68), XII, p. 142; Taylor, p. 103.

26. Originally "his death." See Supplement, p. 277 (*Pap*. IV B 97:6); Historical Introduction, p. xx.

27. See *JP* I 1072 (*Pap*. IV C 75).

28. On the category of "the interesting," see Supplement, p. 326 (*Pap*. IV A 169); *Fear and Trembling*, pp. 82-83, *KW* VI (*SV* III 131), and note 4.

29. In contrast to the position of the Eleatics, Heraclitus maintained that nothing is, that all changes, that everything is becoming its opposite.

30. "Mediation" is the Danish (and English) version of the German *Vermittelung*. See, for example, Hegel's *Wissenschaft der Logik, Werke*, III, pp. 100, 105, 110; IV, p. 75; *J.A.*, IV, pp. 110, 115, 120, 553; *Hegel's Science of Logic* (tr. of *W. L.*, Lasson's ed., 1923; Kierkegaard had 2 ed., 1833), tr. A. V. Miller (London: Allen and Unwin; New York: Humanities Press, 1969), pp. 99, 103, 107, 445; *Encyclopädie der philosophischen Wissenschaften, Erster Theil, Die Logik*, para. 65, 70; *Werke*, VI, pp. 133-34, 138; *J.A.*, VIII, pp. 171-72, 176; *Hegel's Logic* (tr. of *E. W.*, 3 ed., 1830; Kierkegaard's ed., 1840, had the same text), tr. William Wallace (Oxford: Clarendon Press, 1975), pp. 101, 105; *Anxiety*, pp. 81-93, *KW* VIII (*SV* IV 350-63). See *JP* II 1578; III 3072, 3294 (*Pap*. II A 454; III A 108; IV A 54). See note 34.

31. See "the moment" or "the instant," Plato, *Parmenides*, 156 d; *Collected Dialogues*, p. 947. In *Platonis opera*, III, p. 79, τὸ ἐξαίφνης is translated into Latin as *momentum*. See *Anxiety*, pp. 86-90, *KW* VIII (*SV* IV 356-60).

32. See, for example, Plato, *Parmenides*, 160; *Platonis opera*, III, pp. 86-89; *Collected Dialogues*, pp. 950-51; "Interlude," *Fragments*, *KW* VII (*SV* IV 235-51); *Anxiety*, pp. 82-84, *KW* VIII (*SV* IV 351-54 fn.).

33. See, for example, Plato, *Parmenides*, 138 c; *Platonis opera*, III, pp. 32-33; *Collected Dialogues*, p. 932; Aristotle, *Physics*, III, V–VII; *Aristoteles graece*, I–IV, ed. Immanuel Bekker (Berlin: 1831; *ASKB* 1074-75), pp. 200-05, 225-50; *The Works of Aristotle*, I–XII, ed. J. A. Smith and W. D. Ross (Oxford: Clarendon Press, 1908-52), X. See *Fragments*, *KW* VII (*SV* IV 236-39); *JP* I

258, 260 (*Pap.* IV C 47, 80); Wilhelm Gottlieb Tennemann, *Geschichte der Philosophie*, I–XI (Leipzig: 1798-1819; *ASKB* 815-26), I, pp. 37, 39-40; III, pp. 125-28.

34. See Hegel on transition and becoming, for example, *Die Naturphilosophie, Encyclopädie der philosophischen Wissenschaften,* para. 349; *Werke,* VII¹, p. 548; *J.A.,* IX, p. 574; *Hegel's Philosophy of Nature* (tr. of part 2 of *E. W.,* 4 ed., 1847, 2 ed. *Werke*; Kierkegaard had 1 ed. *Werke,* 1841), tr. A. V. Miller (Oxford: Clarendon Press, 1970), p. 350; *Wissenschaft der Logik, Werke,* III, pp. 78-111; *J.A.,* IV, pp. 88-121; *Science of Logic,* pp. 82-108. See note 30.

35. See note 4.

36. See *Fragments, KW* VII (*SV* IV 240).

37. The pagan view of life. See *Anxiety,* pp. 18, 21, *KW* VIII (*SV* IV 290, 293); *JP* I 895 (*Pap.* IV C 86) (this note replaces note 490, *JP* I, p. 533).

38. This sentence is quoted in *Anxiety,* p. 18, *KW* VIII (*SV* IV 290 fn.).

39. Johann Georg Hamann (1730-1788), in a letter to J. G. Lindner, *Hamann's Schriften,* I–VIII¹⁻², ed. F. Roth (Berlin: 1821-43; *ASKB* 536-44), I, p. 467. The quotation, used as the epigraph to "Problemata" in *Fear and Trembling,* was deleted in the final copy.

40. Tage Algreen-Ussing (1797-1872), Danish politician and jurist, appointed in 1840 as professor of law at the University of Copenhagen. On May 28, 1837, he gave a speech at a meeting in commemoration of the introduction on May 28, 1831, of the new ordinances on the Estates of the Realm. See *Kjøbenhavnsposten,* May 29, 1837, p. 596.

41. The Danish reference is to residents on the Mol peninsula, who are the proverbial butt of stories of density and folly akin to tales about the Gothamites in England. The particular story is printed in *Beretning om de vidt bekjendte Molboers vise Gjerninger og tapre Bedrifter* (Copenhagen: 1829), no. 9, p. 15.

42. Jägerstrasse 57, second floor, Kierkegaard's address on his first visit to Berlin. See *Letters, KW* XXV, Letter 60.

43. The Französische Kirche and the Neue Kirche.

44. See *JP* V 5654 (*Pap.* IV A 101), May 10, 1843, written during Kierkegaard's second visit to Berlin.

45. An allusion to the title of the first section of *Either/Or,* II, *KW* IV (*SV* II 3-140).

46. In an old Roman Catholic Ash Wednesday ceremony, the priest would strew ashes upon himself and the parishioners and repeat the Latin sentence quoted in the text.

47. See *Letters, KW* XXV, Letter 81.

48. On May 25, 1843, the first tunnel under the Thames was opened.

49. See *Letters, KW* XXV, Letter 60.

50. The motto above the stage of the Royal Theater, Copenhagen, was and still is *"Ej blot til Lyst"* (Not only for pleasure).

51. Two well-known Copenhagen restaurants on Allégade and Freder-

iksberg Allé, respectively. Lars Mathiesen's restaurant was frequented particularly by writers and students.

52. *Der Talisman*, a three-act farcical comedy with songs, by Johann Nestroy.

53. German *gestaltend* with a Danish ending.

54. See *Fear and Trembling*, p. 27, *KW* VI (*SV* III 79).

55. In German and Danish, *Posse*: a light dramatic composition that often includes songs and music and is characterized by broad comedy, with a latitude of situations and relations, and not infrequently by a satirical slant. In the 1840s, the *Posse* was a very popular dramatic form in Vienna and Berlin. See Supplement, pp. 326-27 (*Pap.* IV A 178).

56. See *Sickness unto Death*, p. 79, *KW* XIX (*SV* XI 191); *Practice, KW* XX (*SV* XII 173-78).

57. Meïr Goldschmidt, in his recollection of the first time he met Kierkegaard, refers to a singular leap. See *Corsair Affair*, Supplement, p. 138, *KW* XIII. Cf. *JP* III 2316 (*Pap.* II A 655).

58. See *Fear and Trembling*, p. 41, *KW* VI (*SV* III 91).

59. Kierkegaard owned Aloys Blumaur's (1755-1798) travesty on the *Aeneid*, *Virgils Aeneis* (Schwäbisch Hall: n.d.; *ASKB* 1298). Some editions published before 1844, such as the Leipzig 1806 edition, carried on the title page of Vol. III Daniel Chodowiecki's engraving illustrating the founding of Rome. A collection of Chodowiecki's engravings was published in 1790 and 1793 under the title *Taschenbuch zum Nutzen und Vergnügen*. See Hans Peter Rohde, *Gaadefulde Stadier paa Kierkegaards Vej* (Copenhagen: Rosenkilde og Bagger, 1974), pp. 95-100.

60. Presumably an allusion to the humorous article on classifications, *"Om Inddelinger,"* (signed B.C.), in Johan Ludvig Heiberg's *Kjøbenhavns flyvende Post*, no. 40, May 18, 1827, col. 6-8.

61. See Plato, *Phaedrus*, 229 e–230 a; *Platonis opera*, I, pp. 130-31; *Collected Dialogues*, p. 478; *Fragments, KW* VII (*SV* IV 204-06). The text has "changeable" [*foranderligt*] rather than "curious" [*besynderligt*] as in *Fragments*.

62. Friedrich Beckmann (1803-1866), famous German comic actor, from 1824 the leading actor of the Königstädter Theater for many years.

63. Philipp Grobecker (1815-1883), at the Königstädter from 1840.

64. Jens Baggesen, in a review of Oehlenschläger's *Ludlams Hule, Danske Værker*, I–XII (Copenhagen: 1827-32; *ASKB* 1509-20), XII, p. 25.

65. Johan Christian Ryge (1780-1842), a physician and actor, played Salomon Goldkalb in J. L. Heiberg's first vaudeville, *Kong Salomon og Jørgen Hattemager, Skuespil*, I–VII (Copenhagen: 1833-41; *ASKB* 1553-59), II, pp. 303-400.

66. Baron von Münchhausen, when he sank into a bog. See *Fear and Trembling*, p. 109, *KW* VI (*SV* III 155); *JP* III 3249 (*Pap.* I A 153).

67. See note 57.

68. The carnival area in Dyrehaven, a few miles north of Copenhagen.

69. See *Either/Or*, I, *KW* III (*SV* I 126), and *Upbuilding Discourses in Var-*

ious Spirits, KW XV (*SV* VIII 217-18), on the confusion of church and theater.

70. See *The Concept of Irony, KW* II (*SV* XIII 331); *Postscript, KW* XII (*SV* VII 287).

71. Emanuel Hirsch suggests that this is a critical observation on the Fichtean-Kantian idea that life after death is an endless ethical striving and progress toward perfection. Kierkegaard, *Die Wiederholung,* ed. and tr. Hirsch, p. 155, n. 52.

72. No edition of *Robinson Crusoe* or of any other work by Defoe is listed in *ASKB.* Kierkegaard could have read a Danish translation (1826) of *Robinson Crusoe* by L. Kruse.

73. Here Constantin Constantius and Kierkegaard were poles apart. On his second Berlin visit, Kierkegaard had a flood of ideas and almost uninterruptedly wrote the first version of *Repetition.* See *Letters, KW* XXV, Letter 82.

74. Johannes Ewald (1743-1781) was the author of an inscription on a coffee pot, "*Paaskrift paa en Kaffekande,*" *Samtlige Skrifter,* I–IV (Copenhagen: 1780-91; *ASKB* 1533-36), IV, p. 365: "Like friendship, so your juice, thou noble Mocca fruit, / Should be pure and strong and hot and not misused." Kierkegaard wrote from Berlin during his first visit that one café had better coffee than could be had in Copenhagen; *Letters, KW* XXV, Letter 51.

75. In Virgil's *Aeneid* (IV, 698-99), it is told that Dido, queen of Carthage, could not die before Prosperpine, queen of the underworld, had taken a hair from Dido's head. The *Aeneid* is not listed in *ASKB.*

76. Proverbs 19:13.

77. Kierkegaard had Justinus Kerner, *Die Seherin von Prevorst* (Stuttgart, Tübingen: 1838; *ASKB* 596) and *Die Dichtungen* (Stuttgart: 1834; *ASKB* 1734). This anecdote, however, has not been located in Kerner's works. It is possibly a reference to *Njal's Saga,* ch. 75. See *JP* V 5330 (*Pap.* II A 233) and note 461.

78. A character in Johan Ludvig Heiberg, *Kjøge Huskors,* sc. 46, *Skuespil,* V, pp. 399-402.

79. The Danish is a play on "*tage* Alt *igjen*" (*take* everything *again, retake* everything) and "*Gjentagelse*" (literally, *retaking* or *repetition*).

80. Reminiscent of Faust's desire for a moment of experience so satisfying that he could say, "Verweile doch! du bist so schön [Ah, still delay, thou art so fair]!" Goethe, *Faust,* I, 4, l. 1700; *Werke,* XII, p. 86; Taylor, p. 58.

81. *Troilus and Cressida,* I, 2: "a tapster's arithmetic may soon bring his particulars therein to a total." Kierkegaard's Danish version is based on Schlegel and Tieck's German translation, *Shakespeare's dramatische Werke,* I–XII (Berlin: 1839; *ASKB* 1883-88), XI, p. 145.

82. Johann Gottfried Herder, *Volkslieder,* ed. Johannes Falk, I–II (Leipzig: 1825; *ASKB* 1487-88).

83. See Ecclesiastes 1:2.

84. The Cyrenaic philosopher Hegesias (ca. 300 B.C.) spoke so attractively about death that some of his followers committed suicide. See Tennemann, *Geschichte der Philosophie*, II, p. 106. Tennemann cites Cicero, *Tusculanae Disputationes*, I, 34; Diogenes Laertius, II, 86 [-96]; *Valerius Maximus*, VIII, C, 9. See *JP* I 201 (*Pap.* X² A 377).

[PART TWO]

Repetition

1. On the following section (pp. 179-231), see Historical Introduction, p. xx.

2. Domitian is reported to have stayed indoors for hours at a time occupied with a pursuit of flies, which upon capture were placed on pins. See Suetonius, "Titus Flavius Domitianus," *The Lives of the Caesars*, VIII, 3; *Tolv første romerske Keiseres Levnetsbeskrivelse*, I–II, tr. Jacob Baden (Copenhagen: 1802; *ASKB* 1281), II, p. 231; *Suetonius*, I–II, tr. J. C. Rolfe (Loeb Classics, New York: Macmillan, 1914), II, p. 345.

3. In a copy of the first Danish edition (see *Pap.* IV B 99), Kierkegaard corrected a typographical error from *legede* (played) to *levede* (lived).

4. See Horace, *Epistles*, I, 11, 9; *Q. Horatii Flacci Opera* (Leipzig: 1828; *ASKB* 1248), p. 580; *Satires, Epistles and Ars Poetica*, tr. H. Rushton Fairclough (Loeb Classics, New York: Putnam, 1929), p. 323.

5. Lucian, *Demonax*, 11; *Luciani opera*, I–IV (Leipzig: 1829; *ASKB* 1131-34), II, p. 372; *Lucian*, I–VIII, tr. A. M. Harmon (Loeb Classics, New York: Macmillan, 1913), I, p. 151.

6. Greek philosopher (second century B.C.) who defended his not being initiated into the mysteries by saying that if he had been he would have been obliged to recommend them if they were good and to warn against them if they were bad. See *JP* II 1549 (*Pap.* IV A 39), where reference is made to Johann Georg Hamann, *Hamann's Schriften*, VIII¹, p. 307 fn.

7. See Supplement, p. 277 (*Pap.* IV B 97:8), for deletion.

8. An echo of Regine's response to Kierkegaard's breaking of their engagement. See *JP* V 5913, 5999; VI 6273 (*Pap.* VII¹ A 126; VIII¹ A 100; IX A 408).

9. Kierkegaard tried to deceive Regine into thinking he was a deceiver. See Historical Introduction, pp. xi, xiii.

10. See Historical Introduction, p. xviii; *Stages, KW* XI (*SV* VI 34-35).

11. One who writes about last things, including life after death, as did Aristophanes in *The Frogs* and Lucian in his *Dialogues of the Dead*. The particular references are to Johan Ludvig Heiberg, author of *En Sjæl efter Døden* (A soul after death), "an apocalyptic comedy," which appeared in *Nye Digte* (Copenhagen: 1841; *ASKB* 1562), and to Hans Lassen Martensen, who reviewed Heiberg's piece in *Fædrelandet*, no. 398, January 10, 1841, col. 3217.

See also *Prefaces, KW* IX (*SV* V 29); *Postscript, KW* XII (*SV* VII 142); *Pap.* IV B 46, p. 203.

12. *Vox-Doctors,* false doctors, men called doctors without having the qualifications. See Supplement, p. 277 (*Pap.* IV B 97:9).

13. The confusion of actual death and the declarations of a lover is discussed by Constantin Constantius in his banquet speech in *Stages, KW* XI (*SV* VI 55-56).

14. I.e., the frontier of the religious.

15. See *Fear and Trembling,* pp. 34, 35-36, 37, 40, 46-51, 56-57, 59, 69, 99-100, 115, 119, *KW* VI (*SV* III 85, 87, 88, 91, 97-100, 106-07, 109, 118, 147-48, 161, 164).

16. On the distinction between reflexion (*Reflex*) and reflection (*Refleksion*), see *Two Ages,* p. ix, *KW* XIV.

17. See p. 131 and note 4.

18. The Danish term *Ophævelse* is a play on Hegel's use of *Aufhebung* and *aufheben* (the dialectic of contradiction and mediation). The Danish *Ophævelse* together with the verb *gjøre* [to make] means to make a disturbance, a commotion. See *Irony, KW* II (*SV* XIII 332); *Prefaces, KW* IX (*SV* V 48); *Postscript, KW* XII (*SV* VII 38, 69, 315); "That Single Individual," *Point of View, KW* XXII (*SV* XIII 609); *JP* II 1574 (*Pap.* II A 766).

19. See Supplement, pp. 308, 321-22 (*Pap.* IV B 117, p. 288, 118:7).

20. To Archimedes is attributed the saying, "Give me a place to stand [a fulcrum], and I will move the world." See *Either/Or,* I, *KW* III (*SV* I 308); *JP* V 5099 (*Pap.* I A 68).

21. See Job 2:8-11.

[Letters from the Young Man, August 15 to February 17]

1. See Supplement, p. 277 (*Pap,* IV B 97:10), for deletion.

2. See *JP* VI 6476, 6482, 6488, (*Pap.* X^1 A 659, 667; X^2 A 3.

3. See *Letters, KW* XXV, Letters 49-50, in which Kierkegaard, writing from Berlin to his friend Emil Boesen, inquires about Regine.

4. See Supplement, pp. 277-78 (*Pap.* IV B 97:11).

5. *Adresseavisen,* no. 85, April 10, 1843, Supplement, col. 10. See *JP* III 2591 (*Pap.* IV A 78).

6. An expression used for boys in an orphanage because of their clothing. See *Anxiety,* p. 34, *KW* VIII (*SV* IV 306).

7. Adam Wilhelm Schack v. Staffeldt (1769-1826), "Elskovsbaalet," *Samlede Digte,* ed. F. L. Liebenberg, I–II (Copenhagen: 1843; *ASKB* 1579-80), II, p. 327.

8. This hitherto unidentified quotation has been located by Hans Peter Rohde (*Gaadefulde Stadier paa Kierkegaards Vej,* pp. 101-08) as coming from Wilhelm Müller's "Der ewige Jude," *Taschenbuch zum geselligen Vergnügen* (Leipzig: 1823), pp. 10-12.

9. Ecclesiastes 12:1.

10. See Supplement, p. 278 (*Pap.* IV B 97:12), for change.

11. Job 1:21. See "The Lord Gave, the Lord Took Away, Blessed Be the Name of the Lord," *Eighteen Discourses, KW* V (*SV* IV 9-23), the first of *Fire opbyggelige Taler,* published December 6, 1843, two months after the publication of *Repetition* (October 7). See *JP* II 1386, 1536; IV 4683 (*Pap.* X^1 A 196; X^4 A 396, 573).

12. See Job 29:12-15.

13. See Job 7:11.

14. See Job 29:12-15; cf. Matthew 23:14; James 1:27.

15. See Job 9:3; 33:12. See Supplement, pp. 304, 318 (*Pap.* IV B 117, pp. 284, 299).

16. See Job 1:6-12; 2:1-6.

17. See Job 37:4; 38:1; 40:1. In *Repetition,* thunder and thunderstorm are a lower parallel (esthetic-religious) to "by virtue of the absurd" (higher religious) in *Fear and Trembling*: a transcendent possibility where there evidently is no possibility. See p. 185 and note 15.

18. See Job 1:2.

19. See Job 2:7.

20. A stock theatrical figure in comedy and pantomime.

21. The borrowed Dutch-German word *Seelenverko[o]per* (seller of souls) refers to innkeepers and others who deceptively procured unwilling sailors for ships about to sail.

22. Cicero, "In Defense of Sextus Roscius of Ameria," XXX, 84; *M. Tulli Ciceronis opera omnia,* I–VI, ed. Johannes Augustus Ernesti (Halle: 1756-57; *ASKB* 1224-29), II, p. 58; *Cicero: Speeches,* tr. John Henry Freese (Loeb Classics, Cambridge, Mass.: Harvard University Press, 1941), p. 197.

23. With modifications, the two following sentences are the title of the major part of *Stages, KW* XI (*SV* VI 175-459).

24. A character in Ludvig Holberg's popular comedy *Erasmus Montanus.* Per Degn (deacon), ignorant but keen, vanquishes Latin-flaunting Rasmus Berg in a Latin dispute by posing nonsensical questions cast in his own inimitable Latin.

25. Nicolaj Edinger Balle, *Lærebog i den Evangelisk-christelige Religion* (Copenhagen: 1824; *ASKB* 183), ch. 6, III, para. 2; ch. 1, I, para. 2. Balle's catechism is referred to in *From the Papers of One Still Living, KW* I (*SV* XIII 83); *Either/Or,* II, *KW* IV (*SV* II 242, 290); *Prefaces, KW* IX (*SV* V 12); *Stages, KW* XI (*SV* VI 414). *Letters, KW* XXV, Letter 195 (1849), also quotes ch. 6, III, para. 2.

26. Danish script at the time was Gothic or German script, both in handwriting and in print. Latin script means roman, the style used now in most printing and typewriting.

27. *Emplastrum manus dei,* a traditional poultice used for chest colds etc. In *Läkemedelsnamn* (Lund: 1918), John Lindgren states that the particular name came from the general view that medical remedies were regarded as a gift from God's hand. The name is listed in *Pharmacopoea Danica* (Copen-

hagen: 1868); in the next edition (1893), the name is changed to *emplastrum aeruginis compositum*.

28. The range of poetry as a human interpretation of being and existence encompasses Job, who defends himself on the basis of moral excellence (32:1: "for he continued to think himself righteous") until he moves beyond to the religious (42:1-6: "Therefore I melt away; I repent in dust and ashes"). Hence, Job is in a border territory (*confinium*) touching both poetry and the religious.

29. A theme treated by all three of the great Greek tragedians, but only Sophocles' *Philoctetes* survives. In the campaign against Troy, Philoctetes was bitten by a snake and abandoned by his compatriots because they could not bear his lamentations. Philoctetes in his suffering approached the limit of the human, but he did not, like Job, have the possibility of the religious transcending of that limit. See *Either/Or*, I, *KW* III (*SV* I 128, 135-36); *Stages*, *KW* XI (*SV* VI 425-26); *Pap*. III C 38-40; V B 148:35.

30. See *JP* V 5288 (*Pap*. II A 679).

31. See Job 2:13, 3:1.

32. See Job 16:21. Here the translation is according to the older Danish version given in the text.

33. See *JP* IV 3992; V 5186 (*Pap*. II A 19; I A 333, para. 2).

34. See Ecclesiastes 3:1.

35. Here "tempt" [*friste*], meaning "test," is the language of the King James translation and of the Danish Bible of Kierkegaard's time. See *Fear and Trembling*, p. 9, *KW* VI (*SV* III 61), and note 2; *Postscript*, *KW* XII (*SV* VII 226).

36. See Isaiah 40:6-8.

37. See *JP* II 1251 (*Pap*. VII¹ A 181).

38. See Job 32:1-22.

39. Job 19:21.

40. See Job 13:4; translation follows the Danish text.

41. Job 6:5.

42. See *Fear and Trembling*, p. 9, *KW* VI (*SV* III 61), and note 2.

43. Job 1:21.

44. Abraham, the central figure in *Fear and Trembling*, published on the same day (October 7, 1843) as *Repetition*, is called the "father of faith" (p. 18, *KW* VI [*SV* III 70]). Others may be "knights of faith" or "heroes of faith" (pp. 38-41, 51, 66, 74, *KW* VI [*SV* III 89-92, 101, 115, 123]). All of them represent positions beyond that of Job.

45. See Ephesians 6:11.

46. See *Pap*. VI B 41:3.

47. See note 17.

48. See Job 29:4. The older Danish Bible has *Herrens Fortrolighed* (the confidence, intimacy, of the Lord).

49. See Job 42:10-15.

50. See *Either/Or*, II, *KW* IV (*SV* II 306-18), for a lengthy consideration

of this theme. In a copy of *Enten/Eller*, II (*SV* II 306), Kierkegaard wrote: "If a person is most fully in the right, before God he ought always have an even higher expression: that he is in the wrong, for no human being can penetrate his consciousness absolutely" (*Pap*. IV A 256). See *Discourses in Various Spirits, KW* XV (*SV* VIII 348-69); *Sickness unto Death*, pp. 79-87, *KW* XIX (*SV* XI 191-99).

51. See Job 8:1-22.

52. On Regine's and her father's responses to the breaking of the engagement, see *JP* V 5913, 5999 (*Pap*. VII¹ A 126; VIII¹ A 100); VI 6273, 6470, 6538, 6544 (*Pap*. IX A 408; X A¹ 648; X² A 210, 216). This passage was written before Kierkegaard learned of Regine's engagement to Johan Frederik Schlegel.

53. According to old Danish law, if the death sentence was judged too severe, the condemned could be imprisoned for a period dependent upon conduct and other factors. See *Pap*. V B 98:18.

54. See note 17.

55. On the concept of repetition, see Historical Introduction, pp. xiii-xiv fn., xxxiii-xxxiv.

56. Here the extant portion of the original final copy ends. See Historical Introduction, p. xx.

[Incidental Observations by Constantin Constantius]

1. See *JP* IV 4092 (*Pap*. II A 378).

2. For changes in the final copy, see Supplement, p. 278 (*Pap*. IV B 97:13).

3. For an addition and a deletion in the final copy, see Supplement, p. 278 (*Pap*. IV B 97:14).

4. For a change in the final copy, see Supplement, p. 278 (*Pap*. IV B 97:15).

5. For a change in the final copy, see Supplement, p. 278 (*Pap*. IV B 97:16).

6. For a change in the final copy, see Supplement, p. 279 (*Pap*. IV B 97:17).

7. For a change in the final copy, see Supplement, p. 279 (*Pap*. IV B 97:18).

8. For a change in the final copy, see Supplement, p. 279 (*Pap*. IV B 97:19).

9. For a change in the final copy, see Supplement, p. 279 (*Pap*. IV B 97:20).

10. The little multiplication table from 2 to 10 and the big table from 10 to 20.

11. As Regine had done. See *JP* VI 6472, p. 195, 6776 (*Pap*. X⁵ A 149; X¹ A 659).

12. For a change in the final copy, see Supplement, p. 279 (*Pap*. IV B 97:22).

13. For a change in the final copy, see Supplement, p. 279 (*Pap.* IV B 97:23).

14. For a change in the final copy, see Supplement, p. 280 (*Pap.* IV B 97:24).

15. For a change in the final copy, see Supplement, p. 280 (*Pap.* IV B 97:25).

16. For a change in the final copy, see Supplement, p. 280 (*Pap.* IV B 97:26).

17. For a change in the final copy, see Supplement, p. 280 (*Pap.* IV B 97:27).

18. For a change in the final copy, see Supplement, p. 280 (*Pap.* IV B 97:28).

19. For changes in the final copy, see Supplement, pp. 280-81 (*Pap.* IV B 97:29).

[Letter from the Young Man]

1. See Historical Introduction, p. xix.

2. See p. 185 and note 17; Historical Introduction, p. xx. The young man's repetition is not essential like Job's but rather the result of something accidental. See *JP* I 885 (*Pap.* III A 135). The "thunderstorm" is quite different from the one referred to on pp. 212-14.

3. See Job 1:2; 42:10-13.

4. See *Anxiety*, p. 151, *KW* VIII (*SV* IV 417); *Pap.* V B 60, p. 137.

5. The goddess of birth in Greek mythology. See *Iliad*, XIX, 96ff.; Ovid, *Metamorphoses*, IX, 281; Vollmer, *Wörterbuch der Mythologie*, p. 657; Paul Friedrich A. Nitsch, *Neues mythologisches Wörterbuch*, I–II (Leipzig, Sorau: 1821; *ASKB* 1944-45), I, 134; II, 27; *JP* III 3389 (*Pap.* III A 204).

6. See Historical Introduction, pp. xvi-xvii.

[Concluding Letter by Constantin Constantius]

1. For a change in the final copy, see Supplement, p. 281 (*Pap.* IV B 97:30). See also Historical Introduction, p. xx.

2. The Greek Church Father Clement of Alexandria (ca. 150–ca. 220) wrote in allegories so that the uninitiated would not understand (see, for example, *Stromateis*, V, 9). See *JP* II 1724 (*Pap.* III B 5); Supplement, pp. 282-83 (*Pap.* IV B 109). In *Anxiety*, p. 18, *KW* VIII (*SV* IV 290), the allusion is repeated in observations by Vigilius Haufniensis on *Repetition*.

3. An ironical reference to the Hegelian pattern: position, negation, and mediation.

4. This observation and the discussion following are an attack upon Hegel's emphasis upon the universal at the expense of the individual. On the theme of universal and exception, see, for example, *Fear and Trembling*, p. 82, *KW* VI (*SV* III 130).

5. See Luke 15:17.

6. Presumably the addition of the final sentence (*Pap.* IV B 97:31) was

made because the Constantin of the rewritten portions (*SV* III 214-22, 249-52, and 257-64) seems quite different from the earlier Constantin.

7. See Supplement, p. 326 (*Pap.* IV A 169).

8. For a change in the final copy, see Supplement, p. 281 (*Pap.* IV B 97:32).

SUPPLEMENT

1. See pp. 15-23, especially pp. 21-22 and note 21.

2. See p. 9 and note 2.

3. See pp. 10-11.

4. See pp. 94-99 and notes 25, 26.

5. The Danish title, *Mellemhverandre*, is a word coined by Kierkegaard. See Supplement, p. 245 (*Pap.* IV B 80:3); *The Concept of Irony, KW* II (*SV* XIII 232, 262, 362). The literal translation is "between each other."

6. Simeon Stylites (d. 459?), Syrian hermit who lived thirty-five years on a small platform on top of a high pillar—hence, Stylites. Feast day, January 5. See *From the Papers of One Still Living, KW* I (*SV* XIII 54); *JP* II 1188, 1541 (*Pap.* I A 252, 340).

7. Danish: *Stillinger.* See pp. 45-46; *Pap.* II A 799, 801; *JP* V 5791 (*Pap.* VI B 17).

8. See Historical Introduction, p. xxv.

9. See *JP* V 5560 (*Pap.* III A 203).

10. See *JP* V 5560, 5674 (*Pap.* III A 203; IV A 126); *Works of Love, KW* XVI (*SV* IX 343).

11. See p. 25; Supplement, pp. 249-50 (*Pap.* IV B 96:4); *Repetition*, p. 149.

12. A Danish term for penitentiary is *Rasphus* (English: rasphouse), derived from the rigorous prison work of rasping dyewood into powder.

13. See Supplement, p. 243 (*Pap.* IV B 78).

14. The first negative goes along with the second negative in the phrase "not as that old pagan did," and therefore, in reading, the first negative may be omitted. See Supplement, p. 287 and note 45.

15. See *JP* II 2181 (*Pap.* III A 141). The reference is to Horace, *Odes*, III, 1, 40; *Opera*, p. 145; *Horace: The Odes and Epodes*, tr. C. E. Bennett (Loeb Classics, New York: Putnam, 1930), p. 171.

16. See p. 31 and note 14.

17. By extension: all kinds of people. See II Samuel 8:18, 15:18, 20:23.

18. See p. 61.

19. See p. 21.

20. In this case *problemata* refers to the four parts on pp. 10-14. In each version Abraham is represented as preparing for the sacrifice according to the command but as acting without faith. By contrast, the faith of Abraham is accentuated in the main section.

21. See Supplement, p. 252 (*Pap.* IV B 96:1 c); *Repetition*, p. 149, *KW* VI (*SV* III 190).

22. See Acts 8:9-24. Simon, a magician (*Magus* or *Mager*), was baptized

by Philip but was later rebuked by Peter for wanting to purchase the gift of the Holy Spirit. From his name comes the word "simony," the purchase of ecclesiastical offices.

23. *Die blaue Bibliothek aller Nationen*, I–XII (Gotha, Weimar: 1790-1800; *ASKB* 1445-56).

24. See, for example, *Postscript*, *KW* XII (*SV* VII 436-39, 454, 464), on irony as the incognito of the ethical.

25. See Genesis 37:31-34.

26. See Matthew 21:28-30.

27. See Matthew 21:29. The Danish translation at that time includes "but afterwards he repented."

28. *Iphigenia in Aulis*, ll. 1223-26; *Euripides*, tr. Wilster, p. 145; *Complete Greek Tragedies*, IV, p. 359, ll. 1217-18. See p. 118 and note 14.

29. See p. 118 fn.

30. See *Fragments*, *KW* VII (*SV* IV 245-56).

31. See p. 19 and note 12.

32. I.e., Sophocles. See Cicero, *On Old Age*, VII, 22; *M. Tullii Ciceronis opera omnia*, I–VI, ed. J. A. Ernesti (Halle: 1756-57; *ASKB* 1224-29), IV, pp. 938-39; *Cicero: De senectute, De amicitia, De divinatione*, tr. William A. Falconer (Loeb Classics, Cambridge, Mass.: Harvard University Press, 1953), p. 31: "And how is it with aged lawyers, pontiffs, augurs, and philosophers? What a multitude of things they remember! Old men retain their mental faculties, provided their interest and application continue; and this is true, not only of men in exalted public station, but likewise of those in the quiet of private life. Sophocles composed tragedies to extreme old age; and when, because of his absorption in literary work, he was thought to be neglecting his business affairs, his sons haled him into court in order to secure a verdict removing him from the control of his property on the ground of imbecility, under a law similar to ours, whereby it is customary to restrain heads of families from wasting their estates. Thereupon, it is said, the old man read to the jury his play, *Oedipus at Colonus*, which he had just written and was revising, and inquired: 'Does that poem seem to you to be the work of an imbecile?' When he had finished he was acquitted by the verdict of the jury."

33. See *JP* III 3289 (*Pap.* IV A 19).

34. See p. 168.

35. See pp. 68-69, 86-92.

36. See Supplement, pp. 241-42 (*Pap.* IV A 76).

37. Pseudonym of Magnus Eiríksson (1806-1881), Icelandic-Danish theologian. For the title of the pseudonymous work, a critique of *Fear and Trembling*, see Supplement, p. 265 (*Pap.* X⁶ B 69). See *JP* VI 6597 (*Pap.* X² A 601).

38. The entry was written for possible publication in some paper, but it was not submitted.

39. *Postscript*, *KW* XII (*SV* VII 537).

40. Anders Sandøe Ørsted (1778-1860), jurist and statesman and brother of the physicist Hans Christian Ørsted.

41. See p. 84.

42. See pp. 54-67.

43. See pp. 68-81.

44. Carl Wilhelm Jessen (1764-1823), Danish naval captain, later admiral, and governor of the Virgin Islands for a year before his death.

45. See pp. 41-45.

46. Anti-Climacus is the pseudonymous author of *The Sickness unto Death* (July 30, 1849) and of *Practice in Christianity* (September 27, 1850).

47. *Pap.* X^6 B 77-82. For the entries omitted here (*Pap.* X^6 B 78-81), see *JP* I 9-12.

48. See Supplement, p. 263 (*Pap.* X^6 B 68), and note 44.

49. See Supplement, p. 265 (*Pap.* X^6 B 69).

50. See p. 84.

51. See Supplement, pp. 267-68 (*Pap.* X^4 A 338).

52. Silhouette cutting was a popular minor art at the time. Hans Christian Andersen is now the best-known practitioner from that period.

53. *JP* III 3020, 3714; VI 6791 (*Pap.* X^4 A 338, 357, 458).

REPETITION

1. *Johannes Climacus, or De omnibus dubitandum est* (*Pap.* IV B 1), written in 1842-1843 but not published. In the present edition, the work appears together with *Philosophical Fragments*, by Johannes Climacus, *KW* VII.

2. *Johannes Climacus, KW* VII (*Pap.* IV B 1, pp. 146-48).

3. Danish: *Realitet.* In *Johannes Climacus,* the term *Realitet* is used quite differently from the way it is used in Kierkegaard's published works and elsewhere in the *Papirer.* T. H. Croxall in his translation of the work (London: Black, 1958) properly points out on pp. 66, 74, 148, and 149 that *Realitet* is used synonymously with *Virkelighed* (actuality) and that Climacus sometimes shifts from one term to the other without a change in meaning. See *JP* III, pp. 900-03.

4. The Danish term here is *Moment,* not *Øieblik,* which is usually translated "moment" and usually has a special meaning in Kierkegaard's writings (see *JP* III 2739-44 and p. 821; VII, p. 62). Here "moment" is used as it is found in Hegel's works: a vanishing element, factor, or particular in a whole, a constituent or a part of a unity. See, for example, *Wissenschaft der Logik, Werke,* III, pp. 108, 111, 121; *J.A.,* pp. 118, 121, 131; *Hegel's Science of Logic* (tr. of *W.L.,* Lasson ed., 1923), pp. 105, 107, 116.

5. See p. 357, note regarding the title page.

6. See p. 362, note on Philostratus.

7. This particular revision was required because of the replacement of the final section by a new version. See Historical Introduction, p. xx.

8. See note 7.

9. See note 7.

10. Johanne Luise Pätges Heiberg (1812-1890), leading Danish actress and wife of Johan Ludvig Heiberg. In 1848 she was the subject of Kierkegaard's *The Crisis and a Crisis in the Life of an Actress*, published under the pseudonym Inter et Inter (*Fædrelandet*, July 24, 27). The addition of the area to a name signifies a provincial attachment and a diminution of the great, somewhat like "world famous in Dubuque."

11. In Norse mythology, one of the challenges by Utgard-Loke to Thor was to empty a horn in three draughts. Thor failed. Later he learned that the end of the horn was in the sea. Thor nevertheless diminished the sea considerably, and thereafter such a phenomenon was called ebb tide.

12. In "The Seducer's Diary," *Either/Or*, I, *KW* III (*SV* I 394), Johannes says he is getting the "sign Horace wished on all faithless girls—a black tooth." Horace, *Odes*, II, 8, 3; *Opera*, p. 109; Loeb, p. 127.

13. See Henrik Hertz, *Valdemar Atterdag*, V, 1. The work was performed at the Royal Theater on January 12, 21, and 24, 1839, but was not published until 1848.

14. *Urania Aarbog for 1844*, ed. J. L. Heiberg (Copenhagen: 1843; *ASKB* U 57). Johan Christian Lund and Henrik Lund, in their catalog of Kierkegaard's papers, characterize unit 364 (*Pap.* IV B 108-24) as follows: "Heiberg's *Urania* and some *Intelligensblade* with loose aphoristic (generally) notes." This copy of *Urania* is missing. It no doubt was the yearbook for 1844 (published December 1843), which contains Heiberg's "*Det astronomiske Aar*" (The Astronomical Year), a treatise with primary emphasis upon the orderly repetitions of the movements of heavenly bodies. Since "repetition" is the key term in the piece, it is not surprising that it discusses at some length (pp. 97-102) "a recently published book . . . *Repetition*." Kierkegaard wrote replies (*Pap.* IV B 110-17; see Supplement, pp. 283-319) to Heiberg's observations but did not publish them. The pertinent portion of Heiberg's treatise reads (ed. tr.):

. . . [p. 94] In other words: true, authentic change is a *development*— that is, in its repetitions it is new; every time it reproduces its contents, it carries along with it something that was merely a bud in the previous production but that now in the repeated production has been developed into a veritable existence. A development such as this is not found in nature, whose productions, however much they alter in the particular, nevertheless, when examined as a whole, stay at the same point. To be sure, there is a development in all organic life. The seed is a germ that through different stages develops into a flower and then to fruit; but the new seed, which contains the fruit, is identical with the plant from which it germinated; the new plant generation merely repeats the previous one, [p. 95] while, on the other hand, each new generation in the world of spirit goes beyond the previous one and uses its achievements for genuinely new beginnings—that is, for those that lead to something genuinely new. Consequently, it must be acknowledged that the changes that take place in nature do not in the true sense of the word merit the name of variations, but, on the contrary, it [nature] is ruled by the law of repetition; and this is especially discernible in the movements of the heavenly bodies, where the change consists merely of shifting external and contingent combinations, whereas organic nature still brings forth an immanental development from original shoots.

Thus, despite the changes involved in the astronomical year, which in part constitutes its own self-completing orbit, in part is fragments from other periods independent of the solar year but partially encompassed by it, *repetition* remains the predominant point of view from which one may contemplate the astronomical year. With respect to the above statement about repetition, are we to draw the conclusion that the periodic variation which the year produces is monotonous and boring? In that case, it is wrong to transfer the categories of spirit to nature and consequently apply to it a standard that does not correspond to its concept. [p. 96] Unquestionably, pure and simple repetition without any renewed contents is tedious in anything relating to the spiritual world, whose principle is development and where consequently lack of this must be labeled as absence of spirit, thereby annulling the concept of a spiritual world. But this does not presuppose that the same repetition that in the spiritual produces the impression of emptiness should produce the same impression in nature, for we do not come to nature with the same expectations and demands with which we come to spirit. On the contrary, just as the spirit awes us with its ceaseless progress, so nature awes us with its ceaseless repetition, which depends upon the unalterable laws it follows. So it is only to a temporal and empirical contemplation that nature's conformity to law reveals itself as *repetition*; from the standpoint of idea, we say, since it is conformity to law that is repeated and since it would not be conformity to law if it were not constantly the same, then the accent of an intelligent contemplation of nature must fall more upon one and the same *being* in the eternal idea than upon one and the same *becoming* in the temporal repetition. Therefore one must see something far higher in nature's and also spirit's repetitions than mere repetition, although [p. 97] something entirely different in both spheres: that is, in the spirit we should see the *development* that accompanies repetition and that in a way annuls repetition *per se*; in nature, on the other hand, we should see the *resting eternity*, the fixedness, the security and infallibility, that specifically allows repetition to continue in order to be able to manifest itself through it.

In a recently published book that even bears the title *Repetition*,* something very beautiful and appropriate is said about this concept, but the author has not distinguished between the essentially different meanings repetition has in the natural sphere and in the spiritual sphere. He thereby has fallen into the error that *repetition* is supposed to play the same role in future philosophy that "what has mistakenly been called *mediation*" plays in current philosophy.**

Nature, of course, can be said to mediate itself through its lawful repetitions, but in the sphere of the spirit mediation embraces a something different from mere repetition, something already [p. 98] adequately intimated in the above remarks. That in his celebration of repetition the author actually has had the categories of nature especially in view and, perhaps without being aware of it, stretched the validity of the concept beyond its legitimate boundaries seems to be evident in part from his having specifically applied it to a concept from natural philosophy, namely, *movement*, since he thinks that the concept of repetition would be able to bring about a reconciliation between the Eleatics and Heraclitus,† that is to say, between two opposing philosophical schools, one of which denied all motion while the other saw everything in motion, and in part from the author's tendency—not only in this book but in others that undoubtedly are from the same hand—toward what is called a *philosophy of life*. In something like that, a sympathetic association with nature would be an essential factor, but there cannot be sympathy with nature unless one takes pleasure in its repetitions. With this restriction in view, I quote a few of the author's statements that bear out what has been advanced above and facilitate the transition to what follows:

"*Repetition* is a crucial expression for what [p. 99] *recollection* was to the Greeks. Just as they taught that all knowing is a recollecting, modern philosophy will teach that all life is a repetition. — — — Repetition and recollection are the same movement, except in opposite directions, for what is recollected has been, is repeated backward, whereas genuine repetition is recollected forward. — — — One never grows weary of the old, and when one has that, one is happy. He alone is truly happy who is not deluded into thinking that the repetition should be something new, for then one grows weary of it. — — — He who does not grasp that life is a repetition and that this is the beauty of life has pronounced his own verdict and deserves nothing better than what will happen to him anyway—he will perish; for hope is a beckoning fruit that does not satisfy, recollection is petty travel money that does not satisfy, but repetition is the daily bread that satisfies with blessing. When existence has been circumnavigated, it will be manifest whether one has the courage to understand that life is a repetition and has the desire to rejoice in it. — — — If God himself had not willed repetition, the world would not have come into existence. Either he would have followed the superficial plans of hope, or he would have retracted [p. 100] everything and preserved it in recollection. This he did not do: therefore the world continues, and it continues because it is a repetition.†† — — — The dialectic of repetition is easy, for that which is repeated has been—otherwise it could not be repeated—but the very fact that it has been makes the repetition into something new. When the Greeks said that all knowing is recollecting, they said that all existence, which is, has been; when one says that life is a repetition, one says: actuality, which has been, now comes into existence. If one does not have the category of recollection or of repetition, all life dissolves into an empty, meaningless noise. Recollection is the ethical view of life, repetition the modern."§

What is said here is very true and very beautiful if one understands it with the proper limitation and remembers that one must know how to see and to find something more and something higher in repetition than itself. Anyone lacking a sense for repetition is bereft of life and therefore cannot feel the courage to begin it anew, either in the critical epochs allotted to him here on earth [p. 101] or in the new status after death. But the allurement of repetition is not itself but is what a person himself makes of it, and precisely here mediation comes to hold the place that the author erroneously thinks ought to be given over to repetition. But abstract, purely objective repetition that has not been mediated through subjectivity to something higher than itself is boring and devoid of spirit. Who could wish to repeat his life utterly unchanged from the cradle to the grave, to repeat all his errors and misconceptions, all his cares and misfortunes? Indeed, one would rather not repeat unaltered even joy or good fortune, since by its very returning unchanged it would not return as the same. That many pleasures are far less impressive the second time than the first is universally acknowledged in the saying that if one has enjoyed himself someplace once, he should not go back there again. Therefore the author, who was merely seeking repetition, should not have repeated his journey to Berlin. On the other hand, the repetition of the reading of a book, of the enjoyment of a work of art, can heighten and in a way surpass the first impression, because one thereby immerses oneself more deeply in the object and appropriates it more inwardly. But in that case the pleasure is not in the repetition [p. 102] *per se* but in what the repetition carries along with it or in what the person himself makes of it.

The same is true of our observation of nature, and especially of the natural or astronomical year. Nature always speaks the universal language of repetition but allows us to perceive it especially in its periodic cycles: they proclaim it to us as does the pendulum in a clock, which with every second communicates to us the change that is nothing other than repetition, steadily speaking with the same voice. What nature gives us is nothing other than repetition; what we do with it, so that it can continually be something new for us, depends upon us. In other words, nature is merely a setting for the precious stone of our independent activity; according to Calderon's beautiful simile, nature heightens joy for the joyful and sorrow for the sorrowing, just as the bee sucks honey from the same flower from which the spider sucks poison. As one works nature's repetitions into something new and different, this sympathy with nature is one of the primary clues to the true wisdom of life; it is the foundation for all admonishments to enjoy life and to keep young despite the toll of years.

No one has felt this more deeply than Goethe. . . . [P. 103 is a discussion of Goethe's *Werther*; pp. 104-06 are a quotation from *Aus meinem Leben, Dichtung und Wahrheit*, III, 13.]

[P. 106] After this delineation, Goethe goes on to discuss what at that particular period contributed to nourishing the hypochondria he described, namely, the acquaintance Germany had just made with melancholy English [p. 107] literature, and he mentions in this connection Young ("Night Thoughts"), Gray, Milton, and Ossian, the last of whom played such a significant role in *Werther*.

Those golden words embrace the whole dialectic of repetition.

* *Repetition, A Venture in Experimenting Psychology*. By Constantin Constantius. (Copenhagen 1843.)

** P. 33 [148].

† Ibid.

†† P. 3-6 [131].

§ P. 34 [149].

15. "No one will easily deduce from what I write that I regard that age as mad; my opinion is simply that it is mentally depressed . . . . But all depression borders on mental debility, and it is my opinion that against this there is found both prevention and healing in the same bath from which the ancient world derived its admirable equilibrium and peace of mind" (J. L. Heiberg, "Det astronomiske Aar," *Urania . . . 1844*, p. 122, ed. tr.).

16. "The prevention and healing are to be found in astronomy" (ibid., pp. 120-21, ed. tr.). Johan Ludvig Heiberg (1791-1860) was not only the leading writer, literary critic, dramatist, and Danish Hegelian of the time, but he was also an amateur astronomer of considerable competence and had an observatory in his residence on Christianshavn.

17. See note 16.

18. Herr Dapsul von Zabelthau, in Hoffmann's *Die Serapions-Brüder*, E.T.A. *Hoffmann's ausgewählte Schriften*, I–X (Berlin: 1827-28; *ASKB* 1712-16).

19. See, for example, *Kjøbenhavns flyvende Post*, no. 43, April 9, 1830, where Heiberg shifts on a point in his running argument with Carsten Hauch. See note 20 below.

20. Adam Oehlenschläger's *Væringerne i Miklagaard* (1827) was the occasion of a three-year critical attack by Heiberg on Oehlenschläger's work. Carsten Hauch (1790-1872), poet, novelist, and lecturer in natural science at Sorø, was among those who defended Oehlenschläger. For Heiberg, the issue was the nature, status, and level of esthetic feeling, thought, and form. See, for example, *Kjøbenhavns flyvende Post*, no. 41, April 5, 1830.

21. A line from J. L. Heiberg's review of *Either/Or* in "Litterær Vintersæd," *Intelligensblade*, no. 24, March 1, 1843, p. 288.

22. See note 14.

23. *Repetition* (October 7, 1843).

24. See p. 225 and note 2. The wording is not quite the same.

25. See note 14.

26. The author of *Repetition*.

rania . . . 1844, pp. 97, 100.

in the text and in the notes,

tion of the treatise in *Urania.*

V V 26).

d *Erasmus Montanus*, III, 5.

note 14.

r 1, 1842, has an article with

o "The Astronomical Year."

anuary 9, 1846), *The Corsair*

44, pp. 4-60.

to *regula de tri*, an arithmetic

e other three terms are given.

phrase in the style of Hol-

te 14.

nd note 11; *Prefaces, KW* IX

ncilor Rasmus Stiernholm, a

selskab (The United Welfare

10), and note 33.

B 111 refer to *Urania . . .*

are not always exact, but the

nd note 14, also p. 312 (*Pap.*

title page.

Supplement, pp. 290-92 (*Pap.*

4.

11, p. 266, ll. 6-7, omits the

nmas surrounding the phrase:

æg 1, Royal Library.

54. A continuation of the quotation from Heiberg, *Urania . . . 1844*, p. 110.

55. See note 15.

56. Pius Alexander Wolff, *Preciosa*, tr. Claudius Julius Boye (Copenhagen: 1822), p. 25. The piece was performed at the Royal Theater on January 5 and November 26, 1843. See *Stages*, *KW* XI (*SV* VI 114).

57. See *Postscript*, *KW* XII (*SV* VII 243).

58. See p. 229.

59. P. 179.

60. P. 153. Heiberg's last quotation is actually from p. 149, which is p. 34 in the first edition of *Repetition*.

61. See *Urania . . . 1844*, pp. 97, 100; see note 14.

62. Ibid.

63. See Supplement, pp. 283-84 (*Pap.* IV B 110, pp. 258-59).

64. P. 131. *Urania . . . 1844*, pp. 98-99; see note 14.

65. *Urania . . . 1844*, p. 113.

66. See *The Concept of Anxiety*, pp. 18-19, *KW* VIII (*SV* IV 290-91).

67. See note 31.

68. *Urania . . . 1844*, p. 97; see note 14.

69. *Urania . . . 1844*, p. 100; see note 14.

70. See p. 225 and note 2.

71. See notes 14 and 16.

72. *Phaedrus*, 230 d. The translation of Plato here is from Kierkegaard's Danish version of the Greek and Latin in the Astius edition of *Platonis opera*.

73. Johan Ludvig Heiberg, *Perseus, Journal for den spekulative Idee*, no. 2, 1838 (*ASKB* 569), p. 3. See *Prefaces*, *KW* IX (*SV* V 17).

74. See notes 16, 21, 33, and 41.

75. *Urania . . . 1844*, p. 147.

76. *Vitis*, I, p. 70; Riisbrigh, I, p. 66. See *Fragments*, *KW* VII (*SV* IV 181); *Prefaces*, *KW* IX (*SV* V 45-46).

77. P. 223.

78. See note 14.

79. See p. 225.

80. Presumably Johan Nicolai Madvig (1804-1886), whose critical writings, particularly on Cicero, had won acclaim in Denmark and abroad. See *Postscript*, *KW* XII (*SV* VII 542).

81. See Supplement, p. 283 (*Pap.* IV B 110), and note 29. See *Prefaces*, *KW* IX (*SV* V 27-28).

82. See *Prefaces*, *KW* IX (*SV* V 27).

83. *Either/Or*, I, *KW* III (*SV* I 253-72).

84. For a draft of the remainder of the paragraph, see Supplement, p. 320 (*Pap.* IV B 118:1).

85. See p. 226 and note 3.

86. For a draft of the next six lines, see Supplement, p. 320 (*Pap.* IV B 118:2).

pplement, p. 320 (*Pap.* IV B

ence, see Supplement, p. 321

: Heiberg's of celestial recur-
ference to the repetition, the
nic sense. See p. 133; Supple-

vi; title page and note to sub-

pplement, p. 321 (*Pap.* IV B

see Supplement, p. 321 (*Pap.*

plement, pp. 321-22 (*Pap.* IV

ript, *KW* XII (*SV* VII 88-89,
e, I, pp. 37, 39-41.

236-39); *Prefaces*, *KW* IX (*SV*

nent, p. 322 (*Pap.* IV B 118:8).

B 116).
d note 95.
nent, p. 322 (*Pap.* IV B 118:9).
4.
ragraph, see Supplement, pp.

08; *Collected Dialogues*, p. 422.

119. According to J. L. Heiberg's view.

120. See Supplement, p. 287 (*Pap.* IV B 111, p. 262, ll. 7-13).

121. For a draft of the remainder of this sentence and of the next sentence, see Supplement, p. 323 (*Pap.* IV B 118:11).

122. For a draft of the initial portion of this sentence, see Supplement, p. 323 (*Pap.* IV B 118:12).

123. *Urania . . . 1844*, p. 98; see note 14.

124. See Supplement, pp. 320, 324, 326 (*Pap.* IV B 118:1, 120, A 156).

125. For a draft of the following two sentences, see Supplement, p. 323 (*Pap.* IV B 118:14).

126. *Urania . . . 1844*, p. 106; see note 14.

127. Ibid.

128. Ibid.

129. See Supplement, p. 324 (*Pap.* IV B 120, pp. 308-09).

130. See note 31.

131. See *Prefaces, KW* IX (*SV* V 29-30).

132. For a draft of the remainder of this sentence up to the first dash, see Supplement, p. 323 (*Pap.* IV B 118:15).

133. For a draft of the remainder of this sentence and the next, see Supplement, p. 323 (*Pap.* IV B 118:16).

134. *Urania . . . 1844*, p. 97; see note 14.

135. See Supplement, p. 311, and note 118.

136. See Supplement, p. 301, and note 81.

137. For a draft of the remainder of the paragraph, see Supplement, p. 323 (*Pap.* IV B 118:18).

138. *Figaros Givtermaal*, tr. Niels Thorup Bruun (Copenhagen: 1817), IV, 7, p. 124.

139. *Urania . . . 1844*, p. 98; see note 14: "beyond its legitimate boundaries."

140. See Supplement, p. 296 (*Pap.* IV B 111).

141. P. 131. *Urania . . . 1844*, pp. 98-99; see note 14.

142. P. 186.

143. See *Prefaces, KW* IX (*SV* V 49).

144. See Supplement, p. 313 (*Pap.* IV B 117).

145. Friedrich W. J. von Schelling (1775-1854), German philosopher whose lectures Kierkegaard heard in Berlin during the winter of 1841-1842.

146. Schelling, *Philosophische Untersuchungen über das Wesen der menschlichen Freiheit* (Landshut: 1809; *ASKB* 763).

147. See p. 133.

148. See Supplement, pp. 302-05 (*Pap.* IV B 117).

149. See p. 225.

150. See p. 149.

151. In *Papirer*, entry IV B 124 is designated as missing. Only the first line, taken from Barfod's catalog, is given. The two pages of manuscript

are in the Kierkegaard Archives, Royal Library, Copenhagen, and are included in a supplement in *Pap.* XI³.

152. In "Autobiographical Fragments," Heiberg writes of sitting in his room at the König von England in Hamburg "with Hegel on my table and Hegel in my thoughts." Then came a "sudden inner vision, like a flash of lightning, which instantly illuminated the whole region for me and awakened in me the central thought hitherto hidden from me" (*J. L. Heibergs Prosaiske Skrifter,* I–XI [Copenhagen: 1861-62], XI, p. 500, ed. tr.). See *Postscript, KW* XII (*SV* III 153), where this episode is introduced as the experience of one Dr. Hjortespring. In "Autobiographical Fragments" (*Skrifter,* XI, pp. 491-94) Heiberg also writes of his interest in diplomacy and of his associations in diplomatic circles. The major portion of "Autobiographical Fragments" was first published in C. Molbech, *Dansk poetisk Anthologie,* I–IV (Copenhagen: 1830-40), IV, pp. 243ff. See *JP* III 2347 (*Pap.* V C 3).

153. Apparently a free rendition of lines in Ludvig Holberg, *Ulysses von Ithaca,* V, 2.

154. Ludvig Holberg, *Den politiske Kandestøber,* I, 5.

155. Ludvig Holberg, *Den pantsatte Bondedreng,* I, 3.

156. See *Fear and Trembling,* pp. 98-99, *KW* VI (*SV* III 146); *The Concept of Anxiety,* pp. 17-19, *KW* VIII (*SV* IV 289-91 fn.).

157. Gotthard Oswald Marbach, *Geschichte der Philosophie des Mittelalters* (Leipzig: 1841; *ASKB* 643); *Geschichte der griechischen Philosophie* (Leipzig: 1838; *ASKB* 642).

158. See pp. 228-30

159. See pp. 146-48, 172-74.

160. See p. 214.

161. See pp. 150-71.

162. See *Anxiety,* p. 154, *KW* VIII (*SV* IV 420); *Postscript, KW* XII (*SV* VII 70, 306, 366, 401-02, 434, 446-54, 484).

163. See *Postscript, KW* XII (*SV* VII 420, 442, 455, 484).

164. See *Anxiety,* p. 151 fn., *KW* VIII (*SV* IV 417).

165. See *Anxiety,* p. 149, *KW* VIII (*SV* IV 414). The Danish *Oprindelighed,* literally "originality," could also be translated as "primitivity." See *JP* III 3558-61.

166. See p. 179.

167. Karl Rosenkranz, *Psychologie oder die Wissenschaft vom subjectiven Geist* (Königsberg: 1837; *ASKB* 744), pp. 157-58.

168. See *Anxiety,* p. 149, *KW* VIII (*SV* IV 414).

169. See *Postscript, KW* XII (*SV* VII 169).

170. Ibid.

171. Ibid. (*SV* VII 170-71).

172. Ibid.

173. See, for example, ibid. (*SV* VII 114, 171, 195); *Stages, KW* XI (*SV* VI 414).

174. See *Postscript, KW* XII (*SV* VII 134).

175. The first discourse in *Fire opbyggelige Taler* (1843), in *Eighteen Discourses, KW* V (*SV* IV 9-24).

176. Bishop Jakob Peter Mynster's pseudonym, composed of the middle consonants of his three names. The reference is to his article "*Kirkelig Polemik*," which appeared in Johan Ludvig Heiberg's *Intelligensblade*, 1844, pp. 97-114. There he distinguishes between the Job discourse and the others in Kierkegaard's *Fire opbyggelige Taler* (1843), in *Eighteen Discourses, KW* V (*SV* IV 9-68). Mynster (1775-1854) was a friend of Kierkegaard's father, Michael Petersen Kierkegaard; he baptized and confirmed Søren and until the later years was deeply admired and respected by him.

177. Johannes Climacus, the pseudonymous author of *Philosophical Fragments* (1844) and *Concluding Unscientific Postscript* (1846).

178. See Historical Introduction, pp. xxi-xxvi; title page; and note regarding subtitle.

179. *Repetition, Fear and Trembling*, and *Three Upbuilding Discourses* were first available in bookstores on October 16, 1843. *Four Upbuilding Discourses* (with the Job discourse) appeared on December 6, 1843.

180. Part One of *Stages*, "In Vino Veritas," is William Afham's recollection of the banquet and the speeches on love or on the relation between man and woman given on that occasion. *KW* XI (*SV* VI 13-83).

181. Ibid. (*SV* VI 32).

182. Ibid. (*SV* VI 114). See *Postscript, KW* XII (*SV* VII 243 fn.); Supplement, p. 293 (*Pap.* IV B 111, p. 269).

183. In referring to recurrences or repetitions in the ordinary sense, Kierkegaard sometimes uses *Repetition* rather than *Gjentagelse*. In this entry the stress is on the ethical transmutation of recurrences that otherwise would be merely habitual. Judge William takes a similar approach in discussing marriage, work, and friendship. See *Either/Or*, II, *KW* IV (*SV* II, e.g., 115-20, 261-68, 283-91); *Stages, KW* XI (*SV* VI, e.g., 112-14).

184. See note 176.

185. See *Either/Or*, II, *KW* IV (*SV* II 145).

186. See pp. 148-49.

187. Constantin Constantius.

188. See pp. 170-76.

BIBLIOGRAPHICAL NOTE

For general bibliographies of Kierkegaard studies, see:
Jens Himmelstrup, *Søren Kierkegaard International Bibliografi*. Copenhagen: Nyt Nordisk Forlag Arnold Busck, 1962.
Aage Jørgensen, *Søren Kierkegaard-litteratur 1961-1970*. Aarhus: Akademisk Boghandel, 1971.
Kierkegaard: A Collection of Critical Essays, ed. Josiah Thompson. New York: Doubleday (Anchor Books), 1972.
Søren Kierkegaard's Journals and Papers, ed. and tr. Howard V. Hong and Edna H. Hong, assisted by Gregor Malantschuk, I. Bloomington, Indiana: Indiana University Press, 1967.
For topical bibliographies of Kierkegaard studies, see ibid., I–IV, 1967-75.

INDEX

about-face, 216

Abraham, xiv, xix, 9-38, 52-82,
112-20, 239-42, 245-51, 254-56,
258, 263, 266-71, 341, 350, 372,
376; and defensibility of silence,
82-119; as doubter, 248; as father
of faith, 18-19, 55, 66, 68-69, 82,
117, 260, 269, 372; and fulfillment, 43; as great man, 30, 31,
32; greatness of, 16, 249; and
hero, 33, 57, 65; and hypocrisy,
114; and irony, 118; and Jehovah, 270-71; justification of, 62-
63; as man of faith, 57, 72; and
the merman, 99; as murderer,
30, 55, 57, 66, 74, 250; and ordeal, 19, 22, 52-53, 60, 71, 77,
113, 115, 209, 247, 251, 269,
271; and paradox, 33, 52-53, 119;
and poet, 118; preacher on, 28-
29, 52; as prototype, 266-67; and
repentance, 115; and resignation,
37-38, 119, 254; and silence, 12;
as the single individual, 99, 114;
and sleep, 31; and sorrow, 17;
and speaking, 113-19; and spiritual trial, 60, 115, 118; and teleological suspension of the ethical,
56; and his telos, 59; and temptation, 9, 19, 21, 74, 77, 114-20,
239; and time, 19; and the tragic
hero, 57-61, 114-20; and trial,
53, 76-77; understanding of, 113-
15; and the universal, 76-77, 251;
and virtue, 59

Abrahamson, Werner Hans, et al.,
*Udvalgte danske Viser fra Middel-
alderen*, 345

abridging, 245

absolute, the, 56, 62, 70, 120; absolute relation to, 56, 62, 70, 81,
93, 97, 98, 111, 113, 120; duty,
74, 78; duty to God, 68, 70, 72,
81, 349; infinitude, 29; relation to
the demonic, 98

abstract, the, 161

absurd, the, xxxi, xxxii, xxxv, 34-
37, 40-41, 46-59, 69, 99, 101,
115, 119, 185, 259-62, 305, 313,
321, 324, 344, 371; and impossibility, 50, 51; and the improbable, 46; and the unexpected, 46;
and the unforeseen, 46

accidental, the, 162

accidental concretion, 158, 163

Achilles, 113

act: external, 116; of resignation,
46, 48; and thought, 326

action, 319; and philosophy, 98

actors, 161-65

actuality, ix, x, xvii, xviii, xxiii,
xxiv-xxv, 34, 41, 43, 44, 51, 86,
87, 99, 110-12, 133, 140, 146,
149, 158, 161, 163, 184-85, 200,
201-02, 210, 226, 229, 230, 310,
322, 378; artificial, 154-55; ideal,
xxiv; and ideality, xiii, 274-75;
and imagination, 191; and reality, 41, 274-75

Adam and Eve, 158

Adresseavisen, 8, 301, 370

Aeschylus, 256

Agamemnon, 57-58, 61, 79, 87,
114-16, 347

age, the present, 7-8, 46, 83, 84,
92, 100-01, 108, 111, 121, 149

Agnes and the merman, 94-99,
242, 252-53

Library of Congress Cataloging in Publication Data

Kierkegaard, Søren, 1813-1855.
  Fear and trembling; Repetition.

  (Kierkegaard's writings; 6)
  Translation of: Frygt og bæ ven and of Gjentagelsen.
  Bibliography: p.
  Includes index.
  1. Christianity--Philosophy.   2. Sin.   3. Repetition
(Philosophy) I. Hong, Howard Vincent, 1912-
II. Hong, Edna Hatlestad, 1913-   .   III. Kierkegaard,
Søren, 1813-1855. Gjentagelsen. English. 1982.
IV. Title.   V.   Series: Kierkegaard, Søren, 1813-1855.
Works. English.   1982; 6.
BR100.K52 1982   201   82-9006